BAKING IN AMERICA

BAKING IN

Traditional and Contemporary Favorites

 Houghton Mifflin Company   Boston • New York • 2002

AMERICA

from the Past 200 Years

GREG PATENT

For Dorothy,
always

For information about permission to reproduce selections
from this book, write to Permissions, Houghton Mifflin Company,
215 Park Avenue South, New York, New York 10003.

Visit our Web site: www.houghtonmifflinbooks.com.

Library of Congress Cataloging-in-Publication Data is available.

ISBN 0-618-04831-6

Design by Melissa Lotfy
Food styling by Rori Trovato
Prop styling by Joelle Hoverson

Printed in the United States of America

RRD 10 9 8 7 6 5 4 3 2 1

Acknowledgments

One of the joys of writing a cookbook is getting to thank all the people who helped in so many ways along the road.

I wished for and got the editor I wanted and needed, Rux Martin. Her keen, perceptive eye found the book within my manuscript, and she carefully guided me through the process of bringing it to its final form. I cannot thank her enough for her confidence in me and her unwavering passion throughout this project.

I also want to thank the following for their invaluable help: my agent, Judith Weber, for believing in this book from the beginning, and for playing an active role throughout the book's production; associate editor Lori Galvin-Frost, for baking her way through my book and for cheerfully reminding me of deadlines; Deb DeLosa, Houghton Mifflin's cookbook publicist; photographer Anna Williams, food stylist Rori Trovato, and prop stylist Joelle Hoverson, for making my recipes look so inviting and for giving them such life and beauty; and Melissa Lotfy of Houghton Mifflin, for the great design.

I would also like to thank the many librarians and curators who got caught up in the drama of my research. They happily provided me with information and welcomed me to their vaults, archives, and rare book rooms. I am especially grateful to Russell Martin, of the American Antiquarian Society in Worcester, Massachusetts, for allowing me free access to original Boston newspapers from the 1800s for my research; Mark Kepper, of the Baker Library at the Harvard Business School, for giving me access to volumes of the invaluable *Confectioners' Journal;* R. Eugene Zepp, rare book and manuscript librarian, and Jane Duggan, reference librarian of the Boston Public Library, for leading me to important historical sources and providing menus from Boston's Parker House; Carin O'Connor, of the Bostonian Society for sending me copies of old Parker House menus; Helen Haskell, Tom Owen, and Sheila Nash, of the Los Angeles Public Library, for opening its rare book collection to me; Becky Cape and Sue Presnell, of the Lilly Library at Indiana University in Bloomington, for making available all the library's books and ephemera on American baking; Nicholas Graham, reference librarian of the Massachusetts Historical Society, for providing copies of historical Parker House menus; the New York Public Library, for opening its menu collection to me; Constance Malpas, of the New York Academy of Medicine, for allowing me to rummage through its old cookbook and menu collections; Barbara Haber, of the Schlesinger Library at Harvard University, for making it possible for me to visit the Baker Library; Ellen Shea, of the Schlesinger, for assistance in research on the Boston Cream Pie; and Barbara Wheaton, also of the Schlesinger, for making so many well-catalogued boxes of ephemera available to me.

Ruth Murray, of today's Omni Parker House Hotel in Boston, provided the original recipe for the Boston Cream Pie; Gerry Tice, executive chef, and Tuoi Tran, pastry chef, allowed me to watch while they put together a Boston Cream Pie. Flo Braker and Shirley DeSantis generously took the time to test the Golden Butter Layer Cake with Chocolate Frosting to see how it worked at sea level. Karen Hess shared her remarkable knowledge of baking in America. Jan Longone, of the Wine and Food Library, sent me boxes and boxes of ephemera. Sandra Oliver, editor of the newsletter *Food History News,* publishes this invaluable historical resource and sent me her files on the Boston Cream Pie. William Woys Weaver provided information on Pennsylvania Dutch baking and on Eliza Leslie, which I couldn't have found anywhere else. I thank them all.

I am also grateful to the many people who tasted and critiqued what I baked: Pam Adams, Anthony Cesare, Kathy Cross, Dana and Frank D'Andraia, Monte Dolack, Pat and Mike Gray, Phoebe Hunter, Jon Jackson, John Keegan, Karin Knight, Marion and Norman Lavery, Bill Muñoz, Mary Beth Percival, Jane Rechtenwald, and Kay Whitlock.

I am indebted to my friend Pat Gray for her meticulous proofreading.

My wife, Dorothy, tasted and critiqued everything I baked and took loving care of me, and I can't thank her enough.

Finally, I would like to thank the International Association of Culinary Professionals and the James Beard Foundation for awarding me a Linda D. Russo Travel Grant, which allowed me to complete my research for this book.

CONTENTS

NOTE TO THE COOK

Measuring Flour

For the recipes in this book, flour is measured either by the dip-and-sweep method or by sifting the flour and then spooning it into the measuring cup. To measure by the dip-and-sweep method, stir the flour in its container to aerate it slightly, then dip a dry measuring cup into the flour, filling it to overflowing, and sweep off the excess with a narrow metal spatula or a knife. Unless the recipe specifies otherwise, use the dip-and-sweep method.

When a recipe calls for sifted flour, place more flour than you will need into a sifter or strainer set on a sheet of waxed paper, and sift it onto the paper. Spoon the sifted flour into a dry measuring cup, filling it to overflowing. Sweep off the excess.

INTRODUCTION

America's love affair with baking stretches back only two hundred years, yet in this relatively brief period we've developed a large and varied tradition rivaling that of countries that have been around for thousands of years. Where did all these recipes come from? I became fascinated by this question as I leafed through *Seventy-Five Receipts, for Pastry, Cakes, and Sweetmeats* in the cozy wood-paneled rare book room of the Los Angeles Public Library. There, in the earliest American baking book, written in 1828 by Eliza Leslie ("A Lady of Philadelphia"), an unusual recipe called Indian Pound Cake grabbed my attention:

> Eight eggs.
> The weight of eight eggs in powdered sugar.
> The weight of six eggs in Indian meal, sifted.
> Half a pound of butter.
> One nutmeg, grated—or a tea-spoonful of cinnamon.

Stir the butter and sugar to a cream. Beat the eggs very light. Stir the meal and eggs, alternately, into the butter and sugar. Grate in the nutmeg. Stir all well. Butter a tin pan, put in the mixture, and bake it in a moderate oven.

Pound cake, a traditional English cake normally made with fine white flour, had been transformed into something new by the substitution of an authentic American ingredient, cornmeal, known at the time as Indian meal, for the flour. And it was flavored with an entire nutmeg to boot. Intrigued, I wondered what the texture would be like. And would the nutmeg overwhelm the flavor? I couldn't wait to get into the kitchen to find out.

My first attempt didn't work because the regular supermarket cornmeal I used was too coarse, making the cake heavy and gritty. When I switched to fine cornmeal, however, the cake had a deliciously complex texture, tender yet a bit toothsome, the nutmeg adding a marvelous aroma and a not-too-strong spiciness. I was hooked. I searched through other nineteenth-century cookbooks and found many more Indian pound cake recipes. Some were flavored with rose water, or with brandy, or both. Rose water, the distilled extract of rose petals, contributed a floral aroma and flavor, and when I added brandy as well, the taste was exquisite. (Try the recipe on page 180 and you'll see what I mean.)

Baking the almost two-hundred-year-old recipe made me feel an unexpected kinship with Miss Leslie. It was as if she were with me in my kitchen. Past and present coexisted. What other treasures, I wondered, might I find by delving into old cookbooks? Would I be as successful at resurrecting them as I had been with the Indian Pound Cake?

In reading rooms from Los Angeles to Cambridge, Massachusetts, I pored over historic cookbooks, diaries, pamphlets, and old newspapers. My research stretched from the earliest American cookbook, *American Cookery,* by Amelia Simmons—fittingly published a mere twenty years after the signing of the Declaration of Independence—through the first decade or so of the Pillsbury Bake-Off, a cooking contest inaugurated in 1949 that illustrates the ingenuity of American cooks during the last half of the twentieth century. I discovered that from the beginning, American women had created an extraordinary variety of savory and sweet baked goods. Over and over again, I encountered recipes for breads and desserts I had never heard of before: Composition Cake, Silver Cake, Pennsylvania Dutch Tea Rolls, Boston Cream Cakes. Why, I wondered, had these delicious-sounding recipes disappeared from twentieth-century cookbooks? I decided to bake them to see for myself. I soon found that these extinct recipes are as appealing and contemporary today as they were a hundred or more years ago. The Boston Cream Cakes were a revelation: crisp sugar-glazed cream puffs with an especially tender interior and filled with a rich, velvety baked custard flavored with a vanilla bean and cinnamon stick. Made from a buttery, sweet yeast dough, the Pennsylvania Dutch Tea Rolls have an especially light and tender texture.

The old cookbooks I spent my days with were much more than a rich source of recipes. Many contained advice on how to shop, design, furnish a kitchen, and manage servants. And, at a time when medicine was in its infancy, almost all cookbooks gave medical advice and provided recipes for the sick room. These cookbooks were windows on how people lived, and as I baked my way through the recipes, I discovered I was at the same time retracing history.

Like their British ancestors, Americans were terrific bakers, expanding on centuries-old traditions that had been established in Europe. (Just how much Americans used to bake is clear from the fact that in 1900, 95 percent of all flour in America was purchased for home use, compared to just 15 percent in 1970.) Equipment in eighteenth- and nineteenth-century American kitchens was primitive by today's standards—the rotary egg beater wasn't invented until 1870—yet somehow these women managed to make everything we do today: yeast breads, quick breads, all kinds of cakes, cookies, pies, and tarts, even cheesecakes. In that first slim volume of sixty-four pages, for example, Amelia Simmons included more than fifty recipes for baked goods, demonstrating that baking was the primary culinary tradition of this country.

Unlike previous cookbooks, which were merely reprints of books printed in England and featuring English ingredients and cooking methods, *American Cookery* presented American ingredients and addressed the needs and desires of the American housewife, with recipes "adapted to this country and all grades of life." Miss Simmons's message was implicitly democratic: anyone can do this. Each of the approximately 250 recipes I've included in this book shows the hallmarks of American baking that she set forth: simplicity, straightforwardness, and experimentation.

Some of the oldest recipes I found, those for sweet and savory breads, date to the eighteenth and early nineteenth centuries, when baking was done almost exclusively in a brick oven alongside the fireplace. These breads were nearly always leavened with yeast. One of the most popular loaves of the period, Third Bread, a crusty, dense bread, was made with equal amounts of wheat, rye, and cornmeal. The substitution of cheaper rye flour and cornmeal for most of the wheat was common practice. Wheat remained expensive until the 1860s, when wheat growing and milling became established in the Midwest. Wheat, Rye, and Indian Bread (page 66) is my re-creation of the old staple Third Bread. Another example of American ingenuity in the kitchen is Rice Bread, a delightfully chewy loaf, in which some of the costly wheat flour was replaced by rice, which was plentiful in the South's Low Country.

Early cookbooks also revealed many delicious examples of sweet yeast breads. Election Cake, a yeast cake made with raisins and dried currants that dates back to the 1600s, was so good that it was supposedly used to bribe voters. In my version (page 118), I've kept the traditional dough but improvised by adding a variety of dried fruits not available to

A HINT TO THE WORKING CLASSES

If a man, twenty-one years of age, began to save a dollar a week, and put it to interest every year, he would have, at thirty-one years of age, six hundred and fifty dollars; at forty-one, one thousand six hundred and eighty; at sixty-one, six thousand one hundred and fifty; and at seventy-one, eleven thousand five hundred dollars. When we look at these sums, and when we think how much temptation and evil might be avoided in the very act of saving them, and how much good a man in humble circumstances might do for his family by these sums, we cannot help wondering that there are not more savers of one dollar a week.

—Mrs. E. A. Howland,
The New England Economical Housekeeper (1846)

our ancestors. Who knows, you might be able to swing a few votes for your favorite candidate with it!

Mildly spiced nonyeasted loaf cakes, packed with dried currants, raisins, and citron, sweetened and made dark with molasses, were also extremely popular in nineteenth-century American homes. The poet Emily Dickinson was renowned for her Black Cake, a delicious confection that I've resurrected in the fervent hope it will restore fruitcake's good name (see page 206). Doughnuts—balls of deep-fried sweet yeast bread dough—are a venerable tradition that came to us from the Dutch. One quintessentially American doughnut that I happened upon, called Little Pittsburghs, were great favorites with the hungry miners of Leadville, Colorado, who paid a dime apiece for them and gobbled them down with glasses of dried-apple cider.

From the time *American Cookery* appeared in 1796 to the mid-1800s, American bakers, showing a zest for saving time that continues to this day, experimented with various chemical leaveners. The first was pearl ash (potassium carbonate), then came saleratus (sodium carbonate) and baking soda (sodium bicarbonate). When baking powder arrived in the late 1850s, yeast breads rapidly gave way to quick breads, and the traditional leaveners, eggs and yeast, were abandoned in favor of chemical ones. An advertisement in an 1856 edition of the *Boston Daily Evening Transcript* touted the virtues of baking powder, called "nutritive yeast powder" by its manufacturers: "We introduce this new article to the public with the greatest confidence that it will be found the best and cheapest to rise bread, hot biscuits, griddle cakes, and all kinds of sweet

WEIGHTS AND MEASURES

Wheat Flour, one pound is one quart.
Indian Meal, one pound two ounces is one quart.
Butter, when soft, one pound is one quart.
White Sugar powdered, one pound one ounce is one quart.
Best Brown Sugar, one pound two ounces is one quart.

Liquids
Sixteen large table-spoonfuls are half a pint.
Eight   "   "   "   are one gill.
Four   "   "   "   are half a gill, or one glass.
Twenty-five drops are equal to one tea-spoonful.
A common wine-glass to half a gill.
A common tumbler to half a pint.

—Mrs. E. A. Howland, *The New England Economical Housekeeper* (1846)

cakes, gingerbreads, etc. Bread made with this powder requires no saleratus or soda, and no time to rise."

Is it any wonder baking powder proved to be irresistible to the harried housewife?

Over time she exercised her penchant for experimentation by incorporating produce from her garden—carrots, pumpkin, zucchini—into quick breads. She also varied her breads by adding dried currants, raisins, coconut, or fresh berries to loaves and muffins. Dense fruit cakes, which kept well, were now shunned in favor of cakes made puffy and light with the newfangled leaveners. Even old-fashioned pound cakes were "improved upon" by cutting back on the eggs, reducing the beating time, and lightening their textures with baking powder or baking soda.

The invention of baking powder as well as other innovations in the kitchen made possible the rise of tall, glamorous layer cakes. At first glance, these fancy cakes would seem to be at odds with the American spirit of simplicity seen in the plainer loaf cakes and pound cakes of earlier eras, but they are the culmination of the American fascination with speed and ease. The chocolaty, fluffy Devil's Food Cake I found while leafing through a promotional pamphlet for shortening and the light, tender Orange Chiffon Cake that was created by an ingenious California insurance salesman in the 1920s show that by the twentieth century, the American kitchen had taken a giant leap forward.

Time-saving kitchen equipment and utensils like electric refrigerators, freezers, ovens with reliable thermostats, and especially electric mixers allowed women to bake many more cakes than they had in the past and make them taller and fluffier too.

One such cake, the classic Lady Baltimore Cake, a spectacularly high three-layer cake spread with a sugary walnut filling between the layers and frosted with a billowy, white icing made by beating egg whites and sugar over boiling water, became a favorite in Charleston, South Carolina, in the first decade of the 1900s. Another impressively tall and delicious cake I found, the four-layer Chocolate and Gold Ribbon Cake, a prize winner originally called Regency Ribbon Cake from the Pillsbury Bake-Off in 1955, is filled and frosted with a luxuriously smooth chocolate icing. You'll find both these cakes in this book.

When it came to ingredients, American bakers again proved themselves to be innovators rather than hidebound traditionalists. Instead of making her piecrusts with simple mixtures of flour, butter, and water, Amelia Simmons added eggs. And rather than confining herself to the traditional English pie fillings of apples, apri-

RECIPE OR RECEIPT?

Most nineteenth-century cookbooks use the word "receipt" instead of "recipe." There are *Miss Leslie's New Receipts for Cooking; The Godey's Lady's Book Receipts; Seventy-Five Receipts, for Pastry Cakes, and Sweetmeats;* and so on. How did "recipe" ultimately triumph over "receipt"?

Jessup Whitehead, author of several cookbooks in the late 1800s and influential food columnist for Chicago's *Daily National Hotel Reporter,* summed up the conflicting usage of the day in the seventh edition of *The American Pastry Cook:*

> *Of half a dozen different articles on the grocer's shelves, four have recipes printed on the packages while others give receipts. Of six persons talking together, four or five will say recipe, the rest receipt. The label on the bottle tells you that the sauce beside your plate was prepared from the receipt of a nobleman of the county. But the nobleman's only authoritative English cook-book uses recipe. . . . Both words are right, but which is better?*

After using the word "recipe" in hundreds of pages of his column, Mr. Whitehead eventually decided to buck the tide and opt for "receipt" instead. His choice boiled down to the number of syllables. In Mr. Whitehead's view, it was pretentious to use three syllables when two would do.

In making his decision, he cited Harpers, which had just published a cookbook he considered especially authoritative. It made "extreme correctness a special feature. . . . It was typographically perfect. It hyphenated every cocoanut. It split hairs on teaspoonful . . . and adopted receipt instead of recipe." Mr. Whitehead concluded, "There was no more room for doubt. Higher precedent there could not be, and so, if the reader pleases, as far as this column is concerned, we will render unto the doctors the Latin trisyllable which is theirs, and use only the humbler but safer English receipt."

cots, cherries, gooseberries, lemons, and oranges, she boldly incorporated the new fruits and berries she found in America: cranberries, currants, grapes, peaches, quince, and pumpkin. Since then, of course, the variations dreamed up by American bakers in both crusts and fillings—from Hazelnut Streusel Sweet Potato Pie to Blueberry Pie with Amaretti Crust—have confirmed the national love of experimentation.

The willingness of the American baker to embrace new ingredients intensified in the nineteenth and twentieth centuries and is nowhere more apparent than in the cookie recipes that began to proliferate then. The most famous example is the all-time favorite chocolate chip cookie, invented in the 1930s by an enterprising innkeeper named Ruth Wakefield, who tossed chopped chocolate into her cookie dough when she'd run out of walnuts. (Until the 1880s, chocolate was almost exclusively used as a beverage in the home.) Oatmeal and peanuts, two of our most beloved additions to cookies today, were originally used for animal feed until the Civil War. Since Ruth Wakefield's time, cooks have outdone her by incorporating a host of new ingredients into chocolate chip cookies: candied ginger, white chocolate, macadamia nuts, and crushed candies.

Though American bakers have always been unusually open to new products, whether cream cheese or coconut, our baked goods have never lost the charming straightforwardness that has characterized them since the beginning. Old cookbooks abound with simple fruit desserts that show a frugal determination to use what was on hand. The same creative spirit motivated early cooks to stir stale bread crumbs into a mixture of stewed spiced apples for a brown Betty or top fruits with a simple mixture of flour, butter, sugar, and oats for a crisp, or with biscuit dough for a cobbler. And who but an American baker would think of baking a pineapple cake in a cast-iron skillet, then upending tradition by turning the whole thing upside down?

In selecting recipes from old cookbooks and pamphlets, I paid close attention to recipes that appeared repeatedly in many sources by different authors. That, I felt, was a good indication of a recipe's popularity and intrinsic worth. After several years of testing, I've chosen only the best for this book.

In re-creating recipes from the past, I looked upon them as a blueprint or guide, a suggestion of something that might be. Cookbook language, especially in older books, is often hard to follow, full of strange ingredients such as "grown flour" (flour that had been spoiled by dampness and could not be made into proper bread), or "barm" (a type of sourdough made by adding flour to fermenting beer or ale), and measurements like "gills," "wine glasses," and "tumblers." Often the recipes I encountered were simply a string of ingredients separated by commas, with no mixing details, pan sizes, oven temperatures, or baking times. Exceptional food writers such as Eliza Leslie and Maria Parloa wrote in paragraph form, as was the norm, but they gave specific ingredient amounts and provided detailed directions and visual clues to guide the cook. Only a handful of cookbook authors began a recipe with a list of ingredients followed by instructions for preparation. Sarah Tyson Rorer, in *Mrs. Rorer's Philadelphia Cook Book* of 1886, set the standard for recipe writing that we still use today, with a list of ingredients followed by the method.

As I tested, I also had to remind myself that the sugar and butter, ovens, and cooking equipment we use today are entirely unlike those of the past. Sugar, for example, was not the pure white granulated kind we buy today but was likely to contain some molasses. It was solidified into cones and had to be cut with special snippers and crushed before using. Wheat flour was often "unbolted," or whole grain. Only after the mid-nineteenth century did "cleaner" white flours became available because of newer milling and sifting techniques. I was amazed, however, to see how many spices home cooks used a hundred or more years ago. Allspice, cinnamon, cloves, ginger, mace, and nutmeg were regularly added in far greater quantities than they are today.

Because of these differences, making these old recipes exactly as written was all but impossible. I've tried to be true to their spirit while filling in the missing details. Whenever possible, I've relied on time- and labor-saving equipment, such as electric mixers and food processors. In addition, while many of the recipes in this book faithfully reproduce ones I encountered in old cookbooks, others are my own creations, loosely based on those of the past. Some were inspired by ingredients our ancestors lacked, such as dried blueberries and cranberries or white chocolate. I hope you'll feel comfortable enough with these recipes to conduct your own ongoing experiments in the great American tradition of improvisation, throwing in a little something here or there to see what happens—just as Amelia Simmons and Ruth Wakefield would have done.

FROM FIREPLACE TO ELECTRIC RANGE

In eighteenth-century America, the fireplace was the center of life in the kitchen. Roasting was done on spits over wood coals, and vegetables, soups, and stews were cooked in cast-iron pots suspended on metal arms that could be swung above or away from the fire to give some control over temperatures. A single loaf of bread might be baked in a Dutch oven nestled into the hot coals of the fireplace, but most baking took place in wood-fired brick ovens.

To make the fire, the housewife had to load the logs into the oven and ignite them. Since the oven had no flue, she regulated the heat by keeping the door ajar to allow oxygen in. After about two hours, when the wood had been reduced to coals and ashes and the oven was hot enough to bake bread, she swept out the oven and put in her doughs. Small loaves could bake directly on the hearth surface. Larger loaves were baked in pans.

In most New England homes, the oven was built into the side of a large fireplace. The Pennsylvania Dutch cooked their food in kitchen fireplaces but did their baking in brick ovens in bakehouses that were completely separate from their homes. In the larger plantations of the South, the kitchens themselves were separate from the house, which made sense not only because of the hot climate but also from the standpoint of safety. Kitchens often caught on fire, and if they burned down, at least the large mansions would be spared.

Though they were extremely laborious, requiring a thorough mastery of heat regulation, something that was only attained after years of experience, brick ovens made superior breads with marvelous crusts and moist textures—and they are still the ovens of choice for professional bakers. They also retain heat for a long time, the temperature falling gradually over many hours. This allowed the housewife to bake a variety of breads, pies, cookies, and custards, in that order, each item going into the oven at the appropriate level of heat.

Brick ovens required huge amounts of wood. During the first two hundred years of settlement by colonists, forests were depleted to such a degree that another source of fuel had to be found. In the late 1700s, a new kind of oven was designed, the cast-iron range, which replaced both the brick oven and the fireplace as the primary choice for cooking. The range—popularly known as the iron monster—was enormous and unwieldy, but it economized on fuel. It could burn coal or wood, or later, oil or gas. Women had a devil of a time getting used to this huge interloper that came with flues, dampers, and all sorts of other controls. But the one feature it lacked was a thermostat.

More than half a century after the cast-iron range began finding its way into homes, housewives still needed instruction in its use. Cookbook author Sarah Tyson Rorer provided this advice in *Mrs. Rorer's Philadelphia Cook Book* (1886):

> *Study the draughts of your range. . . . Close the dampers, and this will throw the heat around the oven. Pull the dampers out only when you wish the heat or gas to escape into the chimney. . . . Open the draughts and dust damper, rake the fire well, until free from every particle of ashes; then open the top and brush the soot and the small pieces of coal, if any, from the top of the oven into the fire. See that the corners are free from ashes, and fill the fire-box even full with coal. . . . If you add more coal than this, you cut off the upper draught, and, of course, lose much heat. Now clean out the ashes, and carry them away.*

The technological leap from the cast-iron range to modern gas and electric ovens with reliable thermostats occurred in the late 1920s, a mere thirty years or so from the time Mrs. Rorer wrote of struggling with the iron monster. By the mid-1930s, the new ranges had become standard kitchen appliances. When a woman wanted to bake, she simply turned a dial and set it to the desired temperature. She no longer needed to be a woodsman and engineer. Instead, she could devote her energies to the creative acts of cooking and baking.

ABOUT THE INGREDIENTS

When I was in my teens, I learned a valuable baking lesson from a lady named Edna Allen, who told me, "You have to put in good to take out good." Using only the best ingredients is particularly important in baking, where inferior flours, fats, or flavorings will ruin something you've put your heart and soul into making.

Flours, Cornmeals, Grains, and Starches

FLOUR

About Flour In the United States, which grows some of the world's best wheat, there are basically two separate species. They include more than one hundred distinct varieties that are cultivated today. Wheat is classified according to the season in which it's sown. *Winter wheat* is planted in the fall and reaped in the late summer or autumn of the following year. *Spring wheat* is sown in the spring and harvested in the fall of the same year.

Both winter and spring wheats can be "hard" or "soft," depending on their protein content. Generally speaking, the higher the amount of protein, the harder the wheat. The color of the wheat grain is another indicator of protein content. You may see bags of flour in the grocery store labeled "hard red spring wheat" or "hard red winter wheat," which are ideal for making bread. Soft red winter wheat flour is best used in cakes and pastries. Other soft wheat flours include *winter* and *spring white wheat* flours. The important point to keep in mind is to choose the proper flour for what you are going to bake. If it's a cake or pastry, you'll want a soft wheat flour, low in protein (8 to 9 percent). If you're baking a chewy, yeasty bread, then opt for a hard wheat flour (11 to 13 percent). Check the label on the flour package for protein content to determine if it's milled from soft or hard wheat. For each ¼ cup flour, soft wheat cake flour will have 2 grams protein, all-purpose unbleached flour 3 grams, and hard wheat bread flour 4 grams.

I use *organic flours* in baking whenever possible. They are better for the planet and more healthful for us. These flours are becoming increasingly available in supermarkets. The all-purpose brand I use routinely is Gold Medal Organic Unbleached Flour. For most breads, I use a hard wheat organic bread flour made by either Giusto's or King Arthur. Both can be ordered by mail if you can't find a local source (see Sources, pages 525–26).

Wheat Proteins Wheat flour contains many kinds of proteins. Two of the main ones, *glutenin* and *gliadin,* are what give the wheat its "strength." When glutenin and gliadin come into contact with liquid, they knit together to form a network called *gluten.* The more of these proteins the flour contains (the harder the wheat), the more gluten is formed, and the stretchier the dough will become. Therefore, hard flours are best used for yeast breads. Low-protein soft flours are ideal for cake and pastry.

All-Purpose Wheat Flour All-purpose flour is a blend of soft and hard wheat flours, with a medium percentage of protein content. Not all so-called all-purpose flours are equal. White Lily flour, for example, a wonderful flour milled in Knoxville, Tennessee, is labeled all-purpose, but it is really a soft wheat flour best suited for making cakes, biscuits, and pastries. Another well-known all-purpose flour, King Arthur, contains more protein than other common supermarket brands. These differences can affect the outcome of a recipe. Many years ago, we lived in North Carolina for a little over a year, and the first recipes I baked there, including ones I'd made many times before, failed. It turned out the flour I was using was actually a soft wheat flour with an extremely low protein content, yet the bag was labeled all-purpose. Be sure to check the protein content listed on the bag!

All-purpose flour can be *bleached* or *unbleached.* After the bran and germ have been removed from wheat, the resulting flour is unbleached, with a creamy cast. To make flour pure white, it is treated chemically with chlorine dioxide, benzoyl peroxide, and acetone peroxide. This bleaching process destroys vitamins E and members of the B-complex group, so bleached flour must then be "enriched" by adding these vitamins. Bleached all-purpose flour contains slightly less protein than unbleached. Many bakers prefer to use bleached flour for cakes, cookies, and pastries because they say the results are more delicate.

Although all-purpose flour is supposed to be ideal for any use, that is not generally the case. I far prefer cake flour or an unbleached soft wheat flour when making a cake, and I often use a mixture of cake flour and all-purpose flour for a pastry. All-purpose flour with a protein content of 10 to 11 percent (Gold Medal or Pillsbury) is good for some cakes, however, as well as yeast breads and some yeast pastries.

Bread Flour An unbleached hard wheat flour with a protein content of 11 to 13 percent, bread flour makes breads with a springy, chewy texture. It is available in many supermarkets, but you can substitute unbleached all-purpose flour. Do not use bread flour for cakes or pie doughs.

Cake Flour Cake flour is a bleached soft wheat flour with a protein content of 8 to 9 percent. It makes light-textured, tender cakes and biscuits. It is too low in gluten to be used successfully in yeast breads. It is sold in supermarkets in 2-pound boxes under the brand names Softasilk and Swans Down. Avoid self-rising cake flours.

Whole Wheat Flour Whole wheat flour contains all the components of the wheat kernel: the endosperm, which makes up the bulk of the grain (80 to 85 percent) and is mainly starch and protein; the tiny germ, or embryo of the plant (2 to 3 percent of the kernel), which is packed with minerals, vitamins (including vitamin E), proteins, and fats; and the bran, or tough outer husk (about 15 percent of the grain), a rich source of fiber. Consequently, whole wheat flour has a high nutritional value and depth of flavor. If you can find stone-ground whole wheat flour, by all means buy it. Because less heat is generated by stone-grinding than regular steel milling, more of the nutrients in the flour are preserved. And because it has been ground between two stones, the flour has an uneven texture, which imparts an interesting toothsome quality to breads. But be careful how you use whole wheat flour. Don't just substitute it for white flour because it's better for you: it may not produce the best results.

Graham Flour Graham flour is a coarsely ground whole wheat flour. It gives breads a marvelous texture and a rich, nutty taste. Use it in yeast breads or quick breads.

White Whole Wheat Flour Milled from a new variety of wheat, white whole wheat flour has a milder taste than regular whole wheat flour but the same nutritional benefits. A rich golden tan, it is unbleached and contains no added chemicals. Use it as you would regular whole wheat flour. As far as I know, only King Arthur (see Sources, page 525) offers this flour.

Flour Storage Store white flours in airtight containers in a cool, dry place (if you live in a humid area, this is especially important). Buy only what you think you can use in a couple of months, since flour can take on an off taste after prolonged storage. Because the oil in whole-grain flours can turn rancid if stored at room temperature, these flours should be refrigerated or frozen. Measure or weigh what you'll need for a recipe, and bring the flour to room temperature before use.

Measuring Flour For directions on how to measure flour, see page viii.

Cornmeal Supermarket cornmeal, whether white or yellow, has most likely had its vitamin-rich germ removed. Degerming prolongs shelf life, but a lot of the flavor and texture is lost. If you can find stone-ground cornmeal, which contains the entire grain, use it (see Sources, page 526). Its medium-coarse texture makes it excellent in corn breads, muffins, and yeast breads. Whole-grain cornmeal, like whole-grain flour, is perishable. Store it in the freezer, where it will keep for at least 1 year.

Fine cornmeal, ground almost to a powder, is the kind suitable for using in a cake batter. You can use either the yellow or white variety. If you can't find packages that specifically say the cornmeal is finely ground, then use masa harina, a fine yellow cornmeal used in Mexican and southwestern cookery. Many supermarkets carry bags or containers of it.

Oatmeal Oatmeal is highly nutritious because it contains the bran, germ, and endosperm of the grain. Only the indigestible outer hull is removed in processing. I like to use the quick-cooking or old-fashioned rolled oats for the chewy texture and nutty taste they give to cookies and breads; do not use instant oatmeal. Oatmeal can be stored at room temperature.

Cornstarch Cornstarch is the dried and powdered endosperm of the corn kernel. It has a fine texture and adds tenderness to many kinds of cakes and pastries.

Rice Flour White rice flour is ground from husked rice kernels. It has an ultrafine texture and a pure white color. Since it contains no gluten, there is no danger of overbeating batters made with rice flour. Rice flour is available in some supermarkets, usually in 2-pound bags, or through mail-order (see Sources, page 526). Rice flour is a good alternative for people who are sensitive to gluten.

Rye Flour Rye flour can make dense, chewy, delicious breads. But because it is low in gluten, breads made with only rye flour turn out on the gummy side and hardly rise at all. In most cases, wheat flour (white or whole wheat) is added to the dough for texture and volume. Rye flour has a rich, nutty, slightly tart taste, and a little of it adds a marvelous tang to wheat-flour doughs. Two basic types of rye flour are sold in the United States: *dark,* or *pumpernickel rye,* and *light,* or *medium rye.* The whole grain is ground to make dark rye flour. It is coarse-textured and loaded with protein, vitamins, and minerals. Dark rye flour, because of its stronger taste and grittier texture, is great in bread doughs. Light rye has had the germ and sometimes the bran removed during milling, giving it a lighter color, finer texture, and less nutrition than dark rye flour. But both have their uses in baking.

Soy Flour Ground from whole soybeans, golden soy flour is rich in protein and fats. The brand I use is Bob's Red Mill, which you can find in the flour aisle in many supermarkets. Because it is gluten-free, it cannot be used as the only flour in breads. A small amount added to a standard bread dough boosts the protein content considerably. Doughs containing soy flour often smell like soy, which can be off-putting to some, but the odor disappears in baking, leaving only a deliciously nutty taste. Full-fat soy flours must be refrigerated, or they will turn rancid.

Leaveners: Yeast, Baking Soda, and Baking Powder

YEAST

The three basic types of yeast available today are fresh, active dry, and instant. Fresh is the purest form of yeast, and it has the highest amount of living cells — 100 percent — of any type of yeast. Some supermarkets carry foil-wrapped cakes of fresh yeast (0.6 ounces each), but it is not widely available. Fresh yeast is perishable: it must be stored in the refrigerator, and it should be used no later than 1 to 2 weeks after the expiration date on its wrapping.

Active dry yeast contains fewer living yeast cells than fresh yeast. It must be dissolved in warm water before being used so that the dead yeast cells can fall away, exposing the living cells. The major brands of active dry yeast available today are Fleischmann's and Red Star. Supermarkets everywhere carry them, and you can buy them in units of three conjoined packets containing 1/4 ounce (2 1/4 teaspoons) each, in 4-ounce jars, or in 1-pound vacuum-packed bags. SAF also makes an active dry yeast, SAF Traditional Active Dry Perfect Rise Yeast. It can be dissolved in warm water before using or added directly to the dry ingredients.

Instant yeast is faster to use because it is added directly to the flour. Once the liquid is added during the mixing of the dough, the yeast dissolves and becomes active. Because instant yeast has more living cells than active dry yeast, it causes doughs to rise faster. This isn't necessarily desirable, since doughs develop much more flavor when yeast acts slowly. However, doughs rich in butter, which are normally slow to rise, will profit from the addition of instant yeast. The two major brands of instant yeast are SAF and Fermipan. I use SAF; it is sold under a couple of names: SAF Perfect Rise Gourmet Yeast and SAF Instant Yeast. The Perfect Rise yeast is sold in double ¹/₄-ounce (2¹/₄-teaspoon) packets and in 3-ounce resealable pack-ages. SAF Instant Yeast is also available in 1-pound vacuum-packed bricks—handy if you bake a lot of bread. Many supermarkets carry SAF yeast. It can also be ordered by mail (see Sources, page 525).

Dry yeast, active dry or instant, should be stored in the refrigerator, where it will remain viable for up to 1 year. Check the expiration date before you buy.

BAKING SODA

Baking soda, or sodium bicarbonate, is one of the most potent chemical leaveners. An alkali, it is used to neutralize acid ingredients in batters as well as to leaven them. Molasses, honey, chocolate, sour cream, and buttermilk, for example, are all acidic, and baking soda counteracts the acidity. In large amounts, baking soda can give an off-taste to foods, so it is always used in small amounts.

BAKING POWDER

Double-acting baking powder, the major kind sold today, contains baking soda, an alkali, and one or more acids. Some leavening action begins when the batter is mixed, but a second, stronger action takes place in the oven under the influence of heat. One of the most commonly available brands is Calumet; its acidic ingredients include sodium aluminum sulfate, calcium sulfate, and monocalcium phosphate. Rumford baking powder contains only a single acid, calcium acid phosphate, and it is aluminum-free. Both these and other double-acting baking powders contain cornstarch, which acts to absorb moisture and to keep the acid and alkali ingre-dients separate from one another so they won't react in the can. I've used both aluminum and nonaluminum baking powders successfully, but I prefer Rum-ford because aluminum baking powders can impart a slightly metallic flavor to baked goods. There are several brands of nonaluminum baking powder available nationally.

All baking powders have expiration dates printed on their containers. Once opened, they lose their potency within a few months. I replace mine every 4 months or so. To test whether or not your baking powder is still viable, stir 1 tea-spoon into ¹/₂ cup hot water. If it bubbles gently, it's fine. If you have a can that's been sitting in your cupboard for a year or more, toss it out.

Sugar and Other Sweeteners

GRANULATED SUGAR

Granulated white sugar is the most refined of sugars. There are two kinds of granulated sugar: cane, derived from the tropical sugarcane, and beet, made from sugar beets. Beet sugar is cheaper than cane sugar. Chemically, beet and cane sugar are the same sucrose molecule, made up of a glucose molecule joined to one of fructose. In baking, they are interchangeable, but if you're melting sugar for a caramel, be sure to use cane sugar, because beet sugar doesn't melt as smoothly. How do you know if you're buying cane or beet sugar? Read the label. Containers of cane sugar will say "pure cane sugar." If a bag just says "sugar," it's most likely beet sugar.

CONFECTIONERS' (POWDERED) SUGAR

This is white granulated sugar that has been pulverized into a fine powder, with a small amount of cornstarch added to prevent clumping. Older cookbooks sometimes called it 10X sugar, meaning it was ten times finer than granulated sugar. It is used mostly to make icings and frostings and to dust baked cookies, cakes, or cupcakes. It may become lumpy, especially if you live in a humid climate. Be sure to store it airtight, and if it is very lumpy, sift it before measuring.

BROWN SUGAR

The most readily available brown sugars are light and dark brown sugar, sold in 1-pound boxes or 2-pound resealable plastic bags in any supermarket. Both are refined white granulated sugar with some of the extracted molasses replaced. Dark brown sugar has more molasses, giving it a deeper and richer taste than light brown sugar. In recipes where you want a delicate molasses flavor, use light brown sugar. The more assertive dark brown gives cakes and cookies a delicious toffeelike flavor. Brown sugar is moist and clumpy, and it's measured by packing it into dry measuring cups. The sugar has a tendency to dry out and become hard as a brick over time. You can soften it by adding a cut apple to the bag or box, closing it up, and waiting a day or two. A quicker way is to smash the dried sugar into clumps, put them into a shallow pan, and spritz them lightly with water. Cover tightly with foil and heat the sugar in a warm oven (about 225°F) for about 15 minutes, until it is soft. Cool before using. To keep any unused brown sugar moist, store leftovers with a cut apple in a tightly closed container.

SUCANAT AND RAPADURA SUGAR

These brown sugars have a richer, deeper flavor than ordinary brown sugar because nothing is removed from the cane syrup during processing. Sucanat, an acronym for "sugarcane natural," is sugarcane juice that's been evaporated without chemical processing. It has a granular consistency, like active dry yeast, and is deep golden brown. Rapadura sugar is made the same way; Rapunzel is another brand name. Both Sucanat and Rapadura are sold in bulk in health food stores, and I've found Rapunzel in some supermarkets. Both of these highly flavorful sugars can be used successfully in baking instead of ordinary brown sugar. Measure them as you would granulated sugar.

CORN SYRUP

Corn syrup comes in light and dark varieties. Not as sweet as sugar, it adds moistness to baked goods, and it helps to prevent the crystallization of granulated sugar when it is cooked to make syrups and fondants. *Light corn syrup* is a combination of dextrose and fructose. *Dark corn syrup* is a mixture of light corn syrup and a darker syrup produced during the refining of sugar. It is often used in pecan pie fillings, where a deeper, more butterscotchlike taste is wanted.

HONEY

Orange blossom, clover blossom, sage blossom, and buckwheat are four of the most commonly used honeys. Mild in flavor, they add moisture without dominating other flavorings—such as extracts or spices. Various other imported honeys are also available, but taste them before using to make sure they won't overwhelm the other flavors. Sometimes honey crystallizes after prolonged storage. To liquefy it, put the jar of honey in a saucepan of water and heat over low heat until the crystals dissolve.

MAPLE SYRUP

Maple syrup comes in different grades: Fancy, A, and B, ranging in color from a very light gold to a dark amber. The lighter the syrup, the milder the flavor and the higher the price. Use light syrups for anything from pouring onto waffles or pancakes to cookie doughs and cake batters. The darker Grade B is also suitable for both eating and for baking. It works wonderfully in soft ginger cookies and in gingerbread instead of molasses. Whatever maple syrup you buy, be sure the label says "pure maple syrup."

MOLASSES

Molasses is a syrupy byproduct of the refining of cane sugar. It is very slightly more nutritious than white sugar. It has a distinctive taste and aroma—assertive and inviting, with coffee and butterscotch nuances. Brer Rabbit and Grandma's are the two most common brands.

Fats

BUTTER

There is no substitute for butter. Its sweet flavor adds immeasurably to the taste of whatever you're baking. I always use unsalted butter because salt tends to mask the rich flavor undertones of the cream used to make the butter. Over the years I've tried many brands, both regional and national, and the one with the most consistently good results has been Land O' Lakes. The foil wrapper keeps out unwanted flavors and odors better than paper does. If you do lots of baking, buy several pounds of unsalted butter when it's on sale, and store it, well wrapped in foil, in the freezer. Thaw it in the refrigerator a day or two before you plan to use it.

Many recipes in this book call for creaming room-temperature butter together with sugar. "Room temperature" means anywhere from 65° to 75°F. What's important is that the butter be malleable so that it creams easily and aerates as much as possible when beaten with the sugar. It should not be too soft or look oily, or it will never have the structure to create the small air cells necessary for expansion during baking.

The microwave is handy for softening cold butter. Unwrap the butter, set it on a piece of waxed paper, and microwave at 30 percent power for 30 seconds. Test the butter to see if it feels cool and waxy and your finger leaves an impression when you press it. If not, turn the stick(s) over and microwave again. If you don't own a microwave but your kitchen is very warm, you can take the butter straight from the refrigerator and beat it on low speed with an electric mixer until it becomes softer. Then increase the speed to medium and beat until it is smooth and creamy.

When butter is cut into flour to make pastry, it should be very cold, so that the pieces remain firm. During rolling, the butter flattens out, forming flakes that remain haphazardly arranged within the dough. In the oven, the melting butter forms air pockets within the dough, making the pastry flaky.

LARD

A little lard in combination with butter makes far flakier piecrusts than butter alone. Part of the reason is that lard is virtually water-free. Even small amounts of water produce gluten formation in wheat flour, and butter contains about 16 percent water. For delicious, flaky pastry, substitute lard for half the amount of butter.

For the best lard, you should render your own, as our forbears did when they lived on farms and raised hogs. But since this is usually not practical, you can use a good commercial variety, such as John Morrell's. Check the package to be sure the lard is pure, with no additives. Store in the refrigerator.

VEGETABLE SHORTENING

To make vegetable shortening, liquid vegetable oils are hydrogenated: through some chemical wizardry, extra hydrogen atoms are attached to the atoms in oils to turn them into a saturated fat. In America's most popular brand, Crisco, the addition of nitrogen gas helps extend its shelf life and contributes to its pure white color. Vegetable shortening is softer than butter, is easy to measure (Crisco now comes in premeasured sticks), needs no refrigeration, and makes wonderfully flaky, tender pastries and fluffy cakes. The problem is it has no taste. For these reasons, when I use shortening, I use a higher proportion of butter to shortening in my recipes.

Recently vegetable shortenings have come under scrutiny because their hydrogenated fats are made up of trans fatty acids. Health professionals say that trans fats are worse for us than the plain old saturated fats found in butter because they accelerate the production of cholesterol in our bodies.

MARGARINE

I don't use it.

VEGETABLE OILS

The most commonly used oils in cooking and baking are canola, corn, safflower, sunflower, and peanut. For quick-bread batters, I use corn or safflower oil. For frying, peanut oil is my first choice because it has a high smoking point, meaning it won't burn until the oil reaches very high temperatures. It adds a mild nutty flavor to fried foods.

Eggs, Milk, and Other Dairy Products

EGGS

All recipes in this book call for US Grade A large eggs, which weigh about 2 ounces each in the shell. Whenever possible, try to buy eggs laid by cage-free chickens fed organic feed. I buy eggs at a local health food store, where local egg purveyors make deliveries every few days. The eggshells may be white, brown, or even green or blue, depending on the breed of hen; the color of the shell has nothing to do with the quality of the egg. Fresh whole eggs increase in volume more than stale eggs when beaten, and I try to buy the freshest eggs possible. Many supermarkets now carry eggs laid by hens that are not confined to cages.

MILK

For baking, I always use whole milk. It makes pastry creams smooth and silky, gives custards body, and contributes more rich flavor to cakes, cookies, and other baked goods than low-fat milks do.

BUTTERMILK

Buttermilk contributes tenderness and a delightful tang to baked goods. I am particularly fond of it in layer cakes, where its acidity acts as a counterpoint to the sweetness of the sugar. When butter used to be churned at home, the watery liquid left over after the cream solidified into butter was buttermilk. Today buttermilk is cultured. It has a thick, creamy texture but it is low in fat. Buttermilk keeps very well in the refrigerator for several weeks. Over time, it tends to separate into a heavier, thicker layer on the bottom and a thin, watery layer on top. Shake the carton a few times before using.

SWEETENED CONDENSED MILK

This extremely sweet, thick, cream-colored product is made by evaporating whole milk and cooking it with sugar. I use it in some cheesecakes, where it contributes a silky smoothness. Be sure not to confuse it with evaporated milk, which is shelved near it.

CREAM, CREAM CHEESE, SOUR CREAM, AND YOGURT

Heavy Cream and Whipping Cream Both these creams can be whipped, but heavy cream has a higher butterfat content (36 percent) than whipping cream (30 to 36 percent). The unfortunate practice of ultrapasteurization, which extends shelf life, has a negative effect on the taste and texture of cream. Ultrapasteurized creams taste less sweet, and they take longer to whip. If you can find regular pasteurized cream, by all means buy it. Organic Valley markets an organic heavy cream that is pasteurized and sold in pint cartons; the half-pint cartons are ultrapasteurized cream.

Sour Cream Real, full-fat sour cream is cultured with lactic acid bacteria and has a butterfat content of about 14 percent. It adds tang, moistness, and richness to baked goods. Because of its fat content, it also has a tenderizing effect in cakes and pastries. Low-fat sour cream can be used if you prefer. Do not use fat-free sour cream. Yogurt can be substituted for sour cream in many baking recipes, but some of that sublime richness is sacrificed.

Cream Cheese Regular cream cheese comes in dense, thick 3- and 8-ounce blocks. It's smooth and spreadable and contains at least 33 percent milk fat. Made with pasteurized milk, cheese cultures, and salt, with gum arabic as a stabilizer, it works better in recipes than the "natural" cream cheeses made without stabilizers. Cheesecakes made with natural cream cheese often curdle during baking. Kraft makes a cream cheese with one-third less fat that works perfectly well in cheese-cakes but less well in frostings, where just a little overbeating can soften the frost-ing so much that it will never set. The recipes in this book specify which type of cream cheese to use. Never use nonfat cream cheese, which has a gluey texture and off-putting flavor.

Yogurt A food staple for centuries in parts of Europe, the Middle East, and Asia, yo-gurt has made inroads into American baking as a lower-fat substitute for sour cream. In many cases it works extremely well, especially if turned into yogurt "cheese" by putting the yogurt in a cheesecloth-lined strainer and draining off the excess liquid. Yogurt is made by culturing lactobacillus or acidophilus bacteria in milk—whole, low-fat, or skim—causing it to thicken and turn sour. The milk of cows, goats, and sheep all make excellent yogurt, but in this country the most com-monly available kind is made with cow's milk. Avoid yogurts that contain artificial gums (some of the cheesecake recipes in this book will not work with such yo-gurts). I only use plain unflavored yogurt in baking.

Flavorings

VANILLA BEANS AND EXTRACT

The fruit of an orchid native to Central America, vanilla must be hand-pollinated, making it quite costly. Then the pods (fruits) undergo a months-long process of fermentation and ripening before they are aged for up to two years and finally brought to market. Today we can buy vanilla from Mexico, Madagascar, Indonesia, and Tahiti.

Be sure to buy *vanilla beans* that are soft, plump, and pliable. They add an intense flavor to sauces, cakes, all sorts of desserts, and sugar. For sauces, split the bean lengthwise, scrape out the small black seeds with a teaspoon, and add the seeds and pod to the milk or cream. Steeping over low heat for about 30 minutes releases vanilla's heady aromatic compounds. The pod can be rinsed, dried, and reused two or three times. For cakes, I like to grind the bean with some sugar in a coffee or spice grinder until both are pulverized and the sugar is saturated with vanilla's taste and aroma. Then I cream the vanilla sugar with the butter. The vanilla sugar is also delicious sprinkled over cookies when they come hot from the oven or stirred into a steaming mug of tea, coffee, or cocoa. To store vanilla beans, wrap them tightly in plastic, seal them in a glass jar or in a zip-top plastic freezer bag, and place them in a cool cupboard. The beans will stay fresh for 4 to 6 months. Do not freeze vanilla beans.

To make *pure vanilla extract,* the mature beans are chopped and steeped in a water-alcohol solution for a few months. I use double-strength vanilla extract, a highly concentrated essence, for its great depth of flavor. It comes with a vanilla bean inside the bottle. I order it from Penzey's (see Sources, page 526). Avoid imitation vanilla. It is made from artificial ingredients and contains no vanilla at all.

ALMOND AND COCONUT EXTRACTS

Until recently only imitation almond and coconut extracts were available, but today you can buy the real, pure extracts. (If these extracts are not sold in your supermarket, see Sources, page 527.)

LEMON AND ORANGE EXTRACTS

Made by distilling concentrated solutions of essential oils from the fruit zests, these extracts add an authentic citrus flavor to all kinds of desserts. Always use pure extracts, readily available in supermarkets. Imitation extracts contain artificial substances and flavors.

ROSE WATER

One of the oldest and most aromatic of all flavorings, rose water is an extract distilled from the petals of roses. I love its sophisticated flavor and aroma and use it in pound cakes, cookies, and other baked goods. You can buy rose water in specialty food shops and in stores that sell Middle Eastern foods. The bottles should be stored in a cool, dark place after opening. Rose water keeps indefinitely.

ORANGE FLOWER WATER

Orange flower water is distilled from the petals of orange blossoms. Like rose water, its use goes back centuries. Middle Eastern and Moroccan cooks use it in salads, syrups, and some savory dishes. I like it in custards, cakes, and cookies. Middle Eastern stores and some Italian delis sell bottles of orange flower water. Keep it in a cool, dark place after opening. It keeps indefinitely.

Chocolate

COCOA

Once all the cocoa butter (which is used in chocolate) has been removed from roasted and ground cacao beans, the dried cake that's left, called cocoa liquor, is ground into a fine powder, cocoa. Cocoa powder is bitter because it contains no sugar, but it imparts a deep, rich chocolate flavor to baked goods and other desserts. Hershey's is probably the best-known *natural,* or *nonalkalized, cocoa. Dutch-process cocoa* is cocoa that's been treated with an alkali to neutralize its acidity. It is darker in color than natural cocoa and gives baked goods a deeper chocolate flavor. Droste, made in Holland, is one of the most popular brands.

Some baking recipes call specifically for one type of cocoa, and in that case it's important you don't substitute one for the other. Since natural cocoa is acidic, it needs some alkali to work properly, and baking soda is usually used for that purpose. But if you substituted Dutch-process cocoa for natural, you would need an acid such as baking powder, not an alkali, to balance it.

UNSWEETENED CHOCOLATE

This has the most concentrated of chocolate flavors in solid form. It is made from chocolate liquor with some of the cocoa butter added back, and nothing else. After the two are combined, the mixture undergoes a lengthy process, called conching, that can last from several hours to a week and mixes, kneads, and beats air into the chocolate, giving it a smooth texture. (The device originally used for this process, a long, stone trough, was curved like a shell, hence the name of the process.) *Unsweetened chocolate* contains no sugar and is as bitter as cocoa. It must always be melted before being used in cakes, brownies, or cookies. It has a fairly high fat content, about 14 grams per ounce. Baker's and Hershey's are the two most common supermarket brands.

BITTERSWEET CHOCOLATE

Unsweetened chocolate with the addition of some sugar and vanilla flavoring, bittersweet chocolate is marvelous for baking because of its strong chocolate flavor. Some imported brands, such as Valrhona, contain anywhere from 55 percent to 70 percent cocoa solids, and I highly recommend them. American brands contain far less, around 35 percent.

SEMISWEET CHOCOLATE

Semisweet chocolate has a lower percentage of cocoa solids and more sugar than bittersweet chocolate. Unless you like chocolate on the bitter side, semisweet makes the best eating chocolate. Lindt makes semisweet chocolate in 3.5-ounce bars; some other European companies, like Valrhona, market it in larger bars. Baker's and Hershey's sell semisweet chocolate in convenient 1-ounce squares, but I strongly recommend the European brands because of their superior flavor.

WHITE CHOCOLATE

This really isn't chocolate at all, but cocoa butter mixed with sugar, vanilla, milk solids, and emulsifiers, poured into molds, and solidified. Inferior brands of white chocolate substitute vegetable shortening for the cocoa butter, so always check the label! Avoid the white chocolate coating sold in supermarkets; it has a waxy consistency, a granular texture, and a sickeningly sweet taste. Use instead the Swiss Lindt white chocolate or the Belgian Callebaut white chocolate.

Spices

Spices contain volatile aromatic oils, and over time they lose their flavor. Buy small quantities of ground spices at a time and keep them in tightly closed small jars in a cool, dry place, or grind your own in a spice grinder or coffee mill reserved for that purpose.

CINNAMON

Cinnamon comes from the inner bark of an evergreen tree grown in several parts of the world. The outer bark is stripped away and the inner bark is rubbed with a heavy brass rod to loosen it. Cuts are made around the bark, and it is carefully cut off the trunk in two sections. The bark is scraped clean, and each piece rolled into scrolls or quills. It's dried and cut into cinnamon sticks or ground into a powder.

GINGER

Ginger is a tropical or semitropical plant that grows as a rhizome, an underground stem. It is not a root. Stalks shoot up from it and produce beautiful big flowers. Fresh ginger can be grated and used in savory or sweet dishes. Dried and ground, it becomes the familiar spice in our kitchen cupboards. Crystallized ginger is often used in cookies and cakes.

NUTMEG

Nutmeg grows on tall tropical trees. The seed of the tree's fruit, nutmeg is wrapped in a webbing of mace, used as a spice on its own. Buy whole nutmegs and grate your own. Preground nutmeg has a faint aroma and a pallid taste in comparison to freshly ground.

MACE

Mace, the lacy covering that surrounds nutmeg, is not interchangeable with it. In large amounts, mace has a medicinal taste, but in small amounts, it adds a sweetness and mild spicy flavor that is most welcome. In the South, mace is a traditional flavoring in pound cakes.

Nuts

The most important thing to remember about nuts is that they're perishable. They keep far better in the shell than out, and they'll stay fresh much longer if whole rather than chopped. Store shelled nuts in the freezer and bring them to room temperature before using.

ALMONDS

Almonds are sold whole with skins on (unblanched, or natural), whole without skins (blanched), slivered (without skin), or sliced (with or without skin). I always buy the slivered or sliced nuts precut. If you use a lot of almonds in cooking, buy the whole unblanched nuts. They'll keep better than the blanched, and it's an easy job to remove the skins. Put the almonds into a bowl and pour boiling water over them to cover. Let stand for a few minutes, then remove the almonds from the water with a slotted spoon a few at a time, and pinch the skins off the nuts. Drain the nuts on paper towels. To dry the almonds, spread them in a shallow pan and bake for 5 to 7 minutes at 350°F, stirring or shaking them once; do not allow them to brown. Cool completely and store in airtight plastic bags. Or, if you want to toast the almonds, bake them a few minutes longer, until they turn pale golden brown. Toast slivered and sliced almonds the same way—since they're smaller, they'll be ready in less time.

BLACK WALNUTS

Black walnuts grow in the eastern United States. They have a very hard shell that's tough to crack, and unless you live near where they're grown, you're most likely to find them in your market shelled and chopped. The nuts have an intense, smoky flavor, and they lend distinction to many cookies and cakes. Brown sugar goes particularly well with black walnuts, as do coffee, chocolate, and many spices.

CHESTNUTS

Because the American chestnut was wiped out by blight many years ago, most chestnuts sold in this country are imported. Fresh chestnuts from Italy are available in the late fall. They are delicious roasted and eaten as is, or they can be cooked and used in desserts. To peel and cook chestnuts, use a sharp knife to cut an X on their flat sides and boil them in water for about 30 minutes until tender. Cool slightly, then remove the shells and inner skins. To puree them, put them through a potato ricer or food mill. It may seem like a lot of work, but it's worth it. You can buy canned unsweetened chestnut puree, but it won't taste as good or perform as well in many desserts, because it's lost its airy, fluffy quality. (Avoid jarred or canned chestnuts, which are usually roasted.) Chestnuts are much starchier than other nuts.

When buying chestnuts, select them carefully. Hold each nut in your hand and press on the shell. It should feel full. Make sure there are no breaks in the shell and no moldy spots. Store them in a paper bag—they need to breath—in a cool spot, and plan on using them soon after buying them, within a few days at most.

HAZELNUTS

Hazelnuts, small acorn-shaped nuts in brown skins and thin shells, are also called filberts. They should be toasted before using to bring out their deep, rich, nutty taste.

To toast hazelnuts, spread them in a single layer on a shallow baking sheet and bake them in a 350°F oven for about 10 minutes, until they begin to smell fragrant and their skins have partially split. Gather the hot nuts in a clean kitchen towel and let them cool for a few minutes, then rub them vigorously through the towel to rub off most of the skins, which have a slightly bitter taste. A few patches of skin won't hurt. Hazelnuts are difficult to chop because of their shape. I use a meat pounder with a flat round head. I tap on the nuts gently, breaking them up into smaller pieces, then chop them finer if necessary.

MACADAMIA NUTS

Native to Australia, macadamias are now grown in Hawaii. They are tough to crack, which helps account for their high price. They are also the richest of nuts, having the highest percentage of fat. Ounce for ounce, macadamia nuts have as much fat as butter, but the fat is mostly monounsaturated, the kind that's good for our hearts.

Macadamia nuts are usually sold whole, either salted or unsalted; the salted ones are much more common. Because of their round shape, they're hard to chop. I use a meat pounder with a round flat head and tap the nuts gently until they break into smaller pieces. Recently, however, chopped salted or unsalted macadamias in 6- or 8-ounce plastic bags have come on the market. Opt for the unsalted kind in baking. If only the salted nuts are available, you will usually need to decrease or eliminate the salt in the recipe. Because these nuts are so high in fat, they are even more perishable than other nuts. Always store them in the freezer.

PEANUTS

This is definitely the all-American nut, even though it's not really a nut at all, but a subterranean legume. Loved for their roastiness and crunch, peanuts are about 70 percent fat, 17 percent protein, and 13 percent carbohydrate. The fats in peanuts are "good" fats, mostly unsaturated, and recent studies have shown that eating a few peanuts daily can decrease one's risk of heart disease. Peanuts are also known as ground nuts, goobers, or goober peas.

My favorite *peanut butter* to eat and to cook with is the natural kind, with nothing added. Before using it, stir the oil that will have accumulated on the surface back into the thick nut paste below it with a fork or knife. As long as the oil and nut paste are thoroughly mixed, they will not separate during baking. Left at room temperature, natural peanut butter stays nice and soft. If it is refrigerated, the small amount of saturated fat in the oil hardens, making the peanut butter fairly stiff. Homogenized peanut butter, often with sugar added, is smooth (or crunchy) and easy to use, but I prefer the flavor of natural. Store opened jars of peanut butter in the refrigerator.

PECANS AND WALNUTS

The pecan is a native American nut, and the trees flourish in the central southern region of the United States, especially Texas and Georgia. Pecans are a type of hickory nut (as are walnuts), and their name comes from the Algonquin Indian *paccan,* which means hickory. The best time to buy pecans is when the nuts are gathered in late fall; November and December are the peak months. The nuts in the shell keep well at room temperature for over a year. Store shelled nuts in the freezer, where they should keep for at least 1 year. Thaw before using.

Buy pecans and walnut halves rather than pieces, if possible, because they stay fresher longer. If a recipe calls for coarsely chopped or broken nuts, break them into smaller pieces with your fingers. To chop nuts, I use a chef's knife, not a food processor, because the processor makes pieces that are uneven in size, with lots of powder, and it can easily overprocess the nuts and make them too oily. If you do use a food processor, process the nuts with a little of the recipe's sugar to prevent them from turning oily or pasty. Grind them to a fine, powdery mixture, but watch carefully so that you don't overprocess.

Both ordinary English walnuts (not black walnuts) and pecans profit from a light toasting in the oven to bring out their rich flavor. Place them in a single layer on a heavy baking sheet. Bake for 4 to 5 minutes, stirring once or twice, until fragrant. They should color only lightly: your nose will be the best indicator of when they're ready.

Fruits

DRIED FRUITS

The dried fruit available in supermarkets is most often sold in sealed packages. Dried fruit should be moist and supple when used in baking, so be sure to close the packages tightly after opening. Or better yet, transfer the contents to a zip-top plastic bag. Dried fruit sold in bulk is apt to be fresher than packaged fruit. Transfer it to zip-top bags for storage. Store in the refrigerator, where the fruit will keep better and longer than at room temperature. If the fruit does dry out, you can soften it by steaming it in a wire strainer set over boiling water for a few minutes. Pat the fruit dry on paper towels, and it's ready to use. If you need diced or cut fruit, steam large pieces and cut them after steaming.

CANDIED CITRON

Candied citron is made from the thick, knobby rind of a large lemonlike member of the citrus family. The fruit is cut in half, the flesh removed, the rind soaked in brine, and then candied. Top-quality citron is naturally green and is tender and has a waxy texture (see Sources, page 526). Citron is sold chopped or as half-rinds. It's best to buy the larger pieces, which keep better, and cut them to suit your needs. Store citron tightly wrapped in plastic in a cool place for 4 to 6 months, or freeze it for up to 8 months.

FRESH APPLES

Even though some apple varieties can be kept in controlled-atmosphere holding chambers for a year, apples always taste best at harvest time. Use apples from New Zealand during our off-season. For baking, Braeburn is my favorite all-purpose apple. It is tart and sweet and firm-textured, and the slices hold their shape in baking. Honeygold is another excellent variety, usually available in October. I rarely use Granny Smith or Golden Delicious, since both of these varieties are picked underripe and so never develop their full flavor potential. New-crop McIntosh apples are wonderful in crisps, but do not use them alone in pies; they are too soft and will make the filling mushy. An apple pie tastes better made with three or more varieties, each with a slightly different taste and texture. A combination of one third each of Braeburn, new-crop McIntosh, and Jonagold, for example, makes an excellent pie. Try to use locally grown varieties whenever possible.

ABOUT THE EQUIPMENT

Measuring Equipment

CUPS AND SPOONS

Dry and liquid ingredients must be measured in different kinds of cups. For liquids, use Pyrex measuring cups with a spout. They come in sizes ranging from 1 cup to 2 quarts. If you do a lot of baking, it's convenient to have at least two each of the 1-cup and 2-cup measures.

To measure sticky liquids like honey or molasses, either brush the inside of the cup lightly with tasteless vegetable oil or coat the cup very lightly with cooking spray: the liquid will then slide right out of the cup.

For dry ingredients, you'll need one or two sets of nested stainless steel measuring cups with straight sides, ranging in size from $1/4$ cup to 1 cup. Some sets are sold now with odd measures, including $2/3$ cup and $3/4$ cup. Heavy stainless steel is far more durable than lightweight stainless, which can dent and become misshapen easily, making your measurements less accurate.

To measure most dry ingredients, fill the cup to overflowing, then sweep off the excess with a narrow metal spatula or straight-edged knife. Measure granulated sugar by scooping the cup into the sugar container and sweeping off the excess.

Measuring spoons come in sets of four and include $1/4$ teaspoon, $1/2$ teaspoon, 1 teaspoon, and 1 tablespoon. Heavy stainless steel spoons are the best. To use measuring spoons, dip the spoon into the container, filling it to overflowing, and level it by sweeping off the excess. When measuring baking soda, cream of tartar, or ground ginger, which tend to clump, break up the lumps with the spoon before measuring.

SCALES

A kitchen scale, although it can be considered an optional piece of equipment, is useful for those times when you want to be absolutely accurate. And when making yeast rolls, it's a simple matter to weigh out portions of dough so that the rolls will be the same size. I have two favorites: a Cuisinart portion scale, which weighs ingredients up to 10 ounces, and a Cuisinart digital scale, which weighs ingredients up to 6 pounds. Many kinds of scales are available from specialty gourmet stores and mail-order catalogs (see Sources, page 524).

Candy, or Deep-Fry, Thermometer Candy or deep-fry thermometers take the guess-work out of cooking sugar syrups and deep-fat frying. Two types are available: a rectangular stainless steel model and a digital probe electronic model made by several manufacturers. The stainless steel thermometer has a sturdy clamp for attaching to the side of your cooking vessel and it can measure up to 400°F. The digital model has a long curved stainless steel probe that easily clips onto the rim of your cooking pot. It has a range of 14° to 392°F. The probe model is useful for small quantities of liquid: you can tilt the pan so that its contents pool into a corner and dip the tip of the probe into the liquid.

Oven Thermometer For accuracy's sake, you should take your oven's temperature before baking. You can either use a digital probe or a stainless steel thermometer. I prefer the latter because I can leave it in the oven and monitor the temperature during baking.

Oven temperatures drift over the course of time. If you're unfamiliar with the way your oven heats, it's essential you check it. Place a rack in the center position and place the thermometer in the center of the rack. Turn the oven on to 200°F and check the temperature on the thermometer after 15 to 20 minutes. Then increase the thermostat in 25-degree increments every 15 to 20 minutes until you reach 450°F, and take the successive readings. If the thermometer and your oven dial are in agreement, you're in luck. If they're off by 25 to 50 degrees, you should have your oven recalibrated by a professional. Even if your oven seems to be behaving perfectly, it's a good idea to check it with the oven thermometer at least once a year.

Instant-Read Thermometer If you're not sure if the water's too hot or too cold for your bread dough, the instant-read thermometer will give you the answer in a few seconds. The thermometer, a long metal probe topped by a dial, responds within a few seconds after being placed into a liquid. (The thermometer should not be left in the liquid, or other food, once a reading has been made.) Digital probe thermometers can also be used for this purpose.

Mixing Equipment

WOODEN SPOONS

You'll need two or three wooden spoons for stirring batters and sauces.

RUBBER SPATULAS

It's handy to have two medium and two large rubber spatulas for cooking, stirring, and folding batters. I buy only heatproof spatulas, instead of having some that are and some that are not, to save storage space and money. A large-bladed rubber spatula ($4^1/_4$ inches long and $2^3/_4$ inches wide) is extremely useful for folding flour into delicate cake batters.

WHISKS

Whisks are great for beating or for smoothing out lumpy mixtures, like cornstarch-thickened sauces or pastry cream. A small whisk is useful for mixing small amounts, either in a small bowl or small saucepan. A medium one can be used for stirring muffin batters or for beating a few eggs or egg whites. A large whisk, sometimes called a balloon whisk, is good for beating large amounts of batter, whites, or cream.

ELECTRIC MIXERS

Hand-held Electric Mixer A hand-held electric mixer is great for mixing cake and cookie batters, whipping egg whites or cream, or beating a boiled icing to thick, shiny peaks over a pan of simmering water. Various powerful hand-held mixers are available today, each adjustable to several speeds.

Stand Mixer If you don't already have one, you will bless the day you splurged on a heavy-duty mixer. I've had my KitchenAid for more than thirty years, and I would be lost without it. It has a 5-quart bowl, a whip attachment, a flat beater (also called a paddle attachment), and a dough hook. An extra bowl is a good idea, handy when the recipe calls for separately beaten egg whites and egg yolks. I use the whip attachment only for beating whole eggs, egg whites, egg yolks, chiffon cake bases, or heavy cream. For pound cake and layer cake batters, I use the paddle attachment, and for yeast breads, the dough hook. KitchenAid mixers come in three bowl sizes: $4^1/_2$-quart, 5-quart, and the new 6-quart model. Any one of these will cut the time for beating cake batters, whipping egg whites, and kneading heavy yeast doughs to mere minutes.

Although you can certainly make any of the cakes in this book with a hand-held electric mixer, a stand mixer frees you to do other things. And despite what some manufacturers say, a hand-held electric mixer isn't up to the job of kneading yeast doughs.

Food Processor Piecrusts mixed in a food processor are especially flaky and tender.

The machine can knead whole wheat bread doughs, which are very wet and heavy, in about 2 minutes. It grinds or finely chops nuts in seconds. And it can chop chocolate for ganache and puree fruits for sauces in moments. Two consistently highly rated and dependable brands are Cuisinart and KitchenAid.

Mixing Bowls Stainless steel or glass bowls are best. Plastic bowls tend to hang on to grease, no matter how thoroughly they're washed, inhibiting the beating of egg whites.

You'll need bowls in a range of sizes. The following are useful: 2 cups, 1 quart, 1 1/2 quarts, 2 quarts, 3 quarts, 4 quarts, 5 quarts, and 6 quarts.

Pastry Tools

PASTRY CLOTH

A canvas pastry cloth is helpful for rolling out dough without using too much flour, which can make the dough tough. A piece of canvas about 24 x 18 inches is big enough for just about any rolling job; the cloth can be purchased at fabric shops and cut to order or found in gourmet shops. Rub flour thoroughly into the canvas before using it for the first time and shake off the excess. Before rolling out a pastry or cookie dough, dust the canvas lightly with flour and coat both the top and bottom surfaces of the dough lightly with flour, then roll away. After you have finished rolling, shake the canvas to remove any excess flour and particles of dough. Fold the pastry cloth up and store it in a zip-top plastic bag in a cool, dry place.

ROLLING PINS

A ball-bearing pin, with two handles, or a plain cylinder of boxwood is your best choice. Both types are excellent, and you should choose which one feels best for you. Avoid heavy marble rolling pins; they compress dough too much.

PASTRY BLENDER AND PASTRY SCRAPER

A pastry blender is a tool made of five or six curved blades attached to a wood, plastic, or metal handle. It does a quick job of cutting fats into flour when making a piecrust. Pastry blenders with flat stainless steel blades are sturdier than those with thin wire ones. An up-and-down chopping motion is the most efficient way to use one.

A pastry scraper, or bench scraper, is a flat piece of metal attached to a wooden or metal handle. If you roll doughs out on a countertop, these scrapers do a quick job of cleaning up any mess.

PASTRY BRUSHES

Pastry brushes are used to dab syrups onto cake layers and to brush egg or sugar glazes onto yeast breads or cookies. Buy a narrow one (1 to 1 1/2 inches) and a wide one (2 to 3 inches) made of natural bristles. Wash them in soapy water, rinse well, and shake out the excess water. Dry the bristles in a towel, and store the brushes in a cool, dry place. They should last for years.

POT HOLDERS AND OVEN MITTS

Equip yourself with several heat-resistant pot holders and oven mitts. Replace them when they begin to show signs of wear. There's nothing more shocking than reaching into a hot oven, grasping a pan with a pot holder, and searing your fingers.

Baking Pans, Pan Liners, and Double Boilers

LAYER CAKE PANS

Lightweight or heavy aluminum round layer cake pans, with or without a nonstick surface, are best. The recipes in this book use only 9-inch diameter pans. The standard depth is 1 1/2 inches, and these pans usually have slightly sloping sides; you should have at least two, or, ideally, four. Straight-sided pans are usually 2 inches deep; have two on hand for those recipes specifying that depth.

RECTANGULAR AND SQUARE BAKING PANS

I like straight-sided pans made of sturdy aluminum, with lips that make it easy to grasp them with a pot holder without touching the batter. They will not dent or bend out of shape. The pans I have are made by Magic Line; Doughmakers makes equally excellent pans. Specialty cookware shops are likely to carry both these brands. I've used regular lightweight aluminum pans, with slightly sloping sides, and they work fine too. It's nice to have one or two of each of the following: 8 x 8 x 2 inches, 9 x 9 x 2 inches, and 13 x 9 x 2 inches. Chicago Metallic makes heavy dark aluminum baking pans with a Silverstone coating in these sizes; darker pans conduct heat better than light-colored pans, giving cakes a browner exterior.

LOAF PANS

They come in several sizes and are used mostly for baking yeast breads and loaf cakes. The two most common sizes are the 6-cup (8 1/2-x-4 1/2-x-2 3/4-inch) and 8-cup (9-x-5-x-3-inch) pans. My preference for an 8-cup loaf cake is the LaForme pan made by Kaiser, a German company, a heavy, dark gray, nonstick pan that measures 10 x 4$\frac{1}{2}$ x 3 inches; specialty cookware shops sell it. Because it is narrower than the standard 8-cup pan, the loaves bake taller and have a prettier shape. It's a good idea to have two each of the standard 6- and 8-cup pans and one of the longer, narrower 8-cup pan.

BAKING SHEETS

Baking sheets may be rimmed or rimless. The rimmed ones can be used for jelly rolls, cinnamon rolls, and all sorts of cookies. Rimless sheets are for cookies and for pastries that don't need sides to contain them. The two most common sizes for rimmed baking sheets are 15$\frac{1}{2}$ x 10$\frac{1}{2}$ x 1 inch, which is the standard one for jelly rolls, and 17 x 12 x 1 inch (also called a half-sheet pan), for just about any kind of roll or cookie. When making batches of cookies, it's convenient to have at least two of either size pan.

Rimless sheets, or sheets with one or two low rims, often called cookie sheets, come in many sizes. Heavy aluminum ones are my favorites. The most convenient are the 14-x-17-inch pans, and it's nice to have two of them.

Insulated cookie sheets, with a layer of air between two layers of aluminum, prevent burning, but cookies tend to take longer to bake on them, and sometimes even when they finally do cook through, the texture is too soft. I don't use them.

TUBE PANS

Bundt pans are tube pans with scalloped sides. The most common size measures 10 inches across by almost 4 inches tall and has a 12-cup capacity. The pans are made of cast aluminum and almost always have a dark nonstick finish. A word of caution: do not wash this type of pan in a dishwasher! The new machines are so powerful that even a single washing will ruin the nonstick finish (although it will still look just fine). Instead, wash it in hot sudsy water, using a nonabrasive scrubber.

A Kugelhopf pan, named for the classic multi-ridged German cake, is very handy. I use it whenever I want an attractive fluted edge for a cake, pound cake, or yeast bread. The pan is made of shiny tin and has fluted sides. It comes in several sizes, but the most common measures 8$\frac{1}{2}$ inches across the top and 4 inches deep and has a 9-cup capacity. The tube extends about 1 inch above the rim of the pan.

The standard angel food cake pan is made of aluminum, with a removable central tube portion, and measures 10 x 4 inches. Small "feet" extending from the rim allow air to circulate when the pan is turned upside down after baking. Do not use a pan with a nonstick coating: you want the cake to stick to the pan as it rises so that it can attain its maximum height. Angel food cake pans are also used for sponge cakes, chiffon cakes, pound cakes, and some sweet yeast cakes. A 9-x-3-inch one-piece tube pan, used in some of the recipes, is also nice to have.

PIE AND TART PANS

Pie Pans Pyrex pie plates absorb heat readily instead of reflecting it, ensuring that crusts bake through and giving them a beautiful golden brown color.

Tart Pans These are 1-inch-deep round pans, usually with scalloped sides and a removable bottom. I use French black steel pans because they conduct heat well. It's nice to own a 9-inch, 10-inch, and 11-inch pan. Be sure to dry the pans thoroughly after washing, or they may develop rust patches (these are easy to remove by washing and drying).

PIZZA PAN

A 13-inch pizza pan is useful for some of the tart recipes in this book.

MUFFIN PANS

These come in mini, standard, and "Texas" sizes. The mini-muffin pans have 12 cups. The standard pans have either 6 or 12 cups. The "Texas" pans have 6 cups. I prefer nonstick muffin pans. It's good to have two of each size. Standard-sized pans are also used for cupcakes, in which case I line the pans with paper cupcake liners.

SPRINGFORM PAN

These round cake pans have removable sides with spring-loaded hinges. They are great for cheesecakes and other cakes that bake higher than 2 inches or cakes that would otherwise be difficult to unmold. They're made of shiny or dark aluminum or of stainless steel. I use aluminum pans that are 2½ to 3 inches deep. Have one each with a diameter of 8 inches, 9 inches, and 10 inches.

BAKING PAN LINERS

Cooking parchment, available in rolls or precut sheets, can be cut to fit any size baking sheet, and it makes an excellent natural nonstick surface for baking all kinds of cookies, pastries, and breads. I like the new reusable silicone liners even better, especially for cookies. There's no buttering the pan and no spraying. Simply lay the liner on your baking sheet, and when you're through, wash it in sudsy warm water, then rinse and dry it. Although they are expensive, they'll last forever.

DOUBLE BOILER

A double boiler is a nested set of two pans; the bottom pan is filled with an inch or so of water, and the smaller pan set on top. A double boiler is useful for gentle cooking: for melting chocolate, cooking boiled icings, and making certain custard sauces. It's easy to improvise a double boiler from two saucepans of different sizes or a heatproof bowl and a saucepan.

BAKING STONE

A preheated baking stone gives a sudden jolt of heat to yeast breads, making them rise higher than they would if baked directly on the oven rack. Baking stones come in round or rectangular shapes; I find the rectangular much more useful. A stone that is about 14 x 16 inches fits perfectly on an oven rack with space to spare around the sides. It takes a while to preheat, so plan on turning your oven on about 1 hour before your dough is ready. I like to bake freeform or sandwich loaves this way. Baking stones are sold at specialty cookware shops and through mail-order (see Sources, page 524).

CAKE TESTERS

Wooden toothpicks or skewers are best for testing the doneness of cakes. Stick the skewer into the center or thickest part of the cake when you think it's done. The skewer should come out clean and dry or for some cakes slightly moist with a few crumbs. You can also use a clean broom straw as a tester.

WIRE COOLING RACKS

You'll want two or three round, square, or rectangular wire racks for cooling cakes. Cake layers are often unmolded onto one rack, covered with another, and inverted again to cool right side up; for a two-layer cake, you'll need three racks. The racks stand on short wire "feet" that allow air to circulate under them. A large rectangular wire rack is useful for rectangular cakes and for large batches of cookies.

Other Useful Tools: Knives, Graters, Sifters, Strainers, etc.

KNIVES

A *paring knife* is useful for releasing baked cakes from the sides of pans; making slits in a pie's top crust; cutting apples into quarters, coring, and peeling them; and cutting dried fruits into smaller pieces. A *chef's knife* with an 8- or 10-inch blade is useful for chopping nuts and chocolate and for cutting cakes and pies into serving portions. A *serrated knife* with at least a 10-inch blade is wonderful for splitting cake layers horizontally and for slicing sponge-type cakes into portions. When dividing a cake layer, you want a blade that is longer than the diameter of the cake for the best control. A *thin-bladed knife,* such as a boning or filleting knife, is the best tool for loosening angel food cakes, sponge cakes, and chiffon cakes from the pan.

SCISSORS

Inexpensive kitchen shears do the best job of snipping dried dates into smaller pieces and cutting parchment or waxed paper for lining baking pans.

GRATERS

Patterned after woodworking rasps, *microplane graters* do the best job of removing zest (the colored part of the rind) from citrus fruits without any of the bitter white pith. You run the fruit down the length of the rasp, and fine wisps of zest emerge on the underside. These graters come with holes of different sizes. If you buy only one, get the one designed for zests. Microplane graters are sold at specialty cookware shops and may be ordered by mail (see Sources, page 524).

Nutmeg graters, inexpensive small metal graters with a curved surface of small grating holes, are sold at specialty cookware shops and in some hardware stores. A microplane grater is also fine for this job.

SIFTERS

Single-mesh sifters are straightforward: they have a single screen of wire mesh. You put the flour into the sifter, turn the handle, and a curved metal wire rotates, aerating the flour as it falls onto the surface below. If some of the flour stays in the sifter, push it through with your fingers. Sifters do not need to be washed. Simply shake them out and store them in a cool, dry place. If you live in a humid area, wrap them airtight in a large plastic bag to keep any little critters away. Lacking a sifter, use a medium-fine strainer or sieve.

STRAINERS AND DREDGERS

A *medium-mesh strainer* is ideal for removing tiny lumps from sauces. They come in several diameters. Sometimes you'll want to dust cocoa or confectioners' sugar over cakes or cookies, in which case you can use a small fine strainer or a *dredger.*

CHERRY PITTER

A cherry pitter that clamps to the side of your kitchen counter is a dream tool if you cook with cherries a lot. You place a handful of stemmed cherries in the hopper and push on the plunger: one by one, the pits fall into a plastic container and the cherries roll into a bowl. You can prepare enough sour cherries for a pie this way in about 10 minutes. Many hardware stores carry these during the summer months.

COOKIE, BISCUIT, AND DOUGHNUT CUTTERS

Cookie and biscuit cutters come in all shapes and sizes. You can buy nested sets of round cutters in a whole range of sizes from 1 to 4 or 5 inches, with either smooth or scalloped sides. For most cookies and biscuits, though, all you really need are two sizes: a 2-inch cutter for biscuits and smaller cookies, and a 3-inch cutter for larger cookies and shortcake. The cutting edge should be sharp and the cutters should be sturdy.

For doughnuts, I use a cutter about 3 inches across with a $3/4$- to 1-inch hole. Buy a sturdy stainless steel one. A bagel cutter, which is a bit larger, also works well. Lacking these, you can always use a kitchen glass to cut out the large circles of dough and a shot glass for the holes.

Cake Decorating Equipment

ICING SPATULAS

These are metal spatulas that come in different widths and lengths. A small one with a 4-inch blade about 1-inch wide does a fine job on layer cakes. I also use this spatula to sweep off the excess flour heaped into a measuring cup. A 6- or 8-inch spatula is also nice to have. An offset metal spatula, with the blade bent at a right angle near the point it joins the handle, is useful for icing a cake in its baking pan.

CAKE TURNTABLE

If you make lots of cakes and like to give them smooth coatings of icing, you might consider buying a cake turntable. It makes icing a cake quick and simple. You turn the cake with one hand as you spread the icing with a metal spatula held in the other hand, resulting in icing that is smooth all the way around the sides. Ateco makes a turntable with a heavy ceramic stand and a rotating aluminum platform. It is sold in specialty baking supply stores (see Sources, page 524).

PASTRY BAG AND TIPS

Plastic-coated pastry bags are useful for piping cream puffs and éclairs, some doughnut shapes, macaroons, and meringues, and for decorating cakes. Have a 14-inch and an 18-inch bag. Plain round or star tips also come in different sizes. A small, medium, and large one of each will be adequate for a wide range of uses. Wash the bags in hot soapy water, rinse them well, and set them on a countertop to dry.

1 Savory Yeast Breads

Bread heads the list of foods for man.

—*Mrs. Rorer's Philadelphia Cook Book,* 1886.

Breads, glorious breads—crusty, chewy, many made with whole grains—were the foundation of a housewife's baking repertoire during the early European settlement of our country. Before housewives eventually succumbed to the convenience of commercial bakeries, producing nourishing loaves of yeast bread was a regular once-a-week activity. And judging from the quantities of flour in recipes from old cookbooks (some called for 32 cups!), women made a lot of loaves.

They also worked hard at it. The housewife had to sift her flour before use to remove any insects that might have taken up residence in the barrel. She usually prepared her dough in stages: the night before baking, she laboriously stirred together a batterlike mixture called a "sponge," which would help develop the bread's natural flavor. On baking day, she had to stoke the wood-burning oven and work the rest of the flour into the sponge. Then came the kneading. Kneading so much dough took an enormous amount of energy.

Working with yeast in those days could be tricky, because it didn't always behave reliably. Compressed foil-wrapped yeast cakes were not available until 1868, and dry yeast did not appear until the 1940s, so housewives had to find their own sources, such as distilleries, breweries, and bakeries. "Barm," a kind of sourdough made with fermenting beer or ale, provided much of the yeast for baking. Once women found a good source of yeast, they would keep a supply on hand, making new batches as needed and adding some of the old batch to "start" the new. But without refrigeration, yeast did not keep for long, so cooks had to renew their supply every few weeks. The summer months, in particular, could be hard on yeast, because it was easy for it to overferment

THE GIFT OF LIFE

On any given day, a dough you've made many times may act uppity. It might need a bit less or a bit more flour to achieve the right consistency. Or it might need a bit more kneading. Use these recipes as guides, and make adjustments accordingly. Humidity, the dryness or wetness of the flour, the temperature in your kitchen—all these are factors that affect a dough's feel and its behavior. Yeast breads are the most alive of all baked goods (before, of course, they reach the killing heat of the oven!), and living things are often unpredictable. For this reason, yeast baking is some of the most interesting and satisfying of all cookery.

and sour. One solution was to make homemade dry yeast, which could be hydrated when needed and was perfectly stable in hot or cold weather.

But despite all the labor, or perhaps because of it, homemade bread was venerated, considered far superior to bakery bread. In 1846, Catharine Beecher, sister of Harriet Beecher Stowe, asserted, "The only kind of bread which is always good for the health, and always acceptable to every palate, is sweet, well-raised home-made yeast bread." It went without saying that the flour in that bread was wholesome and unrefined. Milling methods used in the early- to mid-nineteenth century produced flours that retained a portion of the vitamin-rich germ and fiber-rich bran, imparting the natural sweetness that Beecher praised and making the addition of sugar unnecessary.

The superior flavor and nutritional value of early American flours was soon undermined, however, by the unfortunate English association of white bread with the upper classes and brown bread with the working classes. From the mid-nineteenth century on, millers strived to rid bread of all its brown "impurities," and the demand for pure white flour skyrocketed. By the 1880s, when Midwest millers Cadwallader C. Washburn, John Crosby, and Charles and John Pillsbury had completely replaced the grindstones in their mills with more efficient steel rollers, the "purification" of flour was complete.

Although its nutrients had been somewhat reduced, homemade bread continued to be the mainstay of the home baker at the beginning of the twentieth century. Housewives purchased 95 percent of all American flour in 1900, a good deal of it for bread. With an increasing number of men working far away from home instead of on the farm, portable lunches of sandwiches ensured they'd get something homemade. But in the 1950s, housewives too began to work away from the home, and baking became a leisure-time activity, not a necessity. In 170 years, the move from a rural to urban existence, with both men and women working, pretty much spelled the end of bread making by the home cook, and by 1970, home bakers were buying only 15 percent of American flour.

Over the past twenty years, however, bread making has enjoyed a renaissance, partly because time- and labor-saving heavy-duty mixers, food processors, and bread machines have become standard equipment in many kitchens. But you don't need a machine to make yeast breads. A few minutes of quiet, contemplative kneading will give you a loaf that Miss Beecher would have applauded.

BUTTERMILK BREAD

Makes 2 large loaves

Sometimes there's simply nothing that satisfies more than good old-fashioned white bread. And that's exactly what this is. It's sensational when warm, cut into thick slices, and slathered with peanut butter. It's also great with butter and jam, it makes marvelous sandwiches, and it is my favorite bread for toasting. It gets its special character from buttermilk. In the early 1800s, butter was usually churned at home and buttermilk, the watery liquid that remained after the butter separated out, was often saved to flavor breads and cakes. The cultured buttermilk we buy today isn't the same as the homemade kind, but it delivers irresistible tang to baked goods. I've made this bread with and without sugar. If you want to omit it, add the untoasted wheat germ, which acts as a natural sweetener.

2 cups warm buttermilk (105°–115°F)

½ cup warm water (105°–115°F)

1 ¼-ounce package (2¼ teaspoons) fast-rise active dry yeast

7 cups bread flour or unbleached all-purpose flour, plus more as needed

4 tablespoons (½ stick) unsalted butter, at room temperature

1 large egg

¼ cup sugar or ½ cup untoasted wheat germ (see above)

1 tablespoon salt

1 In a mixer bowl or another large bowl, stir the buttermilk, water, yeast, and 3 cups of the flour together with a wooden spoon. Beat until smooth, cover tightly with plastic wrap, and set aside at room temperature until doubled in volume and bubbly, 1 to 1½ hours.

2 *If using a stand mixer,* add the butter, egg, sugar or wheat germ, salt, and the remaining 4 cups flour to the bowl. Attach the dough hook and knead on low to medium speed for 5 to 8 minutes, until the dough is smooth and elastic, cleans the sides of the bowl, and is only slightly sticky. Knead in a bit more flour if the dough seems too wet and sticky.

   If making the dough by hand, stir in only 3 cups flour after adding the other ingredients. Sprinkle about half the remaining 1 cup flour on your work surface, scrape the dough onto it, and dust the dough with the rest of the flour. Knead the dough for 8 to 10 minutes, folding it over on itself and pushing it away from you in a rhythmic motion, until it is smooth, supple, and only slightly sticky. Add a small amount of additional flour if necessary.

3 Lightly oil a 6-quart bowl, or coat with cooking spray. Add the dough, turn to coat all surfaces, and cover tightly with plastic wrap. Let rise at room temperature until almost tripled in volume, about 1 1/2 hours.

4 Butter or grease two 9-x-5-x-3-inch loaf pans, or coat with cooking spray; set aside. Turn the dough out onto a lightly floured work surface and pat it gently to remove any air bubbles. Divide the dough in half, and shape each piece into a loaf. Place the loaves in the prepared pans. Cover loosely with lightly oiled (or sprayed) plastic wrap and set aside at room temperature

HOW THEY BAKED

In the eighteenth and early nineteenth centuries, baking of any kind was a huge project. Half the day might be spent chopping the wood to heat the oven, building the fire, and waiting the two hours or so for the oven to get sufficiently hot. Then, before anything could go into the oven, the housewife had to shovel out the coals and sweep the oven floor with a broom so that no ashes were left to contaminate the baked goods. Preparing the bread dough or cake batter also took time, but that could be done while the oven was heating up. Often doughs were begun the night before and allowed to rise for several hours during the cool early hours of the morning.

When the oven was ready, the bread was put in first, since a very hot oven was ideal. Later the pies went in, followed by cakes, gingerbread, and finally custards. The oven temperature fell gradually during baking, so that by the time the custards went in, the heat was gentle enough that the eggs wouldn't curdle.

In the absence of thermometers, how did one test to see if the oven was the right temperature? It was all done by feel. Here's how Miss Eliza Leslie did it: "If you hold your hand within the mouth of the oven as long as you can distinctly count twenty, the heat is about right. Pies, puddings, &c., require less heat."

until the centers of the loaves have risen 1½ to 2 inches above the rims of the pans, about 1 hour.

5 About 30 minutes before the loaves are ready to bake, adjust an oven rack to the lower third position and preheat the oven to 375°F.

6 Remove the plastic wrap from the loaves and place in the oven, leaving a few inches between the pans. Bake for 35 to 45 minutes, until the loaves are well browned and sound hollow when you remove them from the pans and rap their bottoms. They will not rise much. Cool on wire racks. You can eat this bread while it's still warm, or let cool completely, 3 to 4 hours, then wrap airtight.

If you plan on eating the bread within a few days, it's best to slice it after it's completely cool and store in airtight plastic bags in the freezer. Then you can take out the slices you need and thaw them for sandwiches, or pop them into the toaster straight from the freezer. For longer storage, up to 1 month, wrap uncut loaves airtight and freeze them.

THE SPONGE METHOD

Most of the recipes in this chapter use the "sponge" method for making bread. This is an old technique that served the housewife well. She could mix up the dough the night before, using some, but not all of the flour. The soft batter rose all night in the cool kitchen and by early morning, the dough had developed an airy, spongy texture with a wonderful yeasty (not sour!) aroma. In the process, it also developed a lot of flavor, due to the slow action of the yeast's enzymes on the flour.

I don't use an overnight sponge. Even a preliminary rise of 1 hour or so allows the sponge mixture to develop much more flavor than breads made without this step. But if you'd like to use the overnight method, prepare the sponge before going to bed and refrigerate it. Bring it to room temperature the next day and complete the dough.

CORNELL WHITE BREAD

*Makes
2 large
loaves*

Cornell bread was developed many years ago at Cornell University by nutrition researcher Dr. Clive McKay. A true Cornell bread must include three ingredients, which boost the nutritive value of refined flour: wheat germ, soy flour, and nonfat dry milk powder. This is the foundation recipe for all Cornell breads. The Ithaca Co-op food store, where this bread was first sold in the 1950s, dubbed it "Golden Triple Rich." It is a marvelous all-purpose sandwich bread. I add sugar and butter to this dough to make all kinds of sweet yeast breads.

6$^1/_2$ cups bread flour or unbleached
    all-purpose flour, plus more as
    needed
1 $^1/_4$-ounce package (2$^1/_4$
    teaspoons) fast-rise active
    dry yeast
$^1/_2$ cup soy flour

$^1/_2$ cup untoasted wheat germ
$^3/_4$ cup nonfat dry milk powder
2$^2/_3$ cups warm water (105°–115°F)
$^1/_4$ cup vegetable oil
$^1/_4$ cup honey
4 teaspoons salt

1 In a mixer bowl or another large bowl, stir together 4 cups of the flour, the yeast, soy flour, wheat germ, and dry milk powder.

2 *If using a stand mixer,* add the water and beat on low speed with the paddle attachment until the flour is moistened. Increase the speed to medium and beat for 6 minutes. The dough will be ropy and sticky and will mass up on the beater. Stop the machine occasionally to scrape the dough off the beater if it climbs up too high. Remove the bowl from the mixer, cover tightly with plastic wrap, and let the dough rise at room temperature until doubled in volume, about 1 hour.

If making the dough by hand, beat in the water with a wooden spoon and continue to beat until the dough is very thick and ropy, about 8 minutes. Cover tightly with plastic wrap, and let rise until doubled.

3 *If using a stand mixer,* attach the dough hook and add the oil, honey, salt, and the remaining 2$^1/_2$ cups flour to the dough. Knead on low speed until the flour is incorporated. Then knead on medium speed for 6 to 8 minutes, until the dough is moist, smooth, and elastic and almost cleans the sides of the bowl. The dough will still be sticky. If it seems too wet, knead in a small amount of additional flour.

If making the dough by hand, stir in the remaining ingredients and $1^1/2$ cups more flour. Sprinkle about half the remaining 1 cup flour on your work surface, scrape the dough onto it, and dust the dough with the rest of the flour. Knead the dough for 8 to 10 minutes, folding it over on itself and pushing it away from you in a rhythmic motion, until it is smooth and supple but still slightly sticky. If necessary, add a small amount of additional flour.

4 Lightly oil a 6-quart bowl, or coat with cooking spray. Scrape the dough into the bowl and turn to coat all over. Pick up the dough and work it briefly with your hands to form a smooth ball; it should feel supple, smooth, and elastic. Return the dough to the bowl and cover tightly with plastic wrap. Let rise at room temperature until almost tripled in size, 1 to $1^1/2$ hours.

5 Butter or grease two 9-x-5-x-3-inch loaf pans, or coat with cooking spray; set aside. Turn the dough out onto a lightly floured work surface and pat it gently to removely any air bubbles. Divide the loaf in half, and shape each piece into a loaf. Place the loaves in the prepared pans. Cover loosely with lightly oiled (or sprayed) plastic wrap and set aside at room temperature until the centers have risen $1^1/2$ to 2 inches above the rims of the pans, about 1 hour.

6 About 30 minutes before the loaves are ready to bake, adjust an oven rack to the lower third position and preheat the oven to 375°F.

7 Remove the plastic wrap from the loaves and place in the oven, leaving a few inches between the pans. Bake for 35 to 45 minutes, until the loaves are well browned and sound hollow when you remove them from the pans and rap their bottoms. Cool completely on wire racks, 3 to 4 hours, then wrap airtight. The loaves can be frozen for up to 1 month.

BUTTERMILK WHEAT GERM BREAD

Makes 2 large loaves

This makes a great sandwich bread. The wheat germ adds a nutritional boost and gives the bread an appetizing speckled look. Be sure to use untoasted, or raw, wheat germ. Toasted wheat germ would make the texture a bit too crunchy.

6 cups bread flour or unbleached all-purpose flour, plus about $1/2$ cup more

1 cup untoasted wheat germ

1 $1/4$-ounce package ($2 1/4$ teaspoons) fast-rise active dry yeast

6 tablespoons ($3/4$ stick) unsalted butter, at room temperature

$1 1/2$ cups buttermilk

$3/4$ cup water

$1/4$ cup honey

2 large eggs

4 teaspoons salt

1 In a mixer bowl or another large bowl, stir together the 6 cups flour, the wheat germ, yeast, and butter until the butter is incorporated.

2 Heat the buttermilk, water, and honey in a medium saucepan over medium heat, stirring occasionally, until the mixture is just warm to the touch. Remove from the heat and stir in the eggs and salt with a fork. Add to the flour mixture.

3 *If using a stand mixer,* attach the dough hook and knead on low speed until the dough is well mixed. Knead on medium speed for about 8 minutes, until the dough is smooth, elastic, and only slightly sticky. Add up to $1/2$ cup more flour, 1 tablespoon at a time, if the dough feels very wet and sticky, kneading well after each addition.

 If making the dough by hand, stir all the ingredients together well with a wooden spoon. Sprinkle about $1/2$ cup additional flour on your work surface, scrape the dough onto it, and dust the dough with a bit more flour. Knead the dough for 8 to 10 minutes, folding it over on itself and pushing it away from you in a rhythmic motion, until it is smooth, elastic, and only slightly sticky.

4 Lightly oil a 6-quart bowl, or coat with cooking spray. Scrape the dough into the bowl and turn to coat all surfaces. Pick up the dough and knead it briefly between your hands. It should be soft, smooth, elastic, and only very slightly sticky. Return to the bowl and cover tightly with plastic wrap. Let rise at room temperature until the dough has almost tripled in volume, about 1 1/2 hours.

5 Butter or grease two 9-x-5-x-3-inch loaf pans, or coat with cooking spray; set aside. Turn the dough out onto a lightly floured work surface and pat it gently to remove any air bubbles. Divide the loaf in half, and shape each piece into a loaf. Place the loaves in the prepared pans. Cover loosely with lightly oiled (or sprayed) plastic wrap and set aside at room temperature until the centers have risen about 1 1/2 inches above the rims of the pans, about 1 hour.

6 About 30 minutes before the loaves are ready to bake, adjust an oven rack to the lower third position and preheat the oven to 375°F.

7 Remove the plastic wrap from the loaves and place in the oven, leaving a few inches between the pans. Bake for 40 to 50 minutes, until the loaves are well browned and sound hollow when you remove them from the pans and rap their bottoms. Cool completely on wire racks, 3 to 4 hours, then wrap airtight. The loaves can be frozen for up to 1 month.

THE BEST FIREWOOD FOR BAKING

The best wood for fires is the hickory, hard maple, white ash, black birch, yellow birch, beech, yellow oak, and locust. The following are inferior in quality. Elm, soft maple, white birch, pepperage, and pine. The following are not fit to burn, either because they snap, or will not burn. Chestnut, butternut, cedar, sasafras, red oak, and buckeye. Any person can learn to distinguish each kind by a little attention and instruction.

—Catharine Beecher,
Miss Beecher's Domestic Receipt-Book (1846)

FOOD PROCESSOR CHALLAH

Makes 1 large braid

This bread is traditionally made for the Jewish Sabbath, but bakeries all over the country make and sell it on a daily basis. It's usually braided from three, four, or even six strands of dough. The entwined strands symbolize love. Challah is a firm-textured bread with a delicious taste, which results from letting the dough rise twice before it is shaped for its final rise. Because of the Jewish injunction against working on the Sabbath, the dough in traditional homes is usually kneaded on Thursday, allowed to rise overnight, and shaped and baked on Friday so that it will be ready to eat by sundown. The easiest way to make challah is with a food processor. Leftovers make terrific French toast or bread pudding.

¼ cup warm water (105°–115°F)

1 0.6-ounce cake compressed yeast or one ¼-ounce package (2¼ teaspoons) active dry yeast

¼ cup vegetable oil

3 large eggs

½ cup cold water

3½ cups unbleached all-purpose flour, plus more as needed

1½ teaspoons salt

1 large egg yolk, whisked together with 2 teaspoons water

1–2 teaspoons sesame seeds or poppy seeds

1 Place the warm water in a 2-cup glass measure or small bowl. Crumble the cake of yeast into it or sprinkle in the dry yeast. Stir, and let stand for about 10 minutes, until dissolved.

2 Add the oil, eggs, and cold water to the yeast mixture and mix well with a fork. Add the 3½ cups flour and salt to a food processor and pulse to mix. With the machine on, gradually add the liquid, taking 20 to 30 seconds. Once the dough gathers into a ball, process for 1 full minute to knead. The dough should clean the sides of the work bowl and should feel soft, smooth, elastic, and not at all sticky. If the dough is too wet, add a small amount of flour.

3 Lightly oil a 3-quart bowl. Shape the dough into a ball, place it in the bowl, and turn to coat all surfaces. Cover tightly with plastic wrap and let rise at room temperature until doubled in volume, about 1 hour. Press an index finger into the dough. When you remove it, the depression should remain; if the dough springs back, cover and continue to let rise.

4 Gently deflate the risen dough with your fingers. Lift it up and shape into a ball, then return to the bowl. Cover tightly and let rise a second time until doubled in volume, 1 to 1¹/₂ hours.

5 Lightly butter or oil a 12-x-17-inch baking sheet; set aside. Turn the dough out onto a lightly floured surface. Divide it into 3 equal pieces and shape each into a ball. Cover loosely with a towel and let rest for 15 minutes.

6 Roll each ball of dough into a 15-inch-long rope. Braid the strands of dough together. Pinch the ends to seal and tuck them under. Place the braid diagonally on the baking sheet. Cover loosely with a sheet of plastic wrap lightly coated with cooking spray and let rise at room temperature until puffed and doubled in size, 1 to 1¹/₂ hours.

7 About 30 minutes before the bread is ready to bake, adjust an oven rack to the lower third position and preheat the oven to 375°F.

8 Remove the plastic wrap from the braid and brush with the egg yolk mixture. Sprinkle with the sesame or poppy seeds. Bake for about 35 minutes, until the challah is a rich golden brown and sounds hollow when you remove it from the pan and rap its bottom. Remove from the baking sheet and cool on a wire rack before slicing. The loaves may be wrapped airtight and frozen for up to 1 month.

YEAST FOR BREAD

As poor yeast is the chief cause of poor bread, pains should be taken to make yeast properly and to keep it well. It must never be allowed to stand in a warm room after it has risen, and the jug in which it is kept should be carefully washed and scalded *each time the yeast is renewed. As much care must be taken with the stopper as with the jug.*

When it is convenient to get fresh cakes of Fleischmann's compressed yeast, it will be much better and cheaper to use them than to make your own.

—Maria Parloa, *Miss Parloa's New Cook Book* (1886)

OATMEAL-RAISIN LOAVES

*Makes
2 large
loaves*

The practice of adding oatmeal to yeast breads had become common by the late 1800s. Fannie Farmer's *The Original Boston Cooking School Cook Book* of 1896 features a recipe for oatmeal bread using water, molasses, and white flour. I prefer milk to water, since it tenderizes the dough, and I use a mixture of whole wheat and all-purpose flour. A little maple syrup adds just a hint of sweetness. This bread is excellent when still warm, cut into thick slices, and spread with sweet butter. It also makes sensational bread pudding or French toast.

2 cups milk	2 large eggs
1¹/₂ cups quick-cooking (not instant) or old-fashioned rolled oats	¹/₃ cup pure maple syrup
	¹/₄ cup water, plus more if needed
4 tablespoons (¹/₂ stick) unsalted butter	1 tablespoon salt
2 cups whole wheat flour	3¹/₂ cups unbleached all-purpose flour, plus more as needed
1 ¹/₄-ounce package (2¹/₄ teaspoons) active dry yeast	1¹/₂ cups golden raisins or a mixture of dark and golden raisins

1 Bring the milk almost to a boil in a large saucepan. Remove from the heat and add the oats and butter. Stir well with a wooden spoon until the butter melts. Cool the mixture until it feels just warm to the touch.

2 *If using a stand mixer,* scrape the oatmeal mixture into the bowl and add the whole wheat flour, yeast, and eggs. Beat on medium speed with the paddle attachment for 5 minutes. Scrape the bowl and beater.

   If making the dough by hand, transfer the oatmeal mixture to a large bowl and stir in the whole wheat flour, yeast, and eggs with a wooden spoon. Beat vigorously until the batter is ropy, about 5 minutes.

   Cover the dough tightly with plastic wrap and let rise at room temperature until almost tripled in volume, 1 to 1¹/₂ hours.

3 *If using a stand mixer,* stir the maple syrup, ¹/₄ cup water, salt, and 1 cup of the all-purpose flour into the oatmeal mixture. Attach the dough hook and, kneading on low speed, add the remaining 2¹/₂ cups flour, ¹/₂ cup at a

time, kneading well after each addition. Increase the speed to medium and knead for 5 to 8 minutes, until the dough cleans the sides of the bowl and feels firm, smooth, and elastic. Add a small amount of additional water or flour if necessary.

If making the dough by hand, stir in the maple syrup, $^1/_4$ cup water, salt, and $2^1/_2$ cups of the all-purpose flour. Sprinkle about half the remaining 1 cup flour on your work surface, scrape the dough onto it, and dust the dough with the rest of the flour. Knead the dough for 8 to 10 minutes, folding it over on itself and pushing it away from you in a rhythmic motion, until it is firm, smooth, and elastic. Knead in a small amount of additional flour if necessary.

4 Lightly oil a 6-quart bowl, or coat with cooking spray, and transfer the dough to the bowl. Turn to coat all surfaces. Pick up the dough and knead briefly between your hands; it should feel slightly firmer. Return the dough to the bowl, cover tightly with plastic wrap, and let rise at room temperature until almost tripled in volume, about 2 hours.

5 Butter or grease two 9-x-5-x-3-inch loaf pans, or coat with cooking spray; set aside. Turn the dough out onto a lightly floured work surface and pat it gently to remove any air bubbles. Sprinkle the raisins over the dough and knead them in. Cut the dough in half, and shape each piece into a loaf. Place the loaves in the prepared pans. Cover loosely with lightly oiled (or sprayed) plastic wrap and set aside at room temperature until the centers have risen about 2 inches above the rims of the pans, about 1 hour.

6 About 30 minutes before the loaves are ready to bake, adjust an oven rack to the lower third position and preheat the oven to 375°F.

7 Remove the plastic wrap from the loaves and place them in the oven, leaving a few inches between the pans. Bake for 40 to 45 minutes, until the loaves are well browned and sound hollow when you remove them from the pans and rap their bottoms. Cool completely on wire racks, 3 to 4 hours, then wrap airtight. The loaves can be frozen for up to 1 month.

RICE BREAD

*Makes
2 loaves*

Nineteenth-century cookbooks featured recipes using rice and rice flour in all kinds of breads and cakes. For breads, rice, which has no gluten, was always combined with wheat flour to provide the all-important gluten network and springy texture. This extremely satisfying bread is as simple as can be. It has a natural sweetness from the rice, a pleasing rich taste, and a chewy, open texture, with lots of small to medium holes. Use any long- or short-grain rice. My own favorite is basmati, because of its nutty flavor. The bread browns only very slightly, becoming a pale golden brown at most. Serve it warm with butter, use it for sandwiches, or toast it. Jams, jellies, and preserves are all great companions.

1/2 cup basmati or other long-grain or short-grain rice	1 teaspoon fast-rise active dry yeast
2 3/4 cups cold water	2 teaspoons salt
6 cups bread flour or unbleached all-purpose flour, plus more as needed	

1 Combine the rice and 1 1/2 cups of the water in a medium saucepan. Bring to a boil, cover, and cook over the lowest heat until all the water is absorbed and the rice is tender, about 20 minutes. Remove from the heat and set aside, covered, for 30 minutes to cool; it should not be hot when mixed into the dough.

2 In a mixer bowl or another large bowl, stir the rice together with the remaining 1 1/4 cups cold water. Feel the temperature with your finger—it should be warm but not hot; an instant-read thermometer should register between 110° and 115°F. Add 2 cups of the flour and the yeast and beat well with a wooden spoon to make a thick batter. Cover with plastic wrap and set aside at room temperature until the sponge has doubled in size and is covered with bubbles at the surface, about 1 1/2 hours.

3 With a wooden spoon, stir 2 more cups of the flour and the salt into the sponge, just to incorporate.

4 *If using a stand mixer,* attach the dough hook and, kneading on low speed, gradually add the remaining 2 cups flour, kneading until it is completely absorbed. Increase the speed to medium and knead for 5 to 6 minutes more, until the dough is smooth, elastic, and only slightly sticky. It should eventually mass up on the dough hook and clean the sides of the bowl. Knead in a bit more flour if necessary.

    To make the dough by hand, gradually stir 3 cups of the flour and the salt into the sponge. Sprinkle about half the remaining 1 cup flour on your work surface, scrape the dough onto it, and dust the dough with the rest of the flour. Knead the dough for 8 to 10 minutes, folding it over on itself and pushing it away from you in a rhythmic motion, until it is smooth, elastic, and only slightly sticky. Knead in a small amount of additional flour if necessary.

5 Butter or grease two $8^1/2$-x-$4^1/2$-x-$2^3/4$-inch loaf pans, or coat with cooking spray; set aside. Lightly flour your work surface and transfer the dough to it. Turn the dough in the flour and knead it a few strokes so it is completely smooth. Divide the dough in half and shape each piece into a loaf. Place the loaves in the prepared pans. Cover loosely with a kitchen towel and set in a warm place (80° to 85°F) to rise until the centers are about 2 inches above the rims of the pans, about 1 hour.

6 About 30 minutes before the loaves are ready to bake, adjust an oven rack to the lower third position and preheat the oven to 375°F.

7 Uncover the loaves and place the pans in the oven, a few inches apart. Bake for about 50 minutes, until they are just lightly colored and make a hollow sound when you remove them from the pans and rap them on their bottoms; they will rise only slightly. Cool on wire racks.

    Slice with a sharp serrated knife. The bread keeps well for several days stored at room temperature in a paper bag. It can be frozen, well wrapped, for up to 1 month.

HONEY WHOLE WHEAT BREAD

*Makes
2 large
loaves*

This is another delicious all-purpose sandwich bread, made with half whole wheat and half white bread flour. Honey brings a depth of flavor without actually sweetening the bread. It makes great toasted cheese sandwiches.

3½ cups whole wheat flour

1 ¼-ounce package (2¼ teaspoons) fast-rise active dry yeast

1½ cups warm water (105°–115°F)

2 large eggs

3½ cups bread flour or unbleached all-purpose flour, plus more as needed

¼ cup vegetable oil

¼ cup honey

½ cup room-temperature water

4 teaspoons salt

1 In a mixer bowl or another large bowl, stir together the whole wheat flour and yeast. Add the warm water and eggs.

2 *If using a stand mixer,* beat on medium speed with the paddle attachment for 4 minutes. Scrape the bowl and beater.

  If making the dough by hand, beat the whole wheat flour mixture vigorously with a wooden spoon until the batter is ropy, 3 to 4 minutes.

  Cover the bowl with plastic wrap and let rise at room temperature until doubled in size, about 1 hour.

3 *If using a stand mixer,* add the 3½ cups bread flour or all-purpose flour, oil, honey, room-temperature water, and salt to the dough. Attach the dough hook and knead on medium speed for 5 to 8 minutes, until the dough cleans the side of the bowl and is smooth, elastic, and only slightly sticky. Knead in a bit more flour if the dough seems too wet and sticky.

  If making the dough by hand, add the oil, honey, room-temperature water, and salt to the dough. Stir in only 2½ cups of the 3½ cups bread flour or all-purpose flour after adding the other ingredients. Sprinkle about half the remaining 1 cup flour on your work surface, scrape the dough onto it, and dust the dough with the rest of the flour. Knead the dough for 8 to 10 minutes, folding it over on itself and pushing it away from you in a rhythmic motion, until it is smooth, elastic, and only slightly sticky. Add a small amount of additional flour if necessary.

4 Lightly oil a 6-quart bowl, or coat with cooking spray. Scrape the dough into the bowl and turn to coat all over. Pick up the dough and work between your hands to form a smooth ball. Return to the bowl, cover tightly with plastic wrap, and let rise until almost tripled in volume, 1 to 1½ hours.

5 Butter or grease two 9-x-5-x-3-inch loaf pans, or coat with cooking spray; set aside. Turn the dough out onto a lightly floured work surface and pat it gently to remove any air bubbles. Divide the dough in half, and shape each piece into a loaf. Place the loaves in the prepared pans. Cover loosely with lightly oiled (or sprayed) plastic wrap and set aside at room temperature until the centers have risen 1½ to 2 inches above the rims of the pans, about 1 hour.

6 About 30 minutes before the loaves are ready to bake, adjust an oven rack to the lower third position and preheat the oven to 375°F.

7 Remove the plastic wrap from the loaves and place in the oven, leaving a few inches between the pans. Bake for 35 to 45 minutes, until the loaves are well browned and sound hollow when you remove them from the pans and rap their bottoms; they will not rise much. Cool completely on wire racks, 3 to 4 hours, then wrap airtight. The loaves freeze well for up to 1 month.

FOOD PROCESSOR 100-PERCENT WHOLE WHEAT BREAD

Makes 1 loaf

Bread made with only whole wheat flour sometimes seems more like a hockey puck than a tender loaf. Kneading all-whole-wheat doughs can cause problems: the tiny pieces of bran are sharp and can break down the gluten strands, thus robbing the bread of the spring it needs.

Food processor to the rescue! Making a sponge with some of the flour serves to soften the bran and make it far less abrasive during kneading. Working with a fairly wet dough and beating it with the food processor dough blade really develops the flour's gluten and gives the dough a silky-smooth elasticity. The bread you will get is light, tender, and altogether delicious. This recipe is for a standard food processor, but it can be doubled (double everything) if you have a larger model.

3 cups whole wheat flour, plus more as needed

1 $\frac{1}{4}$-ounce package (2$\frac{1}{4}$ teaspoons) fast-rise active dry yeast

$\frac{3}{4}$ cup plus 2 tablespoons warm water (105°–115°F), plus more if needed

2 tablespoons vegetable oil

3 tablespoons molasses (I use Grandma's)

1 large egg

2 teaspoons salt

1 Add 1 cup of the flour and the yeast to a food processor fitted with the metal blade. With the motor running, quickly pour in the warm water and process for 15 seconds. Stop to scrape the work bowl, and process for another 15 seconds. Scrape the bowl again, cover with the lid, and let stand until the sponge has doubled in volume, 30 minutes to 1 hour or more, depending on the temperature of your kitchen.

2 Add the oil, molasses, egg, and salt and process for 15 seconds. Carefully remove the metal blade, scraping it clean, and insert the plastic dough blade. Sprinkle the remaining 2 cups flour in a ring on top of the sponge, and process for 1 minute. Scrape the work bowl well—the dough will be very

sticky—and let stand for 3 minutes to allow the flour to absorb the liquid.

3 Process for another $1^1/_2$ minutes, or until the dough gathers into a ball and almost cleans the sides of the work bowl. The dough should be very moist, sticky, and very elastic. If necessary, add a bit more water (or flour)—one key to the success of this recipe is the moistness of the dough.

4 Lightly oil a 3-quart bowl, or coat with cooking spray. Scrape the dough into the bowl and turn to coat all surfaces. Pick up the dough, squish it between your hands, and shape it into a ball; it should be very soft and supple, not sticky. Return to the bowl, cover tightly with plastic wrap, and let rise at room temperature until the dough has tripled in volume and almost reaches the top of the bowl, 1 to $1^1/_2$ hours.

5 Butter or grease an $8^1/_2$-x-$4^1/_2$-x-$2^3/_4$-inch loaf pan, or coat with cooking spray; set aside. Turn the dough out onto a lightly floured work surface and pat it gently to remove any air bubbles. Shape into a loaf. Place the loaf in the prepared pan. Cover loosely with lightly oiled (or sprayed) plastic wrap and set aside at room temperature until the center has risen about $1^1/_2$ inches above the rim of the pan, about 1 hour.

6 About 30 minutes before the loaf is ready to bake, adjust an oven rack to the lower third position, place a heavy baking sheet on the rack, and preheat the oven to 375°F.

7 Remove the plastic wrap from the loaf and place the pan on the baking sheet. Bake for 30 to 35 minutes, until the loaf is well browned and sounds hollow when you remove it from the pan and rap its bottom. Cool completely on a wire rack, 3 to 4 hours, then wrap airtight. The loaf can be frozen for up to 1 month.

FOOD PROCESSOR WHOLE WHEAT CORNELL BREAD

Makes 1 loaf

Made of whole wheat flour, this bread is enriched with the three signature ingredients of Cornell bread: soy flour, wheat germ, and nonfat dry milk. The milk powder causes the bread to brown considerably during baking. It is full of flavor and toasts well. Over the years, many variations of this recipe have appeared in print.

3 cups whole wheat flour, plus more as needed	3 tablespoons soy flour
1 $^1/_4$-ounce package (2$^1/_4$ teaspoons) fast-rise active dry yeast	1$^1/_4$ cups warm water (105°–115°F)
	3 tablespoons molasses (I use Grandma's)
$^1/_4$ cup untoasted wheat germ	2 tablespoons vegetable oil
$^1/_3$ cup nonfat dry milk powder	1 large egg
	2 teaspoons salt

1 Add 1 cup of the whole wheat flour, the yeast, wheat germ, dry milk, and soy flour to a food processor fitted with the metal blade. With the motor running, quickly pour in the warm water and process for 15 seconds. Stop to scrape the work bowl, and process for another 15 seconds. Scrape the bowl again, cover with the lid, and let stand until the sponge has doubled in volume, 30 minutes to 1 hour or more, depending on the temperature of your kitchen.

2 Add the molasses, oil, egg, and salt and process for 15 seconds. Carefully remove the metal blade, scraping it clean, and insert the plastic dough blade. Sprinkle the remaining 2 cups whole wheat flour in a ring on top of the sponge, and process for 1 minute. Scrape the work bowl well—the mixture will be very sticky—and let stand for 3 minutes to allow the flour to absorb the liquid.

3 Process for another 1$^1/_2$ minutes, or until the dough gathers into a ball and almost cleans the sides of the work bowl. The dough should be very moist, sticky, and very elastic. If necessary, adjust the consistency with a bit more

water (or flour)—one key to the success of this recipe is the moistness of the dough.

4 Lightly oil a 3-quart bowl, or coat with cooking spray. Scrape the dough into the bowl and turn to coat all surfaces. Pick up the dough, squish it between your hands, and shape it into a ball; it should be very soft and supple, not sticky. Return the dough to the bowl, cover tightly with plastic wrap, and let rise at room temperature until it has tripled in volume and almost reaches the top of the bowl, 1 to $1\frac{1}{2}$ hours.

5 Butter or grease an $8\frac{1}{2}$-x-$4\frac{1}{2}$-x-$2\frac{3}{4}$-inch loaf pan, or coat with cooking spray; set aside. Turn the dough out onto a lightly floured work surface and pat it gently to remove any air bubbles. Shape into a loaf. Place the loaf in the prepared pan. Cover loosely with lightly oiled (or sprayed) plastic wrap and set aside at room temperature until the center has risen about $1\frac{1}{2}$ inches above the rim of the pan, about 1 hour.

6 About 30 minutes before the loaf is ready to bake, adjust an oven rack to the lower third position, place a heavy baking sheet on the rack, and preheat the oven to 375°F.

7 Remove the plastic wrap from the loaf and place the pan on the baking sheet. Bake for 30 to 35 minutes, until it is well browned and sounds hollow when you remove it from the pan and rap its bottom. Cool completely on a wire rack, 3 to 4 hours, then wrap airtight. The loaf can be frozen for up to 1 month.

ON KNEADING BREAD

To knead, *double up your hands, put them deep into the dough, and work it with your knuckles, exerting all your strength. When the dough sticks to them no longer, but leaves your bent fingers clean and clear, it is time to cease kneading, for you have done enough for that time.*

—Eliza Leslie, *Miss Leslie's New Cookery Book* (1857)

BUTTERMILK, WHEAT, AND RYE BREAD

Makes 2 large loaves

My wife, Dorothy, made up this sandwich bread many years ago, when she was experimenting with different flours and liquids for yeast bread. Good with meats, cheese, even peanut butter and jelly, it is one of our favorite breads. It also makes delicious bread puddings.

3 cups bread flour or unbleached all-purpose flour, plus more as needed

1½ cups whole wheat flour

1½ cups light rye flour

1 ¼-ounce package (2¼ teaspoons) fast-rise active dry yeast

4 teaspoons salt

6 tablespoons (¾ stick) unsalted butter, at room temperature

1½ cups buttermilk

½ cup water, plus more as needed

⅓ cup honey

2 large eggs

1 In a mixer bowl or another large bowl, stir together all three flours, the yeast, salt, and butter until the butter is incorporated.

2 Combine the buttermilk, ½ cup water, and honey in a medium saucepan and heat over medium heat, stirring occasionally, until the mixture is just warm to the touch. Remove from the heat and stir in the eggs with a fork.

3 *If using a stand mixer*, attach the dough hook. Add the liquid to the flour mixture and knead on low speed until the flour is moistened, then knead on medium speed for 5 to 8 minutes, until the dough cleans the sides of the bowl and is soft, moist, elastic, and just a tad sticky. Add a bit more flour or water if necessary.

If making the dough by hand, stir in the liquid mixture with a wooden spoon. Lightly flour your work surface, scrape the dough onto it, and dust with a bit more flour. Knead the dough for 8 to 10 minutes, folding it over on itself and pushing it away from you in a rhythmic motion, until it is smooth, elastic, and only slightly sticky. Add a small amount of additional flour only if necessary.

4 Lightly oil a 6-quart bowl, or coat with cooking spray. Scrape the dough into the bowl and turn to coat all surfaces. Pick up the dough, and knead it

briefly between your hands; it should feel soft, smooth, and supple. Return to the bowl and cover tightly with plastic wrap. Let rise at room temperature until almost tripled in volume, about 1 1/2 hours.

5 Butter or grease two 9-x-5-x-3-inch loaf pans, or coat with cooking spray; set aside. Turn the dough out onto a lightly floured work surface and pat it gently to remove any air bubbles. Divide the dough in half, and shape each piece into a loaf. Place the loaves in the prepared pans. Cover loosely with lightly oiled (or sprayed) plastic wrap and set aside at room temperature until the centers have risen about 1 1/2 inches above the rims of the pans, about 1 hour.

6 About 30 minutes before the loaves are ready to bake, adjust an oven rack to the lower third position and preheat the oven to 375°F.

7 Remove the plastic wrap from the loaves and place them in the oven, leaving a few inches between the pans. Bake for 35 to 40 minutes, until the loaves are well browned and sound hollow when you remove them from the pans and rap their bottoms. Cool completely on wire racks, 3 to 4 hours, then wrap airtight. The loaves can be frozen for up to 1 month.

THE IMPORTANCE OF GOOD FLOUR

It is best economy to purchase the best flour, even at an extra cost. Good flour adheres slightly to the hand, and if pressed in it, shows the impress of the lines of the skin. Dough made of it is a yellowish white, and does not stick to the hands after sufficient kneading. There is much bad flour on the market, which can in no way be made into nutritious food.

—Mrs. Cornelius, *The Young Housekeeper's Friend* (1859)

WHEAT, RYE, AND INDIAN BREAD

*Makes
2 large
loaves*

Rye and Indian bread was a mainstay of the early colonists. I've taken the basic combination of cornmeal and rye flour, added wheat flour for gluten, and molasses for flavoring. Versions using this grain combination were known as Third or Thirded Bread in the eighteenth and nineteenth centuries. It's a dense, fine-crumbed, flavorful bread that does not taste sweet, and it cuts beautifully into very thin slices. It's wonderful with cheese.

Although you can bake it in loaf pans, it's crustier and chewier if allowed to rise in bannetons and baked free-form on a baking stone.

1 cup stone-ground yellow cornmeal	2¹/₂–3 cups bread flour or unbleached all-purpose flour, plus more as needed
2 cups water	
1¹/₂ cups milk	2 cups whole wheat flour
¹/₂ cup molasses (I use Grandma's)	1 ¹/₄-ounce package (2¹/₄ teaspoons) fast-rise active dry yeast
2 cups light rye flour	
	1 tablespoon salt

1 In a medium heavy saucepan, combine the cornmeal with 1¹/₂ cups of the water and the milk. Cook, stirring, over medium heat, until the mixture boils and thickens. Continue cooking, stirring constantly, for 2 minutes. Remove from the heat and stir in the remaining ¹/₂ cup water and the molasses. Transfer the mixture to a mixer bowl or another large bowl. Let stand, stirring occasionally, until the mixture cools but still feels very warm (110° to 115°F).

2 *If using a stand mixer,* add the rye flour, 2 cups of the bread flour or all-purpose flour, the whole wheat flour, yeast, and salt to the cornmeal mixture. Attach the dough hook and knead on medium-low speed for 5 minutes. The dough will be wet and sticky. Add ¹/₂ cup more bread flour or all-purpose flour and knead on low to incorporate, then knead on medium speed for 5 minutes, or until the dough cleans the sides of the bowl and is firm but still slightly sticky. Add some or all of the remaining ¹/₂ cup bread flour or all-purpose flour if necessary, but no more, or the bread will be dry and crumbly.

If making the dough by hand, stir in 2 cups of the bread flour or all-purpose flour after adding the other ingredients. Sprinkle about half the remaining 1 cup flour on your work surface, scrape the dough onto it, and dust the dough with the rest of the flour. Knead the dough for 8 to 10 minutes, folding it over on itself and pushing it away from you in a rhythmic motion, until it feels firm and is only slightly sticky. Add a small amount of additional flour only if absolutely necessary.

Lightly oil a 6-quart bowl, or coat with cooking spray. Put the dough into the bowl and turn to coat all surfaces. Cover tightly with plastic wrap and let rise at room temperature until the dough has doubled in volume, about 2 hours.

3 Transfer the dough to a lightly floured surface and divide it in half. Shape each half into a ball by rolling it in a circular motion. Pinch the seams that form on the underside of the balls firmly to seal well. Rub two bannetons (see Sources, page 524) or cloth-lined baskets generously with flour so that all ridges and nooks and crannies are coated; tap out the excess flour. Place the balls of dough seam side up in the bannetons or baskets. Put each banneton or basket in a large plastic bag. Gather the edges of the plastic together to make a small opening, and blow in the bag to inflate it. Twist it closed, and seal with a twist-tie. Let rise at room temperature until the dough has doubled in volume, about 2 hours.

4 Meanwhile, about 1 hour before the dough is ready to bake, adjust an oven rack to the lower third position and place a baking stone on the rack. Preheat the oven to 450°F.

5 Lightly dust a baker's peel or rimless baking sheet with cornmeal. Unmold a loaf onto the cornmeal, seam side down, and slash the top of the loaf in 3 places with a razor blade or very sharp knife, making the slashes at about a 45-degree angle and 1 to 2 inches apart. Mist the walls of the oven and the baking stone with a fine spray of water and close the oven door. Grab the peel or baking sheet, open the oven door, and quickly slide the loaf onto a far corner of the baking stone. Mist the oven walls (but not the surface of the bread) again with water, and close the oven door. Repeat the procedure with the second loaf, sliding it onto a near corner of the baking stone,

misting the oven walls again with water, and closing the oven door. After 5 minutes, mist the oven for the last time. Bake for 35 to 45 minutes in all, until the loaves are well browned and crusty and sound hollow when you remove them from the pans and rap their bottoms. Cool completely on wire racks.

6 Cut the bread with a sharp serrated knife, and store leftovers in a brown paper bag. The bread keeps well at room temperature for 3 or 4 days, or it can be frozen, wrapped airtight, for up to 2 weeks. To refresh, unwrap the frozen bread, thaw at room temperature, and reheat on a baking sheet in a 350°F oven for 10 minutes. Cool completely before slicing.

GO WEST FOR WHEAT

At home, the English made many breads with oats. When they arrived in North America they found corn but no oats. Because cornmeal and oatmeal behaved similarly in cooking, they substituted one for the other. Rye soon entered the picture, because it grew better than wheat in the North. At first, wheat flour was too expensive for daily use, and it was reserved for special-occasion treats like cakes and pastries. But by the 1860s, the settlers had discovered that it would grow well in the Midwest and that it could be transported cheaply by way of the Erie Canal, so they began using it for everyday baking.

WHOLE WHEAT SUNFLOWER BREAD

Makes 2 large loaves

This nutty-tasting loaf is great for all sorts of sandwiches, and it makes terrific toast. The bread's special moistness comes from mashed potatoes and potato water, a technique first used by nineteenth-century bakers and still employed by bakers today. Barley malt syrup is sold in health food stores.

1 large russet potato (8 ounces)

2 cups water

1 cup unsalted raw sunflower seeds

3 cups whole wheat flour

1 ¼-ounce package (2¼ teaspoons) fast-rise active dry yeast

¼ cup barley malt syrup (see above)

2 large eggs

2–3 cups bread flour or unbleached all-purpose flour, plus more as needed

½ cup untoasted wheat germ

¼ cup vegetable oil

4 teaspoons salt

1 Peel the potato and cut it into eighths. Combine with the water in a small saucepan and cook at a low boil until very tender, about 20 minutes. Drain the potato, reserving the potato water, and return the potato to the pan. Mash until smooth and free of lumps. You'll have about 1 cup. Set aside. You should have 1¾ cups potato water; if not, add water as necessary. Set aside to cool; use when it is still warm.

2 Process the sunflower seeds in a food processor for 2 minutes, or until finely ground, stopping to scrape the bowl once. Set aside.

3 In a mixer bowl or another large bowl, stir together the whole wheat flour and yeast. In a medium bowl, stir the barley malt syrup with the potato water until smooth. Add to the flour mixture, along with the eggs.

4 *If using a stand mixer,* beat on medium speed with the paddle attachment for 4 minutes. Scrape the bowl and beater, cover the bowl tightly with plastic wrap, and let rise at room temperature until the sponge has doubled in volume, about 1 hour.

If making the dough by hand, beat the whole wheat flour mixture vigorously with a wooden spoon until the batter is ropy, 3 to 4 minutes. Cover tightly with plastic wrap and let rise until doubled.

5 *If using a stand mixer,* add the mashed potato, ground sunflower seeds, 2 cups of the bread flour or all-purpose flour, the wheat germ, oil, and salt to the whole wheat mixture. Attach the dough hook and knead on low speed until thoroughly mixed. Add the remaining 1 cup bread flour or all-purpose flour and knead on medium speed for 5 to 8 minutes, until the dough is moist, only slightly sticky, and elastic. If the dough seems too wet, gradually knead in a small amount of additional flour.

If making the dough by hand, stir in 2 cups of the bread flour or all-purpose flour after adding the mashed potato and the other ingredients. Sprinkle about half the remaining 1 cup flour on your work surface, scrape the dough onto it, and dust the dough with the rest of the flour. Knead for 8 to 10 minutes, folding the dough over on itself and pushing it away from you in a rhythmic motion, until it is smooth, supple, and only slightly sticky. Add a small amount of additional flour only if the dough seems too wet.

6 Lightly oil or coat with cooking spray a 6-quart bowl. Scrape the dough into the bowl and turn to coat all over. Pick up the dough and work it between your hands to form a smooth ball, then return it to the bowl. Cover with plastic wrap and let rise until almost tripled in volume, 1 to 1^1/$_2$ hours.

7 Butter or grease two 9-x-5-x-3-inch loaf pans, or coat with cooking spray; set aside. Turn the dough out onto a lightly floured work surface and pat it gently to remove any air bubbles. Divide the dough in half, and shape each piece into a loaf. Place the loaves in the prepared pans. Cover loosely with lightly oiled (or sprayed) plastic wrap and set aside at room temperature until the centers have risen 1^1/$_2$ to 2 inches above the rims of the pans, about 1 hour.

8 About 30 minutes before the loaves are ready to bake, adjust an oven rack to the lower third position and preheat the oven to 375°F.

9 Remove the plastic wrap from the loaves and place in the oven, leaving a

few inches between the pans. Bake for 35 to 45 minutes, until the loaves are well browned and sound hollow when you remove them from the pans and rap their bottoms; they will not rise much. Cool completely on wire racks, 3 to 4 hours, then wrap airtight. The loaves freeze well for up to 1 month.

THE IMPORTANCE OF GOOD BREAD

However improbable it may seem, the health of many a professional man is undermined, and his usefulness curtailed, if not sacrificed, because he habitually eats <u>bad bread.</u>

—Mrs. Cornelius,
The Young Housekeeper's Friend (1859)

BULGUR BREAD

Makes
2 loaves

I got this recipe more than 20 years ago from a friend who found it in the *Detroit Free Press.* I've changed it over time and streamlined the method to use instant yeast. With a nutritional boost from both the bulgur (steamed and dried cracked wheat) and whole wheat flour, a peanut butter and jelly sandwich never had it so good.

$^2/_3$ cup medium bulgur	2 large eggs
1$^1/_3$ cups unsweetened apple juice	2$^1/_2$ cups bread flour or unbleached
2$^1/_2$ cups whole wheat flour	all-purpose flour, plus more
1 $^1/_4$-ounce package (2$^1/_4$	as needed
teaspoons) fast-rise active	$^1/_4$ cup vegetable oil
dry yeast	2–4 tablespoons water
1 cup warm water (105°–115°F)	4 teaspoons salt

1 Combine the bulgur and apple juice in a medium saucepan and bring to a boil over medium heat, stirring occasionally. Reduce the heat to low and cook, stirring occasionally, until the bulgur is tender and the juice is absorbed, about 10 minutes. Remove from the heat and set aside.

2 In a mixer bowl or another large bowl, stir together the whole wheat flour and yeast. Add the warm water and eggs.

3 *If using a stand mixer,* beat on medium speed with the paddle attachment for 4 minutes. Scrape the bowl and beater. Cover tightly with plastic wrap and let rise at room temperature until the sponge doubles in volume, about 1 hour.

   If making the dough by hand, beat the egg mixture vigorously with a wooden spoon until the dough is thick and ropy, 3 to 4 minutes. Cover and let rise until doubled, about 1 hour.

4 *If using a stand mixer,* add the bulgur, 2$^1/_2$ cups bread flour or all-purpose flour, oil, 2 tablespoons of the water, and the salt to the sponge. Attach the dough hook and knead on low speed for about 8 minutes, until the dough cleans the sides of the bowl and is moist, elastic, and only slightly sticky. If the dough is too dry, knead in some or all of the remaining 2 tablespoons water. If it is too wet, knead in a small amount of bread or all-purpose flour.

If making the dough by hand, add the bulgur, 2 cups of the bread flour or all-purpose flour, the oil, 4 tablespoons water, and the salt to the sponge and beat with a wooden spoon to make a thick, moist dough. Sprinkle most of the remaining $1/2$ cup bread flour or all-purpose flour on your work surface, scrape the dough onto it, and dust with the rest of the flour. Knead the dough for 8 to 10 minutes, folding it over on itself and pushing it away from you in a rhythmic motion, until it is smooth, elastic, and only slightly sticky. Add a small amount of additional bread flour or all-purpose flour if necessary.

5   Lightly oil a 6-quart bowl, or coat with cooking spray. Scrape the dough into the bowl, turning to coat all over. Pick up the dough and work between your hands to form a smooth ball. Return the dough to the bowl, cover tightly with plastic wrap, and let rise until almost tripled in volume, 1 to $1^{1}/_{2}$ hours (it will almost fill the bowl).

6   Butter or grease two $8^{1}/_{2}$-x-$4^{1}/_{2}$-x-$2^{3}/_{4}$-inch loaf pans, or coat with cooking spray; set aside. Turn the dough out onto a lightly floured work surface and pat it gently to remove any air bubbles. Divide the dough in half, and shape each piece into a loaf. Place the loaves in the pans. Cover loosely with lightly oiled (or sprayed) plastic wrap and set aside at room temperature until the centers have risen $1^{1}/_{2}$ to 2 inches above the rims of the pans, about 1 hour.

7   About 30 minutes before the loaves are ready to bake, adjust an oven rack to the lower third position and preheat the oven to 375°F.

8   Remove the plastic wrap from the loaves and place in the oven, leaving a few inches between the pans. Bake for 35 to 45 minutes, until the loaves are well browned and sound hollow when you remove them from the pans and rap their bottoms; they will not rise much. Cool completely on wire racks, 3 to 4 hours, then wrap airtight. This bread freezes well for up to 3 weeks.

GRAHAM CARROT BREAD

Makes 2 large loaves

Graham flour is whole wheat flour that has had only the coarsest bran removed. The carrot juice gives these light-textured sandwich loaves a stunning orange color. If you don't have a vegetable juicer, you can find carrot juice (choose pure juice, not a blend) either on the shelf in cans or in the frozen food section of many health food stores, or buy it at the juice bar in your market or health food store. This bread makes terrific toast.

4 cups graham flour

1 1/4-ounce package (2 1/4 teaspoons) fast-rise active dry yeast

1 1/2 cups carrot juice

1 cup water

1/3 cup vegetable oil

1/3 cup molasses (I use Grandma's)

2 large eggs

4 teaspoons salt

2 1/2 cups bread flour or unbleached all-purpose flour, plus more as needed

1 In a mixer bowl or another large bowl, stir together the graham flour and yeast. In a saucepan, heat the carrot juice and water only until warm (105°–115°F). Add to the flour mixture, stirring well with a rubber spatula. The sponge will be very thick. Cover tightly with plastic wrap and let rise at room temperature until doubled in volume, about 1 hour.

2 Add the oil, molasses, eggs, and salt to the batter.

3 *If using a stand mixer,* beat with the paddle attachment on low speed until dough is well mixed, then beat on medium speed for 4 to 5 minutes. The dough may pull away from the sides of the bowl and mass on the beater; scrape the dough off the beater. Attach the dough hook and turn the mixer to low. Add the bread flour or all-purpose flour about 1/2 cup at a time, waiting until each addition is incorporated before adding the next. Then knead on medium speed for 5 to 8 minutes, until the dough is smooth, elastic, and slightly sticky. When you pinch it, it will stick to your fingers. Knead in a bit more flour only if the dough seems too wet and sticky.

If making the dough by hand, beat the molasses mixture with a wooden spoon until it is ropy, about 5 minutes. Stir in 1 1/2 cups of the bread flour or all-purpose flour. Sprinkle about half the remaining 1 cup flour on your work surface, scrape the dough onto it, and dust the dough with the rest of the flour. Knead the dough for 8 to 10 minutes, folding it over on itself and pushing it away from you in a rhythmic motion, until it is smooth, elastic, and still a bit sticky. This dough is wetter than most; add only a small amount of additional flour if necessary to keep it from sticking to your hands.

4 Lightly oil a 6-quart bowl, or coat with cooking spray. Scrape the dough into the bowl. Turn the dough to coat all surfaces lightly, then pick up the dough, knead briefly between your hands, and shape it into a ball; it should feel soft, smooth, and supple. Return the dough to the bowl and cover tightly with plastic wrap. Let rise at room temperature until almost tripled in volume, about 1 hour.

5 Butter or grease two 9-x-5-x-3-inch loaf pans, or coat with cooking spray; set aside. Turn the dough out onto a lightly floured work surface and pat it gently to remove any air bubbles. Divide the dough in half, and shape each piece into a loaf. Place the loaves in the prepared pans. Cover loosely with lightly oiled (or sprayed) plastic wrap and set aside at room temperature until the centers have risen about 1^1/2 inches above the rims of the pans, about 1 hour.

6 About 30 minutes before the loaves are ready to bake, adjust an oven rack to the lower third position and preheat the oven to 375°F.

7 Remove the plastic wrap and place the loaves in the oven, leaving a few inches between the pans. Bake for 40 to 50 minutes, until the loaves are well browned and sound hollow when you remove them from the pans and rap their bottoms. Cool completely on wire racks, 3 to 4 hours, then wrap airtight. The loaves can be frozen for up to 1 month.

YEASTED CORN BREAD

Makes one 13-x-9-inch pan

Before chemical leaveners gained a foothold in kitchens, corn bread was made with yeast. You'll find this bread a revelation. It has a marvelous corn bread taste, but it isn't the least bit crumbly. It's a batter bread, and there's no kneading involved. It is wonderful hot, spread with a generous amount of butter. Be sure to use fine-textured cornmeal.

This bread makes an excellent base for a turkey stuffing. When cool, cut it into cubes and spread them on two large baking sheets. Set aside, uncovered, overnight to dry.

2 cups fine stone-ground yellow cornmeal	2 teaspoons salt
2 cups unbleached all-purpose flour	2 cups milk, warmed to 105°–115°F
1 ¼-ounce package (2¼ teaspoons) fast-rise active dry yeast	8 tablespoons (1 stick) unsalted butter, melted and cooled slightly
	2 large eggs

1 Butter a 13-x-9-inch baking pan, or coat with cooking spray; set aside. Using a rubber spatula, stir the cornmeal, flour, yeast, and salt together in a large bowl. Add the milk, melted butter, and eggs and stir to moisten the dry ingredients. Continue to beat with the rubber spatula for about 2 minutes to make a smooth batter.

2 Scrape into the prepared pan and cover the pan tightly with plastic wrap. Let rise until doubled in volume (the pan will be slightly more than half full), about 1 hour.

3 Meanwhile, adjust an oven rack to the center position and preheat the oven to 375°F.

4 Remove the plastic wrap and bake for 20 to 25 minutes, until the bread springs back when lightly pressed and a toothpick inserted into the center comes out clean. Cut into squares and serve hot. This bread does not freeze well.

JALAPEÑO, CORNMEAL, AND CHEDDAR BREAD

Makes 2 loaves

The aroma of this bread as it bakes will drive you wild. It's packed with the flavors of the American Southwest—jalapeños, corn, cornmeal, and some onions for good measure. The onions must be cooked before being added to the yeast dough, or the dough will not rise. You can shape the dough into two large loaves or use half the dough to make dinner rolls or hamburger buns. This is great with meats and cheeses of all kinds. Or try jams and jellies, especially spicy jalapeño jelly, with it. You can also serve this with jalapeño butter, made by whirring 1 stick of room-temperature unsalted butter, 1 seeded jalapeño pepper, cut into chunks, and 1 teaspoon salt together in a food processor until smooth.

1 tablespoon olive oil	4 teaspoons salt
1 cup chopped yellow onion (1 medium)	6 tablespoons ($3/4$ stick) unsalted butter, at room temperature
$2/3$ cup finely chopped seeded jalapeño peppers (6–8 peppers)	1 $1/4$-ounce package ($2 1/4$ teaspoons) fast-rise active dry yeast
$4 1/2$ cups bread flour or unbleached all-purpose flour, plus more as needed	8 ounces extra-sharp cheddar cheese, shredded (2 cups)
$3/4$ cup stone-ground yellow cornmeal	$1/2$ cup milk, plus more as needed
$1/4$ cup sugar	1 cup canned cream-style corn
	2 large eggs

1 Heat the olive oil in a large skillet over medium heat. Add the onion and jalapeño, and stir and cook for 1 minute. Cover the pan, reduce the heat to low, and cook for 5 to 6 minutes, stirring occasionally, until the onion is tender and translucent but not browned. Set aside to cool.

2 In a mixer bowl or another large bowl, stir together the flour, cornmeal, sugar, salt, butter, yeast, and cheese. Heat the milk and corn in a small

saucepan until just warm to the touch. Remove from the heat and stir in the eggs with a fork.

3 *If using a stand mixer,* attach the dough hook and add the liquid and the onion mixture. Knead on low speed until the flour is moistened, then knead on medium speed for about 8 minutes, until the dough cleans the sides of the bowl and is smooth, elastic, and only slightly sticky. Add a bit more flour or milk if necessary.

If making the dough by hand, stir in the liquid and the onion mixture with a wooden spoon. Lightly flour your workspace, scrape the dough onto it, and dust with a bit more flour. Knead the dough for 8 to 10 minutes, folding it over on itself and pushing it away from you in a rhythmic motion, until it is smooth, elastic, and only slightly sticky. Add a small amount of additional flour only if necessary; the dough should be moist.

4 Lightly oil a 6-quart bowl, or coat with cooking spray. Scrape the dough into the bowl and turn to coat all surfaces. Pick up the dough and knead briefly between your hands; it should be soft, smooth, very supple, and just slightly sticky. Return to the bowl and cover tightly with plastic wrap. Let rise at room temperature until almost tripled in volume, about 1½ hours.

5 Butter or grease two 8½-x-4½-x-2¾-inch loaf pans, or coat with cooking spray; set aside. Turn the dough out onto a lightly floured work surface and pat it gently to remove any air bubbles. Divide the dough in half, and shape each piece into a loaf. Place the loaves in the prepared pans. Cover loosely with lightly oiled (or sprayed) plastic wrap and set aside at room temperature until the centers have risen about 1½ inches above the rims of the pans, about 1 hour.

6 About 30 minutes before the loaves are ready to bake, adjust an oven rack to the lower third position and preheat the oven to 375°F.

7 Remove the plastic wrap from the loaves and place them in the oven, leaving a few inches between the pans. Bake for 35 to 40 minutes, until the loaves are well browned and sound hollow when you remove them from the pans and rap their bottoms. Cool completely on wire racks, 3 to 4 hours, then wrap airtight.

Variations

For rolls, divide half the risen dough into 15 equal portions (shape the rest into a loaf, let rise, and bake as described above). Shape each piece into a ball, pinching the dough on the underside of the ball to make a smooth surface on top. Place the rolls in a greased 13-x-9-inch baking pan (5 the long way and 3 the short way), spacing them slightly apart. Cover loosely with a towel and let rise at room temperature until they are doubled in size and touching one another, about 1 hour. Bake for 20 to 25 minutes, until the rolls are well browned and spring back when lightly pressed. Serve warm.

For hamburger buns, divide half the risen dough (shape the rest into a loaf, let rise, and bake as described above) into 8 equal portions. Shape into balls as described for the rolls. Grease a 17-x-12-inch rimmed baking sheet; don't use cooking spray—the rolls must stick to the pan when you shape them, so butter or shortening are the best fats to use. Place the balls several inches apart on the baking sheet, cover loosely with a towel, and let rest for 10 minutes to relax the gluten. Then flatten each ball into a 3- to 4-inch circle with the palm of your hand. Cover loosely with a towel and let the buns rise until puffy, light, and doubled in size, 45 minutes to 1 hour. Bake the buns for about 25 minutes until they are browned and spring back when lightly pressed. Cool completely on wire racks.

Loaves, rolls, and buns can be frozen for up to 1 month.

PARKER HOUSE ROLLS

Makes about 18 rolls

These rolls, which became famous at Boston's Parker House Hotel around 1860, have a special cleft or fold and were beloved by all who ate them. Early recipes used very little sugar and hardly any butter. The rolls were crisp on the outside and chewy inside. As time went on, the rolls became sweeter and richer, with more and more sugar and butter added.

Jessup Whitehead, author of several cookbooks and a food writer for Chicago's *Daily National Hotel Reporter* in the 1870s and 1880s, said they evolved out of a one-upsmanship between Boston hotels of the day. Charles Wood, a lifetime baker at Boston's Tremont Hotel, was most likely the inventor, but they eventually became the specialty of the Parker House. Travelers dining there quickly spread the word about them on their journeys, a fact that helps to explain why the recipe for the rolls appeared in print relatively soon after their introduction.

The following recipe is adapted from *Miss Parloa's Kitchen Companion*, published in 1887. Miss Parloa used a small amount of yeast (compressed cakes in her day) and long, slow rises, so that the dough had ample time to develop its own flavor. The rolls are best when freshly baked, and the recipe can be doubled.

3 cups unbleached all-purpose flour, plus more as needed	1 teaspoon fast-rise active dry yeast
1 tablespoon cold unsalted butter	1 cup plus 2 tablespoons milk, warmed (105°–115°F)
1½ teaspoons sugar	3–4 tablespoons butter (unsalted or not), at room temperature
1 teaspoon salt	

1 Put the 3 cups flour into a mixer bowl or another large bowl. Add the cold butter, and rapidly work it into the flour with your fingertips until the mixture is the consistency of fine meal. Stir in the sugar, salt, and yeast. Add the milk and stir with a rubber spatula until the dough gathers into a mass.

2 *If using a stand mixer,* attach the dough hook and knead on low speed for 2 minutes. Then knead on medium speed for 4 to 5 minutes, until the dough is supple, smooth, elastic, and not sticky. It should feel quite firm. Knead in a small amount of flour or milk if necessary.

If making the dough by hand, lightly dust your work surface with flour, scrape the dough onto the surface, and dust with a tiny bit more flour. Knead the dough for 8 to 10 minutes, folding it over on itself and pushing it away from you in a rhythmic motion, until it is firm, smooth, and elastic. Knead in a small amount of additional flour if necessary.

3 Lightly oil a 3-quart bowl, or coat lightly with cooking spray. Put the dough in the bowl and turn to coat all surfaces. Pick up the dough and knead briefly between your hands. It will not be at all sticky. Shape it into a ball, and return it to the bowl. Cover tightly with plastic wrap and let rise at room temperature until tripled in volume, 2 to 3 hours.

4 Turn the dough out onto a lightly floured surface, knead it briefly, and cover it loosely with a towel. Let stand for 15 to 30 minutes to relax the gluten.

5 Lightly butter a 10-x-15-inch jelly roll pan. To shape the rolls, roll the dough to a 12-inch circle and a thickness of a scant $^1/_2$ inch. Cut into circles with a floured 2$^1/_4$- to 2$^1/_2$-inch cookie cutter. Make a deep crease in each circle of dough slightly off center by pressing a chopstick or the edge of a rubber spatula handle firmly into the dough, without cutting through. Put a dab—about $^1/_2$ teaspoon—soft butter on the crease, fold the circle in half to form a half moon, and press gently to enclose the butter. Repeat with the cut circles of dough and the remaining butter. Place the rolls almost touching on the prepared jelly roll pan. Cover the rolls loosely with a kitchen towel and let rise in a warm place until light and puffy, about 45 minutes. Meanwhile, gather the scraps of dough and knead them together briefly, then cover with a towel, let rest 15 minutes, and cut out and shape more rolls. Place on the pan to rise with the other rolls.

6 While the rolls are rising, adjust an oven rack to the center position and preheat the oven to 400°F.

7 Uncover the rolls and place the pan in the oven. Bake for 15 to 20 minutes, until the rolls are crusty and golden brown. With a wide metal spatula, transfer the rolls to a cooling rack and let stand until warm or cool.

Note: To freeze rolls, seal the cooled rolls in zip-top freezer bags and freeze for up to 2 months. To reheat, wrap the frozen rolls in aluminum foil, and place them in a 350°F oven for about 15 minutes.

CAMBOZOLA CHEESE BUNS

Makes 12 large buns

The dough for these buns rises only once, so you can start it just a couple of hours before dinner, and have hot buns ready. Cambozola, a soft creamy Italian blue cheese, gives them a hearty, zesty flavor. Feel free to try other soft cheeses, such as very ripe Brie or Camembert. Chèvre is also good, but in that case, add 1 tablespoon chopped fresh thyme to the batter and substitute olive oil for the butter.

½ cup lukewarm water	1 large egg
1 ¼-ounce package (2¼ teaspoons) active dry yeast	2 tablespoons unsalted butter, melted
5 ounces Cambozola cheese, rind removed, cut into 1-inch pieces	½ teaspoon salt
	2 cups unbleached all-purpose flour
2 tablespoons sugar	

1 Put the water in a mixer bowl or another large bowl and sprinkle in the yeast. Let stand for 5 minutes to soften. Add the cheese, sugar, egg, melted butter, salt, and 1 cup of the flour.

2 *If using a stand mixer,* beat with the paddle attachment on low speed for 1 minute, then beat on medium speed until the cheese is thoroughly incorporated, 1 to 2 minutes more. On low speed, gradually add the remaining 1 cup flour. Beat on medium speed for 1 to 2 minutes longer. The batter will be thick.

   If making the dough by hand, beat the cheese mixture with a wooden spoon until very smooth and thick, about 3 minutes. Gradually stir in the remaining 1 cup flour and beat vigorously for about 5 minutes, until the batter is thick, smooth, and elastic.

3 Butter a standard-size 12-cup nonstick muffin pan, or coat with cooking spray. Divide the batter evenly among the cups. Drape a sheet of lightly oiled plastic wrap loosely over the pan. Let rise in a warm place (80° to 85°F) until the cups are completely filled, about 1 hour.

4 Meanwhile, adjust an oven rack to the center position and preheat the oven to 375°F.

5 Remove the plastic wrap from the rolls and bake for about 15 minutes, until they are golden brown and spring back when gently pressed, and a toothpick inserted in the center comes out clean. Cool in the pan for 1 to 2 minutes, then transfer them to wire racks to finish cooling. Serve warm or at room temperature. The cooled rolls may be wrapped airtight and frozen for up to 1 month.

THE 1900 BREAD MACHINE

Many people assume that bread machines—those modern electric gadgets that do all the mixing for you—are a 1980s invention. In fact, a manual bread maker made of tin and steel was first marketed in America around 1900. To make bread effortlessly and without mess, all the housewife had to do was put the ingredients into the bucket of the machine, affix the lid with an attached kneader on top, and turn the handle. The bread maker was capable of kneading the dough for several loaves of bread in just a few minutes, or so the ads claimed.

One pamphlet, entitled "How to Make Bread," shows a scowling middle-aged woman with her hands immersed in a mass of dough in a large pan. The adjacent page shows a beautiful smiling young woman, looking as though she just emerged from her dressing room, with her hand barely touching the knob of the cranking mechanism. The selling point of the product was noted in the accompanying copy: "The hands do not touch the dough, which is mixed and kneaded thoroughly in three minutes by this machine."

2 Quick Breads, Biscuits, and Muffins

Long before commercial baking powders were available to home bakers in the mid-1850s, Amelia Simmons included an early chemical leavener, pearl ash, or potash (potassium bicarbonate), in several of her cake, cookie, and gingerbread recipes in *American Cookery* (1796). This early use suggested housewives were looking for faster ways than yeast to make their baked goods rise. But pearl ash was hard to dissolve and mix evenly into batters and doughs, and it sometimes caused foods to discolor. It did, however, work quickly. An alkali, it neutralized acid ingredients such as honey, molasses, and sour milk, and the tiny bubbles of gas formed by this interaction expanded in the heat of the oven and caused batters and doughs to rise.

Saleratus, an early form of baking soda, served the same purpose as pearl ash, and it was easier to use. Like pearl ash, it functioned alone to neutralize acidic ingredients, or it could be mixed with cream of tartar, an acid formed as a natural by-product of winemaking, to make baking powder. Baked goods made with it were light and tender, and the whole leavening action was accomplished in minutes instead of the hours required by yeast.

The first baking powders that appeared on the market in the mid-1850s were single-acting ones, meaning they became active as soon as they were mixed into a wet batter or dough. It was important to get quick breads and other such baked goods into the oven as soon as possible before the baking soda, which is highly soluble in water, lost its oomph. These single-acting powders were mixtures of one part baking soda and two parts cream of tartar plus some cornstarch, which acted much like a referee in a boxing match, keeping the active ingredients apart so they wouldn't start interacting in the can.

Baking powder manufacturers competed furiously with one another to come up with a still better product, and around 1890, double-acting baking powders replaced their single-acting forerunners. These powders also contained baking soda but substituted the acidic cream of tartar with one or more other acids that became active twice, once when mixed into the batter, and the second time in the oven's heat. These powders were more stable in the can and they gave the baker wiggle room.

Baking powders, also called yeast powders in their early days, met with mixed reactions among the nation's cookbook authors. Eliza Leslie, a disciple of the renowned cooking teacher and pastry chef Mrs. Elizabeth Goodfellow of Philadelphia, shunned them. As part of the old guard, these two accomplished cooks were suspicious of chemicals introduced into foodstuffs. "We do not approve of the introduction of these substances into cakes," Eliza Leslie wrote in *Miss Leslie's New Cookery Book* (1857). "They give a sort of factitious lightness very different from that honestly produced by a liberal allowance of egg and butter, genuine yeast, and good beating and stirring—but they destroy the taste of the seasoning, and are certain destruction to the taste of lemon, orange, strawberry, pine-apple, and every kind of fruit flavoring."

After baking powders containing aluminum phosphates (so-called alum powders) had made their way into markets, a baking powder war began between the makers of tartrate and aluminum phosphate powders, the tartrate manufacturers contending that their product was superior and safe for human consumption, whereas the alum powders were not. The Royal Baking Powder Company, in its 1877 cookbook, *The Royal Baker,* claimed,

> It is poor economy, in trying to save a few pennies on baking powder, to sacrifice your health. Acid Phosphate of Lime [burnt bones], Patent Cream Tartar, Alum, Terra Alba, in fact, every cheap trashy substitute so nearly resemble a genuine baking powder that is impossible for the housekeeper to distinguish the difference by the appearance. It is therefore of the utmost importance to get a well-known brand like the Royal, which has stood the test of years, and is indorsed by the highest authorities for its sterling qualities and absolute purity.

A "baking powder controversy" then ensued, and the fight for supremacy was on. As in many of today's product wars, the profit motive was really what drove the battle, the makers of the more expensive tartrate baking powders striving to eliminate their cheaper competition. The fight became a legal one, with years and lots of money spent in litigation. In the end, there was insufficient evidence to support the health claims, and alum baking powders continued to be sold, as they are to this day. Many experienced bakers, myself included, however, avoid alum-based powders—not because of health concerns but because they can have an unpleasant metallic aftertaste. Since double-acting baking powders that don't contain alum are readily available in supermarkets (one brand is Rumford), that's what I use.

SOUTHERN BISCUITS

Makes about 12 biscuits

This is a traditional Southern biscuit—tender, flaky, and wonderful with butter, honey, honey butter, jam, or sorghum. The traditional fat for biscuits is lard, and if you like it, by all means use it. Your biscuits will be more tender and flaky than those made with butter. But perhaps more important than which fat you use is your choice of flour: you must use a soft wheat flour. Cake flour is the most readily available, but if you live in an area where White Lily all-purpose flour is sold, use it. My own preference is for an unbleached soft wheat flour made by Great Valley Mills in Pennsylvania (see Sources, page 526). This pale yellow flour is low in gluten, and it has not been treated with any of the chemical bleaching agents found in ordinary cake flour.

2 cups unbleached soft wheat flour or cake flour (see above)

³/₄ teaspoon salt

2 teaspoons baking powder, preferably nonaluminum

4 tablespoons (¹/₂ stick) cold unsalted butter or ¹/₄ cup lard

¹/₂ cup buttermilk

1 Adjust an oven rack to the center position and preheat the oven to 425°F.

2 Put the flour, salt, and baking powder in a medium bowl and stir to combine well. Cut the butter or lard into 6 pieces and work them into the flour mixture with a pastry blender, two knives, or your fingertips until the particles are the size of peas. Flatten the pieces of fat with your fingertips, rubbing the flour and fat between your fingers rapidly so the fat doesn't soften.

3 Add the buttermilk and fold and stir it in with a rubber spatula until the mixture just gathers into a moist mass; don't beat it or be rough with it. Turn the dough out onto a lightly floured work surface and turn to coat all the surfaces with flour. Pat the dough to a thickness of about ¹/₂ inch. Cut biscuits with a sharp 2-inch round cutter: Dip the cutter into flour each time, stamp out each biscuit without turning the cutter, and place the biscuits about 1 inch apart on an ungreased baking sheet. If a biscuit sticks, simply shake the cutter gently to release it. Gather the dough scraps, gently reshape them into a ¹/₂-inch-thick cake, and cut out 2 or 3 more biscuits.

4 Bake for 12 to 15 minutes, until the biscuits are golden brown. Serve immediately.

Variation

For an entirely different but delicious effect, use 2 cups whole wheat pastry flour or a half-and-half mixture of whole wheat pastry flour and cake flour instead of the soft wheat flour or cake flour. You may have to add a bit more buttermilk, but do so a few drops at a time.

BAKING POWDER PROPAGANDA

To make old-fashioned *Soda Biscuits, substitute two teaspoonsfuls of Royal Baking Powder for every two teaspoonsfuls of Cream Tartar and one of Soda, and you cannot fail of perfect success. Your biscuits will be free from yellow streaks, and when eaten hot will not destroy the teeth or produce distress in people of weak stomachs or weak digestive organs.*

—Royal Baking Powder Company, *The Royal Baker* (1877)

RHUBARB-STRAWBERRY PIE *(page 476)*

above: **CHOCOLATE BUTTERMILK LAYER CAKE** *(page 273)*
right: **MAPLE-FROSTED MAPLE CUPCAKES** *(page 236),* **GINGER CUPCAKE TRIPLE PLAY** *(page 238),*
and **CHOCOLATE-FROSTED COCONUT CUPCAKES** *(page 230)*

LINDY'S CHEESECAKE *(page 356)*

CRANBERRY MUFFINS FROM NANTUCKET *(page 105)* and
PUMPKIN-DATE LOAF WITH CREAM CHEESE SWIRL *(page 98)*

BOSTON CREAM PIE *(page 332)*

ELECTION CAKE *(page 118)*

BIG LEMON-FROSTED SUGAR COOKIE SQUARES *(page 406)*, CASHEW AND GOLDEN RAISIN BISCOTTI WITH WHITE CHOCOLATE GLAZE *(page 418)*, PEPPERED GINGERSNAPS *(page 396)*, and WHITE CHOCOLATE CHUNK BROWNIES *(page 420)*

LEMON SPONGE CLOUD *(page 314)*

RAISED POTATO DOUGHNUTS *(page 138)*

LEMON GÉNOISE WITH WHITE CHOCOLATE BUTTERCREAM AND RASPBERRIES *(page 350)*

NECTARINE-RASPBERRY CRISP *(page 442)*

COCONUT LAYER CAKE *(page 286)*

WHITE CORNMEAL SKILLET BREAD

Makes one 10-inch round bread

In South Carolina's Low Country, this is how John Martin Taylor, like generations of Southerners before him, makes corn bread: no flour, no sweetening, just cornmeal, eggs, buttermilk, salt, and leavening. The recipe is adapted from Taylor's book *Hoppin' John's Lowcountry Cooking*. My favorite cornmeal—both for taste and texture—is white cornmeal made from the whole grain. Because it is perishable, you should store it in the freezer. You can order it from hoppinjohns.com.

You'll need a well-seasoned 10-inch cast-iron skillet to give the bread its unique golden brown crust. Serve with lots of butter. The bread is wonderful with all kinds of soups, stews, chilis, and gumbos.

1 tablespoon vegetable oil or bacon grease

2 large eggs

2 cups buttermilk

3/4 teaspoon salt

2 cups white cornmeal, preferably stone-ground

1 tablespoon baking powder, preferably nonaluminum

1 Rub a 10-inch cast-iron skillet with the oil or bacon grease and put the pan on the center shelf of a cold oven. Turn the oven on to 450°F and preheat for 15 to 20 minutes.

2 While the oven heats, whisk together the eggs, buttermilk, and salt in a large bowl. Add the cornmeal 1 to 2 tablespoons at a time, whisking it in to make a smooth batter.

3 When the oven is ready, add the baking powder to the batter and whisk it in rapidly. Carefully remove the skillet from the oven and immediately scrape the batter into the pan. It will sizzle and sputter. Bake for 15 to 20 minutes, until the top of the corn bread is golden and flecked with darker brown spots, a toothpick inserted into the center comes out clean, and the bread has shrunk from the sides of the pan. Cool in the pan for 5 to 10 minutes before cutting into wedges and serving.

TEXAS JALAPEÑO CORN BREAD

Makes one 10-inch round bread

I got this recipe many years ago from a great lady named Vi Campbell, who got it from a Texas friend. The bread is moist and spicy and contains cornmeal and whole kernel corn, but no flour. Vi always made this with bacon drippings, and for the best taste, that is really the fat of choice, though you can substitute lightly salted butter. For best results, use a 10-inch cast iron skillet. If you don't have one, use a well-greased 9-inch square baking pan.

1	cup yellow cornmeal, preferably stone-ground	1	garlic clove, minced
1	teaspoon baking soda	3	jalapeño peppers, seeded and finely chopped
1	teaspoon sugar	1	cup fresh corn kernels, or thawed frozen corn
1/2	teaspoon salt		
3	large eggs	1 1/2	cups Monterey Jack cheese (or pepper Jack cheese), shredded (6 ounces)
1	cup milk		
1	(2-ounce) jar pimientos, drained and diced		
1/2	cup finely chopped yellow onion	1/3	cup bacon drippings or 5 tablespoons salted butter, melted

1 Grease a 10-inch cast-iron skillet generously with vegetable shortening and put the pan on the center shelf of the oven. Turn the oven on to 450°F and preheat for 15 minutes.

2 In a large bowl, stir together the cornmeal, baking soda, sugar, and salt. In a medium bowl, beat the eggs lightly with a fork, then stir in the milk, pimientos, onion, garlic, jalapeños, corn, 1 cup of the cheese, and the bacon drippings or butter. Add the liquid to the dry ingredients and stir with a rubber spatula to make a smooth batter.

3 Carefully remove the pan from the oven and immediately scrape the batter into the pan. Sprinkle the remaining 1/2 cup cheese on top. Bake for about 20 minutes, until the corn bread is golden brown and a toothpick inserted into the center comes out clean. Cool for 10 to 15 minutes before serving.

BLUEBERRY BUTTERMILK SCONES

Makes 8 large scones

One secret of tender, flaky scones is to keep the butter in large flakes, not small pieces. Another secret is to use a soft wheat flour, such as White Lily or Great Valley Mills (page 526). I use a mixture of all-purpose flour and soft wheat or cake flour. These moist scones will melt in your mouth. The combination of blueberries, lemon zest, and buttermilk give them a wonderful tang. If fresh blueberries are not available, you can substitute frozen unsweetened whole berries. Other fruits work well too: diced firm but ripe apricots, for example, or raspberries or cranberries.

1 cup unbleached all-purpose flour	8 tablespoons (1 stick) cold unsalted butter, cut into tablespoon-sized pieces
1 cup unbleached soft wheat flour or cake flour	Finely grated zest of 1 lemon
1/2 teaspoon baking soda	1 1/2 cups fresh or frozen (not thawed) blueberries
1/2 teaspoon salt	1 1/4 cups buttermilk
1/4 cup sugar	

1 Adjust an oven rack to the center position and preheat the oven to 350°F. Line a large baking sheet with cooking parchment or a silicone liner; set aside.

2 Sift the flours, baking soda, salt, and 2 tablespoons of the sugar into a large bowl. Add the butter pieces and use a pastry blender or two knives to chop them gently into largish pieces. Then use your fingertips to work the butter rapidly into large flakes. (If your kitchen is warm, chill the flour mixture briefly before proceeding.) Add the lemon zest and blueberries and toss with your fingers to coat evenly.

3 Set aside 1 tablespoon of the buttermilk. Pour the remaining buttermilk into the blueberry mixture and stir and fold gently with a rubber spatula just until the dry ingredients are moistened. The dough will be very thick. Scrape the dough out onto a lightly floured work surface and dust it lightly with flour. With the palms and sides of your hands, shape the dough into an 8-inch circle. Brush the reserved buttermilk on top (or use your fingers to smear it on the dough) and sprinkle with the remaining 2 tablespoons sugar. Cut the dough into quarters with a large heavy knife, then cut each quarter in half, to form 8 wedges.

4 With a spatula, transfer the scones to the lined baking sheet, spacing them about 2 inches apart. Bake for 20 to 25 minutes, until golden brown. Transfer to cooling racks with a spatula and serve warm or at room temperature.

"PERFECT LEAVENING AND MAXIMUM PROTECTION"

Steadily, evenly, hundreds of new tiny bubbles swell through the batter and continue the leavening. Up! . . . up! . . . they keep raising the batter and hold it high and light. Thanks to these two actions, Calumet protects your baking from start to finish.

—General Foods, *All About Home Baking* (1933)

GRAHAM CRACKER BROWN BREAD

*Makes
1 loaf*

Brown bread recipes appeared in cookbooks throughout the nineteenth century. Usually made with cornmeal and whole wheat flour, sometimes with rye added, and flavored with molasses, these early breads were leavened with yeast and either baked or steamed. Later versions substituted baking soda for the yeast, which saved a couple of hours of rising time. This one is streamlined even further. Graham crackers stand in for whole wheat flour, and the bread bakes quickly, in a little over 1 hour. The texture is moist, and the bread not too sweet.

1 cup unbleached all-purpose flour	1 cup graham cracker crumbs
1 teaspoon baking soda	1 large egg
1/2 teaspoon salt	1/3 cup molasses (I use Grandma's)
1 teaspoon freshly grated nutmeg	1 cup buttermilk
4 tablespoons (1/2 stick) unsalted butter, at room temperature	1 cup dark raisins

1 Adjust an oven rack to the lower third position and preheat the oven to 350°F. Butter an 8^1/$_2$-x-4^1/$_2$-x-2^3/$_4$-inch loaf pan and dust the insides all over with fine dry bread crumbs or graham cracker crumbs. Knock out the excess crumbs and set aside.

2 Sift the flour, baking soda, salt, and nutmeg together and set aside.

3 In a large bowl, beat the butter with an electric mixer on medium speed until smooth and creamy, about 1 minute. Gradually beat in the graham cracker crumbs, then beat for 1 to 2 minutes. Add the egg and beat for 1 minute, then beat in the molasses.

4 On low speed, add the flour mixture in 3 additions, alternating with the buttermilk, beginning and ending with the flour and beating only until incorporated. Stir in the raisins. Spread the batter in the prepared pan.

5 Bake for 1 hour to 1 hour and 10 minutes, until the loaf is well browned and springs back when gently pressed and a toothpick inserted in the center comes out clean. Cool in the pan on a wire rack for 15 minutes. Unmold and set right side up on the wire rack to cool.

6 When the bread is completely cool, cut into slices with a sharp serrated knife. This loaf keeps well for several days, wrapped airtight, at room temperature. It can be frozen for up to 1 month.

SYLVESTER GRAHAM

Sylvester Graham followed his father's path to the ministry. Chronic ill health plagued the younger Graham most of his life, and he became a reformist in ideas of diet and health. Today he's known for graham crackers and graham flour and for promoting the healthful benefits of eating breads made with whole wheat flour. Sylvester Graham also stressed a lifestyle known as Grahamism, which included abstinence from alcohol, tobacco, and meat; sleeping on hard mattresses; chastity; cold showers; and vigorous exercise. Interest in Grahamism peaked in the 1830s and faded in the 1840s, after which Graham frequently lectured on biblical topics. He died in 1851 in Northampton, Massachusetts, at the age of fifty-seven.

GOLDEN PUMPKIN LOAF

*Makes
1 large
loaf*

A little cornmeal adds texture to this moist loaf. Be sure to use fine corn-meal, though, or the texture will be gritty. Golden raisins, walnuts, and a mixture of spices make it seem like a holiday bread—but don't wait for a special occasion to make it. I like to have it on hand for a mid-morning or afternoon snack. Cut it into thick slices. It's good plain or with cream cheese.

1$1/4$ cups unbleached all-purpose
  flour
$1/2$ cup fine yellow cornmeal
1 teaspoon baking powder,
  preferably nonaluminum
$1/4$ teaspoon baking soda
$1/2$ teaspoon salt
1 teaspoon ground ginger
$1/4$ teaspoon ground cardamom
$1/4$ teaspoon ground mace

2 large eggs
$3/4$ cup firmly packed dark brown
  sugar
$1/2$ cup sugar
1 cup canned solid-pack pumpkin
  (not pumpkin pie filling)
1$1/2$ teaspoons pure vanilla extract
$1/4$ cup vegetable oil
1 cup golden raisins
$1/2$ cup walnuts, finely chopped

1 Adjust an oven rack to the lower third position and preheat the oven to 350°F. Butter a 9-x-5-x-3-inch or 10-x-4$1/2$-x-3-inch loaf pan, or coat with cooking spray. Set aside.

2 Sift the flour, cornmeal, baking powder, baking soda, salt, ginger, carda-mom, and mace together; set aside.

3 In a large bowl, whisk the eggs for about 1 minute, until frothy. Add both sugars and whisk until creamy and thick, 1 to 2 minutes. Whisk in the pumpkin, vanilla, and oil until smooth. Stir in the raisins and walnuts. Add the sifted dry ingredients and stir gently with a rubber spatula only until the batter is thoroughly combined. Scrape the batter into the prepared pan and smooth the top.

4 Bake for 50 to 60 minutes, until the loaf is well browned and a toothpick inserted into the center comes out clean. Cool in the pan on a wire rack for 15 minutes. Remove from the pan and turn the loaf right side up on the rack to cool completely. Store airtight, and cut with a serrated knife.

APRICOT-MACADAMIA BRAN BREAD

*Makes
1 large
loaf*

This moist, not-too-sweet bread is great at any time of the day. It is wonderful thinly sliced and spread with cream cheese. For the best taste and texture, make it a day ahead.

You can use either salted or unsalted macadamia nuts. The easiest way to chop macadamia nuts is to put them into a large plastic bag, set the open bag on your countertop, and spread the nuts into one layer. Gently tap on the nuts with a meat pounder or rolling pin to crush the nuts into medium-sized pieces.

1¹/₄ cups unbleached all-purpose flour	³/₄ cup sugar
1¹/₄ teaspoons baking powder, preferably nonaluminum	2 large eggs
¹/₄ teaspoon baking soda	1 cup all-bran cereal
¹/₂ teaspoon salt	4 small very ripe bananas (1 pound), mashed with a fork (about 1¹/₃ cups)
8 tablespoons (1 stick) unsalted butter, at room temperature	³/₄ cup diced dried apricots
2 teaspoons pure vanilla extract	³/₄ cup chopped macadamia nuts

1 Adjust an oven rack to the lower third position and preheat the oven to 350°F. Butter a 10-x-4¹/₂-x-3-inch or 9-x-5-x-3-inch loaf pan, or coat it with cooking spray, dust the inside with flour or fine dry bread crumbs, and knock out the excess. Set aside.

2 Sift the flour, baking powder, baking soda, and salt together; set aside.

3 In a large bowl, beat the butter with an electric mixer on medium speed until smooth and creamy, about 1 minute. Add the vanilla and ¹/₄ cup of the sugar and beat on medium-high speed for 1 minute. Beat in the remaining sugar 2 tablespoons at a time, beating for 20 to 30 seconds after each addition. Scrape the bowl and beaters, and beat for 4 minutes. The mixture will be very fluffy. Scrape the bowl and add the eggs one at a time, beating for 1 minute after each. Add the all-bran and beat on low speed for 1 minute. Beat in the flour mixture on low speed in 3 additions, alternating

with the banana, beginning and ending with the flour and beating only until incorporated. With a rubber spatula, fold in the apricots and macadamia nuts. Spread evenly in the prepared pan.

4 Bake for about 1 hour, until the loaf is deep brown and a toothpick inserted into the center comes out clean. Cool in the pan on a wire rack for 20 minutes. Remove from the pan and let cool completely right side up on a wire rack. Store airtight, and cut thin slices with a sharp serrated knife.

THE HEALTH CHAMPIONS

Believe it or not, the dry cereals that provide a quick breakfast to millions of Americans today, and that add taste and texture to many baked goods, began as health foods. Toward the end of the nineteenth century, Dr. John Harvey Kellogg ran the faddish Battle Creek Sanitarium, where people came to solve their health woes. Skinny people were fed twenty-six times a day while lying immobile, weighed down with sandbags. Those with high blood pressure downed pound after pound of grapes.

One of Kellogg's firm beliefs was that gnawing on zwieback would keep the teeth in good condition. Not everyone's teeth were strong enough, however, and one client actually broke a tooth as she struggled to bite through one of the hard, dry biscuits. To solve the problem, Kellogg invented a wheat cereal he called Granose. It sold well, and in 1907 his brother, Will Keith, hit the jackpot with Kellogg's Toasted Corn Flakes. This product remains the country's most popular breakfast cereal to this day.

Inspired by the success of corn flakes, in 1915 the company devised a way of turning wheat bran, a great source of dietary fiber, into a crunchy product they christened Kellogg's All-Bran Cereal. All-Bran is more than just a breakfast food. Added to quick breads, it provides flavor, texture, and healthy fiber.

PUMPKIN-DATE LOAF WITH CREAM CHEESE SWIRL

Makes
1 large
loaf

Dates and pumpkin are a natural combination, and the pumpkin keeps the sweetness of the dates in check. Pumpkin pie spice is a blend of cinnamon, allspice, nutmeg, ginger, mace, and cloves, sold in any supermarket. The bread is best if allowed to stand overnight; make it the day before you plan to serve it.

CREAM CHEESE MIXTURE

- 4 ounces light cream cheese (do not use fat-free)
- 2 tablespoons sugar
- 1 teaspoon pure vanilla extract
- 1 large egg

PUMPKIN LOAF

- 1²/₃ cups unbleached all-purpose flour
- 1 teaspoon baking powder, preferably nonaluminum
- ¹/₄ teaspoon baking soda
- ¹/₂ teaspoon salt
- 1¹/₂ teaspoons pumpkin pie spice
- 2 large eggs
- 1¹/₄ cups firmly packed dark brown sugar
- 1 cup canned solid-pack pumpkin (not pumpkin pie filling)
- ¹/₄ cup vegetable oil
- 1 cup pitted whole dates, each date cut into 6 pieces with scissors (do not use packaged chopped dates)

1 Adjust an oven rack to the lower third position and preheat the oven to 350°F. Butter a 9-x-5-x-3-inch or 10-x-4¹/₂-x-3-inch loaf pan, or coat with cooking spray. Set aside.

2 For the cream cheese mixture, beat together the cream cheese, sugar, vanilla, and egg in a small bowl with an electric mixer until very smooth. Set aside.

3 For the pumpkin loaf, sift the flour, baking powder, baking soda, salt, and pumpkin pie spice together; set aside.

4 In a large bowl, whisk the eggs for about 1 minute, until frothy. Add the brown sugar and whisk for about 1 minute more, until the mixture is creamy and thick. Whisk in the pumpkin and oil until smooth. Stir in the dates. Add the flour mixture and stir gently with a rubber spatula only until thoroughly combined. Scrape the batter into the prepared pan and smooth the top. Pour on the cream cheese mixture and swirl it in with a knife, moving crosswise down the length of the loaf.

5 Bake for 55 to 60 minutes, until the loaf is well browned and a toothpick inserted into the center comes out clean. Cool in the pan on a wire rack for 15 minutes. Remove from the pan and let cool completely, right side up, on a wire rack. Slice with a serrated knife.

PUMPKIN EATERS

Although many of us think of pumpkin as quintessentially American, it isn't. Gourds similar to the pumpkin were grown in Europe long before the first colonists set foot in the new land and were used to make pie. The pumpkins on this continent, while not identical to those our European ancestors knew, were similar enough that they were able to adapt them to their treasured recipes.

PERSIMMON WALNUT BREAD

*Makes
2 loaves*

Packed with persimmon pulp and walnuts, this bread is dense and moist and not too sweet. Be sure to use persimmons that are truly ripe. I adapted this from a recipe in *Mountain Country Cooking: A Gathering of the Best Recipes from the Smokies to the Blue Ridge,* by Mark F. Sohn.

6 fully ripe Hachiya persimmons (about 2 pounds)

3 cups walnut halves or large pieces (about 12 ounces)

3¼ cups unbleached all-purpose flour

2 teaspoons baking powder, preferably nonaluminum

½ teaspoon salt

4 large eggs

1 cup sugar

1 cup firmly packed light brown sugar

1 cup (2 sticks) unsalted butter, melted and cooled

1 Adjust an oven rack to the lower third position and preheat the oven to 375°F. Butter two 8½-x-4½-x-2¾-inch loaf pans; set aside.

2 Pull the stems off the persimmons and cut each fruit lengthwise in half. With a teaspoon or grapefruit spoon, scoop the pulp out into a bowl. Use a pastry blender or a potato masher to chop or mash the pulp into small pieces; you should still have some pieces of persimmon mixed with the pureed pulp. Measure 2 cups and set aside. Eat any leftovers or reserve for another use.

3 Toast the walnuts in a shallow baking pan until fragrant, stirring once or twice, 6 to 8 minutes. Let cool completely.

4 Sift the flour, baking powder, and salt together; set aside.

5 Whisk the eggs in a large bowl until thoroughly combined and slightly frothy. Add both sugars and beat in thoroughly with the whisk. Whisk in the butter. Stir in the persimmon pulp and walnuts with a rubber spatula. Add the flour mixture and stir only until the batter is smooth. Divide the batter between the prepared pans and smooth the tops.

6 Bake for about 1 hour and 5 minutes, until the loaves are well browned and

a toothpick inserted into the center comes out clean. The loaves will be quite dark, especially on the edges, but if they start to brown too much before they are done, lay a piece of aluminum foil, shiny side up, loosely on top during the last 30 minutes or so of baking.

7 Cool in the pans on a wire rack for 20 minutes. Run a small sharp knife around the sides to release the loaves, and carefully unmold them. Set them right side up on a rack to cool completely. Wrap airtight. The loaves can be frozen for up to 2 months.

PERSIMMONS

America has its own native persimmon, *Diospyros virginiana.* About the size of a golf ball, the fruit grows abundantly on tall trees from Pennsylvania to Illinois, all the way south to Florida and west to eastern Texas. The name comes from an Algonquin word, *putchamin.* The persimmon is a voluptuous fruit: the bright orange flesh is smooth and buttery and slides down your throat. To be fully ripe, the fruit must be allowed to fall from the tree, and folks who live where persimmons grow know they must wait for late fall before they pick the fruit—off the ground. Persimmon lovers claim the fruit of each tree is different.

The large orange Asian Hachiya persimmons, available in markets in the fall, make delicious substitutes for our native variety. They must be very soft to have developed their full sweetness and lost their astringency. If you've ever eaten an unripe persimmon, you won't forget that awful puckeriness. Avoid Fuyu persimmons, which are round and squat, rather than teardrop-shaped as are Hachiya persimmons, and crunchy rather than soft in texture. Persimmons will ripen at home in a paper bag. When they feel like a sack of mush, they're ready to eat or to bake with.

BLUEBERRY–LEMON CURD STREUSEL MUFFINS

Makes 12 large muffins

These big, delicate, berry-filled muffins have a delightfully crunchy topping and a hidden surprise of lemon curd in the center. They rise above the rims of their cups, making an attractive brim. A nonstick pan works best for these. They're delicious plain, but butter makes them even better.

STREUSEL TOPPING

- 3 tablespoons unbleached all-purpose flour
- 2 tablespoons sugar
- 2 tablespoons cold unsalted butter, cut into pieces
- 1/2 teaspoon freshly grated nutmeg

MUFFINS

- 1 3/4 cups unbleached all-purpose flour
- 3/4 cup sugar
- 1 teaspoon cream of tartar
- 1/2 teaspoon baking soda
- 1/2 teaspoon salt
- 6 tablespoons (3/4 stick) cold unsalted butter, cut into pieces
- 1 1/2 cups fresh or frozen (not thawed) blueberries
- 1 large egg
- 1/2 teaspoon pure vanilla extract
- 3/4 cup milk
- 1/3–1/2 cup Lemon Curd (page 292)

1 Adjust an oven rack to the center position and preheat the oven to 350°F. Butter a 12-cup muffin pan, preferably nonstick. Set aside.

2 For the topping, combine the flour and sugar in a small bowl. With a pastry blender or your fingertips, work in the butter until it is in small flakes. Stir in the nutmeg. Refrigerate.

3 For the muffins, sift the flour, sugar, cream of tartar, baking soda, and salt together into a large bowl. Add the butter and cut it in with a pastry blender or two knives until the pieces are about the size of small peas. Add the blueberries and toss them in the mixture with your fingers. In a small bowl, beat the egg lightly, then stir in the vanilla and milk. Add the milk mixture to the flour mixture all at once, folding it gently with a rubber spatula just to moisten the dry ingredients. The batter will be stiff.

4 Divide half the batter among the prepared muffin cups. Top each with a small spoonful of lemon curd. Spoon the remaining batter evenly over the lemon curd. Sprinkle the streusel mixture on top of the muffins.

5 Bake for 20 to 25 minutes, until the muffins are golden brown and spring back when gently pressed. Cool in the pan for 5 minutes. Invert the pan onto a baking sheet, wait for a few seconds, and slowly lift off the pan. The muffins should all come out easily; if not, use the tip of a sharp knife to dislodge them. Turn the muffins upright and serve at once.

HUCKLEBERRY MUFFINS

Makes 16 muffins

Wild huckleberries have an intensity and tartness that commercially grown blueberries simply can't match. If you can't get fresh wild huckleberries, use frozen wild blueberries, available in 1-pound bags in some supermarkets. You can mix the dry and liquid ingredients separately the night before (refrigerate the liquids). In the morning, simply combine the two and add the berries—the muffins will be ready for the oven in a matter of minutes.

1³/₄ cups unbleached all-purpose
   flour
1 cup sugar
2 teaspoons baking powder,
   preferably nonaluminum
¹/₂ teaspoon salt
6 tablespoons (³/₄ stick) cold
   unsalted butter, cut into pieces

1 cup buttermilk
1 large egg
1 teaspoon pure vanilla extract
1¹/₂ cups fresh huckleberries or
   frozen (not thawed) wild
   blueberries

1 Adjust an oven rack to the center position and preheat the oven to 350°F. Butter 16 muffin cups, preferably nonstick, and set them aside. (I use one 12-cup muffin pan and one 6-cup pan, filling only 4 cups of the latter.)

2 Sift the flour, sugar, baking powder, and salt together into a large bowl. Add the butter and cut it in with a pastry blender or two knives until the mixture resembles coarse meal.

3 In a small bowl, whisk together the buttermilk, egg, and vanilla to combine well. Add the berries to the dry ingredients and toss them in gently with your hands. Add the milk mixture and fold everything together gently with a rubber spatula just to moisten the dry ingredients. The batter will be very thick. Divide the batter evenly among the muffin cups.

4 Bake for 20 to 25 minutes, until the muffins are golden brown and spring back when gently pressed. Cool in the pans for 5 minutes, then invert the pans onto a baking sheet, wait a few seconds, and carefully lift off the pans. If any of the muffins stick, use the tip of a small sharp knife to dislodge them. Serve at once.

CRANBERRY MUFFINS FROM NANTUCKET

Makes 12 large muffins

These muffins are a specialty of the historic Jared Coffin House, a hotel and restaurant in Nantucket. They are light textured and sweet yet tangy. Chopped cranberries add more color and cook more evenly than whole berries. I adapted the recipe from one given to me many years ago by Sherry Strange, a cook who attended one of my food processor classes.

2 cups unbleached all-purpose flour

2 teaspoons baking powder, preferably nonaluminum

1/2 teaspoon salt

1/2 teaspoon freshly grated nutmeg

1 1/2 cups fresh or frozen cranberries (see note, page 106)

1 large egg

1 large egg yolk

3/4 cup plus 2 tablespoons sugar

4 tablespoons (1/2 stick) unsalted butter, cut into tablespoon-sized pieces, at room temperature

1/4 cup vegetable shortening

1 teaspoon pure vanilla extract

1/2 cup plus 2 tablespoons milk

1 Adjust an oven rack to the center position and preheat the oven to 350°F. Butter a 12-cup muffin pan, preferably nonstick, and set aside.

2 Combine the flour, baking powder, salt, and nutmeg in a food processor and process for 5 seconds. Transfer to a sheet of waxed paper and set aside.

3 Add the cranberries to the processor and pulse 3 to 5 times, until completely chopped. Remove from the work bowl.

4 Add the egg, egg yolk, and 3/4 cup of the sugar to the processor and process for 1 minute. Add the butter, vegetable shortening, and vanilla and process for 1 minute, stopping the machine once to scrape the work bowl. With the machine running, add the milk and process for 5 seconds.

5 Sprinkle the dry ingredients over the mixture in the work bowl. Pulse twice, about 1 second each time. The batter will be thick and some flour will not be incorporated. Scrape most of the batter into a medium bowl.

Pulse the processor for 1 second to spin off any batter clinging to the blade. Scrape the remaining batter into the bowl. Add the cranberries, and fold them into the batter with a rubber spatula.

6 Divide the batter evenly among the muffin cups, filling them quite full. Don't level the batter. Sprinkle the 2 remaining tablespoons sugar over the muffins, using about $^1/_2$ teaspoon for each.

7 Bake for 20 to 25 minutes, until the muffins are light golden and spring back when gently pressed and a toothpick inserted into the center comes out clean. Cool the muffins in their cups for 5 minutes, then carefully remove them to a wire rack. Serve hot, warm, or at room temperature. These are best when very fresh.

Note: If using frozen cranberries, thaw them just until they can be easily pierced with the tip of a sharp knife before chopping.

WHOLE WHEAT, OATMEAL, AND RAISIN MUFFINS

Makes 12 large muffins

These moist, light-textured whole-grain muffins are full of delicious, healthful antioxidants. You can prepare the batter the night before and refrigerate it, then bake muffins fresh in the morning. Bake only as many as you need at a time; the remaining batter will keep, refrigerated, for at least 1 week. The top of the batter will darken after a day or two; be sure to stir well before using.

1 cup whole wheat flour	1½ cups quick-cooking (not instant) rolled oats
2 tablespoons untoasted wheat germ	1 large egg
2 tablespoons wheat bran	1 cup buttermilk
¼ cup sugar	¼ cup vegetable oil
¼ cup firmly packed brown sugar	1 teaspoon pure vanilla extract
1½ teaspoons baking soda	½ cup boiling water
½ teaspoon salt	
1 teaspoon ground cinnamon	
1 cup raisins or mixed dried fruits (I use ⅓ cup each diced dates, raisins, and cranberries; or use dried blueberries, diced apricots, and raisins)	

1 In a large bowl, stir together the flour, wheat germ, bran, sugar, brown sugar, baking soda, salt, and cinnamon. Add the dried fruits and oats and toss to mix well.

2 In a small bowl, beat the egg lightly with a fork. Stir in the buttermilk, oil, and vanilla. Add to the dry ingredients and stir with a rubber spatula until thoroughly moistened. Add the boiling water and stir it in with a rubber spatula. The batter will be fairly thin. Let stand for 15 to 20 minutes before baking, or cover and refrigerate until ready to bake.

3 Adjust an oven rack to the lower third position and preheat the oven to 375°F. Coat a 12-cup muffin pan, preferably nonstick, with cooking spray.

4 Spoon $1/3$ cup batter into each cup. Bake for about 20 minutes (about 25 minutes if the batter is cold), until the muffins are well browned and spring back when gently pressed. Remove the pan from the oven and wait for 1 minute, then carefully remove the muffins and cool briefly on racks. Serve warm.

BUTTERMILK RAISIN-BRAN MUFFINS

Makes 12 large muffins

These moist, not-too-sweet muffins are full of fiber and vitamins, not to mention great taste. In place of the raisins, you could use any dried fruit or a combination, such as cranberries, blueberries, apricots, dates, and sour cherries.

1 cup unbleached all-purpose flour	1/2 cup firmly packed light brown sugar
1 1/2 teaspoons baking soda	1 cup dark raisins
1/2 teaspoon salt	2 cups all-bran cereal
1 teaspoon ground cinnamon	1 large egg
1/2 teaspoon freshly grated nutmeg	1 1/2 cups buttermilk
1/4 cup untoasted wheat germ	1/4 cup vegetable oil
	1 teaspoon pure vanilla extract

1 Butter a 12-cup muffin pan, preferably nonstick. Set aside.

2 Sift the flour, baking soda, salt, cinnamon, and nutmeg together into a large bowl. Stir in the wheat germ and brown sugar. Add the raisins and all-bran cereal and toss with your fingers to combine.

3 In a medium bowl, whisk the egg. Add the buttermilk, oil, and vanilla and whisk together well. Add to the dry ingredients and stir gently with a rubber spatula. Let the batter stand for 15 to 20 minutes so the liquid thoroughly moistens the cereal. Meanwhile, adjust an oven rack to the lower third position and preheat the oven to 375°F.

4 Divide the batter among the muffin cups, filling them almost to the top. Bake for 15 to 20 minutes, until the muffins are a deep brown and spring back when gently pressed. Cool the muffins in the pan for 5 minutes. Then invert the pan onto a large tray and set the muffins on a wire rack to cool further. Serve warm or at room temperature.

PERSIMMON PECAN MUFFINS

Makes 12 muffins

These light-textured, mildly spiced muffins make a great breakfast or brunch treat. Be sure the persimmons are very ripe; they should feel very soft and squishy. The easiest way to prepare the pulp is to chop it with a pastry blender until it is almost smooth, with just a few smallish chunks.

1³/₄ cups unbleached all-purpose flour

2 teaspoons baking powder, preferably nonaluminum

¹/₄ teaspoon baking soda

¹/₂ teaspoon salt

1 teaspoon ground cinnamon

¹/₂ teaspoon freshly grated nutmeg

¹/₂ teaspoon ground allspice

1 large egg

³/₄ cup sugar

1 teaspoon pure vanilla extract

1 cup mashed ripe Hachiya persimmon pulp (from 2–3 persimmons)

5 tablespoons unsalted butter, melted

¹/₂ cup chopped pecans

1 Adjust an oven rack to the lower third position and preheat the oven to 375°F. Butter a 12-cup muffin pan, preferably nonstick, and set aside.

2 Sift the flour, baking powder, baking soda, salt, cinnamon, nutmeg, and allspice together into a large bowl.

3 In a medium bowl, whisk the egg, sugar, and vanilla together for 1 minute. Whisk in the persimmon pulp and butter. Scrape this mixture over the flour mixture, add the pecans, and fold together with a rubber spatula just to moisten the dry ingredients. Divide the mixture evenly among the muffin cups.

4 Bake for 18 to 20 minutes, until the muffins are golden brown and spring back when gently pressed. Cool the muffins in their cups for 1 minute, then carefully transfer them to cooling racks. Serve hot, warm, or at room temperature.

FRESH APRICOT-CARDAMOM MUFFINS

Makes 12 large muffins

When baked, fresh apricots develop a richness and tartness not evident if the fruit is eaten out of hand. Select apricots that are ripe but firm, not mushy ones.

1³/₄ cups unbleached all-purpose flour

³/₄ cup sugar

2 teaspoons baking powder, preferably nonaluminum

¹/₂ teaspoon baking soda

¹/₂ teaspoon salt

¹/₂ teaspoon ground cardamom

6 tablespoons (³/₄ stick) cold unsalted butter, cut into pieces

1¹/₂ cups diced (¹/₂-inch pieces) fresh apricots (about 8 ounces)

¹/₃ cup dried sour cherries, chopped

³/₄ cup buttermilk

1 large egg

1 teaspoon pure vanilla extract

2 tablespoons sugar

¹/₈ teaspoon ground cardamom

1 Adjust an oven rack to the center position and preheat the oven to 375°F. Butter a 12-cup nonstick muffin pan, preferably nonstick, and set aside.

2 Sift the flour, sugar, baking powder, baking soda, salt, and cardamom together into a bowl. Cut in the butter with a pastry blender or two knives until the mixture resembles coarse meal. Stir in the apricots and cherries.

3 In a small bowl, combine the buttermilk, egg, and vanilla, mixing with a fork. Add all at once to the flour mixture and fold together gently with a rubber spatula, scraping the bowl occasionally, until the ingredients are well moistened. The batter will be stiff.

4 Spoon the batter evenly into the muffin cups. Combine the remaining 2 tablespoons sugar and ¹/₈ teaspoon cardamom and sprinkle ¹/₂ teaspoon of the mixture on top of each muffin.

5 Bake for about 25 minutes, until the tops are golden brown and spring back when pressed gently. Cool in the pan for 5 minutes. Cover the muffins with a sheet of waxed paper and a cookie sheet and invert. Carefully lift off the pan. Turn the muffins right side up and transfer them to wire racks. Serve warm or at room temperature.

3 Sweet Yeast Breads and Doughnuts

As you ramble on through life, brother,

Whatever be your goal,

Keep your eye upon the doughnut,

And not upon the hole.

—Murray Banks

In nineteenth-century American homes, sweet yeast breads and doughnuts were just as popular as everyday savory loaves. Recipes for hot cross buns and Sally Lunn—sweet egg-enriched yeast breads—are included in almost all cookbooks from the mid- to late 1800s. These breads were usually served with afternoon tea or coffee. Many kinds of yeasted cakes, including Election Cake and "great cakes," were also made from sweet doughs, with raisins or currants—the two most commonly used dried fruits of the period—kneaded in. Citron, another favorite, might also have been included. Sweet yeast rolls, like Pennsylvania Dutch Tea Rolls, were made from doughs rich with butter and eggs, and housewives also became adept at making brioche, the richest of all sweetened yeast breads.

The same sweet doughs were also made into doughnuts. The original doughnuts, most likely brought to this country by the early Dutch settlers, were tasty nuggets of fried yeasted dough, often containing dried fruits. Washington Irving may have been the first to mention them in print when he described "the simple charms of a genuine Dutch country tea table . . . an enormous dish of balls of sweetened dough, fried in hog's fat, and called doughnuts, or oly kocks . . . and the crisp and crumbling kruller" in *The Legend of Sleepy Hollow*.

While the Northerners had their doughnuts, a different tradition had emerged in the South. In nineteenth-century New Orleans, delicious fried yeasted rice fritters, called calas, were enjoyed with the morning cup of café au lait. According to *The Picayune Creole Cookbook* (1901),

> The Cala woman was a daily figure on the streets till within the last two or three years. She went her rounds in quaint bandana tignon, guinea blue dress, and white apron, and carried on her head a covered bowl, in which were the dainty and hot Calas. Her cry, *'Belle Cala! Tout Chaud!'* ['Beautiful Calas! Piping Hot!'] would penetrate the morning air, and the olden Creole cooks would rush to the doors to get the first fresh, hot Calas to carry to their masters and mistresses with the early morning cup of coffee.

The cala woman is part of history now, but the fried sweet yeasted New Orleans beignet lives on.

Before the doughnut cutter became standard kitchen equipment, cooks cut doughs into different shapes with a "jagging iron"—a rotary wheel mounted on a handle—and fried them. Sometime around 1870, the classic ring-shaped cutters became available. Once the new shape became accepted, the old-fashioned balls of dough—"dough nuts"—fell by the wayside, except in certain traditional recipes. However, doughnuts didn't become a big business until the twentieth century. In 1921, Adolph Levitt, a Russian-American entrepreneur, founded the Donut Machine Corporation. He put an automatic doughnut maker in the window of one of his bakeries in Times Square, and it stopped traffic. His company was so successful that it spawned an entire industry, the walk-in doughnut shop. The cala women had brought doughnuts to the people, but with Mr. Levitt's invention, food became a destination.

BAKE-OFF IRONY

Nowhere is the American love of experimentation in baking more evident than in the Pillsbury Bake-Off. This granddaddy of cooking contests was originally devised in 1949 to encourage cooks to use more flour. For the first sixteen Bake-Offs, all entries had to be homemade and include at least ¹/₂ cup of Pillsbury's Best All-Purpose Flour.

As more women became part of the workforce, however, the contest bowed to the growing trend of convenience cooking, and the imagination of Bake-Off entrants shifted from original flour-based creations to ready-made products used in new ways. By the seventeenth Bake-Off in 1966, shortcut recipes using packaged mixes and other convenience products predominated. The grand prize winner that year, Golden Gate Snack Bread, displayed the incursion of packaged products into home baking, incorporating pasteurized processed cheese spread and dried onion soup mix into a yeast bread.

At subsequent competitions, recipes made with refrigerated biscuits, piecrusts, ready-made cookie doughs, and pizza crusts have won big bucks. As other corporations—Old El Paso and Green Giant—became allied with Pillsbury, salsas, dry taco mixes, and frozen and canned vegetables were added to the list of acceptable products. Baking, or even cooking, for that matter, was no longer a requirement. The contest gradually threw open its doors to recipes for soups, salads, and main dishes that could be prepared in record time.

With the emphasis on ready-made foods and speed—"Fast and Fabulous Treats" prepared in 15 minutes or less—flour was pushed to the back of the cupboard. The end came in 1996 at the thirty-seventh Bake-Off in Dallas, Texas, when the flour category, which had been the reason for the Bake-Off's existence in the first place, was eliminated.

MARTHA WASHINGTON'S CURRANT CAKE

Makes 1 large sheet cake, about 16 servings

This slightly sweet, mildly spiced yeast bread is similar to the Italian panettone, though not as light. The crust is tender with just a touch of crispness, and the texture dense, yet smooth and buttery. Rose water gives the cake a lovely perfume and helps make the dough tender. This version is scaled down eight-fold from a recipe called Great Cake in *Martha Washington's Booke of Cookery,* transcribed by noted food historian Karen Hess.

Because there is so much butter in the cake, it is slow to rise. Allow about 4 hours in a warm place (85° to 90°F). Or double the amount of yeast to speed up the process, if you wish.

1   0.6-ounce cake compressed yeast or one ¼-ounce package (2¼ teaspoons) active dry yeast

¼   cup warm water (110°–115°F)

1   pound (3 cups) dried currants

3½   cups unbleached all-purpose flour, plus more as needed

½   cup whole wheat flour

¾   cup (1½ sticks) cold unsalted butter, cut into tablespoon-sized pieces

¼   cup sugar (or packed brown sugar)

1   teaspoon salt

½   cup heavy cream

¼   cup pale ale

2   large eggs

¼   teaspoon ground cloves

¼   teaspoon ground mace

¼   teaspoon freshly grated nutmeg

2   tablespoons rose water

1 If using compressed yeast, crumble it into the warm water in a small bowl; set aside. If using dry yeast, sprinkle it over the water, stir well, and set aside. Let stand for about 10 minutes to soften. Meanwhile, if the currants are not soft, put them in a strainer set over—not in—a pot of simmering water for 5 minutes to plump. Drain and pat dry.

2 Place both flours and the butter in a mixer bowl or another large bowl. If using a stand mixer, beat with the paddle attachment on low speed for 3 to 5 minutes, until the mixture resembles coarse meal. Or, cut the butter into

the flours with a pastry blender. Stir the sugar, salt, and currants into the flour mixture. Set aside.

3 Combine the cream, ale, eggs, cloves, mace, and nutmeg in a small saucepan and heat just until the mixture feels warm to the touch. Remove from the heat and stir in the softened yeast and the rose water.

4 *If using a stand mixer,* gradually add the cream mixture to the flour, then beat on low speed for about 5 minutes. Scrape the bowl and beater and beat on medium speed for 1 minute. The dough will be wet and sticky.

   If making the dough by hand, stir the liquids into the dry ingredients with a wooden spoon. Turn the dough out onto a lightly floured surface, dust the dough with flour, and knead the dough for several minutes, until it feels only slightly elastic. Knead in a small amount of additional flour if needed.

5 Butter or grease a 13-x-9-inch baking pan and place the dough in it. Using lightly buttered fingers, pat the dough evenly into the pan. Cover tightly with plastic wrap and let rise in a warm place until the dough almost reaches the top of the pan, about 4 hours.

6 About 30 minutes before the cake is ready to bake, adjust an oven rack to the lower third position and preheat the oven to 350°F.

7 Remove the plastic from the dough and bake for 20 minutes. Cover the dough loosely with a sheet of aluminum foil to keep the currants from burning, and bake for another 20 minutes. Remove the foil and continue baking for another 10 to 20 minutes, until the cake is golden brown and springs back when gently pressed and a toothpick inserted into the center comes out clean. Cool in the pan on a wire rack for 20 minutes, then loosen the cake from the sides of the pan with a small sharp knife.

GREAT CAKE!

Great cakes, as this one was originally called, were common in Colonial America, and they were enormous. The yeast was originally supplied by barm, a kind of sourdough made from fermenting beer or ale, and the liquid came from posset, a combination of cream and ale heated until warm. These huge cakes were probably baked freeform on the hearths of wood-fired ovens.

Cover the cake with a wire rack and invert. Remove the pan and cover the cake with another rack. Invert again to allow the cake to cool right side up.

8 When it is completely cool, cut the cake into thin slices with a gentle sawing motion, using a sharp serrated knife: the best way to do this is to cut the cake first into 2- to 3-inch-wide strips, then cut the strips crosswise into slices about $1/2$ inch thick. Wrap leftovers airtight and store at room temperature for 3 to 4 days. Or divide the cake into 3 or 4 portions, wrap airtight, and freeze for up to 2 weeks.

ELECTION CAKE

Food historian William Woys Weaver says election cakes could be just about anything served at musters, election-day picnics, and other festivities, but originally, they were enriched breads. The name goes back to the 1600s. This version is a big, gorgeous yeast bread, flavored with nutmeg, mace, brandy, and Madeira and containing a generous amount of dried fruits. I adapted it from an 1860s recipe in the magazine *Godey's Lady's Book*. It has an extremely light texture, very similar to a panettone, and is one of my favorite sweet yeast breads.

The dough is very soft and sticky and is best made with an electric mixer, but you can make it by hand. The key to success lies in using the minimum amount of flour. Raisins and citron were the two most commonly used dried fruits in election cakes, but I like to use equal amounts of a large variety of fruit, such as dried sour cherries, blueberries, citron, and dark and golden raisins. Feel free to use whatever you like, including dried cranberries, apricots, peaches, nectarines, or figs, cutting the larger fruits into ¹/₂-inch pieces. This cake keeps well for days at room temperature and is wonderful with steaming-hot coffee or tea.

SPONGE

- 3 cups unbleached all-purpose flour, plus more as needed
- 2 ¹/₄-ounce packages (1¹/₂ tablespoons) fast-rise active dry yeast
- 1¹/₄ cups warm milk (105°–115°F)
- ¹/₂ cup sugar
- 8 tablespoons (1 stick) unsalted butter, very soft

DOUGH

- 8 tablespoons (1 stick) unsalted butter, at room temperature
- 1 teaspoon salt
- 1 whole nutmeg, grated (2–2¹/₂ teaspoons)
- ³/₄ teaspoon ground mace
- ¹/₂ cup sugar
- 1 large egg
- 2 tablespoons sweet sherry or Madeira
- 2 tablespoons brandy
- ³/₄ cup unbleached all-purpose flour, plus more as needed
- 1 pound dried fruits (see above)

1 For the sponge, using a rubber spatula, combine the 3 cups flour, yeast, milk, sugar, and soft butter in a mixer bowl or another large bowl.

2 *If using a stand mixer,* attach the dough hook and beat on high speed just until the dough gathers into a ball, about 1 minute. Reduce the speed to medium-low and knead for 6 to 8 minutes, until smooth and elastic. Knead the mixture briefly in the bowl between your hands. It should feel soft, smooth, supple, and not sticky.

   If making the sponge by hand, knead it on a lightly floured surface for 8 to 10 minutes, until elastic and no longer sticky. Return the sponge to the bowl.

   Cover tightly with plastic wrap and let rise at room temperature until almost tripled in volume, about 2 hours.

3 For the dough, beat the room-temperature butter in a medium bowl with an electric mixer on medium speed until smooth. Add the salt, nutmeg, and mace, beating them in well. Gradually add the sugar and beat for 3 to 4 minutes more. Add the egg and beat for 1 minute. Add the sherry or Madeira and brandy and beat on low speed until incorporated, then beat on medium-high speed until the mixture is smooth and fluffy, 1 to 2 minutes.

4 Deflate the dough in the bowl, stirring it down with a wooden spoon. Add the butter mixture.

5 *If using a stand mixer,* attach the dough hook and knead on low speed for 4 to 5 minutes, until the ingredients are completely incorporated and the dough is smooth. On low speed, gradually add the flour, then knead on medium speed for 4 minutes. The dough will be very soft, smooth, and sticky; do not add any additional flour.

   If making the dough by hand, gradually beat in the butter mixture with a wooden spoon until incorporated. Stir in the 3/4 cup flour. Knead on a lightly floured work surface until soft, smooth, and slightly sticky, adding a small amount of flour if necessary. Return the dough to the bowl.

   Cover tightly with plastic wrap and let rise at room temperature until doubled in size, about 2 hours.

6 Knead the dried fruits into the dough with the dough hook on low speed or stir them in with a wooden spoon. Turn the dough out onto a lightly floured surface and knead briefly to make sure the fruits are evenly dis-

tributed. The dough should be moist and only slightly sticky. Knead in a small amount of flour only if the dough seems excessively sticky.

7 Butter a 10-x-4-inch tube pan with a removable bottom. Shape the dough into a ball. Use your fingers to make a hole in the center and expand the hole so that the dough will fit around the tube. Place the dough in the pan, cover the pan with plastic wrap, and set aside until almost doubled in volume, about 2 hours (the dough will fill the pan by about two-thirds).

8 About 30 minutes before you're ready to bake, adjust an oven rack to the lower third position and preheat the oven to 350°F.

9 Remove the plastic wrap and bake for about 1 hour and 20 minutes, until the cake is a deep golden brown and springs back when gently pressed and a toothpick inserted into the thickest part comes out clean. Cool the cake in the pan for 30 minutes.

10 Run a knife around the sides of the cake to release it from the pan, and lift the cake out of the pan by its tube. Run a thin-bladed knife between the cake and the bottom of the pan to release it, and invert onto a cooling rack. Turn the cake right side up, and let stand until completely cool. Stored at room temperature in an airtight plastic bag, the cake will keep for several days. The cake can also be frozen for up to 1 month. To serve, cut it into slices with a sharp serrated knife.

PENNSYLVANIA DUTCH TEA ROLLS

Makes 20 rolls

These soft, light-as-air sweet rolls are good for serving with tea or coffee. Originally, they were known as rusks. The recipe has been made in this country for well over two hundred years. Amelia Simmons, author of *American Cookery,* the first American cookbook (1796), has six recipes for rusks, which were justifiably popular. Her yeast sponge was started the night before, and the baking schedule arranged so that the rolls would be ready by about 3 P.M. the following day. I adapted this recipe from one in *The Boston Cooking School Cook Book* by Mrs. D. A. Lincoln.

If you like your rolls to have browned bottoms, as I do, bake them on a preheated baking stone. Serve them warm or at room temperature, plain or with butter and jam.

½ 0.6-ounce cake compressed yeast, crumbled, or 1 teaspoon active dry yeast

¼ cup warm water (105°–115°)

1 cup milk, warmed (105°–115°F)

3½ cups unbleached all-purpose flour, plus more as needed

4 tablespoons (½ stick) unsalted butter, at room temperature

½ cup sugar

1 teaspoon salt

1 large egg

Milk for brushing

Poppy seeds, sesame seeds, or additional sugar for sprinkling

1 Add the yeast to the warm water in the bowl of an electric mixer or another large bowl; stir and set aside until softened, about 5 minutes. Add the milk and 1¾ cups of the flour, beating well with a wooden spoon. Cover tightly with plastic wrap and let stand at room temperature for at least 6 hours, or, preferably, overnight. The sponge will have risen and be full of bubbles.

2 Add the remaining 1¾ cups flour, the butter, sugar, salt, and egg. Beat well with a wooden spoon (the dough will be thick and sticky), or use the dough hook to knead on low speed for a few minutes. Scrape the dough onto a lightly floured surface and toss it about to coat it lightly with flour. Knead in a small amount of flour if the dough is too sticky. Wash and dry the bowl and brush it lightly with oil. Return the dough to the bowl, brush

the top with oil, and cover tightly with plastic wrap. Let the dough rise until doubled, either at a cool room temperature, which may take 3 to 4 hours, or in a warm place (85° to 90°F), 1½ to 2 hours.

3 Butter or grease a 13-x-9-inch baking pan. Scrape the dough out onto a lightly floured surface, dust it with flour, and gently pat it into a rectangle measuring about 8 x 10 inches. Don't knead the dough or be rough with it: for a light-textured result, the less handling the better. Using a large sharp knife, cut the dough lengthwise into four 2-inch strips, then cut each strip into five 2-inch squares, making 20 pieces in all. This dough will be very soft. Gently shape each piece into a ball and place them close together in the prepared pan, 5 balls the long way and 4 the short way. If the dough tends to stick to your hands, lightly flour it as you work. Cover the pan tightly with plastic wrap (to prevent the rolls from sticking to the plastic wrap, coat their tops lightly with cooking spray) and set aside in a warm place until the rolls have doubled in size and almost reach the top of the pan, about 1 hour.

4 Meanwhile, adjust an oven rack to the lower third position. If you are using a baking stone, set it on the rack. Preheat the oven to 375°F. The baking stone will need 45 minutes to get hot.

IT'S *YOUR* FAULT

A recipe for Pennsylvania Rusk from *Godey's Lady's Book Receipts and Household Hints* of 1870 comes with a rather severe admonishment: *"If you do not have the very nicest of rusks after trying this receipt, you must try it over again, as it will certainly be your own fault."*

5 Just before baking, uncover the rolls and brush them lightly with milk. Sprinkle with poppy seeds, sesame seeds, or sugar. Bake for about 25 minutes, until the rolls are well browned and sound hollow when you remove them from the pans and rap their bottoms. Cool the rolls in the pan for 5 minutes, then unmold them onto a wire rack to cool right side up. Serve warm or at room temperature.

Variations

Substitute 2 tablespoons rose water for 2 tablespoons of the milk. For a mildly spicy flavor, add ½ teaspoon freshly grated nutmeg, ground mace, or ground cinnamon.

SPANISH BUNS

*Makes one
13-x-9-inch
cake, about
15 servings*

Food historian William Woys Weaver says this heavenly, delicate-textured sweet bread is called Spanish because it was derived from a cake made in Latin America. The recipe is attributed to the Pennsylvania Dutch. According to Eliza Leslie, the cake was eaten with afternoon tea. I've pretty much followed her original recipe, updating it as necessary.

2½ cups unbleached all-purpose
      flour

1 ¼-ounce package (2¼
      teaspoons) fast-rise active
      dry yeast

1 teaspoon salt

1 cup milk, warmed (105°–115°F)

1 cup (2 sticks) unsalted butter,
      cut into tablespoon-sized
      pieces, at room temperature

¾ cup sugar

4 large eggs

1 whole nutmeg, grated
      (2–2½ teaspoons)

2 tablespoons rose water or
      1 tablespoon pure vanilla
      extract

   Confectioners' sugar for dusting
   (optional)

1 Stir together 1½ cups of the flour, the yeast, and salt in a large bowl. Add the warm milk and stir with a rubber spatula to moisten. With an electric mixer on medium-low speed, beat in the butter pieces one at a time, beating until incorporated after each addition. Beat for 2 minutes on medium speed. Gradually beat in the sugar. Add the eggs one at a time, beating for about 45 seconds after each. The batter will be smooth and creamy, with a texture like softly whipped cream. Beat in the nutmeg and rose water or vanilla on low speed. Gradually beat in the remaining 1 cup flour, then beat on medium speed for 1 to 2 minutes until the batter is thick.

2 Generously butter a 13-x-9-inch baking pan. Scrape the batter into the pan and spread it evenly. The pan will be about half-full. Cover tightly with lightly oiled plastic wrap and set the pan in a warm place (80° to 85°F) until the batter has doubled in volume and almost reaches the rim of the pan, about 1 hour.

3 Meanwhile, adjust an oven rack to the lower third position and preheat the oven to 350°F.

4 Remove the plastic wrap from the pan and bake for 30 to 35 minutes, until the cake is a rich brown and springs back when gently pressed and a toothpick inserted into the center comes out clean. Set the pan on a wire rack to cool completely.

5 To serve, cut into squares with a sharp serrated knife and dust with confectioners' sugar, if desired. This keeps well, covered, for 2 to 3 days at room temperature. Well wrapped, it may be frozen for up to 1 month.

RUSSIAN CAKE BREAD

*Makes
2 loaves,
20 to 24
servings*

I first fell in love with this sweet, buttery, cakelike bread at the tenth Pillsbury Bake-Off, where it won $5,000 for Lillian Jehlik. Mrs. Jehlik adapted a recipe her mother had brought to this country from Russia. The bread is extremely easy to make. The three rises before baking give it an exceptionally fine crumb and flavor. The bread is especially good warm. Serve plain or spread with butter and/or jam.

3 cups unbleached all-purpose flour, plus more if needed	1 teaspoon salt
1 1/4-ounce package (2 1/4 teaspoons) fast-rise active dry yeast	8 tablespoons (1 stick) unsalted butter
1/2 cup sugar	1 1/4 cups milk
	2 large eggs, lightly beaten
	2 teaspoons pure vanilla extract

1 Stir together 1 cup of the flour, the yeast, sugar, and salt in a large bowl.

2 Melt the butter in a small saucepan over low heat. Stir in the milk and heat the mixture until very warm (110° to 115°F). Reserve 1 tablespoon of the beaten eggs for glaze. Add the remaining eggs, the warm milk mixture, and the vanilla to the dry ingredients and stir with a wooden spoon until they are well moistened, then beat until the batter is smooth. Gradually add the remaining 2 cups flour, beating until smooth after each addition. The batter will be very thick and elastic. Add a bit more flour if necessary to bring the dough to the right consistency. Scrape the bowl, and cover it tightly with plastic wrap. Let the dough rise in a warm place (85° to 90°F) until doubled in volume, 1 to 1 1/2 hours.

3 Stir the dough down with a wooden spoon, cover it, and let it rise again in a warm place until doubled, 45 minutes to 1 hour.

4 Butter two 8 1/2-x-4 1/2-x-2 3/4-inch loaf pans. Divide the batter evenly between the pans. Cover loosely with a kitchen towel, and let rise in a warm place until doubled and very light.

5 Meanwhile, adjust an oven rack to the lower third position and preheat the oven to 350°F.

6 Gently brush the loaves with the reserved egg: try not to let any egg run down between the dough and the sides of the pans, or the dough may stick and rise unevenly. Bake 30 to 35 minutes, until the tops of the loaves are a deep golden brown and spring back when gently pressed. Cool in the pans on a wire rack for 10 to 15 minutes. Run a knife around each loaf to release it, and carefully remove from the pans. Set upright on wire racks to cool completely. To serve, cut the bread with a sharp serrated knife. Well wrapped, the loaves freeze well for up to 1 month.

BRIOCHE MORAVIAN SUGAR CAKE

*Makes one
9-inch
square cake,
16 servings*

Moravian Sugar Cake is at least 150 years old. Usually baked on a Saturday so that it could be served for evening supper, it was made slightly differently by each Moravian community, according to food historian William Woys Weaver. In the recipe here, I have taken the basic idea of the cake—a sweet yeast dough dimpled with lumps of cinnamon, butter, and brown sugar—and added a new twist by using a buttery brioche dough, which gives it an exceptionally light and airy texture. This cake is so tender and delicious you may not be able to stop eating it!

1 pound chilled Brioche Dough (page 128)

4 tablespoons ($\frac{1}{2}$ stick) unsalted butter, at room temperature

$\frac{1}{3}$ cup firmly packed light brown sugar

$1\frac{1}{2}$ teaspoons ground cinnamon

1 Butter a 9-inch square baking pan. Roll out the dough on a lightly floured surface to fit into the bottom of the pan. Pat the dough in place. Cover the pan tightly with plastic wrap, pulling it taut so that it will not touch the dough as it rises. Let rise in a warm place (80° to 85°F) until tripled in volume, about 3 hours; the dough will reach halfway up the sides of the pan and be puffy and light.

2 Meanwhile, adjust an oven rack to the center position and preheat the oven to 350°F.

3 Mash the butter with a fork in a small bowl. Add the brown sugar and cinnamon and stir with the fork until smooth. Place 16 small spoonfuls of the sugar mixture on top of the risen dough, spacing them evenly and making 4 rows of 4 sugar dabs each. Gently push on each dab with a fingertip so it sinks partway into the dough. If the dough forms bubbles as you do this, simply break them by pinching them.

4 Bake for about 20 minutes, until the cake is well browned and the sugar pools are slightly bubbly. Set the cake in its pan on a wire rack to cool. Serve warm (which is best!) or at room temperature, cut into squares with a serrated knife.

BRIOCHE DOUGH

Makes about 2 1/2 pounds dough

If the American cooking teacher Mrs. Rorer was right, this classic French dough was being made by American home cooks in the 1880s. The hallmarks of brioche are a light texture with a fine crumb and a buttery, eggy flavor. The dough has many uses besides being shaped into the classic rolls with topknots.

Brioche dough must be made at least a day ahead, and it will keep well in the refrigerator for 3 to 4 days. For maximum flavor and texture, the dough is made in stages: a sponge and a final dough. Each requires a few hours of rising, but with no attention on your part. Plan your time accordingly. You're about to embark on a baking adventure. (For best results, do not double the recipe.)

SPONGE

- 1 0.6-ounce cake compressed fresh yeast or one $1/4$-ounce package (2$1/4$ teaspoons) fast-rise active dry yeast
- $1/3$ cup milk, warmed (105°–115°F)
- 1 tablespoon sugar
- 2$3/4$ cups bread flour or unbleached all-purpose flour
- 2 large eggs, at room temperature

DOUGH

- $1/2$ cup sugar
- 1 teaspoon salt
- $1/4$ teaspoon ground mace
- 2 large eggs, at room temperature
- 1 cup (2 sticks) unsalted butter, cut into 10 pieces, very soft
- $1/2$ cup bread flour or unbleached all-purpose flour, plus more as needed

1 For the sponge, if using compressed yeast, crumble it into a mixer bowl or another large bowl and add the warm milk and sugar. Let stand for 5 minutes, then stir in $3/4$ cup of the bread flour or all-purpose flour with a wooden spoon to make a firm, sticky lump of dough. If using dry yeast, combine it with the sugar and $3/4$ cup flour in the bowl. Pour in the warm milk and stir well with a wooden spoon.

2 *If using a stand mixer,* add the eggs to the bowl and beat with the paddle attachment on medium speed until the mixture is smooth.

If making by hand, use a sturdy wire whisk and beat until the mixture is smooth.

Scrape the bowl and beater (if using), and sprinkle the remaining 2 cups flour over the batter; *do not mix it in.* Cover the bowl tightly with plastic wrap and set aside at room temperature for about 3 hours, until the yeast mixture has bubbled up and almost completely engulfed the flour.

3 For the dough, add the sugar, salt, mace, and eggs to the sponge.

4 *If using a stand mixer,* beat with the paddle attachment on low speed for about 1 minute, just to combine all the ingredients. Increase the speed to medium and beat for $1\frac{1}{2}$ minutes.

   If making the dough by hand, beat well with a wooden spoon until smooth.

5 Add the butter one piece at a time, beating on low speed or with the wooden spoon until each piece is incorporated (15 to 20 seconds if using a mixer). Scrape the bowl and beater, then beat for 2 minutes more on medium speed or for 5 minutes by hand.

6 *If using a mixer,* attach the dough hook. Add the $\frac{1}{2}$ cup flour and knead it in thoroughly on low speed, then knead on medium speed for 2 to 3 minutes. The soft, sticky dough will ball up on the hook and slap around the sides of the bowl. Scrape the dough off the hook and scrape down the sides of the bowl. Sprinkle the top of the dough with 2 to 3 tablespoons flour to prevent a crust from forming, cover the bowl tightly with plastic wrap.

   To finish the dough by hand, stir in the $\frac{1}{2}$ cup flour, then beat with a wooden spoon for at least 5 minutes. Scrape the bowl and sprinkle the dough with 2 to 3 tablespoons flour. Cover tightly with plastic wrap.

   Let rise at room temperature until tripled in volume, 5 to 6 hours.

7 Refrigerate the risen dough—don't deflate—for 1 hour.

8 Carefully remove the dough from the bowl with a large plastic scraper and place it on a lightly floured work surface. Gently pat it into an 8-x-12-inch rectangle. Fold the dough in thirds, like a business letter, enclose it tightly in plastic wrap, and refrigerate it for at least 8 hours, or overnight. The dough is now ready to use in recipes. (Do not freeze: this dough does not take well to very cold temperatures.)

BRIOCHE CINNAMON-RAISIN-PECAN ROLLS

*Makes
15 rolls*

You can make wonderful cinnamon rolls with almost any yeast dough, but brioche takes them to a new dimension. These rolls are especially tender and light and have a scrumptious filling. I like to brush the hot rolls with a confectioners' sugar glaze, but if you'd like a nonsweet shiny glaze, use the egg yolk and milk.

1 1/2 pounds chilled Brioche Dough
(page 128)

FILLING

1/2 cup pecan halves or large pieces

3/4 cup dark raisins

2/3 cup firmly packed light brown
sugar

2 teaspoons ground cinnamon

5 tablespoons unsalted butter, at
room temperature

1 teaspoon pure vanilla extract

EGG GLAZE

1 large egg yolk

2 teaspoons milk

OR

CONFECTIONERS' SUGAR GLAZE

1 1/2 cups confectioners' sugar

3 tablespoons milk

1 teaspoon pure vanilla extract

1 Roll the dough on a lightly floured surface into a 9-x-15-inch rectangle. Turn the dough if necessary, so that a long side faces you. Cover loosely with a kitchen towel.

2 For the filling, put the pecans in a food processor and pulse 5 or 6 times, until coarsely chopped. Remove the nuts and set aside.

3 Add the raisins, brown sugar, and cinnamon to the work bowl and process for about 10 seconds, to coarsely chop the raisins. Add the butter and vanilla and process for 10 seconds. Add the pecans and pulse 5 times.

4 Distribute the filling evenly over the dough in small gobs, then use a narrow metal spatula to spread the filling so that it covers all but 1/2 inch along the long side farthest from you. Roll the dough up tightly, starting with the long side nearest you, and pinch the seam securely to seal it. Turn the roll

seam side down and use a very sharp knife to cut the roll into 1-inch-thick slices.

5 Butter a 15¹⁄₂-x-10¹⁄₂-inch jelly roll pan. Arrange the slices in the pan in rows cut sides up, with 5 the long way and 3 the short way, leaving about 1 inch between the rolls. Cover loosely with a kitchen towel and let rise in a warm place (80° to 85°F) until tripled in volume. The rolls will be light in texture and touching each other.

6 Meanwhile, adjust an oven rack to the center position and preheat the oven to 350°F.

7 *If using the egg yolk glaze,* beat the egg yolk and milk with a fork in a small bowl to combine well. Brush the mixture evenly over the rolls. Bake the rolls for about 20 minutes, until they are a rich golden brown and spring back when gently pressed and a toothpick inserted into the center of a roll comes out clean.

8 *If using the confectioners' sugar glaze,* prepare it a few minutes before the rolls are done. Whisk together the confectioners' sugar, milk, and vanilla in a small bowl until smooth. As soon as the rolls come out of the oven, spoon the glaze evenly over them, then use a pastry brush to spread it.

9 Set the rolls in their pan on a wire rack to cool. Serve warm or at room temperature. Wrapped in aluminum foil, the rolls freeze well for up to 1 month. To reheat them, place the frozen rolls—in their aluminum foil wrapping—on a baking sheet and warm in a preheated 350°F oven, about 15 minutes.

CINNAMON RAISIN-NUT CRISPS

Makes 24 large pastries

These crisp, flaky, chewy pastries are irresistible. The dough is made with cream instead of butter. Even though there's lots of folding and rolling, the pastries are surprisingly quick and simple to make.

DOUGH

- 1 0.6-ounce cake compressed fresh yeast or one 1/4-ounce package (2 1/4 teaspoons) active dry yeast
- 1/2 cup lukewarm water
- 2 large eggs
- 1 cup heavy cream, heated until lukewarm
- 3 tablespoons sugar
- 1 1/2 teaspoons salt
- 1 teaspoon pure vanilla extract
- 4 cups unbleached all-purpose flour, plus more for kneading

FILLING

- 1 cup firmly packed light brown sugar
- 2 teaspoons ground cinnamon
- 3/4 cup slivered almonds
- 1/2 cup dark raisins
- 4 tablespoons (1/2 stick) unsalted butter, melted

About 1 cup all-purpose flour for shaping

About 1 cup sugar for shaping

1 For the dough, crumble or sprinkle the yeast into the lukewarm water in a small bowl and set aside for 5 minutes to soften.

2 Beat the eggs well with a fork in a mixer bowl or another large bowl. Stir in the cream, sugar, salt, vanilla, and yeast mixture. Stir in 3 cups of the flour, and sprinkle the remaining 1 cup flour on top.

3 *If using a stand mixer,* knead with the dough hook on low speed to incorporate the flour, then knead on medium speed for 2 to 3 minutes, until the dough is smooth, supple, and elastic. It will feel soft and only slightly sticky.

If making the dough by hand, beat with a wooden spoon to make a soft, smooth dough. Scrape the dough out onto a lightly floured surface, knead it briefly between your hands, and shape it into a ball.

4 Lightly oil a 6-quart bowl, or coat with cooking spray. Add the dough and turn to coat all sides. Cover the bowl tightly with plastic wrap and let rise at room temperature until doubled in volume (or a bit more), about 1^1/$_2$ hours.

5 For the filling, mix the brown sugar and cinnamon together in a medium bowl. Put the almonds and raisins in a food processor and pulse 8 to 10 times to chop them. Turn the dough out onto a lightly floured surface and roll it to a 24-x-20-inch rectangle. Brush with 2 tablespoons of the butter and sprinkle with half the cinnamon sugar. Fold in the long sides of the dough to meet in the center, then fold over again to make a 4-layered rectangle. Turn the dough 90 degrees and roll out to a 24-x-12-inch rectangle. Flour the dough lightly if it is sticky.

6 Add the almonds and raisins to the remaining cinnamon sugar and mix well. Brush the remaining 2 tablespoons melted butter over the dough and sprinkle with the nut mixture. Pat gently in place. Roll the dough up tightly like a jelly roll, starting from a long side. Pinch firmly to seal. Turn the dough seam side down. Use a ruler to mark the roll into twenty-four 1-inch pieces, and cut them with a sharp knife.

7 Adjust two oven racks to divide the oven into thirds and preheat the oven to 375°F. Lightly butter two large baking sheets or jelly roll pans.

8 To shape the pastries, place a mound each of flour and sugar on your work surface. Dip one piece of pastry into the flour to coat generously, then place it flour side up on the sugar. Roll out to a 4-inch-long oval no thicker than ^{1}/$_4$ inch. If the dough sticks, dust it with more flour. Place the pastry sugar side up on a prepared baking sheet. Repeat with 11 more pieces of dough, placing 6 pastries on each baking sheet, about 1 inch apart. Cover loosely with kitchen towels and let stand for about 15 minutes. Meanwhile, roll out the remaining pieces of dough and set them sugared side up on sheets of waxed paper; cover with kitchen towels until the baking sheets are available.

9 Place the baking sheets in the oven and bake for 20 to 25 minutes, rotating the sheets from top to bottom and front to back once during baking to ensure even browning, until the pastries are an even golden brown; do not overbake. With a wide metal spatula, transfer the pastries to wire racks to cool completely. Wash and dry the baking sheets if necessary, butter them, and bake the remaining pastries. The pastries are best when freshly baked, but they can be frozen for up to 1 month.

KEYS TO DEEP-FRYING

Much of the bad rap deep-frying has gotten is due to improper technique, resulting in soggy, greasy fried foods. If you follow the points outlined here, you'll have excellent results every time.

1. Always start with fresh oil. Choose an oil with a high smoking point. Peanut oil is my first choice, although corn oil also works well.

2. Choose a heavy deep pot. A 5- to 7-quart cast-iron or enameled cast-iron Dutch oven about 6 inches tall is ideal. Cast iron is a good conductor of heat and it is able to keep the oil at a relatively constant temperature.

3. Use plenty of oil. One cause of greasy fried foods is cooking too much food in too little oil. Have about 3 inches of oil in your fryer.

4. Attach a digital probe thermometer or deep-fat thermometer to the side of the pot to monitor the temperature. Heat the oil over medium-high heat. In a 6-quart cast-iron pot, it will take 30 to 40 minutes to reach 365°F, the ideal temperature for most deep-frying.

5. Cook only a few pieces of food at a time, so that the oil temperature never falls below 360°F. The food should swim in the oil. Move it around in the oil to ensure thorough cooking, and turn it frequently for even browning. Wooden chopsticks, tongs, or two forks are handy tools for turning doughnuts and fritters.

6. Remove the food from the oil with a slotted spatula or spoon, letting the excess oil drain back into the pot. Place the food on a wire rack set over a baking dish to allow any remaining oil to drain off; if you set the food on paper towels or crumpled brown paper, it's more likely that the oil would be absorbed by the food than the paper. (After draining on the rack for a few minutes, you can set the food on paper towels to blot any oil still adhering to it.)

7. Make sure to return the oil temperature to 365°F each time before adding more food. When finished cooking, let the oil cool, then strain it through a coffee filter. Store the oil in the refrigerator. You'll be able to use it once or twice more. Every time you reheat cooking oil, the smoking point goes down, which means there's a greater likelihood of the oil burning and ruining whatever you're cooking.

ELIZA LESLIE'S DOUGHNUTS

Makes 24 to 30 doughnuts

This is my updating of Miss Leslie's recipe from the 1851 edition of her classic work, *Directions for Cookery*. The dough is made in two stages, starting with a sponge. Cinnamon, nutmeg, and rose water, the holy trinity of flavorings from the nineteenth century, add great taste and aroma. This dough can be used for many different kinds of doughnuts. You could do as Miss Leslie did, and cut the dough into diamonds or squares, or just about any shape you like, and simply sprinkle them with sugar or coat them with the glaze.

SPONGE

2¹/₂ cups unbleached all-purpose flour

1 ¹/₄-ounce package (2¹/₄ teaspoons) fast-rise active dry yeast

1¹/₂ cups milk, warmed (105°–115°F)

DOUGH

5¹/₂ cups unbleached all-purpose flour, plus more as needed

³/₄ cup (1¹/₂ sticks) cold unsalted butter, cut into tablespoon-sized pieces

1 cup sugar

1 teaspoon salt

1 teaspoon ground cinnamon

1 whole nutmeg, grated (2–2¹/₂ teaspoons)

1 cup milk, warmed (105°–115°F)

3 large eggs

1 tablespoon rose water

3 quarts vegetable oil for deep-frying

Sugar for coating

OR

MAPLE SUGAR GLAZE

2 cups confectioners' sugar

¹/₄ cup pure maple syrup

2–3 tablespoons milk

1 For the sponge, stir the flour and yeast together in a medium bowl. Add the warm milk, and beat with a rubber spatula until the batter is smooth. Cover tightly with plastic wrap, and set aside at room temperature until doubled in volume and very bubbly, about 1 hour.

2 For the dough, put 3 cups of the flour into a mixer bowl or another large bowl.

3 *If using a stand mixer,* cut the butter into the flour using the paddle attachment on low speed until it is in small flakes, about 3 minutes. Add the sugar, salt, cinnamon, and nutmeg and beat for about 1 minute more. Add the warm milk, eggs, and rose water and beat until thoroughly combined, about 1 minute, then beat on medium speed for 3 minutes.

If making the dough by hand, cut the butter into 3 cups of the flour with a pastry blender or two knives until the mixture is like coarse meal. Stir in the sugar, salt, cinnamon, and nutmeg with a wooden spoon. Add the milk, eggs, and rose water and beat for 3 to 5 minutes with a wooden spoon to make a smooth, thick batter.

4 Add the sponge and stir it in with a rubber spatula.

5 *If using a stand mixer,* add 1 1/2 cups more flour and mix it in with the paddle attachment on low speed. Scrape the bowl and attach the dough hook. Add 1/2 cup more flour and knead it in on low speed. Add the last 1/2 cup of flour and knead it in, then increase the speed to medium and knead for 2 to 3 minutes more; the dough should be soft, elastic, and slightly sticky. Do not add any more flour.

If making the dough by hand, gradually stir in 2 cups of the flour to make a thick dough. Sprinkle the remaining 1/2 cup flour on your work surface, scrape the dough onto it, and knead for about 8 minutes, until elastic and slightly sticky. Knead in a small amount of additional flour if necessary.

6 Lightly oil a 6-quart bowl, or coat with cooking spray. Scrape the dough into the bowl and turn to coat all surfaces. Lift up the dough and knead it briefly between your hands. Return it to the bowl, cover tightly with plastic wrap, and set aside to rise at room temperature until doubled in volume, about 1 1/2 hours.

7 Line two large baking sheets with cooking parchment or silicone liners. Turn the dough out onto a lightly floured surface and pat or roll it to a thickness of about 1/2 inch. Dip a 3-inch doughnut cutter into flour and cut out doughnuts. Place the doughnuts about 1 1/2 inches apart on the prepared sheets, and put the doughnut holes between them. Knead the dough scraps together briefly, and let them rest, covered, about 15 minutes. Roll and cut more doughnuts, and place on the baking sheets. Cover with towels, and let rise in a warm place (about 80°F) until doubled in size, about 1 hour.

8 Meanwhile, pour the oil into a 5- to 7-quart wide deep pot, such as a cast-iron Dutch oven. Attach a digital probe thermometer or deep-fry thermometer to the side and heat the oil to 365°F over medium-high heat, about 30 minutes. Place a large cooling rack over a large rimmed baking sheet and set aside.

9 When the oil is ready, add 4 doughnuts and cook for about 3 minutes, turning them halfway through the cooking time with forks or wooden chopsticks, until puffed, cooked through, and deep brown. Be sure the temperature of the oil does not drop below 360°F. Remove the doughnuts from the fat with a slotted spatula, allowing the excess oil to drain back into the pot, and place on the rack to drain further. Cook the remaining doughnuts, returning the temperature of the oil to 365°F each time. Fry the doughnut holes last.

10 *If coating the doughnuts with sugar,* put about 1 cup sugar in a large paper bag and add a few warm doughnuts. Shake gently to coat and transfer to a plate. These are best while warm, but they're also great at room temperature.

If using the maple glaze, whisk the confectioners' sugar, maple syrup, and 2 tablespoons of the milk together in a medium bowl to make a thick, creamy, smooth glaze the consistency of sour cream. If the glaze is too thick, whisk in some or all of the remaining 1 tablespoon milk a little at a time, until it is the right consistency. Brush the warm or cool doughnuts with the glaze and serve after it has set.

OUT OF SIGHT, OUT OF MIND

Doughnuts *should not be eaten before November or after April; indeed, they are not very healthful to eat at any time. Keep covered in a stone pot in the cellar.*

—Maria Parloa, *Miss Parloa's Kitchen Companion* (1887)

RAISED POTATO DOUGHNUTS

*Makes
20 to 32
doughnuts*

For many years when our kids were growing up, I made doughnuts on New Year's Eve. Rather than going out and partying, we stayed at home and greeted the New Year by feasting on these yeast-raised indulgences. I'm particularly fond of this yeast dough made with mashed potatoes, which add moistness, flavor, and chewiness.

There's no getting around the fact that homemade raised doughnuts are a major project, but you will feel a real sense of accomplishment as you watch them puff to amazing heights and turn golden brown as they bob about in the oil. Besides, homemade doughnuts taste so much better than any you can buy. I love every step of the process: making the dough, rolling and cutting it, watching the doughnuts rise to just the right size, sliding them gently into the hot oil where I can see the miracle of yeast's leavening action right before my eyes, and glazing the finished doughnuts. But the greatest joy is biting into a fresh homemade doughnut.

For really large doughnuts, I use a 3½-inch diameter cutter with a ¾-inch hole. For a more modest size, I use a 3-inch tin cutter with a 1-inch hole. Use whatever type you have.

Plan to make the dough 1 day ahead, since it needs to be refrigerated overnight after its first rising.

DOUGHNUTS

- 1 large Idaho potato or 2 medium Yukon Gold potatoes (12 ounces)
- ¾ cup milk
- ½ cup sugar
- 1 0.6-ounce cake compressed fresh yeast or one ¼-ounce package (2¼ teaspoons) active dry yeast
- 1 teaspoon salt
- 1 teaspoon freshly grated nutmeg
- 1½ teaspoons pure vanilla extract
- 8 tablespoons (1 stick) unsalted butter, very soft
- 3 large eggs
- 5½ cups unbleached all-purpose flour, plus more as needed
- 3 quarts vegetable oil for deep-frying

GLAZE

- 3 cups confectioners' sugar
- 1 teaspoon pure vanilla extract
- ¼ teaspoon pure almond extract
- About ½ cup milk

1 For the doughnuts, peel the potato(es) and cut into 2-inch chunks. Place in a medium saucepan and cover with 1 inch water. Bring to a boil, reduce the heat to low, and simmer until the potatoes are completely tender when pierced with the tip of a sharp knife, about 20 minutes. Drain well and mash. Measure 1 packed cup potatoes and set aside.

2 Combine the milk and 1 tablespoon of the sugar in a small saucepan and stir over medium heat only until lukewarm. Transfer to a large mixing bowl. Crumble in the fresh yeast or stir in the dry yeast. Let stand for 5 minutes to soften, then add the remaining sugar, the salt, nutmeg, vanilla, butter, eggs, and mashed potatoes. Add 3 cups of the flour and stir well with a wooden spoon to make a soft, sticky batter.

3 Gradually stir in 2 cups additional flour, to make a soft dough. Sprinkle your work surface with the remaining 1/2 cup flour and scrape the dough onto it. Knead until the dough is soft, smooth, elastic, and only very slightly sticky. Add more flour as necessary, but try to keep it at a minimum, since too much flour will make a heavy dough.

4 Lightly oil a 6-quart bowl, or coat with cooking spray. Shape the dough into a ball and place it in the bowl. Turn to coat all surfaces and cover tightly with plastic wrap. Let rise at room temperature until doubled in volume, about 1 1/2 hours.

5 Gently push your fist into the risen dough. Lift it up, reshape the mass into a ball, and return to the bowl. Re-cover with plastic wrap, and refrigerate overnight. The dough will rise again in the refrigerator.

6 Line two large baking sheets with parchment or with silicone liners. Turn the cold dough out onto a lightly floured surface and sprinkle a bit more flour over it. Roll out to a 15-inch circle about 1/3 inch thick. Lightly flour your doughnut cutter (or two circular cutters, one for the doughnut, one for the hole) and cut out the doughnuts. Cut the doughnuts as close to each other as possible. Place them and the doughnut holes about 2 inches apart on the prepared sheets.

7 Form the scraps into a ball of dough, cover, and let rest for 10 minutes. Roll and cut doughnuts as before and place them on the baking sheets. (Any spare bits of dough can be rolled into ropes and formed into figure eights or twists.)

8 If you want to fry the doughnuts soon, let them rise, covered loosely with a kitchen towel, in a warm place (about 80°F) until they are puffy and light. They'll be about 1¹/₂ inches tall (impressive!). If you want to cook them later, cover them loosely with plastic wrap and refrigerate them for up to 3 hours. About 2 hours before frying, remove the plastic wrap, cover them loosely with a kitchen towel, and place them in a warm place (80° to 85°F) to allow them to rise. Refrigerated doughnuts will rise a bit in the refrigerator, so adjust any additional rising time accordingly. If your doughnuts are ready to fry before the oil is hot enough, refrigerate them to prevent them from rising too much.

9 Pour the oil into a 5- to 7-quart wide deep pot, such as a cast-iron Dutch oven. Attach a digital probe thermometer or a deep-fry thermometer to the side and heat the oil over medium-high heat until the temperature reaches 365°F, about 30 minutes.

10 Meanwhile, line your work surface or a couple of baking sheets with brown paper. Place a large wire rack over a large baking sheet for glazing the hot doughnuts. For the glaze, whisk together the confectioners' sugar, vanilla and almond extracts, and about 6 tablespoons of the milk until smooth. Add enough more milk to make a thick but pourable glaze. Cover tightly with plastic wrap and set aside.

11 To fry the doughnuts, carefully slip 3 or 4 into the hot oil. Adjust the heat if necessary so that the temperature never falls below 360°F. Cook for 2 minutes on each side, turning them over carefully with tongs, forks, or chopsticks without piercing them. They will puff up beautifully and turn deep brown, with a pale line running around their equators. Carefully remove the doughnuts from the oil with a slotted spatula and set them on the paper to drain for about 30 seconds. Then place them on the wire rack and brush them generously with the glaze. Turn them over and brush the other sides with the glaze.

12 Continue cooking and glazing the doughnuts 3 or 4 at a time until they're all done. Cook the doughnut holes last, moving them about in the oil frequently. Leave the doughnuts on the rack until the glaze sets into a thin shiny shell, about 30 minutes. The doughnuts and holes are best when absolutely fresh, even a tad warm.

GERMAN PUFFS

*Makes
24 to 32
puffs*

I've never seen or eaten anything else like these huge, incredibly soft yellow puffs. They're rich with butter and egg yolks, yet lighter than air. I adapted the recipe from Jessup Whitehead's *The American Pastry Cook* (1894). You start with a basic bread dough. After it's risen once, you beat in butter, sugar, lots of egg yolks, and more flour. After a second rise, the dough is shaped into balls and, before frying, allowed to rise once more, until puffy and light. You can leave the fried balls of dough plain, or roll them in confectioners' or granulated sugar. They're best when fresh. Make them for a party, where they're sure to be *the* topic of conversation.

5 cups unbleached all-purpose flour, plus more as needed

1 teaspoon salt

1 ¼-ounce package (2¼ teaspoons) fast-rise active dry yeast

1¼ cups milk, warmed (105°–115°F)

1 tablespoon vegetable oil

¾ cup (1½ sticks) unsalted butter, very soft

⅓ cup sugar

10 large egg yolks

3 quarts vegetable oil for deep-frying

Sugar for coating (optional)

1 Stir together 2 cups of the flour, the salt, yeast, ¾ cup of the milk, and the oil in the bowl of a mixer or another large bowl.

2 *If using a stand mixer,* knead with the dough hook on low for 1 minute, then knead on medium speed for 3 to 4 minutes, until the dough is smooth, elastic, and not sticky.

   If making the dough by hand, beat with a wooden spoon to make a smooth, nonsticky dough. Remove the dough from the bowl and knead it briefly between your hands until it feels perfectly smooth and supple. If the dough seems sticky, knead in a small amount of additional flour. Wash and dry the bowl, oil it lightly, and replace the dough.

   Cover tightly with plastic wrap and let rise at room temperature until doubled in volume, about 1½ hours.

3 *If using a stand mixer,* beat in the butter about 2 tablespoons at a time on low speed with the paddle attachment, beating until each addition is thoroughly incorporated before adding the next. Add the sugar and beat on medium speed for 2 minutes. On low speed, slowly dribble in the remaining $^1/_2$ cup milk, beating until incorporated. Scrape the bowl and beater and beat for 1 minute. Beat in 2 of the egg yolks, followed by $^1/_2$ cup of the flour. Repeat with the remaining yolks in 4 additions and the flour in 3 additions, using 2 cups of the flour in all, ending with the yolks. Scrape the bowl and beater and beat for 2 to 3 minutes more. Attach the dough hook and gradually knead in the remaining 1 cup flour on low, then knead for 3 to 4 minutes more on medium speed. The dough should not be sticky. Knead in a small amount of additional flour if necessary. The dough should be perfectly smooth.

If making the dough by hand, gradually beat in the butter with a wooden spoon until smooth. Beat in the sugar, and gradually beat in the remaining $^1/_2$ cup milk. Beat in 2 egg yolks, then $^1/_2$ cup of the flour. Repeat until you have added all the yolks and 2 cups of flour to the dough, ending with the last of the yolks. Dust your work surface with some of the remaining 1 cup flour, scrape the dough onto it, and sprinkle the dough with the rest of the flour. Knead for 5 to 6 minutes to make a smooth, nonsticky dough. Knead in a small amount of additional flour if necessary. Return the dough to the bowl.

Cover tightly with plastic wrap and let rise at room temperature until doubled in volume, about 2 hours.

4 Line two large baking sheets with silicone liners. Remove the dough from the bowl and knead it briefly on a lightly floured surface. The dough will feel soft and smooth and won't be at all sticky. Pat the dough into an 8-x-12-inch rectangle and cut it into twenty-four 2-inch squares. Shape each into a ball and place on the baking sheets, spacing them about 1$^1/_2$ inches apart. Cover loosely with kitchen towels and set aside while you heat the oil.

5 Pour the oil into a 5- to 7-quart wide, deep pot, such as a cast-iron Dutch oven. Attach a digital probe thermometer or deep-fry thermometer to the side of the pan and heat the oil to 365°F (or a bit higher) over medium-high heat, about 30 minutes. Place a large cooling rack over a large rimmed baking sheet and set aside.

6 One at a time, pick up 6 puffs carefully and slip them into the oil. Cook for about 6 minutes, turning after 3 minutes with forks or wooden chopsticks, until the puffs are dark brown with pale equators. Be sure the temperature of the oil does not drop below 360°F during frying. Remove the puffs from the fat with a pair of metal tongs or a slotted spatula, allowing the excess oil to drain back into the pot, and place the puffs on the rack to drain further. Repeat with the remaining puffs, returning the temperature of the oil to 365°F each time.

7 If you want to coat the puffs with sugar, put about 1 cup sugar into a paper bag, add 6 warm puffs, and shake gently until the puffs are coated. Set the puffs on a plate. Repeat until all puffs are coated. Serve warm or at room temperature.

FRYING RULES FROM 1867

To fry requires care, *and nothing fried will taste greasy if it has been dropped in fat properly heated and in enough of it to immerse the object.*

When an object tastes greasy, it is not because it has been fried in grease, but because there was not enough of it, or because it was not properly heated; for, if heated enough it closes the pores of the object and carbonizes the exterior, so that it cannot absorb any.

To ascertain with accuracy when the fat, lard, or oil is hot enough to lay the things in the pan, dip a fork in cold water, the prongs only, so as to retain but one or two drops of water, which drops you let fall in the fat, and if it crackles, it is hot enough.

Another way is, when jets of smoke come out of the fat.

—Chef Pierre Blot, *Handbook of Practical Cookery* (1867)

DUTCH DOUGHNUTS (OLIE-KOECKEN)

Makes 24 to 30 doughnuts

If this isn't one of the best fried yeast things there is, you could've fooled me. This is my adaptation of a recipe for the Dutch doughnuts known as olie-koecken, from *Foods of the Hudson* by Peter G. Rose, a Dutch food historian who draws on the rich heritage of the region. Compared to regular doughnut doughs, olie-koecken dough is rich with butter, nuts, and dried fruits. Ms. Rose adds fresh apples to her dough, but I do not, because pieces of the wet fruit always poke through, causing the oil to spatter.

The outsides are fabulously crunchy, and the insides are tender, chewy, slightly spicy, and packed with fruit and nuts. No sugar is used in the dough, but I roll the olie-koecken in granulated sugar while they're still warm. If you want smaller olie-koecken, cut them in half after cooking and sugaring them.

8 tablespoons (1 stick) unsalted butter

1 1/2 cups dark raisins

1/2 cup dried cranberries, blueberries, sour cherries, and/or finely diced citron

3 1/2 cups unbleached all-purpose flour

3/4 teaspoon salt

2 teaspoons ground cinnamon

1/2 teaspoon ground cloves

1/2 teaspoon ground ginger

1 1/4-ounce package (2 1/4 teaspoons) fast-rise active dry yeast

2 cups milk, warmed (105°–115°F)

1 cup sliced almonds (blanched or unblanched)

3 quarts vegetable oil for deep-frying

Sugar for coating

1 Melt the butter and set it aside to cool slightly.

2 Put the raisins and other dried fruit in a bowl and add boiling water to cover. Let stand for 5 minutes. Drain well and pat dry on paper towels. Set aside.

3 With a wooden spoon, stir the flour, salt, cinnamon, cloves, ginger, and yeast together in a mixer bowl or another large bowl. Add the warm milk and stir to make a soft dough.

4 *If using a stand mixer,* slowly beat in the butter on low speed using the paddle attachment. When the butter is completely incorporated, continue beating on low for 3 minutes. The dough will be like a thick batter, smooth and elastic. Scrape the bowl and beater.

   If making the dough by hand, beat in the butter with a wooden spoon and continue to beat for about 5 minutes.

5 Add the dried fruit and almonds. Beat on low speed to mix in thoroughly, about 2 minutes, then scrape the bowl and beater. Or stir in the nuts with a wooden spoon. Cover the bowl tightly with plastic wrap and set aside at room temperature until doubled in size, about 2 hours.

6 Stir the dough down with a sturdy wooden spoon, re-cover the bowl, and set aside while the cooking oil heats.

7 Pour the oil into a 5- to 7-quart wide deep pot, such as a cast-iron Dutch oven. Attach a digital probe thermometer or a deep-fry thermometer to the side and heat the oil over medium-high heat until the temperature reaches 365°F, about 30 minutes. Line your work surface or a couple of baking sheets with brown paper.

8 Using two soup spoons, one for scooping a ball of dough out of the mixing bowl, the other for pushing it off into the oil, place 6 to 8 balls of dough into the hot oil (they'll be about golf-ball size or a bit smaller). Cook, turning every 1 to 2 minutes with forks or wooden chopsticks, for 6 to 8 minutes, until a deep brown. Monitor the temperature so that the oil stays between 360° and 365°F. To test for doneness, remove one ball from the oil, drain it on the paper, and cut it in half: if the dough is still raw in the center, cook the balls of dough 1 to 2 minutes longer. Remove the cooked olie-koecken with a slotted spoon and set them on the paper to drain briefly. Remove any pieces of dried fruit that have fallen off the dough into the oil with the slotted spoon, and cook the remaining dough.

9 While the olie-koecken are warm, put about 1 cup of sugar in a paper bag, drop a few of them in, and shake them around to coat. Remove the olie-koecken and set them on a plate. Repeat with the remaining olie-koecken, adding more sugar if necessary. These stay fresh for a day or two, but they are at their crunchiest best if eaten within 6 to 8 hours.

LITTLE PITTSBURGH DOUGHNUTS

Makes about 18 large doughnuts

These lip-smackin' brown sugar doughnuts are fantastically crisp on the outside and soft and tender inside. They were favorites of miners in Leadville, Colorado, during the bonanza days of silver mining. I've adapted this recipe from Jessup Whitehead's *The American Pastry Cook* (1894). The doughnuts cost ten cents apiece, a pretty stiff price in those days. One ad for them proclaimed: "O! those Little Pittsburgh doughnuts are so very fine, if you try them once you'll buy them every time, at the Union Bakery." But competitors began cheapening the ingredients and selling their doughnuts for five cents apiece—and eventually the Leadville mining boom went bust and Little Pittsburghs passed into memory.

5½ cups unbleached all-purpose flour, plus more as needed

2 teaspoons salt

1 ¼-ounce (2¼ teaspoons) package fast-rise active dry yeast

1½ cups milk, warmed (105°–115°F)

2 tablespoons vegetable oil

1 cup firmly packed light brown sugar

2 large eggs

6 tablespoons (¾ stick) unsalted butter, melted and cooled slightly

3 quarts vegetable oil for deep-frying

1 Stir together 3½ cups of the flour, the salt, yeast, milk, and oil in a mixer bowl or another large bowl.

2 *If using a stand mixer,* knead with the dough hook on low for 1 minute, then on medium speed for 3 to 4 minutes, until smooth and elastic.

If making the dough by hand, beat the ingredients together with a wooden spoon to make a firm dough. Remove the dough from the bowl and knead it briefly on an unfloured surface until smooth and supple. Wash and dry the mixing bowl and replace the dough.

Cover the bowl tightly with plastic wrap and let rise at room temperature until doubled in volume, about 1½ hours.

3 *If using a stand mixer,* add the brown sugar, eggs, and butter and beat with the paddle attachment on low speed until incorporated, then beat on medium speed for 2 to 3 minutes. Attach the dough hook, add the remaining 2 cups flour, and knead it in on low speed. Increase the speed to medium, and knead for 3 to 4 minutes more. The dough should be soft and smooth and only slightly sticky. Knead in a small amount of flour if necessary, but do not add too much—the dough should be soft, not firm. Transfer the dough to a lightly floured surface and knead a few times to make sure it is completely smooth.

If mixing by hand, add the brown sugar, eggs, and butter and stir with a wooden spoon until incorporated. Beat for 2 to 3 minutes, until smooth. Gradually stir in the remaining 2 cups flour. Turn the dough out onto a lightly floured surface and knead for 6 to 8 minutes, until smooth, elastic, and slightly sticky. Knead in a small amount of flour only if the dough seems too sticky. The dough should be supple, not firm.

4 Lightly oil a 6-quart bowl, or spray with cooking spray. Put the dough in the bowl, turning it to coat all surfaces. Cover tightly with plastic wrap and let rise at room temperature until doubled in volume, 1 1/2 to 2 hours.

5 Line two large baking sheets with silicone liners. Place the dough on a lightly floured work surface, and pat out to a thickness of about 1/3 inch. Dip a 3 1/2-inch doughnut cutter into flour and cut out the doughnuts. Place the doughnuts on the prepared sheets about 1 1/2 inches apart and put the holes in the spaces between. Form the scraps into a ball; cover, and let rest for 10 minutes. Roll and cut doughnuts as before and place them on the baking sheets. Cover loosely with kitchen towels, and let rise at room temperature until almost doubled in volume, about 45 minutes.

6 Meanwhile, pour the oil into a 5- to 7-quart wide deep pot, such as a cast-iron Dutch oven. Attach a digital probe thermometer or deep-fat thermometer to the side and heat the oil to 365°F over medium-high heat, about 30 minutes. Place a large cooling rack over a large rimmed baking sheet and set aside.

7 Carefully slip 4 doughnuts into the oil. Cook for about 4 minutes, turning with forks or wooden chopsticks halfway through cooking, until they are a rich brown. Remove them from the fat with a slotted spoon, and set them on the rack to drain further. Repeat with the remaining doughnuts, returning the temperature of the oil to 365°F each time. Eat the doughnuts while warm (the best!) or at room temperature. Serve these plain—they don't need a thing.

BRIOCHE DOUGHNUTS

*Makes
about 18
doughnuts*

I don't think there's a richer, butterier, more tender doughnut than this. These are at their best within a few hours of frying, so be sure you have a few hungry people around to do justice to your creations. The dough must be prepared a day ahead and refrigerated overnight.

1 recipe Brioche Dough
  (page 128), chilled

3 quarts vegetable oil for deep-
  frying

Sugar for coating

1 Line two large baking sheets with cooking parchment or silicone liners. Lightly dust your work surface with flour and scrape the chilled dough onto the flour. Sprinkle with additional flour and gently pat the dough to a $1/2$-inch thickness. Check frequently to be sure the dough isn't sticking to the surface. With a floured $2^1/2$- to 3-inch doughnut cutter (or two floured round cutters of different sizes), cut out the doughnuts. Place the dough- nuts about 2 inches apart on the prepared pans, and put the holes between them. Gently gather the scraps together, flour lightly, pat out, and cut out more doughnuts.

2 Cover the doughnuts loosely with kitchen towels, and let rest in a warm place (about 80°F) while the oil heats. By the time you are ready to fry them, the doughnuts should be about 1 inch high, puffy, and light. Or, if you're not going to cook the doughnuts within the hour, refrigerate them for up to 3 hours. Bring them to room temperature and let rise before frying.

3 Pour the oil into a 5- to 7-quart wide deep pot such as a cast-iron Dutch oven. Attach a digital probe thermometer or deep-fat thermometer to the side of the pot, and heat the oil to 365°F over medium-high heat, about 30 minutes. Place a large cooling rack over a large rimmed baking sheet and set aside.

4 When the oil is ready, carefully lift up a doughnut—it will be very soft— and add it to the hot oil. Add 3 more doughnuts to the pot and cook for 2 to 3 minutes, turning them over every 30 seconds or so with forks or

wooden chopsticks, until they are puffed, cooked through, and deep brown. Be sure the temperature of the oil does not drop below 360°F during frying. Remove the doughnuts with a slotted spatula, allowing the excess oil to drain back into the pot, and place them on the rack to drain further. Repeat with the remaining doughnuts, returning the temperature of the oil to 365°F each time. Fry the doughnut holes last.

5 Meanwhile, put about 1 cup sugar in a brown paper bag. While the doughnuts are still hot, add 3 or 4 of them at a time to the bag, fold the top down, and shake gently to coat well. Return the doughnuts to the wire rack. Repeat with the doughnut holes. You can serve the doughnuts warm (the best!) or at room temperature.

BRIOCHE APPLE FRITTERS

Makes about 36 fritters

The dough for these fritters is light as air, and when it is combined with apples and fried, well, these are just *too* good. You make the fritters in an unusual way, actually chopping the apples into the chilled dough. You will need to make the brioche at least a day ahead, but preparing and cooking the fritters goes quickly. A powdered sugar glaze gives them a gorgeous shine. Use crisp, sweet/tart apples such as Braeburn, Fuji, Gala, or Gold Rush, or a mixture.

2 medium apples (12 ounces), quartered, cored, and peeled

2 tablespoons sugar

1 teaspoon ground cinnamon

1½ pounds chilled Brioche Dough (page 128)

3 quarts vegetable oil for deep-frying

GLAZE

1½ cups confectioners' sugar

2 tablespoons apple juice

1 tablespoon milk

1 teaspoon pure vanilla extract

1 Cut the apples into ½-inch pieces. Combine the sugar and cinnamon in a small bowl. Add the apples and toss to coat.

2 Pat or roll the brioche on a floured surface into a rectangle measuring roughly 8 x 16 inches. Have one of the long sides nearest you. Spread the apples over one half of the dough, and fold the remaining dough over the apples to cover them, making a 4-x-16-inch rectangle. Press firmly on the dough with the palms of your hands to seal in the apples. With a large heavy chef's knife, start chopping the dough and apples, working in parallel lines in one direction, then at right angles to the first cuts. Continue chopping, going every which way, until the dough and apples are well commingled. With your hands, gently knead the mixture into a moist, slightly sticky mass. Set aside, and clean off your work surface.

3 Line two baking sheets with parchment or silicone liners. Dust the work surface lightly with flour and place the dough on it. Coat the dough lightly with flour and pat the mass out to a ½-inch thickness; the shape doesn't

matter. Cut the dough into strips about 2 inches wide, then cut each strip into 2-inch pieces. The pieces will have more charm if they look a bit ragged. Place the fritters about 1 inch apart on the prepared pans. Cover loosely with kitchen towels, and let rest at room temperature while the oil heats. Or, if you're not going to cook them within the hour, refrigerate them for up to 3 hours. Bring to room temperature before frying.

4   Pour the oil into a 5- to 7-quart wide deep pot, such as a cast-iron Dutch oven. Attach a digital probe thermometer or deep-fry thermometer to the side of the pot and heat the oil to 365°F over medium-high heat, about 30 minutes. Place a large cooling rack over a large rimmed baking sheet and set aside.

5   When the oil is ready, add 5 or 6 fritters and cook for 2 to 3 minutes, turning them over every 30 seconds or so with forks or wooden chopsticks, until they are puffed, cooked through, and deep brown. Be sure the temperature of the oil does not drop below 360°F during frying. Remove with a slotted spatula, allowing the excess oil to drain back into the pot, and place the fritters on the rack to drain further and to cool. Repeat with the remaining fritters, returning the temperature of the oil to 365°F each time.

6   For the glaze, whisk together all the ingredients until smooth in a medium bowl. Hold each cool fritter over the bowl, and brush the top and sides with the glaze. Return the fritters to the rack to let the glaze set—this will take only a few minutes. Serve warm or at room temperature.

CHOCOLATE DOUGHNUTS

Makes 15 to 18 large doughnuts

These are very chocolaty doughnuts, and they get their rising power from baking powder and soda, not yeast, so they are relatively quick to make. The dough is quite soft. The doughnuts are delicious plain, but if you're a diehard chocoholic, dip them into the glaze.

DOUGHNUTS

1³/₄ cups unbleached all-purpose flour, plus more for shaping

1³/₄ cups unbleached soft wheat flour or cake flour

¹/₂ cup nonalkalized cocoa (I use Hershey's)

1 teaspoon baking powder, preferably nonaluminum

1 teaspoon baking soda

³/₄ teaspoon salt

¹/₂ teaspoon ground cinnamon

2 large eggs

2 large egg yolks

1 cup sugar

³/₄ cup buttermilk

6 tablespoons (³/₄ stick) unsalted butter, melted

2 teaspoons pure vanilla extract

3 quarts vegetable oil for deep-frying

CHOCOLATE GLAZE (OPTIONAL)

2 ounces (2 squares) unsweetened chocolate

2 ounces (2 squares) semisweet chocolate

4 tablespoons (¹/₂ stick) unsalted butter

¹/₂ cup milk

¹/₈ teaspoon salt

1¹/₂ cups confectioners' sugar, plus more if needed

2 teaspoons pure vanilla extract

1 For the doughnuts, sift the flours, cocoa, baking powder, baking soda, salt, and cinnamon together; set aside.

2 In a large bowl, whisk together the eggs, egg yolks, sugar, buttermilk, butter, and vanilla until very smooth. Gradually add the flour mixture, stirring very gently with a rubber spatula only until the ingredients are well combined. Do not beat the dough, or the doughnuts will be tough. The dough will be quite soft and wet. Scrape down the sides of the bowl and cover tightly with plastic wrap. Refrigerate for at least 1 hour, or up to 6 hours.

3 Line two large baking sheets with parchment or silicone liners. Lightly dust the work surface with flour and scrape the dough onto it. Sprinkle with additional flour and gently pat the dough to a $1/2$-inch thickness. Check frequently to be sure the dough isn't sticking to the surface. With a 3-inch floured doughnut cutter (or two floured round cutters of different sizes), cut out the doughnuts. Place them about 1 inch apart on the pans, and put the holes among the doughnuts. Gently gather the scraps together, flour lightly, pat out, and cut out more doughnuts.

4 Cover the doughnuts loosely with kitchen towels, and let rest at room temperature while the oil heats up. Or, if you're not going to cook the doughnuts within the hour, refrigerate them for up to 3 hours. Bring to room temperature before frying.

5 Pour the oil into a 5- to 7-quart wide deep pot, such as a cast-iron Dutch oven. Attach a digital probe thermometer or deep-fat thermometer to the side and heat the oil to 365°F over medium-high heat, about 30 minutes. Place a large cooling rack over a large rimmed baking sheet and set aside.

6 When the oil is ready, carefully lift one of the doughnuts off its pan and slip it into the hot oil. Add 2 or 3 more doughnuts and cook for 2 to 3 minutes, turning them every 30 seconds or so with forks or wooden chopsticks, until they are puffed, cooked through, and deep brown. Be sure the temperature of the oil does not drop below 360°F during frying. Remove the doughnuts with a slotted spatula, allowing the excess oil to drain back into the pot, and place them on the rack to drain further. Cook the remaining doughnuts, returning the temperature of the oil to 365°F each time. Fry the doughnut holes last. Serve warm or at room temperature.

7 For the glaze, if using, melt the chocolates with the butter in a small heavy saucepan over very low heat, stirring occasionally. Whisk until smooth, and whisk in the milk and salt. Remove from the heat and whisk in the confectioners' sugar and vanilla. The glaze should be pourable but not runny; adjust the consistency with more confectioners' sugar, if necessary. Dip each doughnut into the glaze to coat one side, invert, and set on the wire rack glazed side up. Let stand until set. These are best fresh.

CRULLERS

Makes 20 to 24 crullers

C ruller recipes go back hundreds of years. *Krul* means "curl" in Dutch, and traditionally crullers (also spelled krullers) were always corkscrew-shaped. To make them, an unleavened butter-sugar-egg dough was cut into strips, wound around the handle of a wooden spoon, and slipped off into deep fat to fry until crisp. Nowadays crullers can be shaped any number of ways: the strips of dough may be folded in half and twisted, two strips of dough may be entwined around each other, or the strips may be twisted in any shape.

The recipes I've seen, starting with one from Miss Leslie in 1828, are fairly consistent, usually differing only in their choice of flavoring. None uses yeast. This recipe is a composite from several sources. I flavor the dough with vanilla extract and lemon zest. The crullers fry up crisp and crunchy on the outside with slightly tender insides. It's hard to stop eating them.

4 tablespoons (¹/₂ stick) unsalted butter, at room temperature	1³/₄ cups unbleached all-purpose flour, plus more for shaping
¹/₂ cup sugar	3 quarts vegetable oil for deep-frying
2 teaspoons pure vanilla extract	
Finely grated zest of 1 lemon	
2 large eggs	Confectioners' sugar for dusting

1 In a large bowl, beat the butter with an electric mixer on medium speed until smooth, about 1 minute. Add 2 tablespoons of the sugar, the vanilla, and lemon zest and beat for 1 minute. Gradually beat in the remaining sugar in 3 additions, beating for about 15 seconds after each addition. Scrape the bowl and beaters and beat for 3 to 4 minutes. Beat in the eggs one at a time, beating for 1 full minute after each. The mixture should be fairly liquid but smooth. Add the flour and beat it in on low just until the dough gathers into a mass on the beaters. The dough will be stiff and slightly sticky.

2 Lightly flour a work surface. Place the dough on the work surface, turn to coat all over with flour, and pat into a 1-inch-thick disk. Wrap securely in plastic wrap and refrigerate for about 1 hour. (The dough can be prepared up to 1 day ahead.)

3 Pour the oil into a 5- to 7-quart wide deep pot, such as a cast-iron Dutch oven. Attach a digital probe thermometer or deep-fry thermometer to the side of the pot and heat the oil to 365°F over medium-high heat, about 30 minutes. Place a large cooling rack over a large rimmed baking sheet and set aside.

4 While the oil heats, roll the dough on a floured surface into a rectangular shape measuring roughly 16 x 10 inches. Don't worry about uneven edges. Use a pastry wheel or sharp knife to cut the dough into 10-inch-long strips about ³/₄ inch wide. When the oil is ready, pick up a strip and wind it tightly around the handle of a wooden spoon to form a corkscrew; don't stretch the dough as you wind. Slide the cruller off the handle and into the oil, and repeat with 3 to 5 more strips of dough. Fry the crullers for about 4 minutes, turning them with wooden chopsticks or forks, until golden brown and cooked through. Don't let the temperature of the oil fall below 360°F. Remove the crullers from the oil with a slotted spatula, letting the excess oil fall back into the pot, and place them on the wire rack to drain further. Repeat with the remaining dough, returning the oil to 365°F each time.

5 When the crullers are cool, dust them generously with confectioners' sugar and serve. Stored airtight, these stay crunchy and delicious for a couple of days.

A WHALE OF A TIME

According to food historian Sandy Oliver, American whalers were uniquely compensated for their labors. For every thousand barrels they produced, the men were treated to a big batch of doughnuts fried in the whale oil. The cook would prepare the dough, and the men would break off small pieces and fry them in vats of boiling oil. Huge skimmers were used to lift the cooked dough balls out of the fat, and the men devoured them to their hearts' content.

BEIGNETS

*Makes
30 to 36
beignets*

These New Orleans classics, made from a pâte à choux, or cream puff dough, have an incredibly delicate golden brown crust and an airy, honeycombed, custardlike interior. When fried or baked, pâte à choux expands to three or more times its size. It takes only a few minutes to mix up the dough with a hand-held electric mixer, or just use a wooden spoon.

I've given these beignets an orange flavor with orange flower water and finely grated orange zest, but you could use vanilla instead of the orange flower water, or lemon extract and lemon zest. Orange flower water is available at gourmet food shops and in Middle Eastern markets. When the beignets are cool, dust them with confectioners' sugar and pile them on a plate. They'll disappear quickly!

3/4 cup plus 2 tablespoons water	4 large eggs
2 tablespoons orange flower water	Finely grated zest of 1 orange
2 tablespoons sugar	3 quarts vegetable oil for deep-frying
1/2 teaspoon salt	
8 tablespoons (1 stick) unsalted butter	Confectioners' sugar for dusting
1 cup unbleached all-purpose flour	

1 Put the water, orange flower water, sugar, salt, and butter in a medium heavy saucepan. Set the pan over medium heat and stir occasionally until the butter is melted. Raise the heat to high and bring to a boil. Immediately dump in the flour and remove the pan from the heat. Stir vigorously with a wooden spoon to make a smooth mixture. Return the pan to medium heat and stir constantly for about 2 minutes, until the dough begins to film the bottom of the pan. Remove from the heat and set aside for 10 to 15 minutes to cool slightly. Stir the dough two or three times as it cools.

2 Beat in the eggs one at a time with an electric mixer on medium to medium-high speed, beating only until each egg is thoroughly incorporated. Scrape the side and bottom of the pan. After the last egg has been

added, beat for 1 minute. The batter should be smooth, thick, and shiny and look creamy. Stir in the orange zest. Set aside.

3 Pour the oil into a 5- to 7-quart wide deep pot, such as a cast-iron Dutch oven. Attach a digital probe thermometer or deep-fry thermometer to the side of the pot and heat the oil to 370° to 375°F over medium-high heat, about 30 minutes. Place a large cooling rack over a large rimmed baking sheet and set aside.

4 When the oil is ready, use two regular teaspoons to shape the beignets, picking up a rounded teaspoon of dough with one of the spoons and pushing it into the oil with the other spoon. Fry only 6 to 8 beignets at a time. Do not crowd the pot; the beignets will swell to at least three times their size as they cook. Cook for about 10 minutes, turning frequently with forks or wooden chopsticks, until the beignets are an even golden brown. Be sure to maintain the temperature of the oil between 365° and 375°F. Lift the beignets out of the oil with a slotted spoon, letting the excess oil drain back into the pot, and set the puffs on the rack to drain further. Repeat with the remaining dough, returning the oil to 370° to 375° each time.

5 When the beignets are cool, dust them with confectioners' sugar, pile them on a platter, like a pyramid, and serve.

Note: You can successfully revive day-old beignets by putting them on a baking sheet and popping them into a 450°F oven for 3 to 4 minutes. Turn them over after 2 minutes. Drain on paper towels, dust with confectioners' sugar, and serve.

Pound Cakes

In no department of cookery does the average housekeeper need less instruction than in cake-making. It is the one thing pertaining to cookery that nearly every American girl learns.

—Maria Parloa, *Miss Parloa's Kitchen Companion* (1887)

Pound cakes, butter cakes with a tender fine crumb, are English in origin. In the 1700s and 1800s, the basic cake formula was based on the pound cake—butter, sugar, flour, and eggs in equal proportions by weight, with no chemical leavening added. The method of making a pound cake was so commonplace that Amelia Simmons, writing in *American Cookery* in 1796, could assume every cook would know how to do it and that these rudimentary instructions would suffice: "One pound sugar, one pound butter, one pound flour, ten eggs, rose water one gill, spices to your taste; watch it well, it will bake in a slow oven in 15 minutes."

Sarah Josepha Hale's instructions in *The Good Housekeeper* (1841) give us a clearer view of the process: "Take one pound of dried and sifted flour, the same of loaf sugar and butter, the well-beaten yolks of twelve, and the whites of six eggs. Then with the hand beat the butter to a cream, add the sugar by degrees, then the eggs and flour; beat it all well together for an hour."

The prerequisite piece of equipment at that time—besides a strong arm—was a scale. Few cooks today own one. But until the late 1800s, it was a standard item in every household. There were two kinds. In the first, the balance scale, weights are placed on one side and food added to a weighing pan on the other until the two sides balance. The second type was the dial scale, which operates on a spring mechanism. Food is placed in a pan on top of the scale and a dial registers the weight. Miss Parloa preferred the balance scale, commenting that "The old-fashioned is the better, as there is nothing to get out of order."

The essential ingredients of these cakes—eggs and butter—were plentiful in rural America. Most people lived on farms and raised cows and chickens. Because of their high fat and sugar content, the cakes had the advantage of keeping well for days at room temperature. Some cooks added caraway seeds, others put in raisins or currants. Eliza Leslie liked to spice things up with a generous amount of nutmeg and cinnamon, and many recipes included flavorings of lemon extract, wine, liquor, or what is considered an exotic addition today, rose water. The flavoring we consider commonplace, vanilla extract, was expensive and used mostly in perfumes at the time.

Pound cakes were wonderful to have on hand for a snack or company, but they

POUND CAKE POINTERS

1. Temperature of the butter. This is all-important. The butter should not be cold, but it must not be so soft that it becomes oily. The ideal temperature for creaming is around 70°F, malleable but not soft. One convenient way of softening it is with a microwave oven. Take the butter straight from the refrigerator, unwrap it, place it on a piece of waxed paper, and microwave it on 30 percent power for 30 seconds. Turn the stick(s) over and microwave for another few seconds. If the butter feels waxy and an impression remains when you press it gently, it's ready to be creamed. If you do use a microwave, bear in mind the power of your oven and how many sticks you're using. Err on the side of less time in your first trials.

2. Creaming the butter. Beat the butter with an electric mixer (with the paddle attachment if using a stand mixer) on medium speed for about 1 minute. This step makes the butter smooth and aerates it slightly, giving it an almost fluffy texture. Now it's ready to be beaten with the sugar.

3. Beating in the sugar. Granulated sugar is best, since the grains are the ideal size for creating air bubbles in the butter. The key is to add the sugar gradually, making sure each addition is completely incorporated before adding the next. Adding the flavoring during this step seems to add to its intensity. Once all the sugar has been combined with the butter, beat the mixture for 5 to 6 minutes on medium-high speed. *This is the most important step in making any butter cake.* The sugar grains are being rubbed against the butter constantly as the beater (or beaters) aerates and fills the mixture with tiny air bubbles. Without these bubbles, the cake will not rise properly.

4. Adding the eggs. When you make a pound cake, you're making an emulsion of fat and water. Eggs contain fat, but they also contain a lot of water. The important thing is to add them slowly, so that the water in them will be incorporated into the batter with-

were hard work. Flour had to be dried by the fire to remove excess moisture—damp flour in a cake could cause it to fall or have a gummy texture. And then there was that hour of beating—Sarah Hale does not say whether it was permissible to cheat a bit—which, of course, had to be done by hand.

With the advent of electric mixers, pound cakes are among the easiest and best of cakes. And while the recipes here are certainly a lot more detailed than Amelia Simmons's, they are simple enough that anyone can make them.

out separating. Fortunately, egg yolks act as an emulsifier, which favors the union of fat and water. The usual practice is to beat the eggs in one at a time and to continue beating after each addition until the egg is thoroughly incorporated and the mixture aerated even further. Do not rush this process. Even if you're very careful with this step, sometimes the batter will have a slightly curdled appearance. Don't be concerned; everything will smooth out once you add the flour.

5. Adding Dry Ingredients. This is the final step, and it must be done gently to maintain as much of the air structure as possible. Cake flour or unbleached soft wheat flour is used because of its tenderness. I prefer unbleached soft wheat flour because it has not been treated with bleaching agents (see page 526 for a source). Have the mixer on the lowest speed as you gradually add the dry ingredients, and mix only until they are thoroughly incorporated and the batter is smooth. In some recipes, you'll be alternating the addition of the flour with a liquid. Make sure each is beaten in only enough to incorporate and to make the batter smooth. It's also important to stop the machine occasionally to scrape the bowl and beater(s) as necessary.

6. Baking. Carefully spoon the batter into your prepared pan and smooth the top. All the pound cakes in this chapter are baked in a tube or Bundt pan, so place spoonfuls of batter all around the central tube and smooth the top with a rubber spatula. Sometimes you can level the batter by grasping the sides of the pan with your hands and rotating briskly right to left and back again on your countertop.

Pound cakes take a long time to bake. There are several ways of testing for doneness and each recipe will tell you how. An old technique is to set the hot cake on your countertop and put an ear close to it: if the cake hisses, it's not done. The cake is talking to you, telling you to put it back in the oven. This is not a loud sound, so listen carefully. A completely baked cake will be silent. Using a wooden skewer will also tell you if the cake's done. Inserted into the thickest part of the cake, the skewer should come out clean.

ELIZA LESLIE'S CHOCOLATE CAKE

Makes one 10-inch Bundt cake, 12 to 16 servings

This is the earliest recipe for a chocolate cake I've found in a cookbook. It comes from Eliza Leslie's *The Lady's Receipt Book,* published in 1847. Although European bakers used chocolate prior to that time, it took American bakers awhile to do so. For a long time, chocolate was consumed only as a beverage, and although I have found older recipes for "chocolate cake" than Miss Leslie's, they actually contain no chocolate, but were meant to be eaten with hot chocolate.

This cake is moist and has a wonderfully fine crumb and a rich chocolate taste. Miss Leslie grated her chocolate instead of melting it, which gives the cake a highly appealing flecked look. A whole grated nutmeg and a generous hit of vanilla extract flavor the cake. In Miss Leslie's day, vanilla was extremely expensive and not many people baked with it.

The cake is delicious plain, but it wouldn't hurt to dust the top with confectioners' sugar. A scoop of vanilla ice cream would make it even more delectable.

3 cups sifted cake flour	2 cups sugar
1/2 teaspoon salt	1 1/2 cups (3 sticks) unsalted butter, at room temperature
1 whole nutmeg, grated (2–2 1/2 teaspoons)	1 tablespoon pure vanilla extract
3 ounces (3 squares) unsweetened chocolate, coarsely chopped	8 large eggs
	2 tablespoons milk

1 Adjust an oven rack to the lower third position and preheat the oven to 350°F. Butter a 10-inch (12-cup) Bundt pan, preferably nonstick, or coat it with cooking spray, and dust it all over, including the tube, with fine dry bread crumbs. Knock out the excess crumbs and set aside.

2 Resift the cake flour with the salt and nutmeg; set aside.

3 Process the chocolate for 30 seconds in a food processor. Add 1/4 cup of the sugar and process for 30 seconds to 1 minute longer, until the chocolate is chopped into very small granules. Set aside.

4 Beat the butter in a large bowl with an electric mixer on medium speed until smooth and creamy, about 1 minute. Add the ground chocolate mixture and vanilla and beat for 1 minute on medium-high speed. Beat in the remaining 1 3/4 cups sugar about 1/4 cup at a time, beating for 20 to 30 seconds after each addition. When all the sugar has been incorporated, beat for 5 minutes. Beat in the eggs two at a time, beating for 1 minute after each addition; stop to scrape the bowl and beaters occasionally.

5 On low speed, gradually add half the flour mixture, beating only until thoroughly incorporated. Beat in the milk, then the remaining flour. Scrape the bowl and beaters with a rubber spatula and stir to make sure the batter is smooth. Spoon the batter into the prepared pan and smooth the top.

6 Bake for 55 to 60 minutes, until a toothpick inserted into the thickest part comes out clean. Any cracks on top of the cake should appear moist, not dry. Cool the cake in its pan for 20 minutes. Use a thin-bladed knife to loosen the cake from the pan, cover the pan with a wire rack, and invert the two. Carefully lift off the pan and let the cake cool completely upside down.

7 When the cake is completely cool, wrap airtight and store overnight before serving. Cut into thin slices with a serrated knife.

THE PROLIFIC MISS LESLIE

Born in Philadelphia in 1787, Eliza Leslie had no intention of studying cookery, let alone becoming one of the most prolific cookbook authors of the nineteenth century. Although her recipe writing is among the most authoritative and detailed of the period, Miss Leslie's hope was that she'd be remembered for her fiction writing—novels, children's books, and stories. She entered the field of cookery through necessity: her widowed mother had sent her to Mrs. Elizabeth Goodfellow's Philadelphia cooking school so that she could help with the family boardinghouse. Eliza took detailed notes, and almost twenty years later, in 1828, she published *Seventy-Five Receipts for Pastry, Cakes, and Sweetmeats,* a collection of recipes she learned from Mrs. Goodfellow. Her definitive work, *Directions for Cookery,* appeared in 1837 and went on to be reprinted at least sixty times. She wrote many more cookbooks, the last, *Miss Leslie's New Cookery Book,* in 1857, the year before she died. To read her books, as the noted food historian Jan Longone has said, "is to open a window into the nineteenth-century American larder."

SOUR CREAM LEMON POUND CAKE

Makes one 10-inch Bundt cake, 12 to 16 servings

Lemon lovers rejoice! This is a big, beautiful pound cake with an extremely fine, tender texture. Make it for a gathering, or for a tea party, or whenever you want that refreshing tang. It will stay fresh for several days, well covered, at room temperature.

CAKE

3½ cups sifted cake flour

½ teaspoon salt

1½ cups (3 sticks) unsalted butter, at room temperature

Finely grated zest of 2 large lemons

2 teaspoons pure lemon extract

2⅔ cups sugar

6 large eggs

1 cup sour cream

GLAZE

⅓ cup fresh lemon juice

½ cup sugar

Confectioners' sugar for dusting

1 Adjust an oven rack to the lower third position and preheat the oven to 350°F. Coat a 10-inch (12-cup) Bundt pan, preferably nonstick, with cooking spray and dust it all over, including the tube, with fine dry bread crumbs. Tap out the excess crumbs and set aside. (If you prefer to butter or grease the pan, be sure to do a thorough job, or the cake may stick to it.)

2 Resift the flour with the salt; set aside.

3 Beat the butter in a large bowl with an electric mixer on medium speed until smooth and creamy, about 1 minute. Add the lemon zest, lemon extract, and ⅓ cup of the sugar, and beat for 1 minute. Beat in the remaining 2⅓ cups sugar about ⅓ cup at a time, beating for 15 to 30 seconds after each addition. When all the sugar has been added, scrape the bowl and beaters well and beat on medium-high speed for 6 minutes. The mixture should be very fluffy and white in color. Beat in the eggs one at a time, beating for about 30 seconds after each addition, then beat for 1 minute.

4 On low speed, add the flour mixture in 3 additions, alternating with the sour cream, beginning and ending with the flour and beating until well combined. Carefully spoon the batter into the prepared pan and level the top with a rubber spatula.

5 Bake the cake for 1 hour to 1 hour and 10 minutes, or until the top is a deep golden brown and springs back when gently pressed and a toothpick inserted into the thickest part comes out clean; do not overbake. The top will have a wide crack revealing a golden, moist-looking crumb underneath.

6 Meanwhile, for the glaze, stir the lemon juice and sugar together in a small bowl. Continue to stir occasionally as the cake bakes, so the sugar dissolves.

7 Cool the cake in the pan on a wire rack for 5 minutes. Cover with another wire rack and invert. Slowly remove the pan, and set the rack with the cake over a baking sheet. With a pastry brush, brush the glaze all over the cake, including the tube portion, using all the glaze. Let stand until completely cool, preferably overnight.

8 Transfer the cake to a platter. Dust with confectioners' sugar and use a serrated knife to cut into thin portions. Store covered at room temperature.

MAKING LIGHT OF IT

It is well *as a general rule in cake making to beat the butter and sugar to a light cream; indeed, in the making of pound cakes, the lightness of the cake depends as much upon this, as upon the eggs being well beaten; then beat the eggs and put them to the butter and gradually add the flour and other ingredients, beating it all the time.*

—Mrs. Crowen, *The American Lady's System of Cookery* (1850)

GOLDEN POUND CAKE

Makes one 9-inch tube cake, 12 servings

Lemon zest and almond extract flavor this cake, which is moist and denser than most pound cakes and has a very fine crumb.

2¹/₂ cups sifted cake flour	Finely grated zest of 1 lemon
¹/₂ teaspoon salt	1 teaspoon pure almond extract
³/₄ cup (1¹/₂ sticks) unsalted butter, at room temperature	1 large egg
	³/₄ cup milk
1¹/₂ cups sugar	8 large egg yolks

1 Adjust an oven rack to the lower third position and preheat the oven to 350°F. Butter a 10-cup Kugelhopf pan or 9-x-3-inch tube pan, or coat it with cooking spray, and dust all over, including the tube, with fine dry bread crumbs. Knock out the excess crumbs and set aside.

2 Resift the cake flour with the salt; set aside.

3 Beat the butter in a large bowl with an electric mixer on medium speed until smooth, about 1 minute. Beat in about ¹/₄ cup of sugar, the lemon zest, and almond extract on medium-high speed, then beat for 1 minute. Beat in ³/₄ cup more sugar 3 tablespoons at a time, beating for 30 seconds after each addition. Beat for 5 minutes. Scrape the bowl and beaters, add the egg, and beat for 1 minute.

4 Pour ¹/₄ cup of the milk into the batter and beat on low speed just to incorporate. Add the flour mixture in 3 additions, alternating with the remaining ¹/₂ cup milk, beginning and ending with the flour and beating just until each addition is thoroughly incorporated.

5 In a medium bowl, beat the egg yolks on medium speed for 5 minutes, or until thick and lemon colored. Beat in the remaining ¹/₂ cup sugar 2 tablespoons at a time, beating for 15 to 30 seconds after each addition. Increase the speed to medium-high and beat for 3 to 4 minutes, until the yolks are very thick and pale.

6 Add half the yolks to the butter-sugar mixture and fold them in gently with a wide rubber spatula in 8 to 10 strokes; don't be too thorough. Add the remaining yolks and fold them in gently just until completely incorporated. Gently spoon the batter into the prepared pan and smooth the top with the spatula.

7 Bake for 55 to 60 minutes, until the cake is deep golden brown and springs back when gently pressed and a toothpick inserted into the thickest part comes out clean. A crack or two may form on the surface. Cool the cake in its pan on a rack for 20 minutes. Cover with a wire rack, invert the two, and slowly lift off the pan. Let cool completely.

8 When the cake is completely cool, cut into thin slices with a serrated knife. Store covered at room temperature.

FRESH BLUEBERRY POUND CAKE

Makes one 9-inch tube cake, 12 to 16 servings

This is a very pretty cake. It's tender, buttery and dense, with a tight, fine crumb, and when you slice into it, the blueberries gleam like amethysts. Feel free to substitute wild blueberries or huckleberries if they're available. You can also use frozen berries (add them to the batter in their frozen state). The batter for this cake is very thick—be careful not to crush the blueberries when folding them in. For the best taste and texture, cut the cake into thin slices. Serve with a steaming cup of tea or coffee.

2¹/₄ cups sifted cake flour	1 tablespoon pure vanilla extract
¹/₂ teaspoon salt	Finely grated zest of 1 lemon
¹/₂ teaspoon ground mace	1¹/₂ cups sugar
2 cups fresh blueberries, picked over	5 large eggs
1 cup (2 sticks) unsalted butter, at room temperature	1¹/₂ tablespoons fresh lemon juice

1 Adjust an oven rack to the lower third position and preheat the oven to 350°F. Butter or grease a 9-x-3-inch tube pan. Line the bottom with waxed paper or cooking parchment, butter the paper or parchment, and dust the inside of the pan, including the tube, all over with all-purpose flour. Knock out the excess flour and set aside.

2 Resift the cake flour with the salt and mace. Place the blueberries in a bowl and add 1 tablespoon of the flour mixture. Toss gently with your fingertips to coat the blueberries; set aside. (If you are substituting frozen berries, reserve 1 tablespoon of the dry ingredients and combine with the berries just before adding them to the batter.)

3 Beat the butter in a large bowl with an electric mixer on medium speed until smooth and creamy, about 1 minute. Add the vanilla, lemon zest, and ¹/₄ cup of the sugar, increase the speed to medium-high, and beat for 1 minute. Beat in the remaining 1¹/₄ cups sugar ¹/₄ cup at a time, beating for 20 to 30 seconds after each addition, then beat for 5 minutes. Beat in the eggs one at a time, beating for 1 minute after each addition.

4 On low speed, gradually beat in about half of the remaining flour mixture, beating only until incorporated. Beat in the lemon juice, then the last of the flour. The batter will be very thick and smooth and look creamy. Add the blueberries and fold them in very gently with a large rubber spatula; take your time. Transfer the batter to the prepared pan and use the spatula to spread it gently in place to avoid air bubbles. Carefully smooth the top.

5 Bake for 1 hour to 1 hour and 10 minutes, until the cake is golden brown and springs back when gently pressed and a toothpick inserted into the thickest part comes out clean. Cool the cake in the pan for 20 minutes. Cover with a wire rack and invert. Remove the pan and paper, cover with another rack, and reinvert to cool right side up.

6 When the cake is completely cool, wrap airtight. Store overnight before serving.

Variation

For a delicate almond flavor, beat in ¼ teaspoon pure almond extract with the vanilla.

SILVER CAKE

Makes 2 loaf cakes, 20 servings

I have seen versions of this tender butter pound cake in many nineteenth-century cookbooks, where it is also sometimes called Lady Cake. The almonds in the cake must be blanched just before use so they'll be soft and easy to break up with a pestle (or processor). When you add a splash of rose water, the almonds turn pure white. The rose water also imparts a beguiling perfume to the cake.

Serve with steaming cups of coffee, tea, or hot chocolate.

1/2 cup unblanched whole almonds	1 1/3 cups plus 1/2 cup sugar
3 tablespoons rose water	1/2 teaspoon salt
1 teaspoon pure almond extract	1 1/3 cups (about 11) egg whites
1 cup (2 sticks) unsalted butter, at room temperature	2 1/2 cups sifted cake flour

1 Butter two 8 1/2-x-4 1/2-x-2 3/4-inch loaf pans. Dust the insides with all-purpose flour, knock out the excess, and set aside.

2 Put the almonds in a bowl and add boiling water to cover. Let stand for 15 to 20 minutes, until the water is sufficiently cool for you to reach into it. Remove a few almonds at a time and slip off their skins. Pat the almonds dry on paper towels.

3 *To crush the almonds with a mortar and pestle,* add 3 or 4 almonds to the mortar and pound to a paste with the pestle. Some small pieces of almond will remain. Add a splash of rose water and mix it in. Continue with the remaining almonds and rose water, crushing only a few nuts at a time. Add the last of the rose water after all the almonds have been pounded, then use the pestle to mix in the almond extract.

To crush the almonds with a food processor, put all the almonds into the work bowl and pulse a few times to chop coarsely. Add the rose water and pulse 4 or 5 times. Scrape the work bowl and continue pulsing until you have a pasty mixture with some texture. There should be some finely chopped pieces of almond visible. Add the almond extract and pulse to blend.

4 Adjust an oven rack to the lower third position and preheat the oven to 350°F.

5 Beat the butter in a large bowl with an electric mixer on medium speed until smooth, about 1 minute. Beat in $\frac{1}{3}$ cup of the sugar and beat for 30 seconds. Beat in another 1 cup sugar $\frac{1}{4}$ cup at a time, beating for about 20 seconds after each addition. Scrape the bowl and beaters and beat on medium-high for 5 minutes. Add the almond mixture and salt and beat on medium speed until incorporated. Add $\frac{1}{3}$ cup of the egg whites and beat for 1 minute.

6 Resift the flour. With the mixer on low speed, add the flour about $\frac{1}{2}$ cup at a time, beating just until it is incorporated and the batter is smooth.

7 Put the remaining 1 cup egg whites in a large bowl. With clean beaters, beat on medium speed until the whites thicken and form softly drooping peaks when the beaters are raised. Beat in the remaining $\frac{1}{2}$ cup sugar 2 tablespoons at a time, beating for 30 seconds after each addition. Raise the speed to medium-high and beat only until the whites form upright peaks that curl slightly at their tips when the beaters are raised; do not overbeat. Add about one-fourth of the whites to the batter and fold them in with a large rubber spatula. Don't be too thorough; it's all right if streaks of white show. Fold in the remaining whites in 3 additions, incorporating the last addition only until no whites show; be as gentle as possible so as not to deflate them. Carefully spoon the batter into the prepared pans and smooth the tops.

8 Bake for 1 hour and 10 to 1 hour and 15 minutes, until the cakes are well browned and the tops show a crack or two and a toothpick inserted into the center comes out clean. Cool the cakes in their pans on wire racks for 20 minutes. Run a small sharp knife around the sides to release them. Cover each cake with a wire rack and invert. Slowly lift off the pans, cover with other wire racks, and invert again. Let cool completely.

9 Wrap the cakes airtight and let them stand for at least several hours, or overnight, before serving. Cut into slices about $\frac{1}{2}$ inch thick with a serrated knife. The cakes keep well at room temperature for about 3 days; they can be frozen for up to 1 month.

CHOCOLATE ALMOND POUND CAKE

*Makes one
10-inch
tube cake,
16 servings*

This is a great big chocolate cake with a fine, moist texture. Almond paste enriches the batter, and finely chopped almonds coat the pan and decorate the top of the cake. The chocolate glaze is almost black and has a beautiful shine. Make this for a party. If you wish, serve each portion with a spoonful of lightly sweetened whipped cream or a small scoop of vanilla ice cream.

Almond paste is widely available in 8-ounce cans or 7-ounce boxes of foil-wrapped tubes (Odense brand, from Denmark); I have used both kinds with excellent results. If you want a more intense almond flavor, add 1 teaspoon pure almond extract with the vanilla.

1/2 cup blanched or unblanched whole almonds	1 tablespoon pure vanilla extract
5 ounces (5 squares) unsweetened chocolate, coarsely chopped	8 large eggs
	1/2 cup sour cream
3 cups sifted cake flour	**CHOCOLATE GLAZE**
1/2 teaspoon salt	1/4 cup water
1/4 teaspoon baking soda	1/4 cup sugar
7 or 8 ounces almond paste (see above)	Pinch of salt
1 1/2 cups (3 sticks) unsalted butter, at room temperature	4 tablespoons (1/2 stick) unsalted butter, cut into pieces
1 3/4 cups sugar	5 ounces (5 squares) semisweet chocolate, coarsely chopped
	1 ounce (1 square) unsweetened chocolate, coarsely chopped

1 Adjust an oven rack to the lower third position and preheat the oven to 350°F.

2 Process the almonds in a food processor until very finely chopped, 20 to 30 seconds; be careful not to overprocess, or the nuts will become oily. Set aside. Butter a 10-x-4 inch tube pan with a removable bottom and line the bottom with cooking parchment or waxed paper. Butter the paper or parchment. Dust the inside of the pan, including the tube, with the almonds, and knock out the excess. Save the almonds that didn't stick to the pan to sprinkle on top of the cake after glazing. Set aside.

3 Place the chocolate in the top of a double boiler or a small saucepan set into a larger pan of hot water over medium heat. Stir occasionally with a rubber spatula until the chocolate melts, being careful not to splash any water into the chocolate. Remove from the heat, leaving the chocolate pan in the water bath.

4 Resift the flour with the salt and baking soda; set aside. Cut the almond paste into small pieces about the size of an almond; place them on a dish and cover with plastic wrap to prevent them drying out.

5 Beat the butter in a large bowl with an electric mixer on medium speed until very smooth, about 1 minute. Beat in the almond paste a piece or two at a time, beating briefly after each addition until incorporated. Add $^1/_4$ cup of the sugar and the vanilla extract and beat on medium-high speed for 1 minute. Beat in the remaining $1^1/_2$ cups sugar $^1/_4$ cup at a time, beating for 20 to 30 seconds after each addition. Beat for 5 minutes. The mixture will be very light colored and fluffy. Stir the chocolate until it is very smooth and remove the pan from the water bath; set aside.

6 Beat the eggs into the butter mixture one at a time, beating for 1 minute after each. Beat in the chocolate on low speed only until incorporated. Beat in the flour mixture in 3 additions, alternating with the sour cream, beginning and ending with the flour and beating only until smooth. The batter will be thick. Spoon the batter into the prepared pan and smooth the top with a rubber spatula.

7 Bake for 1 hour and 10 to 1 hour and 20 minutes, until the cake springs back when gently pressed and a toothpick inserted into the thickest part comes out looking a bit wet with some chocolate sticking to it; do not overbake. The cake will have a few cracks on top. Cool in the pan on a wire rack for 30 minutes.

8 Run a thin-bladed sharp knife around the sides of the cake to release it and lift the cake out of the pan by the tube. Run the knife around the tube and between the paper liner and the bottom of the pan. Cover the cake with a wire rack and carefully invert the two. Remove the pan and paper, and let the cake cool completely.

9 For the glaze, combine the water, sugar, and salt in a small heavy saucepan and bring almost to a boil over medium heat, stirring occasionally. When you can no longer see any sugar crystals, remove from the heat and whisk in the butter and chocolate until the chocolate is melted and the mixture is very smooth. Set aside for a few minutes, stirring occasionally, until the glaze thickens a bit and is spreadable. It should not be runny.

10 Transfer the cake to a serving plate. Spoon the glaze over the top, and spread it with a thin narrow spatula all over the cake, including the tube portion. As the glaze runs down the side of the cake, quickly spread it thinly and evenly with the spatula. Sprinkle the reserved almonds on top. Let stand for an hour or two, until the glaze is set.

11 Cut the cake into thin slices with a serrated knife. Store leftovers covered with a cake dome or an inverted bowl.

BROWN SUGAR POUND CAKE

Makes one 10-inch Bundt cake, 12 to 16 servings

This fine-textured cake has a deep, rich brown sugar flavor. It's lovely plain, but if you want a more festive presentation, serve it with berries and yogurt or whipped cream.

3 1/2 cups sifted cake flour

1/2 teaspoon salt

1 1/2 teaspoons freshly grated nutmeg

3/4 teaspoon ground mace

1 1/2 cups (3 sticks) unsalted butter, at room temperature

2 1/2 cups dark brown sugar, preferably organic, or a 1-pound box regular dark brown sugar

1 tablespoon pure vanilla extract

6 large eggs

1/2 cup milk

1 Adjust an oven rack to the lower third position and preheat the oven to 350°F. Coat a 10-inch (12-cup) Bundt pan with cooking spray and dust the inside all over, including the tube, with fine dry bread crumbs. Tap out the excess crumbs and set aside.

2 Resift the flour with the salt, nutmeg, and mace; set aside.

3 Beat the butter in a large bowl with an electric mixer on medium speed until smooth, about 1 minute. Add 1/4 cup of the sugar and the vanilla and beat for 1 minute. Beat in the remaining 2 1/4 cups sugar 1/4 cup at a time, beating for 20 to 30 seconds after each addition. Scrape the bowl and beaters and beat for 5 to 6 minutes on medium-high speed. Beat in the eggs one at a time, beating for 1 minute after each.

4 On low speed, add the flour mixture in 3 additions, alternating with the milk, beginning and ending with the flour. The batter may look curdled. Scrape the batter into the prepared pan.

5 Bake for about 1 hour, until the cake is dark brown and springs back when gently pressed and a toothpick inserted into the thickest part comes out clean. Cool the cake in its pan on a rack for 30 minutes. Cover with a wire rack, invert, and carefully remove the pan. Cool completely.

6 Transfer to a cake plate. To serve, cut into thin slices with a serrated knife. Store covered at room temperature.

MALTED MILK BLACK-AND-WHITE POUND CAKE

Makes one 10-inch tube cake, 12 to 16 servings

This is a beautiful, mysterious cake. Part of a vanilla batter is spread in the pan, chocolate is added to the remainder, which is poured over the light batter. The two batters are not marbled or swirled. During baking, the chocolate layer is "swallowed" by the lighter batter and is only revealed when you cut into the cake. You can find malted milk powder in supermarkets, where the dry milk is sold.

3^1/$_2$ cups sifted cake flour	7 large eggs
^{1}/$_2$ cup malted milk powder	^{1}/$_2$ cup milk
^{1}/$_2$ teaspoon salt	^{3}/$_4$ cup chocolate syrup (I use Hershey's)
1^1/$_2$ cups (3 sticks) unsalted butter, at room temperature	^{1}/$_4$ teaspoon baking soda
2^1/$_2$ cups sugar	^{1}/$_2$ teaspoon pure almond extract
1 tablespoon pure vanilla extract	

1 Adjust an oven rack to the lower third position and preheat the oven to 350°F. Coat a 10-x-4-inch tube pan, with a removable bottom, with cooking spray and dust all over, including the tube, with fine dry bread crumbs. Tap out the excess crumbs and set aside.

2 Resift the flour with the malted milk and salt; set aside.

3 Beat the butter in a large bowl with an electric mixer on medium speed for 1 to 2 minutes, until smooth and creamy. Add the sugar about ^{1}/$_4$ cup at a time, beating for about 30 seconds after each addition. Add the vanilla and beat for 6 to 7 minutes, until fluffy and light in color. Beat in the eggs one at a time, beating for about 30 seconds after each addition. Increase the speed to medium-high and beat for 1 to 2 minutes more. Scrape the bowl and beaters.

4 On low speed, add half the flour mixture and beat only until incorporated. Beat in the milk, then the remaining flour, beating only until well combined. Scrape 5 cups of the batter into the prepared pan and level the top with a rubber spatula. Add the chocolate syrup, baking soda, and almond extract to the remaining batter and beat only until thoroughly combined. Pour the chocolate batter over the light batter and smooth the top; do not mix the two.

5 Bake for 1 hour and 25 to 1 hour and 30 minutes, until the cake is golden brown on top and springs back when gently pressed and a toothpick inserted into the thickest part comes out clean. Do not overbake.

6 Cool the cake in the pan on a wire rack for 20 minutes. Cover with another rack and invert the two. Carefully remove the pan, cover with another rack, and invert again to cool completely right side up.

7 Transfer to a cake plate and let stand, covered, for several hours, or preferably overnight, before serving. Use a serrated knife to cut into thin slices.

VANILLA BEAN–RUM POUND CAKE

Makes one 9-inch tube cake, 10 to 12 servings

A ground-up vanilla bean and a splash of rum give this cake a tropical flavor. Although it is wonderful plain, I often serve two thin slices per portion with a scoop of vanilla ice cream on the side.

2 cups sifted cake flour	5 large eggs
1/4 teaspoon salt	3 tablespoons dark rum (I use
1 vanilla bean	Myers's)
1 1/2 cups sugar	
1 cup (2 sticks) unsalted butter, at room temperature	

1 Adjust an oven rack to the lower third position and preheat the oven to 325°F. Coat a 9-x-3-inch tube pan with cooking spray and dust all over, including the tube, with fine dry bread crumbs. Tap out the excess crumbs and set aside. (If you prefer to grease the pan instead, be sure to do a thorough job, or the cake may stick to it.)

2 Resift the flour with the salt; set aside.

3 Cut the vanilla bean into 3 or 4 pieces and grind to a fine powder in a spice mill, coffee grinder, or mini grinder. Add 1/4 cup of the sugar and pulse briefly. Set aside.

4 Beat the butter in a large bowl with an electric mixer on medium speed until smooth and creamy, about 1 minute. Add the vanilla bean mixture and beat for 1 minute on medium-high speed. Beat in the remaining 1 1/4 cups sugar 1/4 cup at a time, beating for about 30 seconds after each addition. Scrape the bowl well and beat for 6 minutes. The mixture will be very fluffy and almost white in color. Beat in the eggs one at a time, beating for 1 minute after each and stopping to scrape the bowl and beaters once or twice.

5 On low speed, add half the flour mixture and beat only until incorporated. Beat in the rum, then the remaining flour, beating only until well combined. Carefully spoon the batter into the prepared pan and level the top with a rubber spatula.

6 Bake for 1 hour and 5 minutes to 1 hour and 15 minutes, until the cake is golden brown and springs back when gently pressed and a toothpick inserted into the thickest part comes out clean; do not overbake. Any cracks in the top of the cake should appear moist.

7 Cool the cake in the pan on a wire rack for 20 minutes. Cover with another rack and invert the two. Carefully remove the pan, cover the cake with another rack, and invert again to cool completely right side up.

8 Transfer the cake to a cake plate. Wrap airtight and let stand overnight before serving. Use a serrated knife to cut into thin slices.

Variation

If you want a larger cake, increase all the ingredients, using 3 cups sifted cake flour, $1/2$ teaspoon salt, $1^1/_2$ vanilla beans, $2^1/_4$ cups sugar, 3 sticks butter, 8 eggs, and $1/_3$ cup rum. Bake in a 10-inch Bundt pan for the same amount of time.

INDIAN POUND CAKE

Makes one 10-inch Bundt cake, 12 to 16 servings

This cake is unusual not only in its use of cornmeal, but in the addition of brandy and rose water. These ingredients tenderize the cake and give it a delicious flavor. Make the cake a day before serving, since its texture improves on standing.

The original version of this recipe is from Mrs. Elizabeth Goodfellow, who ran a renowned cooking school in Philadelphia in the early 1800s. Food historian William Woys Weaver reproduced Mrs. Goodfellow's recipe as she taught it, and I've adapted it. Eliza Leslie, a pupil of Mrs. Goodfellow's, published her version of the recipe in *Seventy-Five Receipts* (1828).

It's essential to use a high-quality fine-textured cornmeal for this cake, such as the fine yellow cornmeal from Great Valley Mills or the white corn flour from Hoppin John's (see Sources, page 526). Serve with cups of strong coffee.

2 cups fine yellow cornmeal or white corn flour	1 cup (2 sticks) unsalted butter, at room temperature
1 cup sifted cake flour	2 cups sugar
½ teaspoon salt	7 large eggs
1 whole nutmeg, grated (2–2½ teaspoons)	2 tablespoons rose water
1 teaspoon ground cinnamon	2 tablespoons brandy

1 Adjust an oven rack to the lower third position and preheat the oven to 350°F. Butter a 10-inch (12-cup) Bundt pan, or coat with cooking spray, and dust the inside, including the tube, with fine dry bread crumbs. Knock out the excess crumbs and set aside.

2 Sift the cornmeal or corn flour, cake flour, salt, nutmeg, and cinnamon together; set aside.

3 Beat the butter in a large bowl with an electric mixer on medium speed until smooth and creamy, about 1 minute. On medium-high speed, beat in the sugar about ¼ cup at a time, beating for 20 to 30 seconds after each addition. Beat for 5 minutes. Beat in the eggs one at a time, beating well after each. Scrape the bowl and beaters.

4 Combine the rose water and brandy in a measuring cup. On low speed, add the flour mixture to the butter in 3 additions, alternating with the liquid, beginning and ending with the flour, and beating after each addition only until incorporated. Scrape the batter into the prepared pan and smooth the top.

5 Bake for 50 to 60 minutes, until the cake is well browned and a toothpick inserted into the thickest part comes out clean. Cool in the pan on a rack for 10 minutes. Run a thin-bladed knife around the central tube to release the cake, cover with a wire rack, and invert the two. Carefully lift off the pan and let the cake cool completely.

6 Wrap the cake airtight with plastic wrap and let stand overnight before serving. Cut into thin slices with a serrated knife.

INDIAN POUND CAKE WITH SOUR MASH WHISKEY

Makes one 10-inch Bundt cake, 18 servings

Yellow cornmeal adds texture to this fine-grained cake, and a generous amount of whiskey gives it great flavor and a heady aroma.

3 cups sifted cake flour

1 cup yellow cornmeal (not fine)

½ teaspoon salt

1 teaspoon ground cinnamon

1½ cups (3 sticks) unsalted butter, at room temperature

Finely grated zest of 1 orange

Finely grated zest of 1 lemon

¾ cup firmly packed light brown sugar

1½ cups sugar

6 large eggs

¾ cup Jack Daniel's whiskey

Confectioners' sugar for dusting

1 Adjust an oven rack to the lower third position and preheat the oven to 350°F. Coat a 10-inch (12-cup) Bundt pan with cooking spray and dust the inside all over, including the tube, with fine dry bread crumbs. Tap out the excess crumbs and set aside.

2 Resift the flour with the cornmeal, salt, and cinnamon; set aside.

3 Beat the butter in a large bowl with an electric mixer on medium speed until smooth, about 1 minute. Add both zests and ¼ cup of the brown sugar and beat for 1 minute. Beat in the remaining ½ cup brown sugar and the granulated sugar ¼ cup at a time, beating for about 15 seconds after each addition. Beat for 5 minutes on medium-high speed. Scrape the bowl and beaters. Add the eggs one at a time, beating for about 30 seconds after each addition. Scrape the bowl and beat for 1 full minute.

4 On low speed, add the flour mixture in 4 additions, alternating with the whiskey, beginning and ending with the flour and beating only until smooth. Spread the batter in the prepared pan.

5 Bake for 50 to 55 minutes, or until the cake is golden brown and springs back when gently pressed and a toothpick inserted into the thickest part comes out clean. Cool the cake in its pan on a rack for 30 minutes. Invert onto a cooling rack, carefully remove the pan, and cool completely.

6 Carefully transfer the cake to a cake plate. Just before serving, dust with confectioners' sugar. Cut into thin slices with a serrated knife. Store covered at room temperature.

AN EASY WAY OF MAKING BUTTER IN WINTER

Making butter was a regular housewifely chore in the nineteenth century, requiring several days. Here are Miss Leslie's recommendations.

The following will be found an excellent method of making butter in cold weather for family use. We recommend its trial. Take, in the morning, the unskimmed milk of the preceding evening (after it has stood all night in a <u>tin</u> pan) and set it over a furnace of hot coals, or in a stove; being careful not to disturb the cream that has risen to the surface. Let it remain over the fire till it simmers, and begins to bubble round the edges; but on no account let it come to a boil. Then take the pan carefully off (without disturbing the cream) and carry it to a cool place, but not where it is cold enough to freeze. In the evening take a spoon, and loosen the cream round the sides of the pan. If very rich, it will be almost a solid cake. Slip off the sheet of cream into another and larger pan, letting as little milk go with it as possible. Cover it, and set it away. Repeat the process for several days (meaning milking the cow each day and letting the milk stand overnight each time), till you have thus collected a sufficiency of clotted cream to fill the pan. Then scald a wooden ladle, and beat the cream hard with it during ten minutes. You will then have excellent butter. Take it out of the pan, lay it on a flat dish, and with the ladle squeeze and press hard, till all the buttermilk is entirely extracted and drained off. Then wash the butter in cold water, and work a very little salt into it. Set it away in a cool place for three hours. Then squeeze and press it again; also washing it a second time in cold water. Make it up into pats, and keep it in a cool place.

This is the usual method of making winter butter in the south of England; and it is very customary in the British provinces of America. Try it.

— Eliza Leslie, *Miss Leslie's New Cookery Book* (1857)

SPICE POUND CAKE

Makes one 10-inch Bundt cake, 18 servings

Cinnamon, ginger, nutmeg, and allspice flavor this cake; brown sugar contributes a hint of molasses. Serve it plain or with vanilla ice cream.

3 cups sifted cake flour

1/2 teaspoon salt

2 teaspoons ground cinnamon

1 teaspoon ground ginger

1/2 teaspoon freshly grated nutmeg

1/2 teaspoon ground allspice

1 1/2 cups (3 sticks) unsalted butter, at room temperature

1 1/3 cups sugar

1 cup firmly packed light brown sugar

2 teaspoons pure vanilla extract

6 large eggs

1/2 cup milk

Confectioners' sugar for dusting

1 Adjust an oven rack to the lower third position and preheat the oven to 350°F. Coat a 10-inch (12-cup) Bundt pan with cooking spray and dust the inside all over, including the tube, with fine dry bread crumbs. Tap out the excess crumbs and set aside.

2 Resift the flour with the salt and spices; set aside.

3 Beat the butter in a large bowl with an electric mixer on medium speed until smooth, about 1 minute. Combine both sugars in a small bowl. Add 1/4 cup of the sugar and the vanilla to the butter and beat for 1 minute. Beat in the remaining sugar 1/4 cup at a time, beating for 20 to 30 seconds after each addition. Beat for 5 minutes on medium-high speed. Scrape the bowl and beaters. Beat in the eggs one at a time, beating for 1 minute after each addition. Scrape the bowl and beater.

4 On low speed, add the flour mixture in 3 additions, alternating with the milk, beginning and ending with the flour and beating only until smooth. Spread the batter in the prepared pan.

5 Bake for about 1 hour, or until the cake is dark brown and springs back when gently pressed, and a toothpick inserted into the thickest part comes out clean. Cool in the pan on a wire rack for 20 minutes. Invert onto a cooling rack, carefully remove the pan, and cool completely.

6 Wrap the cake airtight and let stand overnight. Just before serving, dust with confectioners' sugar. Cut into thin slices with a serrated knife.

BANANA POUND CAKE

Makes one 10-inch Bundt cake, 12 to 16 servings

A generous amount of banana liqueur gives this cake a decided banana flavor and delicious aroma. Fine-textured and moist, the cake is wonderful plain. The poppy seeds make a great addition.

3¹/₂ cups sifted cake flour	2 teaspoons pure vanilla extract
1 teaspoon freshly grated nutmeg	6 large eggs
¹/₂ teaspoon salt	¹/₂ cup crème de banane liqueur
1¹/₂ cups (3 sticks) unsalted butter, at room temperature	¹/₄ cup poppy seeds (optional)
2 cups sugar	Confectioners' sugar for dusting

1 Adjust an oven rack to the lower third position and preheat the oven to 350°F. Butter a 10-inch (12-cup) Bundt pan, or coat with cooking spray, and dust the inside all over, including the tube, with fine dry bread crumbs. Tap out the excess crumbs and set aside.

2 Resift the flour with the nutmeg and salt; set aside.

3 Beat the butter in a large bowl with an electric mixer on medium speed until smooth, about 1 minute. Add ¹/₄ cup of the sugar and the vanilla and beat for 1 minute. Add the remaining 1¹/₄ cups sugar ¹/₄ cup at a time, beating for 20 to 30 seconds after each addition. Scrape the bowl and beaters, and beat for 5 minutes on medium-high speed. Add the eggs one at a time, beating for 1 minute after each.

4 On low speed, add the flour mixture in 3 additions, alternating with the banana liqueur, beginning and ending with the flour and beating only until smooth. Stir in the poppy seeds, if using. Spread the batter in the pan.

5 Bake for 50 to 55 minutes, or until the cake is golden brown and springs back when gently pressed and a toothpick inserted into the thickest part comes out clean. A crack may develop in the top. Cool in the pan on a rack for 30 minutes. Invert onto a cooling rack, carefully remove the pan, and cool completely.

6 Carefully transfer the cake to a cake plate. Just before serving, dust with confectioners' sugar. Cut into thin slices with a serrated knife. Store covered at room temperature.

BLACK WALNUT BOURBON
POUND CAKE

*Makes one
9-inch tube
cake, 10 to
12 servings*

Black walnuts have a lusty flavor that blends beautifully with bourbon. And brown sugar highlights both. Black walnuts are often sold already chopped, but they need to be finely chopped for this recipe. Use a chef's knife, which does a better job than a food processor. If your market doesn't carry black walnuts, you can order them by mail (see Sources, page 522). They are worth seeking out. When they arrive, freeze them to preserve their freshness. Bring them to room temperature before using. If you can't get black walnuts, however, substitute ordinary walnuts.

Serve this cake cut into thin slices. It tastes better that way, and you'll get a more powerful aroma than with thick slices.

2 cups sifted cake flour	1½ cups firmly packed dark brown sugar
½ teaspoon salt	
1 teaspoon ground cinnamon	5 large eggs
2 cups (8 ounces) finely chopped black walnuts	2 tablespoons bourbon or Jack Daniel's whiskey
1 cup (2 sticks) unsalted butter, at room temperature	

1 Adjust an oven rack to the lower third position and preheat the oven to 325°F. Coat a 9-x-3-inch tube pan with cooking spray and dust all over, including the tube portion, with fine dry bread crumbs. Tap out the excess crumbs and set aside. (If you want to grease the pan instead, be sure to do a thorough job, or the cake might stick to it.)

2 Resift the flour with the salt and cinnamon. Combine the black walnuts with ¼ cup of the dry ingredients, tossing to coat well; set aside.

3 Beat the butter in a large bowl with an electric mixer until smooth and creamy, about 1 minute. On medium-high speed, add the brown sugar about ¼ cup at a time, beating for about 30 seconds after each addition. Scrape the bowl well and beat for 5 to 6 minutes. The mixture will be very fluffy. Beat in the eggs one at a time, beating for 1 minute after each. The batter may look curdled, but that's okay.

4 On low speed, beat in half the flour mixture, beating only until incorporated. Beat in the bourbon or whiskey, then the remaining flour, beating only until well combined. Stir in the walnuts. Carefully spoon the batter into the prepared pan and level the top with a rubber spatula.

5 Bake for 1 hour to 1 hour and 10 minutes, until the cake is dark brown on top and springs back when gently pressed and a toothpick inserted into the thickest part comes out clean; do not overbake. Any cracks in the top of the cake should appear moist.

6 Cool the cake in the pan on a wire rack for 20 minutes. Cover with another rack and invert the two. Carefully remove the pan, cover with another rack, and invert again to cool completely right side up.

7 Transfer the cake to a cake plate. Let stand, covered, for several hours, preferably overnight, before serving. Use a serrated knife to cut into thin slices. Store covered at room temperature.

MRS. GOODFELLOW'S DOVER CAKE

Makes one 10-inch Bundt cake, 16 servings

This pound cake, from the early 1800s, is attributed to the famous nineteenth-century cooking teacher Mrs. Elizabeth Goodfellow. It is made with rice flour, which lacks gluten and produces an extremely fine-grained cake. Because rice flour is much finer and lighter in texture that wheat flour and was abundantly available in the nineteenth century, it was used in many baked goods of the time. The cake is delicious all by itself, but it is wonderful served with fresh berries, peaches, or ice cream.

1 cup (2 sticks) unsalted butter, at room temperature
$^1/_2$ teaspoon salt
2 cups sugar
8 large eggs
$^1/_4$ cup brandy

$^1/_4$ cup dry Madeira or sherry
1 tablespoon orange flower water
$2^3/_4$ cups rice flour (spooned into cup and leveled)

Confectioners' sugar for dusting

1 Adjust an oven rack to the lower third position and preheat the oven to 325°F. Butter a 10-inch (12-cup) Bundt pan, or coat with cooking spray, and dust the inside all over, including the tube, with fine dry bread crumbs; knock out the excess crumbs and set aside.

2 Beat the butter in a large bowl with an electric mixer on medium speed until smooth and creamy, about 1 minute. Add the salt and $^1/_4$ cup of the sugar and beat for 20 to 30 seconds. Beat in the remaining $1^1/_2$ cups sugar about $^1/_4$ cup at a time, beating for 20 to 30 seconds after each addition. Beat on medium-high speed for 5 minutes. Beat in the eggs one at a time, beating for 1 minute after each addition.

3 Combine the brandy, Madeira or sherry, and orange flower water in a measuring cup. On low speed, add the rice flour to the butter mixture in 3 additions, alternating with the liquid, beginning and ending with the rice flour and beating only until each addition is incorporated. Scrape the batter into the prepared pan and smooth the top.

4 Bake for 50 to 55 minutes, until the cake is golden brown and springs back when gently pressed and a toothpick inserted into the thickest part comes

out clean. Cool in the pan for 20 minutes. Cover with a wire rack and invert. Remove the pan, and cool the cake completely.

5 Transfer the cake to a cake plate. Just before serving, dust with confectioners' sugar. Cut into thin slices with a sharp serrated knife. Wrapped airtight, the cake keeps well at room temperature for several days; it can be frozen for up to 1 month.

A GOOD RULE

Before commencing to make a cake or pudding, see that all the ingredients required are ready and at hand: the butter and sugar in the pan, eggs broken, flour weighed, and all other materials needed, ready for use. By so doing the cake or pudding may be made in a very short time, and with much less difficulty.

—Hannah Widdifield, *Widdifield's New Cook Book* (1856)

GREAT BIG CAKE WITH DRIED FRUITS

*Makes one
10-inch
Bundt cake,
18 to 20
servings*

The texture of this cake is dense with a moist crumb, and it's relatively low in fat. You can use almost any mixture of dried fruits that you like —just be sure to include at least one tart variety such as cranberries or sour cherries. The best way to cut large pieces of dried fruit (peaches, pears, and nectarines) is to slice them into strips about ¼ inch wide, then cut the strips crosswise into ¼-inch dice. Snip dates, prunes, and apricots into bite-sized pieces with scissors. Do not use packaged chopped dates, apricots, or prunes; they're inferior in quality and tend to be too dry.

Let the cake stand overnight before serving. It will keep fresh for days at room temperature. It needs no glaze or any adornment, but if you want to glamorize it a bit, dust a little confectioners' sugar on top.

1 packed cup bite-sized pieces dried dates	1 teaspoon baking soda
1 packed cup bite-sized pieces dried prunes	½ teaspoon salt
¾ cup bite-sized pieces dried apricots	8 tablespoons (1 stick) unsalted butter, at room temperature
½ cup dried blueberries	1 8-ounce package Neufchâtel cream cheese
½ cup dried sour cherries	2 cups sugar
½ cup golden raisins	Finely grated zest of 1 orange
3⅓ cups sifted unbleached all-purpose flour	1 tablespoon pure vanilla extract
½ cup cornstarch	4 large eggs
	1 cup low-fat sour cream

1 Adjust an oven rack to the lower third position and preheat the oven to 350°F. Coat a 10-inch (12-cup) Bundt pan with cooking spray and dust all over with fine dry bread crumbs, including the tube. Knock out the excess crumbs, and set aside.

2 In a large bowl, combine the dried fruits with ⅓ cup of the flour; toss with your fingers to coat evenly. Resift the remaining 3 cups flour with the cornstarch, baking soda, and salt; set aside.

3 Beat the butter and cream cheese in a large bowl with an electric mixer on medium-low speed until very smooth, about 1 minute. Add $1/4$ cup of the sugar, the orange zest, and vanilla and beat for 1 minute. Beat in the remaining $1^3/4$ cups sugar about $1/4$ cup at a time, beating for 20 to 30 seconds after each addition. Beat for 5 minutes. Add the eggs one at a time, beating for 1 minute after each. Scrape the bowl and beaters.

4 On low speed, beat in the flour mixture in 3 additions, alternating with the sour cream, beginning and ending with the flour and beating only until the batter is smooth. The batter will be very thick. Add the batter to the dried fruits and fold together with a large rubber spatula. Spoon the batter into the prepared pan and smooth the top.

5 Bake for 1 hour and 15 to 1 hour and 20 minutes, until the cake is golden brown and a toothpick inserted into the thickest part comes out clean. The top may crack. Cool the cake in the pan on a rack for 20 minutes. Invert onto a cooling rack, carefully remove the pan, and cool completely.

6 Wrap the cake airtight and store overnight before serving. Cut into thin slices with a sharp serrated knife.

Variation

You can add 1 cup chopped pecans, walnuts, or macadamia nuts when you fold the batter and dried fruits together.

GINGER–MACADAMIA NUT POUND CAKE

Makes one 9-inch tube cake, 12 to 16 servings

Layers of flavor and texture are the hallmark of this mildly spicy cake, which has a deliciously fine crumb. The ginger taste is more concentrated toward the bottom, where the pieces of crystallized ginger come to rest. Crunchy bits of finely chopped macadamia nuts are fairly evenly distributed throughout the cake, but there will be a bit more toward the bottom.

Crystallized ginger is widely available in supermarkets. Fresh ginger should be finely grated, not shredded or chopped, to remove its tough fibers. Serve thin slices of this cake as part of a dessert buffet or with afternoon tea or coffee.

3 cups sifted cake flour	1 cup (2 sticks) unsalted butter, at room temperature
1/2 teaspoon salt	
3/4 cup salted or unsalted macadamia nuts	1 1/2 cups sugar
	6 large eggs
1/2 cup crystallized ginger, cut into 1/4-inch pieces	1 tablespoon finely grated peeled fresh ginger

1 Adjust an oven rack to the lower third position and preheat the oven to 350°F. Butter a 9-x-3-inch tube pan, or coat with cooking spray, and dust all over, including the tube, with fine dry bread crumbs. Knock out the excess crumbs and set aside.

2 Resift the flour with the salt. Combine the macadamia nuts and 1/2 cup of the flour mixture in a food processor and pulse 4 or 5 times for 1 second each, only until the nuts are chopped medium-fine. You want pieces of varying size, but they should be on the small side. Transfer the mixture to a small bowl, add the crystallized ginger, and toss with your fingers to coat evenly; set aside.

3 Beat the butter in a large bowl with an electric mixer on medium speed until smooth, about 1 minute. Increase the speed to medium-high and beat in the sugar 1/4 cup at a time, beating for 15 to 30 seconds after each

addition. Beat for 5 to 6 minutes. The mixture will be very fluffy and almost white in color. Beat in the eggs one at a time, beating for 1 minute after each. Beat in the grated ginger.

4 On low speed, gradually beat in about half of the flour mixture, beating only until incorporated. Add the macadamia-ginger mixture and beat to incorporate. Gradually add the remaining flour mixture, beating only until no flour shows. Scrape the bowl and spoon the batter into the prepared pan and smooth the top.

5 Bake for 50 to 60 minutes, until the cake is lightly browned and a tooth-pick inserted into the thickest part comes out clean. Cool the cake in the pan on a rack for 30 minutes. Run a thin-bladed sharp knife all around the edge and central tube to release the cake. Cover the cake with a wire rack and invert the two. Slowly lift off the pan, cover the cake with another rack, and invert again to cool completely right side up.

6 Wrap the cake airtight and let stand overnight before serving. Cut with a serrated knife.

5

Loaf Cakes and Sheet Cakes

Loaf cakes are some of the oldest cakes, but historically the word "loaf" was reserved for a particular kind of cake enriched with butter, eggs, sugar, and dried fruit. It didn't mean, as it does today, that the cakes were baked in pans designed for loaves of bread. Some loaf cakes were leavened with chemical leaveners, others with yeast. Amelia Simmons included four loaf cake recipes in *American Cookery* (1796) — all containing yeast, and all with enormous quantities of butter or butter and lard, sugar, eggs, raisins, and spices. Mrs. Putnam, writing in 1849, offered two formulas for loaf cakes that rival those of Miss Simmons in their richness. Because of their high fat content, these cakes would keep without refrigeration for a week or more.

Precursors of our loaf cakes are English in origin, and recipes for this type of cake appeared regularly in seventeenth- and eighteenth-century English cookbooks. *Elinor Fettiplace's Receipt Book*, a cookbook from 1604, contains a Great Cake or Fruit Loaf, a yeasted version of the baking soda–leavened cake in this chapter, with a nice balance of fruit to batter. By the nineteenth century, loaf cakes containing dried fruits—raisins, currants, and citron—with barely enough batter to hold them together had became extremely popular. Black Cake is one such cake, and it's easy to see why it became such a favorite. The fruits are sweet with natural sugars, the cake's texture is tender yet chewy, and the flavor has an appealing spiciness. These cakes bear no relation to the overly sweet, gluey fruit cakes of today, full of fluorescent-hued sticky fruits, that have become the brunt of jokes.

The best late nineteenth- and twentieth-century loaf cakes were made of well-flavored rich, buttery batters, with or without dried fruits. And when dried fruits were used, they were not dyed artificially or saturated with sugar syrup. For example, the recipe for Miss Parloa's Fig Loaf Cake (1887), calls for half a pound of dried figs and raisins in an eggy brown sugar batter leavened with baking powder and flavored with cinnamon, nutmeg, and cloves. A few years later, in 1902, *Mrs. Rorer's New Cook Book* featured a Chocolate Loaf Cake leavened with baking powder and baked in a square pan.

By Mrs. Rorer's time, the rules of baking had been pretty well codified, and cast-iron ranges were in almost every home. Even though the ovens lacked thermostatic controls, it was possible to regulate their heat fairly accurately by adjusting the amount of fuel—gas, coal, or oil. Baking powder had also been accepted wholeheartedly by busy housewives. And once bakers discovered they could put these cakes together fairly quickly, it was simply a question of applying their imagination and deciding what to put in them. The following recipes suggest some of the liberating possibilities.

ELIZA LESLIE'S LAFAYETTE GINGERBREAD

Makes 1 sheet cake, 10 to 12 servings

This spicy gingerbread has an especially light and tender texture. The recipe comes from Eliza Leslie's last cookbook, *Miss Leslie's New Cookery Book* (1857). In the nineteenth century, many baked goods were named in honor of the famous, and the Revolutionary War general Lafayette had died long before her book appeared. Serve the cake warm (fabulous!) or at room temperature. It is divine with a spoonful of softly whipped cream.

3	cups sifted cake flour	
1/2	teaspoon baking soda	
1/2	teaspoon salt	
1	tablespoon ground ginger	
1	teaspoon ground cinnamon	
1/2	teaspoon ground mace	
1/2	teaspoon freshly grated nutmeg	
8	tablespoons (1 stick) unsalted butter, at room temperature	

1/2 cup firmly packed light or dark brown sugar

3 large eggs

1 cup molasses (I use Grandma's)
Finely grated zest of 1 large orange

1/4 cup fresh orange juice

1/2 cup milk

2 tablespoons brandy

1 Adjust an oven rack to the lower third position and preheat the oven to 350°F. Butter a 13-x-9-inch baking pan and set it aside.

2 Resift the flour with the baking soda, salt, ginger, cinnamon, mace, and nutmeg; set aside.

3 In a large bowl, beat the butter with an electric mixer on medium speed for about 1 minute, until smooth and creamy. Add the brown sugar and beat on medium-high speed for 5 minutes, or until light and fluffy. Scrape the bowl and beaters. Beat in the eggs one at a time, beating for 1 minute after each. The batter will look curdled. Add the molasses and beat for 1 minute. Add the orange zest and juice and beat on low speed until incorporated. Don't worry if the batter looks curdled again; it will become smooth when the last of the flour is mixed in.

4 Combine the milk with the brandy in a measuring cup. On low speed, add the flour mixture to the butter mixture in 3 additions, alternating with the

milk mixture, beginning and ending with the flour and beating after each addition only until smooth. Scrape the batter into the prepared pan and level it by shaking the pan gently from side to side.

5 Bake for about 35 minutes, until the cake springs back when gently pressed and a toothpick inserted into the center comes out clean. Cool in the pan on a wire rack. Serve warm or at room temperature. This cake keeps well, covered, at room temperature for 1 to 3 days.

CORNSTARCH CAKE

Makes 1 large loaf cake or Bundt cake, about 16 servings

The inside of this cake is pure white and its texture is incredibly light— it literally melts in your mouth. It's like a butter angel food cake, with a very fine crumb and a crusty macaroonlike top. The cake was very popular in the mid- to late 1800s. William Woys Weaver tells me its origin is Pennsylvania Dutch. Serve thickish slices plain, with tea or coffee, or spoon some berries on top.

1 cup sifted unbleached all-purpose flour	1 cup (2 sticks) unsalted butter, at room temperature
1 cup cornstarch	1$^{1}/_{2}$ cups sugar
1 teaspoon baking powder, preferably nonaluminum	2 teaspoons pure lemon extract
$^{1}/_{2}$ teaspoon salt	$^{1}/_{2}$ cup half-and-half
	6 large egg whites

1 Adjust an oven rack to the lower third position and preheat the oven to 350°F. Butter an 11-x-4$^{1}/_{2}$-x-2$^{3}/_{4}$-inch (10-cup) loaf pan or a 10-inch (12-cup) Bundt pan. Dust the pan all over with fine dry bread crumbs; knock out the excess crumbs and set aside.

2 Resift the flour with the cornstarch, baking powder and salt; set aside.

3 In a large bowl, beat the butter with an electric mixer on medium speed until smooth, about 1 minute. Add $^{1}/_{4}$ cup of the sugar and the lemon extract and beat for 1 minute. Beat in another 1 cup sugar about $^{1}/_{4}$ cup at a time, beating for 20 to 30 seconds after each addition. Raise the speed to medium-high and beat for 5 minutes. Scrape the bowl and beaters.

4 On low speed, add the cornstarch mixture in 3 additions, alternating with the half-and-half, beginning and ending with the cornstarch and beating only until the batter is smooth.

5 In another large bowl, beat the egg whites with clean beaters on medium speed until they form soft peaks. Beat in the remaining $^{1}/_{4}$ cup sugar about 1 tablespoon at a time, beating for a few seconds after each addition. Raise the speed to medium-high and beat for a few seconds, until the whites form shiny upright peaks that curl slightly at their tips when the beaters are raised; do not overbeat. Stir about one fourth of the whites into the batter to lighten. In 3 additions, gently fold in the remaining whites only until no whites show. Scrape the batter into the prepared pan and smooth the top.

6 Bake for 1 hour to 1 hour and 10 minutes, until the cake is well browned and a toothpick inserted into the center comes out clean. If the cake begins to brown too much, lay a piece of aluminum foil loosely over the top of the cake. Cool in the pan on a wire rack for 20 minutes. Carefully remove the cake from the pan and set it right side up on a wire rack to cool completely. Handle gently; the cake is fragile.

7 Cut the cake into slices with a serrated knife. The cake keeps well, wrapped airtight, at room temperature for several days; it can be frozen for up to 1 month.

HOW TO MAKE CORNSTARCH

Before cornstarch was available in boxes, home cooks had to make their own. Here's how:

Gather the corn when it is a proper age for table use; have a large tin grater, and grate the corn into a clean vessel, into which drop the cobs as you grate them until the vessel is about half full; rub the cobs and squeeze them dry as possible, and put them into another vessel of clean water; rub and squeeze them again; the third rinsing will take all the starch out; let it settle, and then pour all the starch together and strain it through a coarse cloth, and then through a flannel, and let it settle until the next morning, when you will find a thick yellow substance under the water, covering the pure white article in the bottom of the vessel; remove the yellow substance and pour clean water on the starch and stir it up; as soon as it settles thoroughly again, pour off the water and put the starch on dishes, and set it in the sun to dry. When you want to use it, moisten it with cold water and pour boiling water on, till it is the right consistency for use. It requires no boiling.

—*A Quaker Woman's Cookbook. The Domestic Cookery of
Elizabeth Ellicott Lea* (1853), facsimile edition, edited by
William Woys Weaver (1982)

MOLASSES MARBLE LOAF

Makes 1 large loaf cake, about 12 servings

Two-toned cakes date back to the mid-1800s. Here, molasses and a generous amount of allspice flavor and marble a vanilla butter cake. The combination is heavenly. A creamy confectioners' sugar icing, scented with cinnamon, glazes the top and sides of the cake. Serve with tea or coffee, as a mid-morning or afternoon snack, or as a light dessert following a luncheon.

CAKE

2 cups sifted all-purpose flour

1 1/2 teaspoons baking powder, preferably nonaluminum

1/4 teaspoon salt

8 tablespoons (1 stick) unsalted butter, at room temperature

1 cup sugar

1 teaspoon pure vanilla extract

2 large eggs

2/3 cup milk

2 tablespoons molasses (I use Grandma's)

1 teaspoon ground allspice

ICING

1 cup confectioners' sugar

1/4 teaspoon ground cinnamon
   Pinch of salt

3 tablespoons heavy cream, plus more if needed

1 teaspoon pure vanilla extract

1/4 cup finely chopped pecans (optional)

1 For the cake, adjust an oven rack to the lower third position and preheat the oven to 350°F. Butter a 10-x-4 1/2-x-3-inch or 9-x-5-x-3-inch loaf pan, dust the inside all over with flour, and knock out the excess; set aside.

2 Resift the 2 cups flour with the baking powder and salt; set aside.

3 In a large bowl, beat the butter with an electric mixer on medium speed until smooth, about 1 minute. Add the sugar about 1/4 cup at a time, beating for 20 to 30 seconds after each addition. Beat in the vanilla. Scrape the bowl and beaters and beat on medium-high speed for 5 minutes. Beat in the eggs one at a time, beating well after each addition.

4 On low speed, add the flour mixture in 3 additions, alternating with the milk, beginning and ending with the flour and beating only until smooth after each addition. The batter will be thick.

5 Transfer about one third of the batter to a small bowl, add the molasses and allspice, and stir to combine well. Spoon the light and dark batters alternately in the prepared pan, then run a knife through the length and width of the batter a few times. Smooth the top with a rubber spatula.

6 Bake for 50 to 60 minutes, until the loaf is well browned and springs back when gently pressed and a toothpick inserted into the center comes out clean. Cool in the pan on a wire rack for 20 minutes. Release the cake from the sides of the pan with a small sharp knife. Invert the cake onto a wire rack, and carefully turn right side up to cool completely.

7 For the glaze, whisk the confectioners' sugar, cinnamon, salt, cream, and vanilla in a small bowl until smooth. The icing should be thick but spreadable. Add a few droplets of cream if necessary.

8 Place the cake on a cake plate and spread the icing over the top and sides (it will be a thin layer) with a long narrow metal spatula. If desired, sprinkle the top with the chopped pecans. Let stand until the icing sets. Slice with a serrated knife. This cake keeps well, covered, for 2 to 3 days at room temperature.

A GREAT CAKE

*Makes 1
sheet cake,
16 servings*

This moist, spicy, tender cake is great to have on hand for midday nibbling or to serve just about anytime. It is good plain or spread with a thin layer of cream cheese. The amounts of batter and fruit are balanced, with neither one dominating.

3½ cups sifted cake flour

½ teaspoon salt

1 cup dried currants

1 cup golden raisins

1 cup dark raisins

¾ cup (1½ sticks) unsalted butter, at room temperature

2 cups sugar

1½ teaspoons ground cinnamon

1 teaspoon freshly grated nutmeg

½ teaspoon ground mace

Finely grated zest of 1 lemon

1 large egg

4 large eggs, separated

2 tablespoons fresh lemon juice

1 cup sour cream

1 teaspoon baking soda

1 Adjust an oven rack to the lower third position and place a baking stone on the rack if you have one. Preheat the oven to 300°F for about 1 hour. Butter a 13-x-9-inch baking pan and dust it all over lightly with all-purpose flour; knock out the excess flour and set aside.

2 Resift the cake flour with the salt. Combine ¼ cup of the flour mixture with the currants and raisins in a bowl, tossing with your fingers to separate the pieces of fruit and to coat with the flour; set aside.

3 In a large wide bowl, beat the butter with an electric mixer on medium speed until smooth and creamy, about 1 minute. Beat in ¼ cup of the sugar, the cinnamon, nutmeg, mace, and lemon zest, and beat for about 1 minute. Beat in 1½ cups more of the sugar ¼ cup at a time, beating for about 15 seconds after each addition. Scrape the bowl and beaters and beat on medium-high for 5 minutes. Add the whole egg and beat on medium speed for 1 minute. Add the egg yolks one at a time, beating until thoroughly incorporated after each. Beat in the lemon juice. Scrape the bowl and beater.

4 In a small bowl, combine the sour cream with the baking soda. The mixture will become thick and foamy. On low speed, beat the remaining flour

mixture into the egg mixture in 3 additions, alternating with the sour cream mixture, beginning and ending with the flour and mixing only until each addition is incorporated. Scrape the beaters, and stir in the fruit mixture with a wooden spoon or spatula.

5 With clean beaters, beat the egg whites in a medium bowl on medium speed until they form soft peaks. Gradually sprinkle in the remaining $1/4$ cup sugar, beating until the whites curl only slightly at their tips when the beaters are lifted but are not stiff. Add half the whites to the batter and, using a wide rubber spatula, fold them in gently just to begin incorporating; don't be too thorough. Add the remaining whites and gently fold them in only until no whites show. Scrape the batter into the prepared pan and spread evenly with the spatula.

6 Place the pan on the baking stone, or just on the oven rack, and bake for about $1^1/2$ hours, until the cake is well browned and pulls away from the sides of the pan and a toothpick inserted into the center comes out clean. Cool in the pan on a rack for 30 minutes. Cover the pan with a cooling rack and carefully invert the two. Lift off the pan, cover the cake with another rack, and invert again to cool completely.

7 Wrap the cake airtight and let stand overnight before serving.

CURRANT INFORMATION

Pick all the stones, bits of dirt and long stems from the currants. Add one pint of flour to two quarts of currants, and rub well between the hands. This starts the stems and dirt from the fruit. Put about a pint of currants in the flour sieve and rub them until all the flour has passed through; then put them in the colander and shake until the stems have passed through. When all the fruit has been treated in this manner, put it in a large pan of cold water. Wash thoroughly, and drain in the colander. Repeat this operation three times. When the fruit is well drained, spread it on boards or flat dishes and dry in a warm place. Put away in jars.

—Maria Parloa, *Miss Parloa's New Cook Book* (1880)

COMPOSITION CAKE

*Makes 1
sheet cake,
16 to 20
servings*

This fine, light butter cake flavored with brandy was extremely popular in the mid-1800s. The reason for the cake's name is obscure. Some recipes I've found call for no dried fruits, others for double the amount here. Use them or not, as you prefer. They will sink to the bottom of the cake, giving the slices an intriguing look. Be sure that the fruits you use are moist and pliant, not dried out.

4²/₃ cups sifted cake flour

¹/₂ teaspoon baking soda

¹/₂ teaspoon salt

1 whole nutmeg, grated
   (2–2¹/₂ teaspoons)

1 teaspoon ground cinnamon

1 10-ounce box dried currants
   (2 cups)

²/₃ cup dried blueberries

²/₃ cup finely chopped citron

1 cup (2 sticks) unsalted butter,
   at room temperature

2 cups sugar

6 large eggs

1 cup milk

3 tablespoons brandy

2 tablespoons rose water or 1
   tablespoon pure vanilla extract

1 Adjust an oven rack to the lower third position and preheat the oven to 350°F. Butter a 13-x-9-inch baking pan and line the bottom with cooking parchment or waxed paper. Butter the paper, and dust the pan all over with fine dry bread crumbs; knock out the excess crumbs and set aside.

2 Resift the flour with the baking soda, salt, nutmeg, and cinnamon. Combine the currants, blueberries, and citron in a medium bowl. Add ¹/₄ cup of the flour mixture and toss with your fingers to coat each piece of fruit well; set aside.

3 In a large bowl, beat the butter with an electric mixer on medium speed until smooth and creamy, about 1 minute. Beat in the sugar ¹/₄ cup at a time, beating for about 20 seconds after each addition. Scrape the bowl and beaters, then beat on medium-high speed for 5 minutes. Beat in the eggs one at a time, beating for about 30 seconds after each.

4 Combine the milk, brandy, and rose water or vanilla in a 2-cup glass measure or small bowl. On low speed, add the flour mixture to the egg mixture

in 4 additions, alternating with the liquid, beginning and ending with the flour and beating only until each addition is incorporated. Stir in the fruit-flour mixture. Spread the batter evenly in the prepared pan.

5 Bake the cake for about 1 hour and 10 minutes, until it is an even deep brown and springs back when gently pressed and a toothpick inserted into the center comes out clean. Cool in the pan on a wire rack for 20 minutes. Run a small sharp knife around the edges of the pan to release the cake, cover the cake with a large wire rack, and invert the two. Carefully lift off the pan and paper. Cover with another rack and invert again to cool completely. Slice with a sharp serrated knife.

SUPERIOR CITRON

A large fruit, 4 to 9 inches long, the citron is valued for its rind rather than its pulp, and was popular in seventeenth- and eighteenth-century baking. Well-prepared candied citron, which can add so much character to all kinds of baked goods, bears no relation to what we buy today in supermarkets.

The fruit undergoes a lengthy treatment before it can be used in baking. When young, it is dark green, but within three months, it turns yellow. For the desired green color favored by dealers of candied citron, the fruit must be picked when only 5 to 6 inches long. The fruits are halved, the pulp removed, and the rind submerged in seawater or salted water to ferment for about forty days. The brine solution is changed every two weeks. When the citron is ready to be shipped, it is put into a stronger brine solution for its journey from southern Italy or Greece, where it is grown, to its destination—generally England, France, or the United States, where it is candied. Following a desalting, the citron is boiled to soften the peel. Candying takes place in a strong solution of sucrose and glucose, after which the rind is dried in the sun or put up in jars for future use.

See Sources, page 526, for information on superior-quality citron.

EMILY DICKINSON'S BLACK CAKE

Makes 2 loaf cakes, 24 servings

The poet Emily Dickinson prided herself on her skill as a cook. She was especially proud of her fruitcake, jam-packed with currants, raisins, and citron, which she called "black cake." This is a scaled-down version of her recipe, which was baked in a milk pail.

Black Cake, which would be splendid for a wedding cake, is easy to make and keeps well in the refrigerator for several months. It requires long, slow baking. The batter is basically a pound cake with the addition of a little brandy and molasses. Dark raisins are essential to the taste; do not substitute golden raisins.

4 cups (1¼ pounds) dark raisins	½ teaspoon ground cinnamon
1 10-ounce box dried currants (2 cups)	¼ teaspoon ground cloves
1 cup finely diced citron	1 cup (2 sticks) unsalted butter, at room temperature
2¼ cups sifted all-purpose flour	1 cup sugar
Scant ¼ teaspoon baking soda	4 large eggs
Scant ½ teaspoon salt	¼ cup brandy, plus more for brushing
1 teaspoon freshly grated nutmeg	
½ teaspoon ground mace	¼ cup molasses (I use Grandma's)

1 Adjust one oven rack to the middle and one to the lowest position. Preheat the oven to 250°F. Butter two 8½-x-4½-x-2¾-inch loaf pans. Line the bottoms of the pans with parchment or waxed paper, and butter the paper. Set aside. Place a 13-x-9-inch baking pan half-filled with hot tap water on the lower oven rack.

2 In a large bowl, combine the raisins, currants, and citron. Add ¼ cup of the flour and toss the fruits with your fingers to coat well. Set aside. Resift the remaining 2 cups flour with the baking soda, salt, nutmeg, mace, cinnamon, and cloves, and set aside.

3 In a large wide bowl, beat the butter with an electric mixer on medium speed until smooth, about 1 minute. On medium-high speed, beat in the sugar 2 to 3 tablespoons at a time, beating for about 20 seconds after each addition. Scrape the bowl and beaters and beat for 5 minutes.

4 In a 2-cup glass measure or small bowl, beat the eggs with a fork. Beating on low speed, drizzle the eggs into the butter mixture in 2- to 3-tablespoon installments, beating until each addition is thoroughly incorporated before adding the next. The batter may look curdled. Scrape the bowl and beat for about 3 minutes; the batter should be smooth and fluffy. Scrape the bowl and beater well.

5 On low speed, add the flour mixture in 3 additions, alternating with the brandy, beginning and ending with the flour and beating only until each addition is thoroughly incorporated. Beat in the molasses.

6 Scatter a handful of the fruits over the batter and stir them in with a wooden spoon until each piece is well coated. Continue adding the fruits a handful at a time, making sure to stir until well coated before adding the next installment. (If you add the fruits too fast, they will tend to stick together in clumps.) The batter will be very stiff once all the fruits are in. Spoon the batter into the prepared pans, then press down with a rubber spatula to remove any air pockets.

7 Place the pans on the middle oven rack and bake for 2 hours. Remove the pan of water and bake the cakes for another 1 to 1 1/2 hours, until they spring back when gently pressed and a toothpick inserted into the center comes out clean. Place the pans on a wire rack and cool completely.

8 Run a thin-bladed sharp knife around the edges of the cakes to release them, and invert the pans onto a countertop. If the cakes don't fall out right away, rap the pans sharply on the counter. Lift off the pans, and peel the paper off the cakes. This cake is far easier to cut when cold: Wrap each cake in plastic wrap and then in foil, and refrigerate them. If you want your cakes to have a little kick, brush them with a spoonful or two of brandy before wrapping them.

9 To serve, place each cake with its bottom side up on a cutting board, and cut into thin slices with a sharp serrated knife. The cakes will keep for up to 3 months in the refrigerator, or they can be frozen for 6 to 8 months.

IRISH WHISKEY FRUITCAKE WITH SPICED WALNUTS AND PECANS

Makes 1 large loaf cake, 16 servings

This terrific cake is packed with dried fruits and nuts, with just enough batter to hold everything together. Feel free to use your favorite dried fruits. However, *never* use any artificially colored and syrupy fruits (such as candied cherries, candied pineapple, and inferior-quality citron, the kinds you're apt to find in supermarkets). The fruits must be soaked in whiskey for at least 24 hours, and the cake should age in the refrigerator for at least a couple of days before eating, so plan accordingly.

FRUIT

- 8 ounces (12–14 dates) pitted Medjool dates, quartered
- 8 ounces Black Mission figs, stems removed, halved
- 8 ounces dried apricots, halved
- 8 ounces dried sour cherries
- 2 cups Irish whiskey

NUTS

- 3 tablespoons unsalted butter
- 2 tablespoons sugar
- 1 tablespoon pumpkin pie spice
- 1/4 teaspoon salt
- 1 generous cup walnut halves or large pieces
- 1 generous cup pecan halves

CAKE BATTER

- 6 tablespoons (3/4 stick) unsalted butter, at room temperature
- 1/2 teaspoon salt
- 3/4 cup sugar
- 2 teaspoons pure vanilla extract Finely grated zest of 1 orange
- 3 large eggs
- 1 whole nutmeg, grated (2–2 1/2 teaspoons)
- 3/4 cup sifted all-purpose flour

1 For the fruit, combine the fruits and whiskey in a 2-quart jar with a screw-top or a 1-gallon zip-top bag. Let stand at room temperature for at least 24 hours, preferably 2 or 3 days, turning the jar or bag several times a day.

2 For the nuts, melt the butter in a heavy 10-inch skillet over medium heat. Add the sugar, pumpkin pie spice, and salt and cook, stirring, for 1 to 2 minutes until aromatic. Add the nuts and continue to cook, stirring, for another

3 to 5 minutes, until they are coated; watch closely so they don't burn. Remove from the heat and set aside, stirring occasionally, until completely cool. (The nuts can be stored airtight at room temperature for up to 1 week.)

3 Turn the fruits and liquor into a large wire strainer set over a bowl and set aside for 1 to 2 hours to drain well. (You'll have about $1/2$ cup of syrupy liquor: mix with white wine—about 2 teaspoons per glass—for a delicious aperitif.)

4 Adjust an oven rack to the lower third position and preheat the oven to 300°F. Butter a 10-x-4$1/2$-x-3-inch or 9-x-5-x-3-inch nonstick loaf pan, or coat with cooking spray. Dust the inside of the pan all over with flour, knock out the excess, and set aside.

5 For the batter, in a large bowl, beat the butter and salt with an electric mixer on medium speed until smooth, about 1 minute. Gradually beat in the sugar a few tablespoons at a time, then beat for 2 to 3 minutes. Add the vanilla and orange zest and beat for 1 minute. Beat in the eggs one at a time, beating for 1 minute after each. Scrape the bowl and beaters as necessary.

6 On low speed, add the nutmeg and then the flour, beating only until incorporated. Using a rubber spatula, stir the drained fruits into the batter in 2 or 3 additions, mixing thoroughly. Add the nuts and stir them in well. The batter will be very thick. Place the batter a little at a time in the prepared pan, pressing each addition tightly with the spatula to remove air pockets. Bang the pan on the countertop to settle the batter further, and smooth the top with the spatula.

7 Bake for 2 to 2$1/4$ hours, until the cake is golden brown and springs back when gently pressed and a toothpick inserted into the center comes out clean. Lay a piece of foil loosely on top of the cake during the last 30 minutes to prevent it from overbrowning. Cool in the pan on a wire rack for 30 minutes. Run a thin-bladed sharp knife all around the cake to release it, and cover the cake with a wire rack. Invert the cake, carefully lift off the pan, and cool the cake completely upside down.

8 Wrap the cake securely in plastic wrap and refrigerate for at least 1 day before serving. To serve, use a sharp serrated knife and cut the cake (bottom side up) into thin slices. The cake keeps well in the refrigerator for 2 to 3 weeks, or you can freeze it for up to 6 months.

PRUNE AND WALNUT LOAF

*Makes 1
large loaf
cake, 12
servings*

Prunes add moistness and great flavor to this loaf. Walnuts are a natural mate for the prunes. I like a mixture of English (ordinary) and black walnuts. The latter add a delicious smokiness. Make this a day ahead to allow the flavors and texture to mature.

$1^2/_3$ cups all-purpose flour

$^1/_4$ teaspoon baking soda

$^1/_2$ teaspoon salt

$^1/_2$ teaspoon ground cinnamon

1 whole nutmeg, grated
    (2–$2^1/_2$ teaspoons)

1 cup moist dried prunes, each
    cut with scissors into 6 pieces

2 cups (8 ounces) walnuts, a
    mixture of English and black
    walnuts or all English walnuts,
    coarsely chopped

8 tablespoons (1 stick) unsalted
    butter, at room temperature

2 teaspoons pure lemon extract

$1^1/_2$ cups sugar

2 large eggs

$^1/_2$ cup buttermilk

1 Adjust an oven rack to the lower third position and preheat the oven to 350°F. Butter a 10-x-4$^1/_2$-x-3-inch or 9-x-5-x-3-inch loaf pan, or coat with cooking spray, and dust all over with flour. Knock out the excess flour and set aside.

2 Sift the $1^2/_3$ cups flour with the baking soda, salt, cinnamon, and nutmeg. Combine the prunes and walnuts in a bowl, add 1 tablespoon of the flour mixture, and toss with your fingers to coat. Set aside.

3 In a large bowl, beat the butter with an electric mixer on medium speed until smooth, about 1 minute. Beat in the lemon extract and $^1/_4$ cup of the sugar, then beat on medium-high speed for 1 minute. Beat in the remaining $1^1/_4$ cups sugar about $^1/_4$ cup at a time, beating for 20 to 30 seconds after each addition. Scrape the bowl and beaters and beat for 4 minutes. Beat in the eggs one at a time, beating for 1 minute after each.

4 On low speed, add half the flour mixture, beating only until incorporated.

Slowly add the buttermilk and beat only until smooth. Add the remaining flour and beat only until it's incorporated. Scrape the bowl and beaters. Add the prunes and walnuts, stirring them in with a rubber spatula. Spoon the mixture into the prepared pan, packing it into the corners, and smooth the top.

5 Bake for 1 hour to 1 hour and 10 minutes, until the loaf is well browned and a toothpick inserted into the center comes out clean. Cool in the pan on a wire rack for 20 minutes. Run a thin sharp knife all around the sides to release the loaf, cover with a rack, and invert the two. Remove the pan, place the loaf right side up on the rack, and cool completely.

6 Wrap the cake airtight and let stand overnight before serving. Cut into thin slices with a sharp serrated knife. The cake keeps well at room temperature for several days, or it can be frozen for up to 2 months.

NAME GAME

We may well owe Louis Pellier, a homesick French gold prospector in California, a huge thank-you for bringing his beloved fruit, the prune, from France to the United States. His brother, Pierre, started things by making the 9,200-mile journey by ship from California to France and back again in 1853; in France, he stuck cuttings of the famous prune d'Agen into raw potatoes, packed them in sawdust, and put them into two leather trunks for the long return voyage. In California, Louis grafted the living cuttings to rootstocks of wild plum trees native to the Santa Clara Valley. Seven years later, in 1863, he proudly exhibited his dried French prunes at the State Fair in Sacramento. By 1870, 650 acres were under cultivation, and by 1890, plum trees occupied 90,000 acres of California. Today, California produces 70 percent of the world's prunes.

Prune is the French word for plum, and the fruit, best when dried, became known in this country as prune. Over time, of course, prunes lost their romantic Gallic associations and became the brunt of jokes. To reverse that trend and get them some respect, the image makers proposed renaming the prune "dried plum." And that's exactly what the California Prune Board—er, Dried Plum Board—has done.

POPPY SEED CAKE

Makes 1 large loaf cake, 12 to 16 servings

Seed cake, a pound cake–like cake usually made with caraway seeds, was quite popular throughout the 1800s. In the 1900s, however, the cake went out of favor, probably because Americans lost their taste for caraway. This recipe uses a combination of poppy seeds and anise seeds. If you like caraway, feel free to add 1 tablespoon of the seeds. Generous amounts of orange and lemon zest gives the cake a fresh-fruit taste, reinforced by the orange and lemon juice in the glaze. Make the cake a day ahead, as its taste and texture improve on standing.

CAKE

- 3 cups sifted all-purpose flour
- 2 teaspoons baking powder, preferably nonaluminum
- $1/2$ teaspoon salt
- 1 teaspoon freshly grated nutmeg
- $3/4$ cup ($1 1/2$ sticks) unsalted butter, at room temperature
- 2 cups sugar
  Finely grated zest of 1 large lemon
  Finely grated zest of 1 large orange
- 4 large eggs
- 1 cup milk
- 2 tablespoons poppy seeds
- 1 tablespoon anise seeds

GLAZE

- $1 1/4$ cups confectioners' sugar
- 1 tablespoon fresh orange juice
- 1 tablespoon fresh lemon juice

1 For the cake, adjust an oven rack to the lower third position and preheat the oven to 350°F. Butter a 9-x-3-inch tube pan. Line the bottom with waxed paper or cooking parchment, butter the paper, and dust the pan all over with fine dry bread crumbs. Knock out the excess crumbs and set aside.

2 Resift the flour with the baking powder, salt, and nutmeg; set aside.

3 In a large bowl, beat the butter with an electric mixer on medium speed until smooth, about 1 minute. Beat in the sugar about $1/4$ cup at a time, beating for 15 to 20 seconds after each addition. Scrape the bowl and beaters, add the lemon and orange zests, and beat on medium-high speed for 5 minutes. Beat in the eggs one at a time, beating well after each.

4 On low speed, add the flour mixture in 3 additions, alternating with the milk, beginning and ending with the flour and beating after each only until incorporated. Stop to scrape the bowl and beaters as necessary. Stir in the seeds. Scrape the batter into the prepared pan and smooth the top.

5 Bake for 60 to 65 minutes, until the cake is well browned and springs back when gently pressed and a toothpick inserted into the center comes out clean. Cool the cake in its pan on a wire rack for 20 minutes. Cover with another rack and invert. Lift off the pan and paper. Set the cake on the rack over a rimmed baking sheet and let stand for 15 to 20 minutes, until the cake feels just warm. (The cake can be frozen, unglazed, for up to 1 month.)

6 For the glaze, whisk together the confectioners' sugar, orange juice, and lemon juice in a small bowl until smooth. Use a teaspoon to spoon and spread the glaze evenly all over the top of the warm cake, letting the excess drizzle down the sides. Let stand until completely cool.

7 Carefully transfer the cake to a cake plate. (The best way to do this is to use a cookie sheet that has only one rim, using it as a spatula, sliding it under the cake and then slowly sliding the cake off the sheet onto a cake plate.) Cover with a cake dome or inverted bowl and let stand overnight before serving. The cake keeps at room temperature for 3 to 4 days.

PERSIMMON LOAF

Makes 1 large loaf cake, 12 servings

Hachiya persimmons, usually available from mid-October through December, are an underused and undervalued fruit. The bright orange, smooth, slippery sweet pulp is delicious all by itself, and it is terrific in all sorts of baked goods as well. Be sure to use very ripe fruit: it should feel squishy to the touch, and the stem should be dry and brownish in color. Underripe fruit is hopelessly astringent and will not do. This loaf is loaded with dates and pecans, and it is mildly spiced so as not to obscure the persimmon's unique sweetness. It's best if made a day ahead. Cut into thick slices and serve it plain, or slather it with cream cheese.

1½ cups pecan halves or large
    pieces
4–5 very ripe Hachiya persimmons
2 cups sifted all-purpose flour
1 teaspoon baking powder,
    preferably nonaluminum
½ teaspoon baking soda
½ teaspoon salt
1 teaspoon ground cinnamon
½ teaspoon ground mace

⅛ teaspoon ground cloves
2 large eggs
1 cup sugar
½ cup firmly packed dark brown
    sugar
2 teaspoons pure vanilla extract
⅓ cup vegetable oil
8 ounces pitted dates, cut into
    ½-inch pieces

1 Adjust an oven rack to the lower third position and preheat the oven to 350°F. Butter a 10-x-4½-x-3-inch or 9-x-5-x-3-inch loaf pan, or coat with cooking spray. Dust the pan all over with flour, knock out the excess, and set aside.

2 Place the pecans on a shallow baking sheet and toast in the oven, stirring occasionally, for about 10 minutes, until they give off a roasty aroma and barely turn light tan. Set aside to cool completely.

3 Pluck the stems off the persimmons, and cut them lengthwise in half. Use a grapefruit spoon or teaspoon to scoop the pulp from the skin. Place the pulp into a medium bowl and break it up with a pastry blender. You want a puree with some texture, so leave a few small lumps. Measure 1½ cups and set aside.

4 Resift the flour with the baking powder, baking soda, salt, cinnamon, mace, and cloves; set aside.

5 In a large bowl, beat the eggs with an electric mixer on high speed for 1 to 2 minutes, until slightly thickened. Beat in both sugars and the vanilla, and beat for 3 to 4 minutes until very thick. Reduce the speed to medium and slowly drizzle in the oil in a thin stream, as though you were making mayonnaise, until thoroughly incorporated. Scrape the bowl, and beat on high speed for 1 minute. Add the persimmon puree and beat on medium speed for 1 minute.

6 On low speed, gradually add the dry ingredients, beating only until thoroughly incorporated. Scrape the beaters. With a rubber spatula, stir in the dates, then the pecans. Scrape the batter into the prepared pan and smooth the top.

7 Bake for 1 hour to 1 hour and 15 minutes, until the loaf is well browned and springs back when gently pressed and a toothpick inserted into the center comes out clean. Cool in the pan on a wire rack for 20 minutes. Run a knife around the sides of the pan to release the cake, and unmold the cake onto a wire rack. Turn the loaf and cool it completely.

8 Cut into portions with a sharp serrated knife. Wrapped airtight, this loaf keeps well for up to 1 week at room temperature; or freeze it for up to 1 month.

TOASTED ALMOND LOAF

Makes 1 large loaf cake, 10 to 12 servings

Blanched almonds add texture to this egg-rich, fine-grained loaf. Cakes like this became popular in the early part of the twentieth century, once baking powder gained a firm foothold in home kitchens. Serve the cake at a brunch or as a mid-morning or afternoon snack, or keep it around to nibble on anytime. Make it a day ahead so the flavors can mellow.

$^3/_4$ cup slivered almonds

2$^1/_4$ cups sifted cake flour

1 teaspoon baking powder, preferably nonaluminum

$^1/_4$ teaspoon salt

8 tablespoons (1 stick) unsalted butter, at room temperature

1 cup plus 1 tablespoon sugar

1 teaspoon pure almond extract

5 large eggs

1 Adjust an oven rack to the lower third position and preheat the oven to 350°F. Butter a 10-x-4$^1/_2$-x-3-inch or 9-x-5-x-3-inch loaf pan and dust it all over with flour. Knock out the excess flour and set aside.

2 Put the almonds in a shallow baking pan and toast them, stirring once or twice, for 8 to 10 minutes, until aromatic and golden brown. Immediately transfer them to a cutting surface, spread them out in a single layer, and let them cool completely. Use a chef's knife to chop the nuts into medium-fine pieces, and set aside.

3 Resift the cake flour with the baking powder and salt; set aside.

4 In a large bowl, beat the butter with an electric mixer on medium speed until smooth, about 1 minute. Beat in the 1 cup sugar $^1/_4$ cup at a time, beating for about 20 seconds after each addition. Add the almond extract, then beat for 3 minutes on medium-high speed. Scrape the bowl and beaters. Beat in the eggs one at a time, beating well after each. Scrape the bowl and beaters.

5 On low speed, gradually add the flour mixture, beating only until the batter is smooth. Stir in the almonds. Spoon the batter into the prepared pan and smooth the top. Sprinkle with the remaining 1 tablespoon sugar.

6 Bake for 50 to 60 minutes, until the cake is golden brown and a toothpick inserted into the center comes out clean. The cake will be domed in the center, and it may have a crack or two on top. Cool in the pan on a wire rack for 20 minutes. Run a small sharp knife around the sides of the pan to release the cake, and unmold the cake onto a wire rack. Turn the loaf right side up and cool completely.

7 Wrap the cooled cake airtight and let stand overnight before serving. Cut into thin slices with a serrated knife.

COCONUT LOAF

Makes 1 large loaf cake, 16 servings

This is a delicate, tender, not-too-sweet golden butter cake. It has chopped shredded coconut and pure coconut extract (see page 527 for sources) for that real coconut taste. A slice of it is a wonderful thing to eat in mid-afternoon with a steaming cup of tea or coffee. You can also top slices of the cake with scoops of ice cream and fruit or butterscotch sauce.

2 cups sifted unbleached all-purpose flour	Finely grated zest of 1 lemon
1½ teaspoons baking powder, preferably nonaluminum	1 teaspoon pure coconut extract
¼ teaspoon salt	4 large eggs, separated
8 tablespoons (1 stick) unsalted butter, at room temperature	2 tablespoons fresh lemon juice
1 cup sugar	½ cup milk
	1 cup (3½ ounces) chopped shredded coconut, preferably unsweetened

1 Adjust an oven rack to the lower third position and preheat the oven to 350°F. Butter or grease a 10-x-4½-x-3-inch or 9-x-5-x-3-inch loaf pan, or coat with cooking spray. Dust it all over lightly with flour, knock out the excess flour, and set aside.

2 Resift the 2 cups flour with the baking powder and salt; set aside.

3 In a large bowl, beat the butter with an electric mixer on medium speed until very smooth, about 1 minute. Reserve 2 tablespoons of the sugar to beat with the egg whites. Beat in the remaining sugar 2 to 3 tablespoons at a time, beating for about 20 seconds after each addition. Scrape the bowl, add the lemon zest and coconut extract, and beat on medium-high speed for 4 to 5 minutes, until the mixture is very pale and fluffy-looking. Beat in the egg yolks one at a time, beating for about 30 seconds after each addition. Beat in the lemon juice.

4 On low speed, add the flour mixture in 3 additions, alternating with the milk, beginning and ending with the flour and beating only until smooth. Scrape the bowl and beaters. Stir in the coconut with a rubber spatula. The batter will be thick.

5 With clean beaters, beat the egg whites in a medium bowl on medium speed until they form very soft peaks. Beat in the reserved 2 tablespoons sugar. Continue beating for a minute or so, until the whites form shiny, upright peaks that curl a bit at their tips when the beaters are raised; do not overbeat. Stir about $^1/_4$ of the whites into the batter to lighten it, then fold in the remaining whites gently just until no whites show. Spread the batter in the prepared pan.

6 Bake for 50 to 60 minutes, until the loaf is golden brown and has a few cracks on top and a toothpick inserted into the center comes out clean. Cool in the pan on a rack for 15 minutes. Run a sharp knife all around the cake to release it and carefully unmold it onto a cooling rack to cool completely.

7 Wrapped airtight, the cake keeps quite fresh at room temperature for several days; it freezes well for about 1 month. Cut into portions with a serrated knife.

CASHING IN

In 1895, Franklin Baker, a Philadelphia miller, received a shipment of coconuts from Cuba instead of cash as payment for his flour. At a loss for what to do with them, Baker searched for coconut dealers in Philadelphia, but he found only one. That enterprise was failing, however, and the dealer was unable to purchase them.

In a moment of inspiration, Baker decided to buy the fellow out. Not knowing anything about the business but recognizing how tedious coconuts were to prepare for cooking, Baker believed he could create a demand for a product that was ready to use. He installed special crackers, peelers, and shredders in his mill. Then he packaged the coconut and marketed it to grocers. It became an instant bestseller, and Baker's Coconut is a hit to this day.

CHEWY BUTTERSCOTCH LOAF

Makes 1 sheet cake, 12 servings

I adapted this unusual and easy-to-make cake from a Pillsbury's Bake-Off contest, where it won $7,500 in 1954—big bucks for a fabulous chewy pecan and butterscotch sheet cake. The cooked brown sugar–butter combination gives the cake an especially rich taste. This moist cake is wonderful all by itself, but it is splendid served with vanilla ice cream or lightly sweetened whipped cream. It is best when very fresh.

2 cups (8 ounces) coarsely chopped or broken pecans	1 teaspoon instant espresso powder (I use Medaglia d'Oro)
1½ cups sifted all-purpose flour	2 cups firmly packed dark brown sugar
1 teaspoon baking powder, preferably nonaluminum	2 tablespoons unsalted butter, cut into a few pieces
¼ teaspoon salt	2 teaspoons pure vanilla extract
4 large eggs	

1 Adjust an oven rack to the center position and preheat the oven to 350°F. Butter a 13-x-9-inch baking pan and dust with flour. Knock out the excess and set aside.

2 Place the pecans in a single layer in a shallow baking pan and toast, stirring occasionally, for about 10 minutes, until they smell toasty and just begin to color lightly. Set aside to cool to room temperature.

3 Resift the flour with the baking powder and salt; set aside.

4 Pour enough water into the bottom of a 2-quart double boiler so that when you put the top part in, the water just touches the bottom. Remove the top part of the double boiler. Set the bottom part over high heat and bring the water to a rolling boil. If you don't have a double boiler, use a medium metal bowl set into a large saucepan of water.

5 Meanwhile, whisk the eggs in the top of the double boiler (or medium bowl) just to combine the yolks and whites. Add the instant espresso, and gradually whisk in the brown sugar until smooth. Add the butter. When the water is boiling, place the top part in place and stir constantly with a heatproof rubber spatula for about 5 minutes, going all around the sides

and across the bottom of the pan, until the mixture feels hot to a fingertip. Remove the top of the double boiler or bowl, immediately add all the dry ingredients, and whisk until smooth. With a rubber spatula, stir in the vanilla and nuts. Spread the batter evenly in the prepared pan.

6 Bake for about 25 minutes, until the cake springs back a little when gently pressed; do not overbake. Cool in the pan on a wire rack.

7 When the cake is completely cool, cut into portions with a sharp knife. The cake can be frozen for up to 1 month.

WHO PUT THE SCOTCH IN BUTTERSCOTCH?

The word "butterscotch" first made its way into print in 1855. The tenth edition of *Merriam Webster's Collegiate Dictionary* defines it as "a candy made from brown sugar, butter, corn syrup, and water." So where did the "scotch" come from? *The Oxford English Dictionary,* which doesn't include an entry for butterscotch, does have almost two pages of definitions for scotch. The very first one, derived around 1450, is "an incision, cut, score, or gash." Recipes for butterscotch candy instruct the cook to pour the cooked mixture onto a surface and, while it is still warm, score it into pieces. Once the candy is cool, it is broken into individual servings along those lines. Could that be how it got its name?

Whatever the origin of the name, butterscotch is not to be confused with caramel, which is sugar cooked with water, not butter or cream, and therefore less rich and lacking the butteriness of butterscotch.

GOOD AS GOLD SHEET CAKE

Makes 1 sheet cake, 16 servings

This is a tender vanilla-flavored cake that will melt in your mouth. It's great to serve at a kids' party. You can substitute 1 teaspoon pure orange or lemon extract for the vanilla, and add the finely grated zest of an orange or lemon, beating them into the creamed butter and sugar mixture. I adapted both the cake and icing recipes from *Meta Given's Modern Encyclopedia of Cooking* (1959). Serve plain or with vanilla ice cream.

CAKE

- 2 1/2 cups sifted cake flour
- 1 1/2 teaspoons baking powder, preferably nonaluminum
- 1/2 teaspoon salt
- 1 cup large egg yolks (about 12)
- 3/4 cup (1 1/2 sticks) unsalted butter, at room temperature
- 1 1/2 cups sugar
- 2 teaspoons pure vanilla extract
- 3/4 cup milk

FROSTING

- 2 cups confectioners' sugar
- 1/3 cup Dutch-process cocoa
- Pinch of salt
- 4 tablespoons (1/2 stick) unsalted butter, at room temperature
- 6 tablespoons heavy cream
- 1 teaspoon pure vanilla extract

1 For the cake, adjust an oven rack to the lower third position and preheat the oven to 350°F. Butter a 13-x-9-inch baking pan. Line the pan with cooking parchment or waxed paper, butter the paper, and dust only the bottom of the pan with all-purpose flour. Knock out the excess; set aside.

2 Resift the flour with the baking powder and salt; set aside.

3 In a large bowl, beat the egg yolks with an electric mixer on high for 3 to 5 minutes, until they are very thick and pale and form a slowly dissolving ribbon when the beater is raised. Scrape the yolks into a medium bowl and set aside. (Don't bother to wash the large bowl.)

4 Add the butter to the large bowl and beat on medium speed until very smooth, about 1 minute. Beat in 1/4 cup of the sugar and the vanilla and beat for 1 minute. Scrape the bowl and beaters. Add the remaining 1 1/4 cups sugar 1/4 cup at a time, beating for about 20 seconds after each addition. Scrape the bowl and beaters and beat on medium-high speed for 5 minutes. The mixture will be very light and fluffy. Beat in the egg yolks on medium speed in 4 additions, beating for about 30 seconds after the first 3 additions and for 1 minute after the last one. Scrape the bowl and beaters.

5 On low speed, add the flour mixture in 4 additions, alternating with the milk, beginning and ending with the flour and beating only until thoroughly incorporated. The batter will be thick and smooth and resemble fluffy whipped cream. Spread the batter evenly in the prepared pan.

6 Bake for 30 to 35 minutes, until the cake is well browned and springs back when gently pressed and a toothpick inserted into the center comes out clean; do not overbake. Cool in the pan on a wire rack for 15 minutes (it will settle). Run a sharp knife all around the cake to release it, cover with a wire rack, and invert the two. Remove the pan and paper. Replace the paper on the bottom of the cake, cover the cake with another rack, and invert again to cool completely (the paper will prevent the cake from sticking to the rack).

7 For the frosting, whisk the confectioners' sugar, cocoa, and salt in a small bowl until thoroughly combined. Beat the butter in a medium bowl with an electric mixer until smooth and creamy. Alternately add the cocoa mixture and the cream in 3 additions, beginning with the cocoa mixture and ending with the cream and beating until smooth after each addition. Beat in the vanilla. The frosting should be thick and smooth.

8 Scrape the frosting into a small heavy saucepan, set the pan over low heat, and stir almost constantly with a rubber spatula, scraping the bottom, for about 5 minutes, until the frosting darkens uniformly and thins out a little. It should be warm, but never hot. Remove from the heat and set aside for 5 to 10 minutes, stirring occasionally, until thick and creamy and spreadable.

9 To frost the cake, cover the cake (still on a cooling rack) with a wire rack and invert the two. Carefully peel the paper off the cake. Place a rectangular serving plate on the cake and invert again. With a narrow metal spatula, spread a thin layer of frosting around the sides of the cake, using about one third of the frosting. Scrape the remaining frosting on top of the cake and spread it smoothly and evenly. It will be a thin layer. Let the cake stand until the frosting is set, then cut into portions with a sharp knife.

KENTUCKY CHOCOLATE SHEET CAKE

*Makes 1
sheet cake,
12 to 16
servings*

This is a rich, chocolaty cake with a silky smooth chocolate frosting made with a food processor. I've adapted the recipe from one in my book *Food Processor Cooking Quick and Easy* (Ten Speed Press, 1992). If you are concerned about egg safety, see page 272 for how to prepare raw eggs for the frosting.

CAKE

- 2 cups sifted cake flour
- 1 teaspoon baking soda
- ¼ teaspoon salt
- 4 ounces (4 squares) unsweetened chocolate, coarsely chopped
- ½ cup boiling water
- ½ cup ice water
- ½ cup buttermilk
- 2 cups sugar
- 2 large eggs
- 1 teaspoon pure vanilla extract
- 8 tablespoons (1 stick) unsalted butter, cut into 6 pieces, at room temperature

FROSTING

- 3 ounces (3 squares) unsweetened chocolate
- ⅔ cup sugar
- 6 tablespoons (¾ stick) unsalted butter, cut into 6 pieces, at room temperature
- 1 teaspoon pure vanilla extract
- 2 large eggs

1 For the cake, adjust an oven rack to the center position and preheat the oven to 350°F. Butter a 13-x-9-inch baking pan, or coat with cooking spray, dust it lightly with flour, and knock out the excess flour; set aside.

2 Resift the cake flour with the baking soda and salt; set aside.

3 Put the chocolate in a food processor and process until finely chopped, about 1 minute. With the machine running, add the boiling water and process for 30 seconds. Stop to scrape the work bowl. The mixture should be smooth and the chocolate completely melted; if necessary, process for a few seconds longer. With the machine on, add the ice water and process for 5 seconds. Add the buttermilk and process for a few seconds. Transfer to a 2-cup measure or a small bowl and set aside to cool completely. (Don't wash the processor bowl.)

4 Add the sugar, eggs, and vanilla to the food processor, and process for 1 minute. Add the butter and process until smooth, about 1 minute. Add the cooled chocolate mixture and process for 10 seconds. The batter will be very thin. Scrape the work bowl well, and spoon the flour mixture in a ring on top of the batter. Pulse the machine very rapidly 4 times, less than a second each; the blade should stop rotating between pulses. Scrape the work bowl well and pulse rapidly 2 more times. If the dry ingredients are not completely incorporated, stir them in with a rubber spatula. The batter may not appear completely smooth, and it will be slightly thicker than heavy cream. Scrape the batter into the prepared pan and let stand at room temperature for 5 minutes.

5 Bake the cake for 30 to 35 minutes, until the top springs back when gently pressed, the edges just begin to pull away from the sides of the pan, and a toothpick inserted into the center has a few chocolate crumbs sticking to it; do not overbake. Cool the cake in its pan on a wire rack for 10 minutes. Run a thin-bladed sharp knife all around the sides to release the cake, cover the pan with a wire rack, and invert the two. Remove the pan, cover the cake with another wire rack, and invert again to cool completely.

6 For the frosting, melt the chocolate in the top of a double boiler or in a small saucepan set into a larger pan of hot water over medium heat, stirring occasionally. When the chocolate is melted, remove the pan from the water and set it aside to cool slightly.

7 Put the sugar, butter, vanilla, and 1 of the eggs into the food processor. Process for 2 minutes, stopping every 30 seconds to scrape the work bowl. Add the remaining egg and process for 30 seconds more. Add the melted chocolate and process for 30 seconds. Scrape the work bowl and process again for a few seconds, until the frosting is very smooth and creamy. The sugar should be completely dissolved: rub a bit of the frosting between your fingers to be sure, and, if necessary, process for a few seconds longer. The frosting thickens as it stands. Use as soon as it is of spreading consistency.

8 Invert the cooled cake onto a serving platter. Spread most of the frosting thickly on top of the cake, and use the remainder for just a thin layer on the sides. Let stand until the frosting has set, about 1 hour, then cut into portions with a sharp knife. Store covered at room temperature.

6 Cupcakes and Cream Puffs

Cup Cake

Take four cups of flour, three of sugar, one of melted butter, one of sour cream, with a teaspoonful of saleratus dissolved in it, and three eggs; season it with brandy and nutmeg; mix and bake it as pound cake.

—Elizabeth Ellicott Lea, *Domestic Cookery* (1853)

Notice anything unusual about the above recipe? It's called "cup cake" but it's baked in a single pan. Many nineteenth-century cookbooks contained recipes for "cup cakes," but the name almost always meant that the ingredients were measured in cups, rather than weighed. This measuring undoubtedly saved the housewife time, since she could simply dip her cup into the ingredients instead of weighing them on a balance scale.

However ordinary that act may sound, it signified a revolutionary shift. By the late 1880s, the American housewife had converted from weighing to measuring. All the recipes for baked goods in *Mrs. Rorer's Philadelphia Cook Book* (1886) and those in *Miss Parloa's Kitchen Companion* (1887) forsake the scale in favor of the cup. But in 1902, Mrs. Rorer gave a recipe for Sponge Cups, a true cupcake complete with icing. From then on, cupcakes appeared regularly in cookbooks, though not necessarily named as such. Chocolate Nut Cakes from *Lowney's Cook Book* (1907–1908) are baked in "gem pans"—cast-iron muffin cups, by then a common household pan. In 1924, Ida Bailey Allen's *Modern Cook Book* provided nine specific recipes for cupcakes, which she says to bake in "small well-oiled pans." Cupcakes had finally been accorded independent status as a bona fide American dessert!

CUPCAKE TIPS

1. When a recipe makes more than 12 cupcakes, use either a 12-cup muffin pan and a 6-cup pan or two 12-cup pans. A 12-cup pan and a 6-cup pan will fit on one oven rack. Adjust two racks to divide the oven into thirds if using two 12-cup pans. Line the number of cups you need with cupcake liners, leaving the remaining cups empty. If using two 12-cup pans, rotate the pans from top to bottom halfway during baking.

2. When mixing, beat only enough to incorporate so as not to toughen the cupcakes.

3. To fill the cupcake liners, use two regular soupspoons, one to pick up the batter and the other to push it off into the cup. Fill to the recommended level.

4. To prevent overbaking, check for doneness at the minimum baking time.

CHOCOLATE CUPCAKES WITH CHOCOLATE FROSTING

Makes 12 cupcakes

Some of the earliest cupcake recipes included chocolate. Once bakers discovered how sensational it was, they used it in all kinds of cakes and pastries. These chocolate cupcakes get their rich flavor from cocoa. Dutch-process (alkalized) cocoa gives a more intense chocolate taste than nonalkalized, but I've made these with regular cocoa, and they come out just fine. The frosting, made in an unusual way, is especially smooth and creamy. Pack these into kids' lunch boxes or keep them for nibbling after school.

CUPCAKES

- 1^1/$_4$ cups sifted all-purpose flour
- ^{1}/$_2$ teaspoon baking soda
- ^{1}/$_4$ teaspoon salt
- ^{1}/$_4$ cup Dutch-process cocoa
- 6 tablespoons (^{3}/$_4$ stick) unsalted butter, at room temperature
- ^{3}/$_4$ cup sugar
- 1 teaspoon pure vanilla extract
- 2 large eggs
- ^{1}/$_2$ cup milk

FROSTING

- 1 tablespoon unsalted butter
- ^{1}/$_4$ cup sugar
- 1 ounce (1 square) unsweetened chocolate, chopped
- ^{1}/$_4$ cup evaporated milk
- 1 teaspoon pure vanilla extract
- 1^1/$_2$ cups confectioners' sugar

1 For the cupcakes, adjust an oven rack to the center position and preheat the oven to 350°F. Line a 12-cup muffin pan with paper liners; set aside.

2 Resift the flour with the baking soda, salt, and cocoa; set aside.

3 In a medium bowl, beat the butter on medium speed with an electric mixer until smooth, about 1 minute. Add the sugar and vanilla and beat on medium-high speed for 3 to 4 minutes, until smooth and fluffy; stop to scrape the bowl as necessary. Beat in the eggs one at a time, beating for about 1 minute after each.

4 With a rubber spatula, stir in about one third of the flour mixture, just until incorporated. Gently stir in half the milk. Stir in half the remaining flour

mixture, then the rest of the milk, and finally the last of the flour, stirring after each addition just to combine well. Divide the batter evenly among the muffin cups; each cup will be about half full. Don't bother to smooth the batter; it will level itself during baking.

5 Bake for 22 to 25 minutes, until the cupcakes spring back when their centers are gently pressed; do not overbake. Cool for 5 minutes in the pan, then remove from the pan and cool completely on a wire rack before frosting.

6 Meanwhile, for the frosting, melt the butter in a small heavy saucepan over medium heat. Add the sugar and chocolate and cook for 3 minutes over medium heat, stirring constantly with a small heatproof rubber spatula. Add the evaporated milk about 1 tablespoon at a time, stirring constantly. Remove from the heat and set aside until completely cool.

7 Add the vanilla to the chocolate mixture. Gradually stir in the confectioners' sugar to make a thick, creamy frosting. Frost each cupcake generously. Let stand for 30 minutes for the frosting to set before serving.

CHOCOLATE-FROSTED COCONUT CUPCAKES

Makes 12 cupcakes

In the nineteenth century, coconut was extremely popular in all sorts of baked goods, from cookies to fancy cakes, but I never came across a recipe for coconut cupcakes. Here I'm using coconut in three ways: a pure extract, coconut milk, and shredded coconut. Coconut lovers of the world, these dainty treats are for you! A luscious chocolate sour cream icing tops the cupcakes. These are best when fresh. Make them for a picnic or kids' party, or for an informal gathering.

CUPCAKES

1 1/2 cups sifted cake flour
1 teaspoon baking powder, preferably nonaluminum
1/4 teaspoon salt
4 tablespoons (1/2 stick) unsalted butter, at room temperature
1/2 cup sugar
1 teaspoon pure coconut extract
1/2 teaspoon pure vanilla extract
2 large eggs
1 large egg yolk
1/2 cup canned unsweetened coconut milk or whole milk
1 cup (3 1/2 ounces) chopped sweetened or unsweetened shredded coconut

CHOCOLATE FROSTING

1 1/2 ounces (1 1/2 squares) unsweetened chocolate
1 tablespoon unsalted butter
3 tablespoons sour cream
1/2 teaspoon pure vanilla extract
Pinch of salt
1 1/2 cups confectioners' sugar
Milk or cream for thinning, if needed

1 For the cupcakes, adjust an oven rack to the lower third position and preheat the oven to 350°F. Line a 12-cup muffin pan with paper liners; set aside.

2 Resift the flour with the baking powder and salt; set aside.

3 In a large bowl, beat the butter with an electric mixer on medium speed until smooth, about 1 minute. Gradually beat in the sugar, 2 tablespoons at a time, beating for a few seconds after each addition. Scrape the bowl and beaters. Add the coconut and vanilla extracts and beat on medium-high speed for 3 to 4 minutes until smooth and fluffy. Add 1 of the whole eggs and the egg yolk and beat for 1 minute. Add the remaining egg and beat for 1 minute.

4 On low speed, add the flour mixture in 3 additions, alternating with the coconut milk, beginning and ending with the flour and beating only until smooth. Stir in the coconut. Divide the batter evenly among the cups, filling them two-thirds to three-fourths full.

5 Bake for about 20 minutes, until the cupcakes are golden, their centers are domed, and a toothpick inserted into the center comes out clean. Cool in the pan for a few minutes, then transfer to a wire rack to cool completely.

6 For the frosting, melt the chocolate and butter in the top of a double boiler or in a small saucepan set into a larger saucepan of hot water over medium heat, stirring occasionally with a small whisk until smooth. Whisk in the sour cream, vanilla, and salt. The mixture will be thick. Remove the pan from the water and gradually whisk in the confectioners' sugar, then whisk until the icing is smooth enough to spread. If it is too thick, add 1 to 2 teaspoons milk or cream.

7 Working quickly (this frosting sets quickly), spoon a rounded teaspoonful of frosting onto each cupcake and spread with the back of the spoon.

APRICOT NECTAR CUPCAKES WITH ORANGE CREAM CHEESE FROSTING

Makes 12 cupcakes

I wanted an apricot-flavored cupcake without pieces of fruit. Apricot nectar was the answer. It's available in cans in supermarkets and health food stores. Just be sure the label says pure nectar.

CUPCAKES

1 1/2 cups sifted cake flour

1 teaspoon baking powder, preferably nonaluminum

1/4 teaspoon salt

1/3 cup (2/3 stick) unsalted butter, at room temperature

1 teaspoon pure orange extract

2/3 cup sugar

1 large egg

1 large egg yolk

2 tablespoons milk

1/2 cup apricot nectar

FROSTING

4 ounces cream cheese (don't use low-fat)

Finely grated zest of 1 orange

1 teaspoon pure orange extract

1 1/2 cups confectioners' sugar

1 For the cupcakes, adjust an oven rack to the center position and preheat the oven to 350°F. Line a 12-cup muffin pan with paper liners; set aside.

2 Resift the flour with the baking powder and salt; set aside.

3 In a large bowl, beat the butter with an electric mixer on medium speed until smooth, about 1 minute. Beat in the orange extract. Gradually beat in the sugar, 2 tablespoons at a time, then beat on medium-high speed for 4 to 5 minutes until smooth and fluffy. Beat in the egg and egg yolk and beat for 1 minute. Scrape the bowl. Add the milk and beat it in on medium-low speed.

4 On low speed, add the flour mixture in 3 additions, alternating with the apricot nectar, beginning and ending with the flour and beating only until smooth after each addition. Divide the batter evenly among the cups, filling each about half full. Don't bother to smooth the batter; it will level itself during baking.

5 Bake for 20 to 25 minutes, until the cupcakes are pale golden and spring back when gently pressed. Cool in the pan for 5 minutes, then carefully transfer them to a wire rack to cool completely.

6 Meanwhile, for the frosting, beat the cream cheese in a medium bowl with an electric mixer on medium speed until very smooth. Add the orange zest and extract and beat until smooth. Gradually beat in the confectioners' sugar on low speed, beating only until it is incorporated. Cover tightly and set aside until the cupcakes are cool.

7 Frost the cupcakes, and let stand until the frosting is set, about 30 minutes.

BANANA WALNUT CUPCAKES WITH ZESTY LEMON FROSTING

Makes 12 cupcakes

I based this recipe on one I remember from my childhood. The cupcakes were made with ordinary walnuts, but I love the character black walnuts give. They must be finely chopped, so get out your chef's knife. Don't use a food processor—it will turn some of the nuts into dust and others into a paste. If necessary, you can substitute English walnuts.

CUPCAKES

1¼ cups sifted all-purpose flour

½ teaspoon baking soda

¼ teaspoon salt

¼ teaspoon freshly grated nutmeg

6 tablespoons (¾ stick) unsalted butter, at room temperature

¾ cup sugar

1 teaspoon pure vanilla extract

2 large eggs

½ cup mashed very ripe banana

¼ cup plain yogurt or buttermilk

¼ cup finely chopped black walnuts

FROSTING

4 ounces cream cheese (don't use low-fat)

Finely grated zest of 1 lemon

½ teaspoon pure vanilla extract

¼–½ teaspoon pure lemon extract

1½ cups confectioners' sugar

1 For the cupcakes, adjust an oven rack to the center position and preheat the oven to 350°F. Line a 12-cup muffin pan with paper liners; set aside.

2 Resift the flour with the baking soda, salt, and nutmeg; set aside.

3 In a medium bowl, beat the butter with an electric mixer on medium speed until smooth, about 1 minute. Add the sugar and vanilla and beat for 3 to 4 minutes on medium-high speed until smooth and fluffy, stopping to scrape the bowl as necessary. Beat in the eggs one at a time, beating for about 1 minute after each. Add the banana and beat for 1 minute.

4 With a rubber spatula, stir in half the flour mixture only until incorpo-

rated. Gently stir in the yogurt or buttermilk, then add the remaining flour mixture, stirring with the rubber spatula just to mix well. Stir in the walnuts. Divide the batter evenly among the muffin cups; each cup will be about half full. Don't bother to smooth the batter; it will level itself during baking.

5 Bake for 22 to 25 minutes, until the cupcakes are golden brown and spring back when their centers are gently pressed; do not overbake. Cool for 5 minutes in the pan, then remove the cupcakes from the pan and set them on a wire rack to cool completely.

6 Meanwhile, for the frosting, beat the cream cheese, lemon zest, vanilla, and lemon extract in a medium bowl with an electric mixer until very smooth. Gradually add the confectioners' sugar, beating on low speed only until the sugar is incorporated. Cover and refrigerate until the cupcakes are cool.

7 Frost each cupcake, making swirls if you wish, and arrange the cupcakes on a serving tray. Refrigerate for about 1 hour. You can keep the cupcakes, well covered, for 2 to 3 days in the refrigerator; bring to room temperature before serving.

MAPLE-FROSTED MAPLE CUPCAKES

Makes 12 cupcakes

Maple syrup—the real thing—goes into the cupcakes and the frosting. I've found that by cutting back on the usual amount of milk, and using the syrup as part of the liquid in the batter, I can get a great maple taste without changing the texture of the cupcakes. Please do not use an imitation maple syrup, which is just plain sugar with a little maple flavoring. If you wish, sprinkle some chopped pecans on top after frosting the cupcakes.

CUPCAKES

$1^{1}/_{2}$ cups sifted all-purpose flour

$1^{1}/_{4}$ teaspoons baking powder, preferably nonaluminum

$^{1}/_{4}$ teaspoon salt

6 tablespoons ($^{3}/_{4}$ stick) unsalted butter, at room temperature

$^{1}/_{2}$ cup sugar

1 teaspoon pure vanilla extract

$^{1}/_{2}$ teaspoon maple extract

2 large eggs

$^{1}/_{4}$ cup pure maple syrup

$^{1}/_{3}$ cup milk

FROSTING

1 tablespoon unsalted butter, at room temperature

$^{1}/_{4}$ cup pure maple syrup

1 tablespoon milk

$^{1}/_{2}$ teaspoon pure vanilla extract

$^{1}/_{2}$ teaspoon maple extract

$^{1}/_{8}$ teaspoon salt

$1^{1}/_{2}$ cups confectioners' sugar

1 For the cupcakes, adjust an oven rack to the center position and preheat the oven to 350°F. Line a 12-cup muffin pan with paper liners; set aside.

2 Resift the flour with the baking powder and salt; set aside.

3 In a medium bowl, beat the butter with an electric mixer on medium speed until smooth, about 1 minute. Add the sugar, vanilla, and maple extract and beat for 3 to 4 minutes on medium-high speed until smooth and fluffy, stopping to scrape the bowl as necessary. Beat in the eggs one at a time, beating for about 1 minute after each.

4 Combine the maple syrup and milk in a small bowl. With a rubber spatula, stir about one third of the flour mixture into the batter only until incorporated. Gently stir in half the milk mixture. (The batter will look curdled.) Stir in half of the remaining flour mixture, then the rest of the milk mixture, and finally the last of the flour, stirring after each addition just to combine well. Divide the batter evenly among the muffin cups; each cup will be about half full. Don't bother to smooth the batter; it will level itself during baking.

5 Bake for about 25 minutes, until the cupcakes spring back when their centers are gently pressed and the tops are golden brown; do not overbake. Cool for 5 minutes in the pan, then remove from the pan and set on a wire rack to cool completely.

6 For the frosting, beat the butter, maple syrup, milk, vanilla, maple extract, and salt together in a small bowl with an electric mixer for 1 minute. The butter may be visible in small bits, which is all right. Gradually beat in the confectioners' sugar to make a smooth frosting.

7 Frost each cupcake generously. Let stand for 30 minutes for the frosting to set.

GINGER CUPCAKE TRIPLE PLAY

Makes 14 cupcakes

Ginger was the most popular spice of the nineteenth century: cookbooks of the period abound with recipes for cakes and cookies highly spiced with ginger. Three types—fresh, ground, and crystallized—flavor these tender cupcakes. Buttermilk adds a welcome tang, and sour cream contributes tartness and creaminess to the white chocolate ganache frosting.

CUPCAKES

- 1 3/4 cups sifted cake flour
- 1/2 teaspoon baking soda
- 1/4 teaspoon salt
- 1 teaspoon ground ginger
- 1/2 teaspoon allspice
- 8 tablespoons (1 stick) unsalted butter, at room temperature
- 1 teaspoon pure vanilla extract
- 1 1-inch cube peeled fresh ginger, finely grated (plus any juice)
- Finely grated zest of 1 orange
- 1 cup firmly packed light brown sugar
- 1 large egg
- 3/4 cup buttermilk
- 1/4–1/3 cup finely chopped crystallized ginger

FROSTING

- 3 tablespoons heavy cream
- 1 3.5-ounce bar white chocolate (I use Lindt), coarsely chopped
- 2 tablespoons sour cream

1 For the cupcakes, adjust an oven rack to the lower third position and preheat the oven to 350°F. Line 14 muffin cups with paper liners; set aside.

2 Resift the flour with the baking soda, salt, ground ginger, and allspice; set aside.

3 In a large bowl, beat the butter with an electric mixer on medium speed until smooth, about 1 minute. Add the vanilla, fresh ginger, orange zest, and 1/4 cup of the brown sugar. Beat for 1 minute. Beat in the remaining 3/4 brown sugar about 1/4 cup at a time, beating for about 20 seconds after each addition. Scrape the bowl and beaters and beat on medium-high speed for 4 minutes until smooth and fluffy. Add the egg and beat for 1 minute.

4 On low speed, add the flour mixture in 3 additions, alternating with the buttermilk, beginning and ending with the flour and beating only until smooth after each addition. Stir in the crystallized ginger. Divide the batter evenly among the muffin cups, filling them about two-thirds full. Don't bother to smooth the batter; it will level itself during baking.

5 Bake for about 25 minutes, until the cupcakes are golden brown and spring back when gently pressed in the center. Cool in the pans for 5 minutes, then remove them to wire racks to cool completely.

6 Meanwhile, for the frosting, heat the cream in a small heavy saucepan over medium heat until it just comes to the boil. Remove from the heat and add the white chocolate. Whisk until the chocolate is melted and the mixture is smooth. Whisk in the sour cream. Set aside, whisking occasionally, until the frosting is completely cool and thickened enough for spreading.

7 Place a teaspoonful of frosting on top of each cupcake and spread evenly with the back of a spoon. Let stand until set before serving.

DOUBLE ESPRESSO CUPCAKES

*Makes 12
cupcakes*

I came up with these on a blustery afternoon when a winter storm kept us indoors. I wanted a cupcake intensely flavored through and through with espresso: an espresso-flavored syrup is spooned over espresso-flavored cupcakes for a double dose of coffee. Instant espresso powder is available in most supermarkets; if you can't find it, pulverize enough instant coffee crystals to equal the amount of powder specified. Would it be too much to suggest serving these with coffee?

CUPCAKES

- 4 teaspoons instant espresso powder (I use Medaglia d'Oro)
- 3 tablespoons boiling water
- $1/3$ cup buttermilk
- $1^{1}/_{2}$ cups sifted all-purpose flour
- $1/2$ teaspoon baking soda
- $1/4$ teaspoon salt
- 6 tablespoons ($3/4$ stick) unsalted butter, at room temperature
- $3/4$ cup sugar
- 2 teaspoons pure vanilla extract
- 2 large eggs

ESPRESSO SYRUP

- $1/4$ cup water
- 2 tablespoons light corn syrup
- $1/4$ cup sugar
- 1 tablespoon instant espresso powder
- 1 teaspoon pure vanilla extract

Confectioners' sugar for dusting

1 For the cupcakes, adjust an oven rack to the center position and preheat the oven to 350°F. Line a 12-cup muffin pan with paper liners; set aside.

2 Dissolve the espresso in the boiling water. Stir in the buttermilk and set aside. Resift the flour with the baking soda and salt; set aside.

3 In a medium bowl, beat the butter with an electric mixer on medium speed until smooth, about 1 minute. Add the sugar and vanilla and beat on medium-high speed for 3 to 4 minutes, until smooth and fluffy, stopping to scrape the bowl as necessary. Beat in the eggs one at a time, beating for about 1 minute after each.

4 With a rubber spatula, stir in about one third of the flour mixture, only until incorporated. Gently stir in half the espresso mixture. The batter will have a curdled appearance, which is all right. Stir in half the remaining flour mixture, then the rest of the espresso mixture, and finally the last of the flour, stirring with the rubber spatula after each addition just to combine well. The batter will still have a slightly curdled appearance. Divide the batter evenly among the muffin cups; each cup will be about half full. Don't bother to smooth the batter; it will level itself during baking.

5 Bake for 20 to 25 minutes, until the cupcakes spring back when their centers are gently pressed; do not overbake.

6 Meanwhile, for the espresso syrup, combine the water, corn syrup, sugar, and instant espresso in a small heavy saucepan. Bring to a simmer over medium heat, stirring frequently, and continue simmering for 3 to 4 minutes. Remove from the heat and stir in the vanilla.

7 As soon as the cupcakes come out of the oven, carefully spoon about 2 teaspoons of the syrup over each one. Try not to let any of the glaze run between the cupcake liners and the muffin pan. Let stand for 10 minutes, then carefully remove the cupcakes from the pan and place them on a cooling rack to cool completely. (If any of the syrup did run down the sides of the cupcakes, wipe the cupcake liners dry with a paper towel.)

8 Just before serving, dust the top of each cupcake with confectioners' sugar.

Variation

Zesty Lemon Frosting (page 234) is also delicious with the espresso cupcakes: Omit the espresso syrup and frost with the icing instead, or use both syrup and icing but omit the dusting of confectioners' sugar.

LEMON–POPPY SEED CREAM CUPCAKES

Makes 10 cupcakes

These tender, delicate, light-textured cupcakes need no icing. The recipe can be doubled.

1/4 cup poppy seeds

1/4 cup milk

1 1/4 cups sifted cake flour

1 teaspoon baking powder, preferably nonaluminum

1/2 teaspoon salt

4 tablespoons (1/2 stick) unsalted butter, at room temperature

1 teaspoon pure lemon extract

Finely grated zest of 1 large lemon

2/3 cup sugar

1 large egg

1/4 cup heavy cream

Confectioners' sugar for dusting (optional)

1 Adjust an oven rack to the center position and preheat the oven to 350°F. Line 10 muffin cups with paper liners; set aside.

2 Combine the poppy seeds and milk in a small cup and set aside. Resift the flour with the baking powder and salt; set aside.

3 In a medium bowl, beat the butter with an electric mixer on medium speed until smooth, about 1 minute. Beat in the lemon extract and lemon zest. Gradually beat in the sugar 2 tablespoons at a time, and beat on medium-high speed for 4 to 5 minutes until smooth and fluffy. Add the egg and beat for 1 minute. Scrape the bowl. Add the milk mixture and beat on medium-low speed until thoroughly incorporated.

4 On low speed, add half the flour mixture, beating until smooth. Beat in the cream, then add the remaining flour, beating only until the batter is smooth. It will be quite thick. Divide the batter evenly among the prepared muffin cups, filling each a little more than half full. Don't bother to smooth the batter; it will level itself during baking.

5 Bake for 20 to 25 minutes, until the cupcakes spring back when gently pressed. Cool in the pan for 5 minutes, then carefully remove them to a wire rack to cool completely.

6 Just before serving, dust the cupcakes with confectioners' sugar, if desired. These are best when fresh, but leftovers can be stored airtight at room temperature for up to 2 days.

A FLOUR IS BORN

In 1856, Levi Igleheart, Jr., and two brothers established a gristmill near Evansville, Indiana. Over the years, the business prospered. Levi's son, Addison, was curious to know why some flours made better cakes than others. He performed a series of baking tests with a variety of flours and discovered that cakes made from soft winter wheat had the most tender, delicate texture. Using soft flour that had been sifted through fine silk screens and ground again, Addison made the finest cakes he had ever tasted.

One morning in 1894, Addison went to the Evansville train station to see a special exhibit of new cooking utensils on display in one of the trains. He noticed a cake-pan salesman who was actually baking cakes right there in the station! The two exchanged a few words, and as the salesman prepared for his next demonstration, he realized he had run out of flour. Addison quickly offered to supply the man with his own. The flour worked so well that the salesman asked for packages to sell to the housewives visiting the train. Addison obliged, and he and his brother continued to send boxes of their fine flour for demonstrations in towns throughout Indiana.

Within a few years, the flour's popularity had spread by word of mouth, and women began writing directly to the Igleharts for it. The time had come to promote the flour nationally. The Igleharts advertised their Swans Down Cake Flour in the June 1898 *Ladies' Home Journal.* The product became an immediate success everywhere it was sold, and today it remains a major brand in supermarkets across the land.

BLUEBERRY-CURRANT CUPCAKES

Makes 18 cupcakes

These tender, light cupcakes are great with afternoon tea, or take them on a picnic. Dried blueberries and currants are given a quick soak in an orange-flavored syrup before being folded into a classic butter cake batter. After they are baked, the cupcakes are brushed with the leftover soaking syrup.

1/2 cup sugar

1/4 cup water

1 tablespoon finely grated orange zest

1/2 cup dried currants

1/2 cup dried blueberries

1 tablespoon Myers's rum or Grand Marnier

2 cups sifted all-purpose flour

2 teaspoons baking powder, preferably nonaluminum

1/2 teaspoon salt

8 tablespoons (1 stick) unsalted butter, at room temperature

2/3 cup sugar

1 teaspoon pure vanilla extract

2 large eggs

3/4 cup milk

Confectioners' sugar for dusting

1 Combine the sugar, water, and orange zest in a small saucepan and bring to a boil over medium-high heat, stirring occasionally with a wooden spoon. Stir in the currants, blueberries, and rum or Grand Marnier. Remove from the heat, cover, and set aside for 30 minutes.

2 Turn the dried fruit into a strainer set over a bowl and drain well. Reserve the fruit and the syrup.

3 Adjust an oven rack to the center position and preheat the oven to 350°F (or, if you are using two 12-cup muffin pans, adjust two oven racks to divide the oven into thirds). Line 18 muffin cups with paper liners; set aside.

4 Resift the flour with the baking powder and salt; set aside.

5 In a large bowl, beat the butter with an electric mixer on medium speed until smooth and creamy, about 1 minute. Gradually beat in the sugar, then beat in the vanilla. Scrape the bowl and beaters and beat for 3 min-

utes on medium-high speed until smooth and fluffy. Beat in the eggs one at a time, beating for about 30 seconds after each addition.

6 On low speed, add the flour mixture in 4 additions, alternating with the milk, beginning and ending with the flour and beating only until each addition is thoroughly incorporated. Using a rubber spatula, fold in the drained fruits. Spoon the batter into the cups, filling them a little more than half full.

7 Bake for 20 to 25 minutes, until the cupcakes are golden brown and spring back when gently pressed. As soon as you remove the cupcakes from the oven, quickly prick each in 3 places with a fork, and brush the tops with the reserved syrup, using it all. Remove the cupcakes from the pans and set them on wire racks to cool completely.

8 Just before serving, dust the cupcakes with confectioners' sugar.

PERSIMMON CREAM CHEESE CUPCAKES

Makes 12 cupcakes

Persimmon adds its unique sweetness and color to these tender, delicate cupcakes. I use Hachiya persimmons, the most commonly available variety during the fall months. Be sure the persimmons are completely ripe: the fruit must feel very soft, or they will be puckery. The easiest way to mash them is with a pastry blender. Use an up-and-down chopping motion. It's all right if a few pieces of pulp remain.

The cupcakes are baked with a not-too-sweet cream-cheese mixture. These are best when very fresh.

FROSTING

- 4 ounces cream cheese, at room temperature (don't use low-fat)
- 1 large egg white
- 1/2 teaspoon pure lemon extract
- 3 tablespoons sugar
  Pinch of salt

CUPCAKES

- 1 1/4 cups sifted all-purpose flour
- 1 1/2 teaspoons baking powder, preferably nonaluminum
- 1/4 teaspoon salt
- 3/4 teaspoon ground cinnamon
- 1/2 teaspoon ground ginger
- 1/4 teaspoon ground allspice
- 6 tablespoons (3/4 stick) unsalted butter, at room temperature
- 2/3 cup sugar
- 1 teaspoon pure vanilla extract
- 1 large egg yolk
- 2/3 cup mashed persimmon pulp (from 2–3 Hachiya persimmons)
- 2 tablespoons milk
- 1 tablespoon sugar for sprinkling

1 For the frosting, beat the cream cheese in a small bowl, with an electric mixer on medium speed until very smooth. Add the egg white, lemon extract, sugar, and salt and beat until smooth. Set aside.

2 For the cupcakes, adjust an oven rack to the lower third position and preheat the oven to 350°F. Line a 12-cup muffin pan with cupcake liners; set aside.

3 Resift the flour with the baking powder, salt, cinnamon, ginger, and allspice; set aside.

4 In a medium bowl, beat the butter with an electric mixer on medium speed until smooth, about 1 minute. Gradually beat in the sugar. Add the vanilla and egg yolk and beat on medium-high speed for 2 minutes. Add the persimmon and beat for 1 to 2 minutes, until the batter is fluffy. On low speed, beat in the milk. Stir in the flour mixture with a rubber spatula, mixing only until the batter is smooth.

5 Divide the batter evenly among the muffin cups. Spoon the cream cheese frosting on top, and sprinkle each cupcake with $1/4$ teaspoon of the sugar.

6 Bake for about 30 minutes, until the cupcakes spring back when gently pressed at their edges and a toothpick inserted into the center comes out clean. Cool in the pan for 2 to 3 minutes, then carefully remove and set on a wire rack to cool completely.

FUDGE-FILLED WHITE CUPCAKES

Makes 16 cupcakes

These are absolutely at their best very fresh, even slightly warm, when the fudge is still slightly gooey. The paper liners may want to stick to the bottoms of the cupcakes when you peel them off—just be patient.

1 cup (6 ounces) semisweet chocolate morsels

1/2 cup sweetened condensed milk (not evaporated milk)

1 1/4 cups sifted cake flour

1 teaspoon baking powder, preferably nonaluminum

1/4 teaspoon salt

6 tablespoons (3/4 stick) unsalted butter, at room temperature

1 teaspoon pure vanilla extract

2/3 cup sugar

4 large egg whites

1/2 cup milk

1/3 cup coarsely chopped slivered almonds

1 *To melt the chocolate in the microwave,* combine the chocolate and condensed milk in a medium microwave-safe bowl and microwave on high for 1 1/2 minutes. Stir the mixture until smooth, and set aside, stirring occasionally, until completely cool.

Or, *to melt it on the stovetop,* put the chocolate in a small heavy saucepan and place the pan in a larger pan of hot water or a double boiler set over medium heat. Stir occasionally until melted and smooth. Add the condensed milk and stir well. Remove the pan from the water and set aside, stirring occasionally, until completely cool.

2 Adjust an oven rack to the lower third position and preheat the oven to 350°F (or if you are using two 12-cup muffin pans, adjust two oven racks to divide the oven into thirds). Line 16 muffin cups with paper cupcake liners; set aside.

3 Resift the flour with the baking powder and salt; set aside.

4 In a large bowl, beat the butter with an electric mixer on medium speed until smooth, about 1 minute. Beat in the vanilla. Reserve 2 tablespoons of the sugar. Gradually beat in the remaining sugar. Scrape the bowl and beaters and beat on medium-high speed for 4 minutes until smooth and fluffy. Add 1 egg white and beat on medium speed for 1 minute.

5 On low speed, add the flour mixture in 3 additions, alternating with the milk, beginning and ending with the flour and beating only until smooth after each addition.

6 In a clean medium bowl, with clean beaters beat the remaining 3 egg whites on medium speed until they form peaks that curl softly at their tips. Gradually beat in the reserved 2 tablespoons sugar. Increase the speed to medium-high and beat just until the whites are thick and form upright peaks that curl a little when the beaters are raised. Place about one third of the whites on the batter and fold together gently with a large rubber spatula; don't be too thorough. Scoop the rest of the whites on top and fold them in gently but thoroughly.

7 Spoon the batter into the cups, filling them half full. Place a well-rounded regular teaspoon of the chocolate mixture in the middle of each; it will sink during baking. Sprinkle each cupcake with about 1 teaspoon of the almonds.

8 Bake for about 25 minutes, until the cupcakes are pale golden brown and spring back when gently pressed. Cool the cupcakes in their pans for 5 minutes, then carefully transfer them to wire racks to cool. Serve slightly warm or at room temperature.

BROWN-EYED-SUSAN PEANUT BUTTER CUPCAKES

*Makes 12
cupcakes*

Even before George Washington Carver transformed our country's perception of the peanut and helped make it one of our most popular foods, housewives were cooking with the legume. Touted as a health food, peanut butter made its public debut in 1904 at the St. Louis World's Fair. By the 1920s, peanut butter was used in brittle, salad dressings, soups, sandwiches, cream sauces, breads, muffins, and macaroons. Each of these cupcakes has a miniature peanut butter cup set into the batter before baking, giving it a built-in filling, and an icing as well.

1 1/2 cups sifted all-purpose flour

1 1/4 teaspoons baking powder, preferably nonaluminum

1/4 teaspoon salt

1/4 cup creamy peanut butter

2 tablespoons unsalted butter, at room temperature

2/3 cup firmly packed light brown sugar

1 teaspoon pure vanilla extract

2 large eggs

1/3 cup milk

12 Reese's miniature peanut butter cups

1 Adjust an oven rack to the center position and preheat the oven to 350°F. Line a 12-cup muffin pan with paper liners; set aside.

2 Resift the flour with the baking powder and salt; set aside.

3 In a medium bowl, beat the peanut butter, butter, brown sugar, and vanilla extract with an electric mixer on medium speed for 3 to 4 minutes. The mixture will be in large granules, not smooth and fluffy. Beat in the eggs one at a time, beating for about 1 minute after each.

4 With a rubber spatula, stir in about half of the flour mixture, only until incorporated. Gently stir in the milk, then the remaining flour. Divide the mixture among the muffin cups; each cup will be about half full. Don't bother to smooth the batter; it will level itself during baking. Press a peanut butter cup into the center of each cupcake until the top of the peanut butter cup is level with the batter. Don't let the batter cover the peanut butter cups.

5 Bake for 20 to 25 minutes, until the cupcakes spring back when their edges are gently pressed and the tops are golden brown; do not overbake. Cool for 5 minutes in the pan, then remove from the pan and cool completely on a wire rack.

THE PEANUT GALLERY

Back in 1902, soon after George Washington Carver began his historic work with peanuts, Mrs. Rorer printed this method for peanut butter:

Roast the nuts, shell and blow off the brown skins. When making it in large quantities, it will pay to have a bellows for this purpose, or put the peanuts on a coarse towel, cover them with another towel, rub them gently, then blow off the skins. If you use salt dust them lightly with it and grind at once. Pack the butter into glass jars or tumblers, cover them and keep in a cool place. This may be used plain or diluted with water.

Mrs. Rorer's peanut butter would separate over time, the oil rising to the top, making it necessary to stir it back into the thick paste underneath. Twenty-one years later, J. L. Rosefield, a California food processor, finally found a way to keep peanut butter from separating. The process was first used commercially by Peter Pan peanut butter. Ten years later, Mr. Rosefield marketed his own brand of peanut butter, calling it Skippy.

BOSTON CREAM CAKES

Makes 12 to 18 cream puffs

How these incredible cream puffs got their name is unclear, but the dessert was very popular on the East Coast in the early to mid-1800s.

FILLING

3 cups heavy cream

1 3-inch cinnamon stick

1 vanilla bean, split lengthwise

1/3 cup sugar

6 large egg yolks

PUFF SHELLS

1 cup milk

8 tablespoons (1 stick) unsalted butter, cut into pieces

1/2 teaspoon salt

1 cup sifted all-purpose flour

4 large eggs

Sugar for sprinkling

1 For the filling, place the cream and cinnamon stick in a small heavy saucepan. Scrape the seeds from the vanilla bean into the cream and add the pod. Bring to a boil over medium-low heat; watch closely, or the cream may boil over. Remove from the heat, add the sugar, and stir until dissolved. Set aside to steep for about 1 hour.

2 Adjust an oven rack to the center position and preheat the oven to 325°F. Have ready a 9-inch ovenproof glass pie plate and a shallow baking pan large enough to contain the pie plate. Bring a kettle of water to a boil.

3 If a skin has formed on top of the cream, stir it back in. Strain through a fine-mesh strainer, and return to the saucepan. Heat the cream until almost boiling. Meanwhile, whisk the egg yolks in a medium bowl. Gradually whisk the hot cream into the egg yolks; don't beat. Strain the mixture through a fine-mesh strainer into the pie plate and set it in the baking pan. Add boiling water to come halfway up the sides of the pie plate and place in the oven.

4 Bake for 20 to 25 minutes, only until set; the tip of a sharp knife inserted into the center should come out clean. Carefully remove the custard from the water bath and set on a wire rack to cool. (The custard can be made ahead, cooled, and refrigerated for several hours, or overnight.)

5 For the puffs, adjust an oven rack to the lower third position and preheat the oven to 425°F (or if you are using two 12-cup muffin pans, adjust two oven racks to divide the oven into thirds). Lightly coat 12 extra-large or 18 standard-sized nonstick muffin cups with cooking spray; set aside.

6 Combine the milk, butter, and salt in a medium heavy saucepan and heat over medium-high heat, stirring occasionally with a wooden spoon, until the mixture comes to a full rolling boil. Remove from the heat, immediately add the flour, and beat with the wooden spoon. Return the pan to medium-high heat and stir constantly for 1 minute. Remove from the heat and set aside.

7 Place the eggs in a medium bowl and beat them with an electric mixer on high speed until very thick and tripled in volume, about 5 minutes. On low speed, beat the eggs into the warm puff mixture in about 4 installments, beating only until each addition is completely incorporated and stopping to scrape the saucepan once or twice. Use two soup spoons to place small even mounds of dough in the pans, one for picking up the dough and one for pushing it off the spoon. Sprinkle each puff lightly with sugar.

8 Bake large puffs for 25 minutes, standard-sized ones for 20 minutes, or until they are very well browned and have puffed tremendously. Do not underbake, or the puffs may collapse as they cool. Carefully remove the puffs from the pans and cool on wire racks.

9 When they are completely cool, split the puffs horizontally and fill each with some of the custard (which may be at room temperature, slightly warm, or cold). Replace the tops of the puffs and serve as soon as you can, with knives and forks.

Filling Variations

1. Fill with 2 cups heavy cream beaten until thick with ¼ cup confectioners' sugar and 2 teaspoons pure vanilla extract.

2. Fill with scoops of ice cream or frozen yogurt.

3. Fill with 1½ cups heavy cream, beaten until thick, with 1 cup sliced fresh strawberries, 1 tablespoon Grand Marnier, and 2 tablespoons sugar folded in.

7 Layer Cakes

Cake is indeed one of the luxuries of our table, yet it might almost claim a place among the necessaries, so universally does it demand at least an occasional use even among those of less than moderate means.

—Mrs. M. E. Porter, *Mrs. Porter's New Southern Cookery Book* (1871)

Layer cakes—two or more layers of tall, tender, fluffy cake filled and frosted with almost any kind of icing—are a quintessentially American creation. They first appeared in cookbooks toward the last quarter of the nineteenth century. Two major developments conspired to make them into icons of American baking: the invention of baking powder and the cast-iron stove.

The range was invented in Europe in the late 1700s by an American, Benjamin Thompson (later called Count Rumford). His basic design was modified in America into the cast-iron range, and by 1834 the first cast-iron stoves had been patented. These black monstrosities weighed hundreds of pounds and dominated the kitchen. Outfitted with numerous doors, fireboxes, and ovens, they were often decorated in a lavish rococo style. As food historian Kathleen Smallzried puts it in *The Everlasting Pleasure*, "The iron monsters, as they were affectionately known, created the first major revolution in cooking since the discovery of fire." Before that, cooking had to be done in the fireplace, and it required an enormous quantity of wood. As the population exploded, forests were in danger of being depleted. The cast-iron stoves conserved vital fuel by burning it much more efficiently.

They were also much more reliable than wood-fired brick ovens. In the latter, the heat was hard to control. Once the oven was hot, the coals and ashes were swept out, and the oven's temperature steadily fell. It took enormous skill to know just when to put a cake in. If the oven was too hot or too cold, the cake would fail. With a range, the heat could be controlled by adjusting the amount of fuel—wood in the first stoves, and in later models, coal, oil, or gas.

By 1856, the year baking powder

JELLY-CAKE, OR WASHINGTON PIE

***Make cup cake** [meaning the ingredients were measured in cups, not weighed], and when the ingredients are well mixed, spread it upon round shallow tins, three table-spoonfuls to each tin. It will bake in ten or fifteen minutes; then turn it upon a hair sieve, the under surface uppermost. While it is warm spread upon it raspberry jam, currant, or other jelly; then lay the second sheet of cake upon it, the under side next to the jelly. If you wish to make several alternate layers of cake and jelly make the sheets of cake very thin; one large spoonful of the batter will be enough for each tin.*

—Mrs. Cornelius, *The Young Housekeeper's Friend* (1859)

became available to the public, most homes were equipped with the new ranges. Housewives welcomed this new addition to the pantry, which allowed them to bake cakes with far less elbow grease. Baking-powder cakes also used less butter and fewer eggs, which saved on grocery bills, as more and more people moved away from the farm to the city. The rotary egg beater, which became available a few years later, further eased the preparation of cakes. As a result, pound cakes gave way to more economical cakes that could be baked in shallower pans in half the time, thus economizing on fuel, too.

Historically, layer cakes were related to "jelly cakes," thin layers of cake baked in shallow tin or graniteware pans and stacked with jelly or jam between them. Sometimes these cakes were frosted, sometimes not. The number of layers in a jelly cake varied, but an 1897 Sears Roebuck catalog included four pans in a set of "essential" cookware. Over time, the pans became deeper, and by the first decades of the twentieth century, layer cake pans achieved the form they maintain to this day.

The golden age of the layer cake began after the electric mixer came on the scene in the mid-1920s and lasted through the 1950s. Home cooks took great pride in their high, fluffy creations and made them the centerpiece of parties. In the early 1950s, the quick-mix "dump cake" became the darling of the moment: all the ingredients were plunked into the mixing bowl and beaten for a few minutes, and the batter was ready for the oven.

Many of the early layer cakes called for excessive amounts of baking powder—3 to 5 teaspoons per cake. With powerful electric mixers doing the job of creaming the butter and sugar and beating in the eggs, today's layer cakes require far less chemical leavening.

Today the homemade layer cake has become an endangered species, as the boxed-mix kind has virtually replaced the from-scratch variety. Why is it that the more convenience gadgets we have, the lazier we get? With an electric mixer, making the batter for a layer cake takes less than fifteen minutes, only ten minutes more than with a package. The results, however, are vastly superior.

LAYER CAKES STEP BY STEP

1. Preparing the cake pans. Lining buttered layer cake pans with rounds of buttered waxed paper or cooking parchment and lightly dusting the bottoms of the pans with flour or fine dry bread crumbs ensures that the cakes will not stick. Coat the bottoms of layer cake pans, but not the sides. (The cakes rise better without flour or crumbs coating the sides.) Sprinkle a small amount of flour or crumbs in the bottom of the pan and tap the side of the pan to make a thin even layer. Turn the pan upside down and knock out the excess. Don't worry if a little sticks to the sides.

2. Sifting. Always sift flour before measuring. Flour bags often say "no sifting necessary" because the flour has been presifted. Ignore the label: flour packs down when it stands. Unsifted flour often contains small, compact flour nuggets that won't mix well into batters and can result in holes in a cake's texture. To sift, place more flour than you need into a sifter set on a sheet of waxed paper. Sift the flour, then spoon it lightly into dry measuring cups to overflowing. Sweep off the excess with a metal spatula and return the flour to the sifter. Add any dry ingredients to be sifted with the flour, and sift them together to ensure thorough mixing. And don't just scoop the dry measure into the flour container and level it off; you'll have too much flour.

3. Shortening or butter? Butter gives a cake great flavor, but shortening results in a lighter, more tender texture. For most cakes, I use all butter, but in some I include shortening for texture. Unsalted butter has the best taste. Always use butter in frostings.

4. Machine mixing. You will find a heavy-duty stand mixer very helpful in making cakes. I use a KitchenAid mixer that has a 5-quart bowl, paddle attachment (flat beater), and whip. You will love the freedom the machine allows, permitting you to do other things while the machine beats away for the 10 minutes or so of creaming the butter with the sugar and beating in the eggs. You can, however, make these cakes with a hand-held electric mixer.

5. Creaming. Perhaps the most critical step in cake making is creaming the butter with the sugar, that is, gradually beating the sugar into the butter and then beating for 5 to 6 minutes. The vigorous action of the sugar with the butter creates small bubbles, which will expand during baking. Do not stint on beating time, or the texture of your cake will suffer.

6. Flavorings. When adding extracts to cakes, I like to beat them in with the butter and sugar. The flavor seems to be more intense that way.

7. Eggs. Add eggs individually to the batter, beating each one in thoroughly before adding the next. Scrape the bowl and beater(s) frequently to ensure even mixing. Eggs beaten in correctly contribute natural leavening power. Some recipes ask you to beat in the egg yolks first, then beat and fold in the egg whites. When beating whites, it's important to beat them enough so that they hold a definite shape, but not until they are stiff and dry. They should be glossy and when the beater is raised, they should form peaks that curl gently at their tips. If you pick up some of the beaten whites with a rubber spatula, they should stay put.

8. Adding the dry and liquid ingredients. Adding the dry ingredients alternately with the liquid results in an even dispersal of the flour particles and a great-textured cake. Beginning and ending with the dry ingredients produces the best results. Beat or stir them in by hand with a rubber spatula or with an electric mixer on the lowest speed. Overbeating will activate the gluten in the flour and toughen the cake.

9. Leveling the batter. If batters don't level themselves in the pans, grasp the pan between your palms and rotate it briskly on your countertop. It's usually not necessary to smooth the top of the batter; that will happen during baking.

10. Placing pans on the oven rack. Arrange the pans on the oven rack in a diagonal arrangement, leaving about 1 inch of space between the pans and the oven walls. If baking more than two layers, adjust two oven racks to divide the oven into thirds; place two pans on the upper rack and one on the lower. Carefully switch the pan positions about two thirds of the way through baking; cakes baked on the lower rack the entire time may get too browned on their bottoms.

11. Checking for doneness. Always test for doneness at the first time specified when a range of times is given. The standard doneness test for many layer cakes is that they just spring back when lightly pressed in the center. This works for some, but not all types. Use the guidelines specified in each recipe. If a cake springs back firmly, chances are it's overdone.

12. Cooling the cakes. Cool cake layers right side up on wire racks. This prevents the tops from getting sticky and makes frosting the cake easier.

13. Icing the cake. When icing cakes, brush away any crumbs with a pastry brush to prevent them from marring the icing. If thin crusty edges formed on the cake layers, carefully trim them away with a small sharp knife before icing. To keep frosting off the cake plate, line the edges of the plate with four narrow strips of waxed paper arranged in a square pattern. Place one layer top side down on the plate; the cake should anchor the paper strips. Use a narrow-bladed metal spatula to spread frosting on top of the layer. Place the second layer right side up on the first layer and frost the sides and top with the remaining icing. Remove each waxed paper strip by tugging on one end and pulling it toward you. If you have a turntable, by all means use it to ice the cake, rotating the cake against the metal spatula for an even, smooth surface.

MAMA'S LITTLE BABY LOVES . . .

Shortening, a manufactured vegetable fat, didn't come on the market until the 1890s. The first product, Cottolene, prided itself in being more digestible than butter. Made with a combination of cottonseed oil and beef suet, it was hardly the pure vegetable product that its supporters claimed. Well-known cooking teacher and author Sarah Tyson Rorer hailed it as "a much more healthful product than lard." Cookbook author Marion Harland also climbed on the bandwagon, proclaiming, "I honestly believe it to be the very best thing of its kind ever offered to the American housekeeper." The medical establishment chimed in, too. Dr. R. Ogden Doremus, Professor of Chemistry, Toxicology, and Medical Jurisprudence, touted its virtues, saying that it "possesses all the desirable qualities of lard without having the objectionable features inherent in all products obtained from swine."

Many other shortenings soon followed, including Crisco, introduced in 1911, the great survivor of the shortening wars. Its pure whiteness comes from tiny nitrogen bubbles, which account for 12 percent of its volume and make for fluffy-textured cakes.

GOLDEN BUTTER LAYER CAKE WITH CHOCOLATE FROSTING

*Makes one
9-inch
2-layer cake,
12 to 16
servings*

I've based this cake on the nineteenth-century 1-2-3-4 cake, made with 1 cup butter, 2 cups sugar, 3 cups flour, and 4 eggs and baked in a loaf pan. Some recipes included baking powder, others did not. Although layer cakes traditionally are made with chemical leaveners, I wanted to see if I could succeed using the natural leavening power of thoroughly beaten butter and sugar, extra whole eggs, and a few additional beaten egg whites. With my modifications, this becomes a classic tall yellow layer cake, not fluffy or airy, but with a moist, fine texture and an even, dense crumb.

The chocolate frosting, made with cream cheese and butter, is smooth, chocolaty, not too sweet, and extremely easy to make.

CAKE

- 1 cup (2 sticks) unsalted butter, at room temperature
- 1/2 teaspoon salt
- 2 cups sugar
- 2 teaspoons pure vanilla extract
- 3 large eggs, separated
- 3 large eggs
- 3 cups sifted cake flour
- 1 cup milk

FROSTING

- 3 ounces (3 squares) unsweetened chocolate
- 8 tablespoons (1 stick) unsalted butter, at room temperature
- 4 ounces Neufchâtel cream cheese
- Pinch of salt
- 2 teaspoons pure vanilla extract
- 2 cups confectioners' sugar

1 For the cake, adjust an oven rack to the lower third position and preheat the oven to 350°F. Butter or grease two 9-inch round cake pans. Line the bottoms with rounds of waxed paper or cooking parchment, butter the paper, and dust the bottoms of the pans with all-purpose flour. Knock out the excess and set aside.

2 In a large bowl, beat the butter with an electric mixer on medium speed until smooth and creamy, about 1 minute. Add the salt, 1/4 cup of the sugar, and the vanilla and beat on medium-high speed for 1 minute. Beat in 1 1/2 more cups of the sugar about 1/4 cup at a time, beating for 20 to 30

seconds after each addition. Stop to scrape the bowl and beaters once or twice. Beat for 5 minutes. Add the egg yolks and beat for 2 minutes. Add the whole eggs one at a time, beating for 1 minute after each addition.

3 On low speed, gradually beat in the flour in 3 additions, alternating with the milk, beginning and ending with the flour and mixing only until the batter is smooth. Scrape the bowl and beaters; set aside.

4 In a medium bowl, with clean beaters, whip the 3 whites on medium speed until they form peaks that curl softly at their tips. Beat in the remaining $1/4$ cup sugar about 1 tablespoon at a time, beating for 10 to 15 seconds after each addition. Increase the speed to medium-high and beat only until the whites form peaks that are shiny and curl slightly at their tips when the beaters are raised; do not overbeat.

5 Transfer about one third of the whites to the batter and fold in gently with a large rubber spatula. Don't be too thorough; it's all right if streaks of white show. Scrape the remaining whites on top of the batter and fold the two together only until no streaks of whites show; handle the batter as gently as possible. Divide the batter evenly between the prepared pans; it will almost fill them. To level the batter, rotate the pans briskly on your countertop.

6 Bake for 30 to 35 minutes, until the layers are deep golden brown and a toothpick inserted into the center comes out clean. The layers may just begin to pull away from the sides of the pans. (Pressing the layers gently and seeing if they spring back is not a good test of doneness. They'll be overbaked by the time that happens.) Cool in the pans for 10 minutes. Run the tip of a small sharp knife around the cakes to release them, cover with a wire rack, and invert. Carefully lift off the pans and papers. Cover the layers with other racks, and invert to cool completely right side up.

7 For the frosting, put the chocolate in the top of a double boiler or in a small saucepan set into a larger pan of hot water over medium heat, stirring occasionally with a small rubber spatula until melted and smooth. Remove from the water and set aside to cool slightly.

8 In a large bowl, beat the butter, cream cheese, salt, and vanilla with an electric mixer on medium speed until very smooth, 1 to 2 minutes. Scrape the bowl. Add the confectioners' sugar and beat on medium-low speed

until incorporated, then beat on medium-high speed for about 30 seconds, until very smooth. Add the chocolate and beat on medium-low speed until completely incorporated. Increase the speed to medium-high and beat for a few seconds more.

9 To frost the cake, carefully trim any crusty edges from the cake layers with a small sharp knife. Place one layer top side down on a cake plate. Spread with about ³/₄ cup of the frosting. Place the second layer right side up on top and frost the sides and top with the remaining frosting. Let stand until the frosting is set. To serve, rinse a sharp knife in hot water and shake off the excess water before making each cut.

WHITE LAYER CAKE

Makes one 9-inch 2-layer cake, 12 to 16 servings

Here's is another American classic: two high, tender layers of white cake filled and frosted with a fabulous Grand Marnier buttercream.

CAKE

3 cups sifted cake flour

1 teaspoon baking powder, preferably nonaluminum

$^1/_2$ teaspoon salt

1 cup (2 sticks) unsalted butter, at room temperature

1 tablespoon pure vanilla extract

$1^3/_4$ cups sugar

8 large egg whites — 6 whites in one bowl, the remaining 2 in another

$1^1/_4$ cups milk

BUTTERCREAM FROSTING

6 large egg yolks

$^3/_4$ cup sugar

$^1/_2$ cup light corn syrup

2 cups (1 pound) unsalted butter, very soft

2 tablespoons Grand Marnier

$^1/_8$ teaspoon salt

1 For the cake, adjust an oven rack to the lower third position and preheat the oven to 350°F. Generously grease two 9-inch round cake pans. Line the bottoms with rounds of waxed paper or cooking parchment. Butter the paper and dust the bottoms of the pans with flour. Tap out the excess and set aside.

2 Resift the cake flour with the baking powder and salt; set aside.

3 In a large bowl, beat the butter with an electric mixer on medium speed until smooth, about 1 minute. Add the vanilla and $^1/_4$ cup of the sugar and beat for 1 minute. Beat in $1^1/_4$ more cups of the remaining sugar about $^1/_4$ cup at a time, beating for 20 to 30 seconds after each addition. Scrape the bowl and beaters well, then beat for 5 minutes on medium-high speed. Add 2 of the egg whites and beat for 2 minutes.

4 On low speed, add the dry ingredients in 4 additions, alternating with the milk, beginning and ending with the flour and beating after each addition only until smooth. The batter may look curdled.

5 In a large bowl, with clean beaters, beat the remaining 6 egg whites on medium speed until they form very soft peaks that droop at their tips when the beaters are raised. Beat in the remaining $^1/_4$ cup sugar 1 tablespoon at a time, beating for about 10 seconds after each addition. Increase the speed to medium-high and beat briefly until the whites are thick and shiny like a marshmallow cream and form peaks with only slightly drooping points; do not overbeat.

6 Transfer about one fourth of the beaten whites to the cake batter with a large rubber spatula. Gently fold in the whites, using 6 or 7 broad strokes; do not be too thorough. Gently fold in the remaining whites in 3 additions, then continue folding until no whites show. Carefully divide the batter between the two pans, handling as gently as possible. To level the batter, rotate the pans briskly on your countertop; the surface of the batter may not be entirely smooth.

7 Bake for 35 to 40 minutes, until the layers are golden brown and a toothpick inserted into the center comes out clean; the layers will barely spring back when gently pressed in the center. Cool in the pans on a rack for 5 minutes. Run a small sharp knife around the sides of the layers to release them, cover with racks, invert, and carefully lift off the pans and papers. Cool the layers upside down for 10 minutes, then cover them with other racks, invert, and cool completely right side up.

8 For the buttercream, in a large bowl, beat the egg yolks with an electric mixer on medium-high speed until very thick, about 5 minutes. Combine the sugar and corn syrup in a small heavy saucepan, set the pan over medium-high heat, and stir constantly with a heatproof rubber spatula until the mixture comes to a full rolling boil. Immediately scrape the mixture into a measuring cup. Pour a dollop of the hot sugar mixture into the yolks and beat on high speed for a few seconds. Stop the machine, add another dollop, and beat it in. Repeat until all the syrup has been added, then beat until the mixture cools to room temperature.

9 On medium speed, add the soft butter about 2 tablespoons at a time, beating after each addition until thoroughly incorporated. The buttercream will be very soft at first, then it will begin to hold its shape and be thick enough to spread. Scrape the bowl and beaters well and beat in the Grand Marnier and salt.

10 Trim any crusty edges from the layers. To frost the cake, place one layer upside down on a plate and spread with about 1 cup of the buttercream. Place the second layer right side up on the first layer and frost the sides and top with the remaining buttercream. Let stand until the frosting is set. To serve, rinse a sharp knife in hot water and shake off the excess water before making each cut. Refrigerate leftovers. Bring to room temperature before serving.

CAKE SENSE

The more quickly *the beating and mixing of the cake are done, the lighter and finer will be the cake.*

—Maria Parloa, *Miss Parloa's Kitchen Companion* (1887)

CALIFORNIA FORTY-NINER CAKE

*Makes one
9-inch
2-layer cake,
12 servings*

Ten egg yolks (and no egg whites) give this cake a marvelous golden color and an especially tender, buttery texture and taste. The frosting is a classic one made by beating egg whites and flavorings over boiling water. These so-called 7-minute icings became all the rage once electric hand-held mixers became household staples in the 1940s. This cake is at its best the day it is frosted.

CAKE

- 2¼ cups sifted cake flour
- ½ teaspoon baking soda
- ½ teaspoon salt
- 10 large egg yolks
- 1½ cups sugar
- ¾ cup (1½ sticks) unsalted butter, at room temperature
- 1 teaspoon pure vanilla extract
- 1 teaspoon pure lemon extract
- 1 cup buttermilk

ICING

- 2 large egg whites
- ¾ cup sugar
- ⅓ cup light corn syrup
- Finely grated zest of 1 lemon
- 1 tablespoon fresh lemon juice
- ¼ teaspoon cream of tartar
- ¼ teaspoon salt

1 For the cake, adjust an oven rack to the center position and preheat the oven to 350°F. Grease two 9-inch round cake pans well. Line the bottoms with rounds of waxed paper or cooking parchment. Butter the paper and dust the bottoms of the pans with flour. Tap out the excess and set aside.

2 Resift the cake flour with the baking soda and salt; set aside.

3 In a large bowl, beat the egg yolks with an electric mixer on medium-high speed until very thick and pale, about 5 minutes. Beat in ½ cup of the sugar about 1 tablespoon at a time, beating for a few seconds after each addition. Scrape the bowl and beaters. Beat for 3 to 4 minutes longer, until the yolks are very thick and form a ribbon when the beaters are raised.

4 In another large bowl, beat the butter on medium speed until smooth, about 1 minute. Add the vanilla, lemon extract, and ¼ cup of the sugar and beat for 1 minute. Beat in the remaining ¾ cup sugar 3 to 4 tablespoons at a time, beating for 20 to 30 seconds after each addition. Scrape the bowl and beaters well, then beat for 5 minutes. Add the beaten yolks in 4 additions, beating for about 30 seconds after each addition. Scrape the bowl, and beat for 1 minute more.

5 On low speed, add the flour mixture in 3 additions, alternating with the buttermilk, beginning and ending with the flour and beating only until smooth. Gently divide the batter between the two pans. To level the batter, rotate the pans briskly on your countertop.

6 Bake for 30 to 35 minutes, until the layers are golden brown and barely spring back when gently pressed and a toothpick inserted into the center comes out clean. Cool on a rack for 5 minutes. Run a small sharp knife around the sides of the layers to release them, cover the pans with wire racks, invert, and carefully lift off the pans. Gently peel off the papers, then replace them on the layers. Cover the layers with other racks and invert to cool completely right side up. (The layers can be made ahead and frozen for up to 1 month.)

7 For the icing, put enough water into the bottom of a double boiler so that the top pan touches the water when inserted. (Or put the water in a large saucepan and place a smaller saucepan on top.) Remove the top pan and bring the water to a boil over high heat. Place all the icing ingredients in the top pan and stir to combine them well. Set the top into the bottom and immediately begin beating the mixture with an electric mixer on medium-high speed. Beat for several minutes, until the icing has greatly increased in volume, is pure white, and forms peaks when the beaters are raised. Remove the pan from the water and beat for 1 to 2 minutes more, until the icing is very thick, forms stiff peaks, and is spreadable. (You can use the icing while it is still warm.)

8 To frost the cake, place one layer upside down on a plate, remove the paper, and spread with about 1 cup of the icing. Place the second layer right side up on the first layer and frost the sides and top with the remaining icing. Make attractive swirls on top with the back of a spoon. Let stand until the icing is set. To serve, rinse a sharp knife in hot water and shake off the excess water before making each cut.

GOLDEN GLORY LAYER CAKE

*Makes one
9-inch
2-layer cake,
12 to 16
servings*

This tender, golden layer cake is filled and frosted with a supremely smooth orange cream cheese icing.

CAKE

2¹/₂ cups sifted cake flour

¹/₂ teaspoon baking soda

¹/₂ teaspoon salt

12 large egg yolks

8 tablespoons (1 stick) unsalted butter, at room temperature

¹/₄ cup vegetable shortening

2 teaspoons pure vanilla extract

1¹/₂ cups sugar

1 cup buttermilk

FROSTING

2 8-ounce packages cream cheese (do not use low-fat), at room temperature

8 tablespoons (1 stick) unsalted butter, at room temperature

Pinch of salt

Finely grated zest of 1 large orange (about 2 tablespoons)

2 teaspoons pure orange extract

2 cups confectioners' sugar

1 For the cake, adjust an oven rack to the lower third position and preheat the oven to 350°F. Butter or grease two 9-inch round cake pans. Line the bottoms with rounds of waxed paper or cooking parchment. Butter the papers and dust the bottoms of the pans with all-purpose flour. Knock out the excess and set aside.

2 Resift the flour with the baking soda and salt; set aside.

3 In a large bowl, beat the egg yolks with an electric mixer on high speed for about 5 minutes, until very thick and pale.

4 In another large bowl, beat the butter and shortening on medium speed for 1 minute, until smooth and creamy. Add the vanilla extract and ¹/₄ cup of the sugar and beat for 1 minute on medium-high speed. Beat in the remaining 1¹/₄ cups sugar about ¹/₄ cup at a time, beating for 20 to 30 seconds after each addition, then beat for 5 minutes. Add about one third of the beaten yolks and beat for 1 minute. Add the remaining egg yolks in 2 installments, beating for 1 minute after each addition.

5 On low speed, add the flour mixture in 3 additions, alternating with the buttermilk, beginning and ending with the flour and beating only until thoroughly incorporated. Divide the batter evenly between the prepared pans. To level the batter, rotate the pans briskly on your countertop.

6 Bake for about 35 minutes, until the layers are a deep golden brown and a toothpick inserted into the center comes out clean. Cool in the pans on wire racks for 10 minutes. Use a small sharp knife to release the layers from the sides, cover with wire racks, invert, and carefully lift off the pans. Gently peel off the liners, then replace them on the layers. Cover with other racks, invert, and cool completely right side up.

7 For the frosting, beat the cream cheese, butter, and salt in a large bowl on medium speed until very smooth and creamy. Beat in the orange zest and extract. On low speed, beat in the confectioners' sugar until incorporated, then beat on medium-high speed for about 1 minute, until the frosting is very smooth.

8 To frost the cake, trim any crusty edges off the cake layers with a small sharp knife. Place one of the layers upside down on a plate and peel off the paper. Using a narrow metal spatula, spread with about 1 cup of the frosting. Place the second layer right side up on the first layer. Frost the sides and top of the cake with the remaining frosting. To serve, rinse a knife in hot water and shake off the excess water before making each cut.

SAGE ADVICE

Do not attempt to make cake without fresh eggs. Cream of tartar, soda and yeast powders are poor substitutes for these. A fresh egg placed in water will sink to the bottom. In breaking eggs, do not break them over the vessel in which they are to be beaten. Break them, one by one, over a saucer, so that if you come across a defective one, you will not spoil the rest by mixing it with them; whereas, if it is a good one, it will be easy to pour the white from the saucer into the bowl with the rest of the whites, and to add the yolk which you retain in the egg-shell to the other yolks.

—Marion Cabell Tyree, editor,
Housekeeping in Old Virginia (1879)

CHOCOLATE AND GOLD RIBBON CAKE

*Makes one
9-inch
4-layer cake,
12 to 16
servings*

The inspiration for this wonderfully old-fashioned cake comes from a prize-winning Pillsbury Bake-Off recipe. You begin by making a golden cake batter, and flavoring half of it with almond extract, cocoa, and espresso powder. A positively luxurious chocolate buttercream frosting goes between the layers and all over the outside. The frosting recipe calls for raw eggs; if you are concerned about egg safety, see page 272 for a perfectly safe method for handling raw eggs.

CAKE

- 1 tablespoon instant espresso powder (I use Medaglia d'Oro)
- 1½ tablespoons unsweetened cocoa
- 1½ tablespoons warm water
- ¼ teaspoon pure almond extract
- 2¾ cups sifted cake flour
- ½ teaspoon baking soda
- ½ teaspoon salt
- ¾ cup (1½ sticks) unsalted butter, at room temperature
- 2 teaspoons pure vanilla extract
- 1½ cups sugar
- 4 large eggs
- 1 cup buttermilk

FROSTING

- 1 12-ounce bag (2 cups) bittersweet or semisweet chocolate morsels
- 8 tablespoons (1 stick) unsalted butter, at room temperature
- 2 teaspoons pure vanilla extract
- 1 cup confectioners' sugar
- 4 large eggs
- 1–2 tablespoons hot water, if needed

1 For the cake, adjust an oven rack to the center position and preheat the oven to 350°F. Butter or grease two 9-inch round cake pans. Line the bottoms with rounds of waxed paper or cooking parchment. Butter the papers and dust the bottoms of the pans with all-purpose flour. Knock out the excess flour and set aside.

2 In a small bowl or a custard cup, stir together the espresso, cocoa, water, and almond extract until very smooth. Cover tightly with plastic wrap and set aside.

3 Resift the cake flour with the baking soda and salt; set aside.

4 In a large bowl, beat the butter with an electric mixer on medium speed until smooth, about 1 minute. Add the vanilla and $1/4$ cup of the sugar and beat on medium-high speed for 1 minute. Beat in the remaining $1^1/4$ cups sugar $1/4$ cup at a time, beating for 20 to 30 seconds after each addition. Scrape the bowl and beaters and beat for 6 minutes. Beat in the eggs one at a time, beating for 30 seconds after each.

5 On low speed, add the flour mixture in 3 additions, alternating with the buttermilk, beginning and ending with the flour and beating only until the batter is smooth. Spoon half the batter ($2^1/2$ cups) into one of the prepared pans. Stir the espresso-cocoa mixture thoroughly into the remaining batter, and scrape it into the second pan. Level the batter by rotating the pans briskly on your countertop.

6 Bake for 30 to 35 minutes, until the layers spring back when gently pressed and a toothpick inserted into the centers comes out clean. Cool in the pans for 10 minutes. Run the tip of a small sharp knife around the layers to release them, cover with wire racks, and invert. Carefully lift off the pans and papers. Cover with other racks, invert, and cool completely right side up.

7 For the frosting, melt the chocolate in the top of a double boiler or in a small saucepan set into a larger pan of hot water, stirring occasionally until smooth. Remove from the water and set aside, stirring occasionally, until the chocolate is completely cool, about 1 hour.

8 In a large bowl, beat the butter with an electric mixer on medium speed until smooth, about 1 minute. Add the vanilla and confectioners' sugar and beat on low speed until incorporated, then beat on medium speed for 1 minute. On medium-high speed, beat in the eggs one at a time, beating for 1 minute after each. Add the cooled chocolate and beat on low speed until smooth and creamy, 1 to 2 minutes.

9 Using a serrated knife, split each layer horizontally in half. Place the top of the chocolate layer upside down on a cake plate. Stir the frosting. If it has set or seems difficult to spread, beat in a little hot water. Using a metal spatula, spread $1/2$ cup of the frosting on the chocolate layer (it will be a very thin layer). Place the bottom half of the yellow cake layer cut side down on top and spread with ¹/₂ cup frosting. Set the bottom half of the chocolate layer cut side up on the yellow layer and spread with ¹/₂ cup frosting. Place the top half of the yellow layer right side up on the chocolate layer and frost the sides and top with the remaining frosting, making it as smooth and even as possible. Let stand until the icing has set. To serve, rinse a sharp knife in hot water and shake off the excess water before making each cut.

MAKING RAW EGGS SAFE

According to the American Egg Board, *Salmonella* bacteria are killed instantly at 160°F. To accomplish this, crack the eggs into a small metal bowl and stir them well with a fork just to break up the yolks and to combine them with the whites. *Do not beat.* Set the bowl in a pan of almost simmering water and stir and scrape gently with a narrow rubber spatula until you see the eggs getting very hot and steamy.

If you have a digital probe thermometer, attach it to the side of the bowl. As soon as the temperature reaches 160°F, remove the bowl from the hot water and set it in a pan of cold water. Stir gently with the spatula until the eggs reach room temperature. They are now safe to use in any recipe. Scrape the eggs into a glass measure and beat in ¹/₄ cup of them at a time where the recipe calls for the addition of 1 egg.

If you have an instant-read thermometer, pour boiling water into a heatproof cup and set it next to the heating eggs. When the eggs look as if they're hot, remove the bowl from the hot water, tip it so that the eggs pool to one side, and insert the thermometer. If the eggs have not reached 160°F, return them to the hot water bath and place the thermometer back in the cup of boiling water (to kill any bacteria that might be present). Repeat the testing (returning the thermometer to the hot water each time) until the eggs reach 160°F (or slightly higher: eggs cook at 180°F, so you have some leeway). Cool them as directed above, and they're ready to use.

CHOCOLATE BUTTERMILK LAYER CAKE

*Makes one
9-inch
2-layer cake,
12 to 16
servings*

This is a tender, light, splendidly high cake that is not too chocolaty. It is frosted with a luxuriously smooth and silky chocolate buttercream. Kids of all ages will love it. It begs to be eaten with a tall glass of cold milk.

CAKE

- 3 cups sifted cake flour
- 1/2 teaspoon salt
- 4 ounces (4 squares) bittersweet or semisweet chocolate, chopped
- 2 tablespoons dark rum (I use Myers's)
- 1 tablespoon hot water
- 3/4 cup (1 1/2 sticks) unsalted butter, at room temperature
- 1 3/4 cups sugar
- 2 teaspoons pure vanilla extract
- 1 large egg, separated
- 3 large eggs
- 2 large egg whites
- 1 1/4 cups buttermilk
- 3/4 teaspoon baking soda

BUTTERCREAM FROSTING

- 1 cup sugar
- 1/2 cup water
- 14 ounces (four 3.5-ounce bars) Swiss bittersweet chocolate, broken into pieces
- 1 tablespoon pure vanilla extract
- 1/8 teaspoon salt
- 1 1/2 cups (3 sticks) unsalted butter, at room temperature
- 5 large egg yolks
  Milk or cream, if necessary

1 For the cake, adjust an oven rack to the lower third position and preheat the oven to 350°F. Butter or grease two 9-inch round cake pans. Line the bottoms with rounds of waxed paper or cooking parchment, butter the papers, and dust the bottoms of the pans with all-purpose flour. Knock out the excess flour and set aside.

2 Resift the cake flour with the salt; set aside.

3 Place the chocolate and rum in a small saucepan and melt the chocolate

over very low heat, stirring occasionally with a small whisk (the chocolate may not be completely smooth). Remove from the heat and whisk in the water. The chocolate will become smooth. Set aside.

4 In a large bowl, beat the butter with an electric mixer on medium speed until smooth and creamy, about 1 minute. Add $1/4$ cup of the sugar and the vanilla and beat for 1 minute. Beat in $11/4$ cups of the remaining sugar about $1/4$ cup at a time, beating for 15 to 20 seconds after each addition. Increase the speed to medium-high and beat for 5 minutes. On medium speed, add the egg yolk, then the 3 eggs one at a time, beating for about 1 minute after each addition. Scrape the bowl and beaters. Add the chocolate mixture and beat on low speed only to incorporate.

5 Stir the buttermilk and baking soda together in a 2-cup glass measure. The mixture will become very bubbly. On low speed, add the flour mixture to the batter in 4 additions, alternating with the buttermilk mixture, beginning and ending with the flour and beating only until each addition is thoroughly incorporated. Set aside.

6 In a medium bowl, with clean beaters, beat the 3 egg whites on medium speed until they hold a soft shape. Beat in the remaining $1/4$ cup sugar about 1 tablespoon at a time, beating for about 15 seconds after each addition. Increase the speed to medium-high and beat until the whites form peaks that curl only slightly at their tips. Transfer about one third of the whites to the chocolate mixture and fold in gently with a large rubber spatula. Don't be too thorough; fold only until no streaks of whites show. Fold in the remaining whites in 2 additions. Divide the batter evenly between the prepared pans. To level the batter, rotate the pans briskly on your countertop.

7 Bake for 35 to 40 minutes, until the layers just begin to pull away from the sides of the pans and the tops barely spring back when gently pressed; do not overbake. Cool in the pans for 10 minutes. Run the tip of a small sharp knife all around the sides of the layers to release them, cover with wire racks, and invert. Carefully lift off the pans and papers. Cover the layers with other racks, and invert to cool completely right side up.

8 For the frosting, combine the sugar and water in a small saucepan and bring to a boil over medium heat, stirring occasionally to dissolve the

sugar. Remove from the heat and whisk in the chocolate until very smooth, then whisk in the vanilla and salt. Set aside, stirring occasionally with a rubber spatula, until the mixture reaches room temperature.

9 In a large bowl, beat the butter with an electric mixer on medium speed until smooth, about 1 minute. Beat in the egg yolks one at a time, beating well after each. On low speed, gradually add about one third of the chocolate mixture, beating only until combined. Beat in the remaining chocolate mixture in 2 installments. The frosting should be thick, smooth, and spreadable. If it seems too thick, thin it with droplets of milk or cream.

10 To frost the cake, place one layer upside down on a cake plate and spread with about 1 cup of the frosting. Place the second layer right side up on the first layer and frost the sides and top with the remaining frosting. Refrigerate for about 1 hour to set the frosting. To serve, rinse a sharp knife in hot water and shake off the excess water before making each cut.

MALTED MILK–CHOCOLATE CAKE

Makes one 9-inch 2-layer cake, 12 to 16 servings

Malted milk gives this cake a subtle and intriguing taste. The chocolate frosting is made first and part of it used in the batter. When the cake is baked and cooled, the rest of the frosting's ready. Malted milk powder and malted milk balls are sold in supermarkets.

FROSTING

- 1 8-ounce package cream cheese (do not use low-fat), at room temperature
- 2 tablespoons unsalted butter, at room temperature
- 2 teaspoons pure vanilla extract
- 6 cups confectioners' sugar
- 3 tablespoons hot water
- 7 ounces (7 squares) unsweetened chocolate, melted and cooled

CAKE

- 2^1/$_2$ cups sifted cake flour
- ^{1}/$_2$ cup malted milk powder (I use Carnation original flavor)
- 1^1/$_2$ teaspoons baking soda
- ^{1}/$_2$ teaspoon salt
- 8 tablespoons (1 stick) unsalted butter, at room temperature
- 4 large eggs
- ^{3}/$_4$ cup buttermilk
- ^{1}/$_3$ cup coarsely crushed malted milk balls

1 Adjust an oven rack to the center position and preheat the oven to 350°F. Butter two 9-inch round cake pans and line the bottoms with rounds of waxed paper or cooking parchment. Butter the papers and dust the bottoms of the pans with all-purpose flour. Knock out the excess and set aside.

2 For the frosting, beat the cream cheese, butter, and vanilla in a large bowl with an electric mixer on medium speed until smooth, about 2 minutes. On low speed, add the confectioners' sugar about 1 cup at a time, beating only until the mixture is smooth. Gradually beat in the hot water. Beat in the chocolate only until incorporated. Scrape the beaters well but don't wash; set them aside. Stir the frosting gently with a rubber spatula to mix thoroughly. Transfer 2 cups of the frosting to a small bowl, cover with plastic wrap, and set aside for icing the cake.

3 For the cake, resift the flour with the malted milk powder, baking soda, and

salt. If any particles of malted milk remain in the sifter, add them to the sifted flour mixture. Set aside.

4 Add the butter to the frosting remaining in the mixing bowl and beat on medium speed for 1 minute. Beat in the eggs one at a time, beating for 1 minute after each.

5 On low speed, add the flour mixture in 3 additions, alternating with the buttermilk, beginning and ending with the flour and beating only until the batter is smooth. Divide the batter evenly between the two pans. To level the batter, briskly rotate the pans on your countertop.

6 Bake for 25 to 30 minutes, until the layers are golden brown and spring back when gently pressed in the center; do not overbake. Cool on a rack for 10 minutes. Run a small sharp knife around the layers to release them from the sides of the pan. Cover the cakes with wire racks, invert, and carefully lift off the pans and papers. Cover the cakes with other wire racks, invert, and cool completely right side up.

7 To frost the cake, trim away any crusty edges with a small sharp knife. Place one layer upside down on a cake plate and spread with about $1/2$ cup of the frosting. Place the second layer right side up on the first layer and frost the sides and top with the remaining frosting. Sprinkle the crushed malted milk balls over the top of the cake. Let stand for about 1 hour until the frosting is set. To serve, rinse a sharp knife in hot water and shake off the excess water before making each cut.

DEVIL'S FOOD CAKE

Makes one 9-inch 2-layer cake, 12 to 16 servings

Chocolate layer cakes arrived in cookbooks around 1880. The name "devil's food" made its appearance in the twentieth century, perhaps because of the cake's redness but more likely as the antithesis of the nineteenth-century angel food cake.

The chocolate custard base in this cake dates back almost one hundred years. I based the recipe on one from 1910 in *Home Helps: A Pure Food Cook Book*, a publicity pamphlet for shortening featuring recipes from culinary luminaries of the day, including Mrs. Rorer and Mrs. Lincoln. The cake is fudgy and tender with an intense chocolate flavor, and the chocolate sour cream frosting is creamy, smooth, and not too sweet.

CHOCOCOLATE CUSTARD

- 1/2 cup milk
- 3 ounces (3 squares) unsweetened chocolate, chopped
- 1 cup firmly packed light brown sugar
- 1 large egg yolk

CAKE

- 2 1/4 cups sifted cake flour
- 1/2 teaspoon baking soda
- 1/2 teaspoon salt
- 8 tablespoons (1 stick) unsalted butter, at room temperature
- 2 teaspoons pure vanilla extract
- 3/4 cup firmly packed light brown sugar

- 2 large eggs, separated
- 1/2 cup milk
- 1 large egg white
- 2 tablespoons sugar

FROSTING

- 4 ounces (4 squares) unsweetened chocolate
- 3 tablespoons unsalted butter
- 3/4 cup sour cream
- 2 teaspoons pure vanilla extract
  Pinch of salt
- 4 cups (one 1-pound box) confectioners' sugar

1 For the chocolate custard, heat the milk in a small heavy saucepan over medium-low heat until steaming hot. Add the chocolate and stir occasionally with a whisk as the chocolate melts, then whisk until smooth. Add the brown sugar and whisk it in until partly dissolved. Stir in the egg yolk with

a heatproof rubber spatula. Increase the heat to medium and stir constantly until the mixture is slightly thickened. Remove from the heat and stir occasionally until the custard reaches room temperature; it will thicken as it cools.

2 For the cake, adjust an oven rack to the lower third position and preheat the oven to 350°F. Butter two 9-inch round cake pans. Line the bottoms with rounds of waxed paper or cooking parchment. Butter the papers and dust the bottoms of the pans with all-purpose flour. Knock out the excess and set aside.

3 Resift the flour with the baking soda and salt; set aside.

4 In a large bowl, beat the butter with an electric mixer on medium speed until smooth, about 1 minute. Add the vanilla and ¼ cup of the brown sugar and beat on medium-high speed for 1 minute. Add the remaining ½ cup brown sugar ¼ cup at a time, beating for 20 to 30 seconds after each addition. Scrape the bowl and beaters and beat for 5 minutes. Add the egg yolks and beat for 1 minute.

5 On low speed, beat in the flour mixture in 3 additions, alternating with the milk, beginning and ending with the flour and beating only until each addition is thoroughly incorporated. Stop to scrape the bowl and beaters as necessary. Add the cooled chocolate custard and beat it in only until incorporated. Set aside.

6 In a medium bowl, with clean beaters, beat the 3 egg whites on medium speed until they form soft peaks that droop at their tips when the beaters are raised. Gradually beat in the sugar. Increase the speed to medium-high and continue beating until the whites form stiff, shiny peaks that curl slightly at their tips when the beaters are raised. Fold the whites into the chocolate batter in 2 additions, folding only until no whites show. Divide the batter between the prepared pans. To level the batter, briskly rotate the pans on your countertop.

7 Bake for 35 to 45 minutes, until the layers barely spring back when gently pressed in the center. (They should not have started to shrink away from the sides of the pans.) Cool in the pans on a wire rack for 10 minutes. Loosen the cakes from the pans by running the tip of a small sharp knife all around them. Cover with wire racks and carefully lift off the pans and

papers. Cover the layers with other racks, invert, and cool completely right side up.

8 For the frosting, melt the chocolate with the butter in a small heavy saucepan over low heat, whisking occasionally until smooth. Remove from the heat and set aside until completely cool. Whisk the sour cream, vanilla, and salt together in a large bowl. Add the confectioners' sugar about one fourth at a time, whisking until very smooth. Whisk in the cooled chocolate until very smooth. If necessary, let stand until spreadable.

9 To frost the cake, trim away any crusty edges with a small sharp knife. Place one layer upside down on a cake plate and spread with about $3/4$ cup of the frosting. Place the second layer right side up on the first layer and frost the sides and top with the remaining frosting. Use the back of a teaspoon to make peaks and swirls in the frosting on top of the cake, if you wish. Let stand about 1 hour until the frosting is set. To serve, rinse a sharp knife in hot water and shake off the excess water before making each cut.

CHOCOLATE ESPRESSO LAYER CAKE

Makes one 9-inch 2-layer cake, 12 to 16 servings

Flavored with cocoa, coffee, and vanilla, this is a dream of a layer cake. The texture is classically light and fluffy, and the frosting is creamy, buttery, and very chocolaty, but not too sweet.

CAKE

2¹/₄ cups sifted cake flour

¹/₄ cup unsweetened cocoa

¹/₂ teaspoon baking soda

¹/₂ teaspoon salt

1 tablespoon instant espresso powder (I use Medaglia d'Oro)

8 tablespoons (1 stick) unsalted butter, at room temperature

¹/₄ cup vegetable shortening

2 teaspoons pure vanilla extract

1¹/₂ cups sugar

4 large eggs

1 cup buttermilk

FROSTING

8 tablespoons (1 stick) unsalted butter, at room temperature

2 large egg yolks

¹/₂ cup unsweetened cocoa

1 tablespoon instant espresso powder

¹/₃–¹/₂ cup heavy cream or milk

2 teaspoons pure vanilla extract

2 cups confectioners' sugar

1 For the cake, adjust an oven rack to the center position and preheat the oven to 350°F. Butter or grease two 9-inch round cake pans. Line the bottoms with rounds of waxed paper or cooking parchment. Butter the papers and dust the bottoms of the pans with all-purpose flour. Knock out the excess and set aside.

2 Resift the flour with the cocoa, baking soda, salt, and espresso; set aside.

3 In a large bowl, beat the butter and shortening with an electric mixer on medium speed for about 1 minute, until smooth. Add the vanilla and ¹/₄ cup of the sugar and beat for 1 minute. Beat in the remaining 1¹/₄ cups sugar about ¹/₄ cup at a time, beating for about 15 seconds after each addition, then beat for 5 minutes on medium-high speed. Add the eggs one at a time, beating for 1 minute after each.

4 On low speed, add the flour mixture in 3 additions, alternating with the buttermilk, beginning and ending with the flour and beating only until the batter is smooth. Divide the batter evenly between the prepared pans. To level the batter, rotate the pans briskly on your countertop.

5 Bake for 35 to 40 minutes, just until the layers spring back when gently pressed. (They should not pull away from the sides of the pans.) Cool in the pans for 10 minutes. Run the tip of a small sharp knife around the sides of the layers to release them, cover with wire racks, and invert. Carefully lift off the pans and papers. Cover the layers with other racks, invert, and cool completely right side up.

6 For the frosting, beat together the butter, egg yolks, cocoa, espresso, $^1/_3$ cup cream or milk, and vanilla in a large bowl with an electric mixer on low speed to combine well. Beat on medium speed for 1 to 2 minutes, until smooth. Add the confectioners' sugar and beat on low speed until incorporated, then beat on medium speed until smooth. Add more cream or milk if necessary to make the frosting spreadable.

7 To frost, place one of the layers upside down on a cake plate. Spread with about one third of the frosting. Place the second layer right side up on the frosting. Spread the remaining frosting over the sides and top of the cake. Let stand about 1 hour until the frosting has set. To serve, rinse a sharp knife in hot water and shake off excess water before making each cut.

BANANA SPLIT LAYER CAKE WITH CHOCOLATE FROSTING

*Makes one
9-inch
3-layer cake,
16 servings*

This gorgeous 4-inch-tall moist, tender cake is packed with banana flavor, in both cake and filling. A smooth bittersweet chocolate frosting cloaks the cake.

FILLING

- ³/₄ cup sugar
- ³/₄ cup evaporated milk
- 2 large egg yolks
- 3 tablespoons unsalted butter, cut into pieces
- ¹/₄ cup mashed ripe banana
- ³/₄ cup finely chopped walnuts
- 1¹/₂ teaspoons pure vanilla extract

CAKE

- 3 cups sifted cake flour
- ¹/₂ teaspoon baking soda
- ¹/₂ teaspoon salt
- ³/₄ cup (1¹/₂ sticks) unsalted butter, at room temperature
- 1³/₄ cups sugar

- 1 teaspoon pure vanilla extract
- 2 large eggs, separated
- 3 large eggs
- 1 cup mashed bananas (2–3 medium bananas)
- ¹/₂ cup buttermilk

FROSTING

- 2 ounces (2 squares) unsweetened chocolate
- 4 tablespoons (¹/₂ stick) unsalted butter, cut into pieces
- ¹/₄ cup milk, plus more if needed
- 2 cups confectioners' sugar
- ¹/₃ cup Dutch-process cocoa
- 1¹/₂ teaspoons pure vanilla extract

1 For the filling, stir together the sugar, evaporated milk, egg yolks, and butter in a medium heavy saucepan set over medium heat. Cook, stirring occasionally with a heatproof rubber spatula until the butter is melted and the sugar dissolved. Increase the heat to medium-high and stir constantly, scraping the bottom, until the mixture boils and thickens and becomes opaque and tan. Cook for about 10 minutes, until the consistency of a thick cream sauce. Remove from the heat and stir in the mashed banana, walnuts, and vanilla. Let cool completely, stirring occasionally. (The filling can be made a day ahead, covered and refrigerated. Bring to room temperature before using.)

2 For the cake, adjust two oven racks to divide the oven into thirds and preheat the oven to 350°F. Butter or grease three 9-inch round cake pans. Line the bottoms with rounds of waxed paper or cooking parchment. Butter the papers and dust the bottoms of the pans with all-purpose flour. Knock out the excess and set aside.

3 Resift the flour with the baking soda and salt; set aside.

4 In a large bowl, beat the butter with an electric mixer on medium speed for about 1 minute, until smooth. Add ¼ cup of the sugar and the vanilla extract and beat on medium-high speed for 1 minute. Beat in 1¼ more cups of the remaining sugar ¼ cup at a time, beating for about 15 seconds after each addition, then beat for 5 minutes. Add the egg yolks and beat for 1 minute. Add the whole eggs one at a time, beating for 1 minute after each. Beat in the banana on medium speed.

5 On low speed, add the flour mixture in 3 additions, alternating with the buttermilk, beginning and ending with the flour and beating only until the batter is smooth.

6 With clean beaters, beat the 2 egg whites in a medium bowl on medium speed until they form soft drooping peaks when the beaters are raised. Beat in the remaining ¼ cup sugar about 1 tablespoon at a time, beating for 15 seconds after each addition. Increase the speed to medium-high and beat only until the whites form shiny peaks that curl slightly at their tips. Using a large wide rubber spatula, fold the whites gently into the batter only until no whites show. Divide the batter evenly among the prepared pans. To level the batter, rotate the pans briskly on your countertop.

7 Place the pans in the oven, two on the upper rack and one on the lower. Bake for 25 to 30 minutes, until the layers are golden brown and spring back when gently pressed in the center. (The layer in the bottom rack will be done first.) Cool in the pans on wire racks for 10 minutes. Run the tip of a small sharp knife around the sides of the layers to release them, cover with wire racks, and invert. Carefully lift off the pans and the papers. Replace the papers on the bottoms, then cover the layers with other racks, invert, and cool completely right side up.

8 For the frosting, melt the chocolate with the butter in a small heavy saucepan over very low heat, stirring occasionally with a whisk. Whisk in the milk. Place the confectioners' sugar in a medium bowl, add the chocolate mixture, and beat with an electric mixer on low speed until very smooth. Beat in the cocoa and vanilla, then beat on medium speed until thick and smooth. The frosting should be spreadable; beat in a few droplets of milk if necessary.

9 To frost the cake, place one of the layers upside down on a cake plate and peel away the paper. Using a narrow metal spatula, spread the layer with half of the banana filling. Remove the paper from a second layer and set it upside down on the filling. Spread with the remaining filling. Place the last layer right side up on top. Spread the chocolate frosting on the sides and top of the cake. Let stand until the frosting has set. (The cake can be made a day ahead and refrigerated, but bring it to room temperature before serving.) To serve, rinse a sharp knife in hot water and shake off excess water before making each cut. Refrigerate leftovers.

BANANA BOATS

Clipper ships were bringing bananas to the eastern states in the 1850s, but it wasn't until the Civil War ended that the fruit began arriving on a regular basis, thanks to the efforts of a railroad builder, Minor C. Kieth. Kieth and his three brothers and thousands of laborers began building a railroad in Costa Rica in 1870. More than four thousand workers died from tropical diseases in the process, along with all of Kieth's brothers. Undeterred, Kieth somehow managed to complete the railroad. Then he looked around to find a crop that would make it profitable. He decided on bananas, and with the help of citizens of Costa Rica, he established some plantations. Within a few years, his fruit was being shipped to New York and New Orleans, and by 1889, bananas were available year-round.

COCONUT LAYER CAKE

Makes one 9-inch 2-layer cake, 12 to 16 servings

This spectacular white cake is flavored with coconut milk and pure coconut extract and filled and frosted with a fluffy white icing. Shredded coconut is generously sprinkled between the layers and along the sides and top of the cake. Make this the day you will serve it, since the icing will not hold up longer than that. My preference is to use fresh coconut, and if you have the time to prepare your own, you'll be well rewarded for your efforts, but packaged sweetened shredded coconut is certainly fine.

CAKE

- 3 cups sifted cake flour
- 1 1/2 teaspoons baking powder, preferably nonaluminum
- 1/2 teaspoon salt
- 1 cup (2 sticks) unsalted butter, at room temperature
- 2 teaspoons pure coconut extract
- 2 teaspoons pure vanilla extract
- 1 1/2 cups plus 1/3 cup sugar
- 8 large egg whites—6 whites in one bowl, the remaining 2 in another
- 1 1/4 cups canned unsweetened coconut milk, stirred well before measuring

ICING

- 4 large egg whites
- 1/8 teaspoon salt
- 1/4 cup light corn syrup
- 2 tablespoons water
- 2 1/2 cups confectioners' sugar
- 1 teaspoon pure coconut extract
- 1 teaspoon pure vanilla extract
- 2 1/2 cups (8 ounces) chopped shredded coconut (fresh or packaged sweetened)

1 For the cake, adjust an oven rack to the lower third position and preheat the oven to 350°F. Butter or grease two 9-inch round cake pans. Line the bottoms with rounds of waxed paper or cooking parchment. Butter the paper and dust the bottoms of the pans with all-purpose flour. Knock out the excess and set aside.

2 Resift the flour with the baking powder and salt; set aside.

3 In a large bowl, beat the butter with an electric mixer on medium speed until smooth, about 1 minute. Add the coconut extract, vanilla, and 1/4 cup

of the sugar and beat on medium-high speed for 1 minute. Beat in 1¹/₄ more cups of the sugar about ¹/₄ cup at a time, beating for 20 to 30 seconds after each addition, then beat for 5 minutes. Add 2 of the egg whites and beat on low speed until incorporated, then increase the speed to medium and beat for 2 minutes.

4 On low speed, add the flour mixture in 4 additions, alternating with the coconut milk, beginning and ending with the flour and beating only until smooth after each addition.

5 In a large bowl with clean beaters, beat the remaining 6 egg whites on medium speed until they form very soft peaks that droop at their tips. Gradually beat in the remaining ¹/₃ cup sugar in 4 installments, beating for about 10 seconds between additions, then increase the speed to medium-high and beat until the whites are thick and shiny like marshmallow cream and form peaks with slightly drooping points. With a large rubber spatula, transfer about one fourth of the whites to the batter. Gently fold in the whites, using 6 or 7 broad strokes; do not be too thorough. Gently fold in the remaining whites in 3 additions. Carefully divide the batter between the two pans, handling it as gently as possible. To level the batter, rotate the pans briskly on your countertop.

6 Bake for 35 to 40 minutes, until the layers are golden brown and just beginning to pull away from the sides and a toothpick inserted into the center comes out clean. Cool in the pans on a wire rack for 5 minutes. Run a small sharp knife around the layers to release them from the pans. Cover the pans with wire racks and invert. Carefully lift off the pans and the papers, then replace the papers on the layers. Cover the cakes with other racks, invert, and cool completely right side up.

7 Place one of the cooled cake layers upside down on a cake plate and remove the paper; set aside.

8 For the icing, you'll need to construct a large water bath; I use a medium saucepan set in a large deep sauté pan (about 12 inches in diameter and 3 inches deep). Put about 2 inches of water in the larger pan and set it over moderate heat. When the water is hot, combine the egg whites, salt, corn syrup, water, and confectioners' sugar in the saucepan. Set the pan in the hot water bath and beat with an electric mixer on high speed for 5 to 6 minutes, until the icing forms stiff peaks when the beaters are raised. Immediately remove the pan from the water bath and scrape the icing into a large bowl. Add both extracts and beat the icing on high speed until it is very thick, like a stiff meringue. You must use the icing right away; work quickly.

9 Combine about one third of the icing with ³/₄ cup of the chopped coconut in a medium bowl and stir to mix, then spread evenly over the layer on the cake plate. Place the second cake layer right side up on top of the coconut icing. Stir the remaining icing to make sure it is perfectly smooth and spread a thick layer over the sides of the cake. Spread the remaining icing on top. Sprinkle ¹/₂ cup of the coconut on top of the cake. Using the palm of one hand, press the remaining 1¹/₄ cups coconut all over the sides. Let stand for about 1 hour (or up to 8 hours) before serving. To serve, rinse a knife in hot water and shake off the excess water before making each cut.

PREPARING FRESH COCONUT

Puncture the three "eyes" on the coconut with a screwdriver or an ice pick and shake out and discard the liquid. Set the coconut in a 400°F oven on a rack adjusted to the lower third position and bake for 30 minutes. Remove the coconut and let it cool until you can handle it, then crack it with a hammer to break it into several large pieces. Peel away the outer shell, then use a vegetable peeler to remove the brown skin. Shred the coconut using a box grater or the fine or medium shredding disk of a food processor. If not using right away, seal the coconut in zip-top plastic bags and refrigerate for 2 to 3 days, or freeze for up to 1 month. One average-size coconut should give you about 1 pound shredded coconut.

BURNT SUGAR CAKE

Makes one 9-inch 2-layer cake, 12 to 16 servings

A real winner! This is an old-fashioned cake with a great caramel taste. In the old days, caramel was called burnt sugar, because you melted white sugar to make it. But you certainly didn't want to burn it! The layers, made without chemical leaveners, are moist, high, and scrumptious.

CAKE

2¼ cups sugar

½ cup milk

1 14-ounce can unsweetened coconut milk

3 cups sifted cake flour

½ teaspoon salt

1 cup (2 sticks) unsalted butter, at room temperature

2 teaspoons pure vanilla extract

3 large eggs

1 large egg, separated

3 large egg whites

FROSTING

8 tablespoons (1 stick) unsalted butter, at room temperature

8 ounces cream cheese (do not use low-fat), at room temperature

2 teaspoons pure vanilla extract

1 1-pound (4 cups) box confectioners' sugar

1 For the cake, heat ½ cup of the sugar in a large heavy skillet over medium heat, stirring with a wooden spoon until the sugar begins to melt. Continue cooking, stirring occasionally, until the sugar is completely melted and turns a deep caramel color, about 10 minutes. Immediately remove the pan from the heat and very gradually stir in the milk. The mixture will seethe and sputter at first. Cook, stirring occasionally, over medium heat, until the caramel has melted again. Transfer to a heatproof 2-cup glass measure. Shake the can of coconut milk well before opening it, and add enough of it to the caramel to make 1¼ cups. Set aside. Refrigerate the leftover coconut milk for another use. (You can prepare the caramel/coconut mixture 1 day ahead. When cool, cover and refrigerate. Bring to room temperature before using.)

2 Adjust an oven rack to the lower third position and preheat the oven to 350°F. Butter or grease two 9-inch round cake pans. Line the bottoms with

rounds of waxed paper or cooking parchment, butter the papers, and dust the bottoms of the pans with all-purpose flour. Knock out the excess and set aside.

3 Resift the flour with the salt; set aside.

4 In a large bowl, beat the butter with an electric mixer on medium speed until very smooth, about 1 minute. Add the vanilla and $1/4$ cup of the sugar and beat for 1 minute. Beat in $1 1/4$ more cups sugar about $1/4$ cup at a time, beating for 20 to 30 seconds after each addition, then beat on medium-high for 5 minutes. Scrape the bowl and beaters. Add the eggs one at a time, beating for 1 minute after each. Add the egg yolk and beat for 1 minute.

5 On low speed, add the flour in 4 additions, alternating with the caramel mixture, beginning and ending with the flour and beating only until the batter is smooth.

6 In a large bowl, with clean beaters, beat the 4 egg whites on medium speed until they form soft peaks when the beaters are raised. Beat in the remaining $1/4$ cup sugar about 1 tablespoon at a time, and continue beating until the whites resemble thick marshmallow cream and form softly drooping peaks. Fold the whites into the batter in 2 additions, just until incorporated. Divide the batter between the prepared pans. To level the batter, rotate the pans briskly on your countertop.

7 Bake for 35 to 40 minutes, until the layers are golden brown and spring back when pressed very gently in the center and a toothpick inserted into the center comes out clean. Cool in the pans on a wire rack for 5 minutes. Run a small sharp knife around the layers to release them from the sides of the pans. Cover with wire racks, invert, and carefully lift off the pans and papers. Cover the cakes with other wire racks, invert again, and cool completely.

8 For the frosting, beat the butter, cream cheese, and vanilla in a large bowl with an electric mixer on medium speed until very smooth and fluffy, 1 to 2 minutes. On low speed, gradually add the confectioners' sugar and beat until incorporated. Increase the speed to medium-high and beat for 1 minute.

9 To frost the cake, place one layer upside down on a cake plate and spread with about ³/₄ cup of the frosting. Place the second layer right side up on the first layer and frost the sides and top with the remaining frosting. Let stand for about 1 hour until the frosting is set. To serve, rinse a sharp knife in hot water and shake off the excess water before making each cut.

LEMON CURD BUTTERMILK LAYER CAKE

Makes one 9-inch 2-layer cake, 12 to 16 servings

This cake is a lemon lover's dream. The tender, golden layers are flavored with lemon zest and lemon extract, and dollops of creamy lemon curd are spooned onto the batter before baking, for moistness and an extra lemony kick. The layers are filled and frosted with a lemon cream cheese and butter icing. Prepare the lemon curd the night before and refrigerate it so it has time to set.

LEMON CURD

- 1 large egg
- 3 large egg yolks
- 1/2 cup sugar
  Pinch of salt
- 1/3 cup fresh lemon juice (grate the zest first)
- 6 tablespoons (3/4 stick) cold unsalted butter, cut into small pieces
  Finely grated zest of 1 lemon

CAKE

- 2 1/2 cups sifted cake flour
- 1/2 teaspoon baking soda
- 1/2 teaspoon salt
- 3/4 cup (1 1/2 sticks) unsalted butter, at room temperature

- 1 1/2 cups sugar
  Finely grated zest of 2 lemons
- 1 teaspoon pure lemon extract
- 4 large eggs
- 1 cup buttermilk

FROSTING

- 12 ounces cream cheese (do not use low-fat)
- 8 tablespoons (1 stick) unsalted butter, at room temperature
  Finely grated zest of 1 lemon
- 1 tablespoon fresh lemon juice
- 3 cups confectioners' sugar

  Candied violets (optional)

1 For the lemon curd, beat the egg, egg yolks, sugar, and salt in a small bowl with an electric mixer on medium-high speed until the mixture thickens, increases in volume, and is pale yellow, 2 to 3 minutes. On low speed, gradually beat in the lemon juice. Scrape the mixture into a heavy 2-quart saucepan, and add the butter. Cook over medium heat , stirring frequently with a heatproof rubber spatula, until the butter melts, then stir constantly, scraping the sides and bottom of the pan, until the mixture thickens and comes to a simmer. Continue cooking, stirring constantly, for 2 minutes more, or until the curd is the consistency of softly whipped cream.

2 Pass the lemon curd through a strainer into a bowl and stir in the lemon zest. Let cool to room temperature, stirring occasionally with the rubber spatula. Cover tightly with plastic wrap, and refrigerate overnight.

3 For the cake, adjust an oven rack to the center position and preheat the oven to 350°F. Butter or grease two 9-inch round cake pans. Line the bottoms with rounds of waxed paper or cooking parchment. Butter the papers and dust the bottoms of the pans with all-purpose flour. Knock out the excess flour and set aside.

4 Resift the flour with the baking soda and salt; set aside.

5 In a large bowl, beat the butter with an electric mixer on medium speed for about 1 minute, until smooth. Add $1/4$ cup of the sugar, the lemon zest, and extract and beat for 1 minute. On medium-high speed, beat in the remaining $1 1/4$ cups sugar $1/4$ cup at a time, beating for 20 to 30 seconds after each addition, then beat for 5 minutes. Beat in the eggs one at a time, beating for 30 seconds after each.

6 On low speed, add the flour mixture in 3 additions, alternating with the buttermilk, beginning and ending with the flour and beating only until the batter is smooth. Divide the batter evenly between the prepared pans. To level the batter, briskly rotate the pans on your countertop.

7 You need half the lemon curd for the cake; save the rest for another use, such as Blueberry–Lemon Curd Streusel Muffins (page 102). Using two small teaspoons, place small mounds of lemon curd all over the batter, using $1/3$ cup for each layer and leaving about 1 inch between the mounds.

8 Bake for about 30 minutes, until the layers are pale golden brown and barely spring back when gently pressed and a toothpick inserted into the center comes out clean. Cool in the pans for 10 minutes. Run the tip of a small sharp knife all around the layers to release them, cover with wire racks, and invert. Carefully lift off the pans and papers. Replace the paper liners, cover the layers with other racks, invert, and cool completely right side up.

9 For the frosting, beat the cream cheese and butter in a large bowl with an electric mixer on medium-high speed until smooth, about 1 minute. Add the lemon zest and lemon juice and beat on medium speed until smooth. On low speed, gradually beat in the confectioners' sugar. Increase the speed to high and beat for just a few seconds, until the frosting is smooth. Overbeating may thin it.

10 To frost the cake, place one of the cooled layers upside down on a cake plate; carefully remove the paper. Spread with about 1 cup of the frosting. Place the other cake layer right side up on the frosting. Spread the remaining frosting over the sides, then the top of the cake, making the frosting on top a bit thicker so that you can then swirl it about with a small spoon. Arrange candied violets, if using, in a circle on top of the cake about 1 inch in from the edge. Refrigerate for at least 1 hour to set the icing. (The cake can be made 1 day ahead.)

11 To serve, slice the cake into portions when cold, and bring the slices to room temperature before serving. Rinse a sharp knife in hot water and shake off the excess water before each cut. Store leftovers in the refrigerator.

SPICY BUTTERMILK PECAN LAYER CAKE WITH PECAN BUTTERCREAM

Makes one 9-inch 3-layer cake, 16 to 20 servings

This magnificent cake is almost 5 inches tall. The layers and the buttercream frosting are packed with pecans toasted with lots of cinnamon and nutmeg, butter, and dark rum. The inspiration came from *Chef Paul Prudhomme's Louisiana Kitchen.* Make this for a special occasion.

TOASTED PECANS

- 2 cups (8 ounces) pecan halves or large pieces
- 1/4 cup firmly packed dark brown sugar
- 2 tablespoons ground cinnamon
- 1 1/2 teaspoons freshly grated nutmeg
- 4 tablespoons (1/2 stick) unsalted butter, melted
- 2 tablespoons dark rum (I use Myers's)

CAKE

- 3 cups sifted cake flour
- 1/2 teaspoon baking soda
- 1/2 teaspoon salt
- 1 cup (2 sticks) unsalted butter, at room temperature
- 2 cups sugar
- 1 tablespoon pure vanilla extract
- 1 large egg, separated
- 3 large eggs
- 2 large egg whites
- 1 cup buttermilk

FROSTING

- 6 large egg yolks
- 3/4 cup sugar
- 1/2 cup light corn syrup
- 2 cups (1 pound) unsalted butter, at room temperature
- 1 tablespoon pure vanilla extract
- 1/8 teaspoon salt

1 For the pecans, adjust an oven rack to the center position and preheat the oven to 350°F.

2 Place the pecans in a single layer on a heavy baking sheet and bake them for 10 minutes, stirring once or twice, until fragrant. Meanwhile, combine the brown sugar, cinnamon, and nutmeg in a medium bowl; use your fingertips to break up any lumps of sugar and to mix everything thoroughly. Stir in the melted butter to make a paste.

3 Add the pecans to the brown sugar mixture and stir to coat them well. Spread evenly on the baking sheet and return to the oven for 10 minutes; stir once or twice. Remove the pan from the oven, drizzle over the rum, and bake for 10 minutes more, stirring once. Remove from the oven and cool completely on the pan. Leave the oven on.

4 Chop the pecans into medium-fine pieces (some pieces will be small, some will be larger; you want a mixture of textures); you'll have about $2^1/2$ cups. Set aside.

5 For the cake, arrange two racks to divide the oven into thirds. Butter or grease three 9-inch round cake pans. Line the bottoms of the pans with rounds of waxed paper or cooking parchment. Butter the papers and dust the bottoms of the pans with all-purpose flour. Knock out the excess and set aside.

6 Resift the flour with the baking soda and salt; set aside.

7 In a large bowl, beat the butter with an electric mixer on medium speed until smooth, about 1 minute. Add $^1/4$ cup of the sugar and the vanilla extract and beat for 1 minute. Beat in $1^1/2$ cups more of the remaining sugar $^1/4$ cup at a time, beating for about 15 seconds after each addition, then beat for 5 minutes on medium-high speed. Beat in the egg yolk and then the whole eggs one at a time, beating for about 30 seconds after each addition. Beat for 1 minute longer.

8 On low speed, add the flour mixture in 3 additions, alternating with the buttermilk, beginning and ending with the flour and beating only until the batter is smooth. Transfer to a large wide shallow bowl; set aside.

9 With clean beaters, whip the 3 egg whites on medium speed in a medium bowl until they form soft drooping peaks when the beaters are raised. Beat in the remaining $^1/4$ cup sugar about 1 tablespoon at a time, beating for 15 seconds after each addition. Increase the speed to medium-high, and beat only until the whites form shiny upright peaks that curl slightly at their tips. Sprinkle $1^1/2$ cups of the pecans over the batter and scrape the whites over the nuts. Using a large wide rubber spatula, fold everything together, folding only until no whites show. Divide the batter evenly among the prepared pans. To level the batter, rotate the pans briskly on your countertop.

10 Place the pans in the oven, two on the upper rack and one on the lower. Bake for 25 to 30 minutes, until the layers are golden brown and a toothpick inserted into the center comes out clean. (The layer on the bottom rack will be done first.) Cool the cakes in their pans for 10 minutes. Run the tip of a small sharp knife around the sides of the layers to release them, cover with wire racks, and invert. Carefully lift off the pans and papers. Cover the layers with other racks, invert, and cool completely right side up.

11 For the frosting, beat the egg yolks in a large bowl with an electric mixer on medium-high speed until very thick, about 5 minutes. Combine the sugar with the corn syrup in a small heavy saucepan. Set the pan over medium-high heat and stir constantly with a heatproof rubber spatula until the mixture comes to a full rolling boil. To stop the cooking, immediately scrape the mixture into a heatproof 1-cup glass measure. With the mixer on high speed, pour a dollop of the hot sugar mixture into the yolks and beat for a few seconds. Repeat the procedure until all the syrup has been added, scraping the cup with a rubber spatula to get as much syrup out as you can. Beat until cooled to room temperature (the mixture must be cool).

12 On medium speed, beat in the butter about 2 tablespoons at a time, beating after each addition until thoroughly incorporated. The frosting will be very soft until the last stick of butter is added, then, miraculously, it will begin to hold its shape and become thick enough to spread. Scrape the bowl and beaters well, and beat in the vanilla and salt. Stir in the remaining pecans.

13 To frost the cake, place one of the cooled layers upside down on a cake plate and spread with about 3/4 cup of the frosting. Set a second layer upside down on the first layer and spread with another 3/4 cup of frosting. Place the third layer right side up on top and frost the sides and top with the remaining frosting. Refrigerate the cake for at least 1 hour to set the frosting.

14 Slice the cake while it is cold. To serve, rinse a large knife in hot water and shake off the excess water before making each cut, then let the slices stand at room temperature for a few minutes so the cake and frosting soften.

OATMEAL LAYER CAKE WITH CARAMEL PECAN FROSTING

Makes one 9-inch 2-layer cake, 16 servings

Oatmeal isn't a usual ingredient in layer cakes, but I've found it works extremely well, making the layers moist and tender. A mixture of butter and vegetable shortening makes the cake especially light textured, and the candylike frosting has a rich caramel flavor.

CAKE

- 1 cup quick-cooking (not instant) rolled oats
- 1 1/2 cups boiling water
- 2 1/4 cups sifted cake flour
- 1/2 teaspoon baking soda
- 1/2 teaspoon salt
- 1 teaspoon ground cinnamon
- 1/2 teaspoon freshly grated nutmeg
- 8 tablespoons (1 stick) unsalted butter, at room temperature
- 1/4 cup vegetable shortening
- 3/4 cup sugar
- 3/4 cup firmly packed dark brown sugar
- 2 teaspoons pure vanilla extract
- 4 large eggs
- 1/2 cup buttermilk

FROSTING

- 4 tablespoons (1/2 stick) unsalted butter
- 1/2 cup firmly packed dark brown sugar
- 6 tablespoons evaporated milk, plus more if needed
- 2 teaspoons pure vanilla extract
- 3 cups confectioners' sugar
- 16 pecan halves

1 For the cake, combine the oats and boiling water in a medium bowl and set aside for 20 to 25 minutes; stir occasionally.

2 Adjust an oven rack to the center position and preheat the oven to 350°F. Butter two 9-inch round cake pans and line the bottoms with rounds of waxed paper or cooking parchment. Butter the papers and dust the bottoms of the pans with all-purpose flour. Knock out the excess and set aside.

3 Resift the flour with the baking soda, salt, cinnamon, and nutmeg, and set aside.

4 In a large bowl, beat the butter and vegetable shortening with an electric

mixer on medium speed until smooth, about 1 minute. Combine both sugars in a bowl. Add $^1/_4$ cup of the sugar mixture and the vanilla to the butter mixture and beat for 1 minute. Beat in the remaining sugar $^1/_4$ cup at a time, beating for 20 to 30 seconds after each addition. Stop to scrape the bowl and beater once or twice. Increase the speed to medium-high and beat for 5 minutes. Beat in the eggs one at a time, beating for 1 minute after each addition. Add the oat mixture and beat for 1 minute.

5 On low speed, add the flour mixture in 3 additions, alternating with the buttermilk, beginning and ending with the flour and beating only until the batter is smooth. Divide the batter evenly between the two pans. To level the batter, rotate the pans briskly on your countertop.

6 Bake for 25 to 30 minutes, until the layers are golden brown and spring back when gently pressed and a toothpick inserted into the center comes out clean; do not overbake. Cool in the pans on a wire rack for 10 minutes. Run a small sharp knife around the layers to release them from the sides of the pans. Cover the cakes with wire racks, invert, and remove the pans and papers. Cover the cakes with other racks, invert, and cool completely right side up.

7 For the frosting, melt the butter in a medium heavy saucepan over medium heat. Add the brown sugar and stir with a wooden spoon for a full 3 minutes, or until the mixture is thick and smooth. Add the evaporated milk 1 tablespoon at a time, then cook for another 3 minutes, stirring constantly. The mixture will be thick and bubbly and resemble caramel sauce. Remove from the heat and cool to room temperature.

8 Stir the vanilla into the cooled brown sugar mixture. Gradually beat in the confectioners' sugar, beating until the frosting is smooth and spreadable. If necessary, add more evaporated milk by droplets.

9 To frost the cake, place one of the layers upside down on a cake plate and spread with about $^1/_2$ cup of the frosting. Place the second layer right side up on the first layer and frost the sides and top with the remaining frosting. Arrange the pecans in a circle on top close to the edge of the cake. Let stand for about 1 hour until the frosting is set. To serve, cut into portions with a sharp knife.

MOLASSES SPICE CAKE WITH ORANGE BUTTERCREAM FROSTING

*Makes one
9-inch
2-layer cake,
12 servings*

A quintet of spices gives these tender layers a seductive flavor. The frosting is essentially a custard flavored with orange and vanilla. Make it first, since it needs to be chilled.

FROSTING

- 1/3 cup all-purpose flour
- 1 1/2 tablespoons cornstarch
- 1/2 cup sugar
- 1 1/2 cups milk
- 2 large egg yolks
  Finely grated zest of 1 orange
- 1 teaspoon pure vanilla extract
- 1/2 teaspoon pure orange extract
- 8 tablespoons (1 stick)
  unsalted butter, at room
  temperature

CAKE

- 2 1/2 cups sifted cake flour
- 1/2 teaspoon baking soda
- 1/2 teaspoon salt
- 1 teaspoon ground cinnamon
- 1 teaspoon ground ginger
- 1/2 teaspoon freshly grated nutmeg
- 1/2 teaspoon ground allspice
- 1/4 teaspoon ground cloves
- 8 tablespoons (1 stick) unsalted
  butter, at room temperature
- 1/4 cup vegetable shortening
- 1 cup sugar
- 1 teaspoon pure vanilla extract
- 4 large eggs
- 1/4 cup molasses (I use Grandma's)
- 3/4 cup buttermilk

1 For the frosting, whisk together the flour, cornstarch, and sugar in a small heavy saucepan. Add 1/2 cup of the milk and whisk to make a smooth mixture. Gradually whisk in the remaining 1 cup milk. Cook over medium heat, stirring constantly with a heatproof rubber spatula, for about 8 minutes, until the mixture begins to thicken and to stick to the bottom of the saucepan. Switch to the whisk and stir constantly for another 2 minutes. Remove from the heat.

2 In a small bowl, blend the yolks with a fork. Add about 1/2 cup of the hot milk mixture and whisk together well. Add to the remaining milk mixture in the saucepan and whisk together thoroughly. Return to the heat and

cook over medium heat, whisking constantly, for 2 minutes more. Remove from the heat and stir in the orange zest, vanilla, and orange extract. Scrape the mixture into a medium bowl and lay a piece of plastic wrap directly on the surface. Refrigerate several hours, or overnight.

3 Beat the chilled frosting base with an electric mixer until very smooth. Add the butter 1 tablespoon at a time, beating thoroughly after each addition. Scrape the bowl, cover with plastic, and set aside at room temperature.

4 For the cake, adjust an oven rack to the center position and preheat the oven to 350°F. Butter two 9-inch round cake pans and line the bottoms with rounds of waxed paper or cooking parchment. Butter the papers and dust the bottoms of the pans with all-purpose flour. Knock out the excess and set aside.

5 Resift the cake flour with the baking soda, salt, and spices; set aside.

6 In a large bowl, beat the butter and shortening with an electric mixer on medium speed until very smooth, about 1 minute. Add $1/4$ cup of the sugar and the vanilla and beat for 1 minute. Beat in the remaining $3/4$ cup sugar about $1/4$ cup at a time, beating for 20 to 30 seconds after each addition, then beat on medium-high speed for 5 minutes. Beat in the eggs one at a time, beating for 30 seconds after each. Add the molasses and beat on medium speed for 30 seconds.

7 On low speed, add the flour mixture in 3 additions, alternating with the buttermilk, beginning and ending with the flour and beating only until the batter is smooth. Divide the batter evenly between the prepared pans. To level the batter, briskly rotate the pans on your countertop.

8 Bake for 25 to 30 minutes, until the layers are golden brown and spring back when gently pressed in the center; do not overbake. Cool on a rack for 10 minutes. Run a small sharp knife around the layers to release them from the pans, cover the layers with wire racks, and invert. Carefully remove the pans and papers. Cover the cakes with other racks, invert, and cool completely right side up.

9 To frost the cake, place one layer upside down on a cake plate and spread with about $2/3$ cup of the frosting. Place the second layer right side up on the first layer and frost the sides and top with the remaining frosting. Refrigerate for 1 hour to set. To serve, cut into portions with a sharp knife.

LADY BALTIMORE CAKE

*Makes one
9-inch
3-layer cake,
16 servings*

This is a wonderful cake for a party or other special occasion. Its golden layers are light textured, it is very tall (about 5 inches!), and it's very sweet. What makes the cake special are the textures of the two different fillings. Both are flavored with vanilla and almond extracts and both contain walnuts, but the first is a slightly cooked sugar syrup with a soft candylike texture and the second is an Italian meringue, made by beating a hot sugar syrup into egg whites. Chopped raisins are folded in, and the mixture is used to frost the cake as well. "Lady Baltimore Cake II" from *Two Hundred Years of Charleston Cooking* and Jean Anderson's rendition of the recipe in *The American Century Cookbook* served as my models.

You will need a candy thermometer. The best way to chop raisins is to partially freeze them in a single layer on a baking sheet just until they lose their squishiness (about 15 minutes), then use a large chef's knife.

CAKE

- 3 cups sifted cake flour
- 1 1/2 teaspoons baking powder, preferably nonaluminum
- 1/2 teaspoon salt
- 3/4 cup (1 1/2 sticks) unsalted butter, at room temperature
- 2 cups sugar
- 3 large eggs, separated
- 1 1/2 cups milk

SOFT FILLING

- 1 1/2 cups sugar
- 1/2 cup water
- 1 cup chopped (medium-fine) walnuts
- 1 teaspoon pure vanilla extract
- 1 teaspoon pure almond extract

HARD FILLING

- 3 large egg whites
- 2 1/2 cups sugar
- 2 tablespoons light corn syrup
- 1/2 cup plus 2 tablespoons water
- 1 teaspoon pure vanilla extract
- 1 teaspoon pure almond extract
- 1 tablespoon fresh lemon juice
- 1 cup coarsely chopped raisins
- 1 cup chopped (medium-fine) walnuts

1 For the cake, adjust two oven racks to divide the oven into thirds and preheat the oven to 375°F. Butter three 9-inch round cake pans, or coat with cooking spray. Line the bottoms of the pans with rounds of cooking parchment or waxed paper, butter or spray the paper, and dust lightly with all-purpose flour. Set aside.

2 Resift the flour with the baking powder and salt; set aside.

3 In a large bowl, beat the butter with an electric mixer on medium speed until smooth, about 1 minute. On medium-high speed, beat in 1³/₄ cups of the sugar about ¹/₄ cup at a time, beating for 20 to 30 seconds after each addition, then beat for 5 minutes. Beat in the egg yolks one at a time, beating for 30 seconds after each.

4 On low speed, add the flour mixture in 4 additions, alternating with the milk, beginning and ending with the flour and beating only until smooth.

5 With clean beaters, beat the egg whites in a medium bowl on medium speed until thick and foamy. Beat in the remaining ¹/₄ cup sugar about 1 tablespoon at a time, then increase the speed to medium-high and beat only until the whites are the consistency of a marshmallow cream and form softly curling peaks. In 2 additions, gently fold the whites into the batter, only until no whites show. Divide the batter among the three pans. To level the batter, rotate the pans briskly on your countertop.

6 Place the pans in the oven, two on the upper rack and one on the lower rack. Bake for 20 to 25 minutes, until the cakes are golden brown, the tops spring back when gently pressed, and the layers just begin to show a hair-

---

A CAKE SENSATION

Lady Baltimore Cake became famous in 1906 when Owen Wister, author of *The Virginian*, described a character eating it in his romantic novel *Lady Baltimore*. The setting is the Lady Baltimore Tea Room in Charleston, South Carolina. The novel's narrator, Augustus, asks the waitress to bring him a slice of a special cake after witnessing a young man ordering it for a wedding.

"And she brought me the cake, and I had my first felicitous meeting with Lady Baltimore. Oh, my goodness! Did you ever taste it? It's all soft, and it's in layers, and it has nuts—but I can't write any more about it; my mouth waters too much."

Wister's description caused a sensation, and bakers vied to recreate the cake in their own homes.

line shrinkage away from the sides of the pan. (The cake on the bottom rack will be done first.) Cool in the pans on a wire rack for 5 minutes. Run a small sharp knife around the sides to release, and invert onto wire racks. Remove the pans and papers, cover with other racks, invert, and cool right side up.

7 For the soft filling, combine the sugar and water in a small heavy saucepan and heat over medium heat, without stirring, swirling the pan gently by the handle from time to time, until the sugar is dissolved and the mixture turns clear and begins to boil. Gradually sprinkle in the walnuts—do not stir. Raise the heat to medium-high, swirling the pan to incorporate the nuts into the syrup. When the mixture returns to a boil, cover the pan and cook for 1 minute to dissolve any sugar crystals sticking to the sides. Uncover, attach a candy thermometer to the side of the pan, and cook the syrup to 220° to 225°F, 1 to 2 minutes. Immediately remove from the heat and set aside to cool to 110°F. Do not stir during cooking.

8 Add the vanilla and almond extracts to the cooled sugar syrup and beat with a wooden spoon to combine well. Divide the filling on top of the 3 cake layers, spreading evenly with a metal spatula. (Don't stack the layers.)

9 For the hard filling, beat the egg whites on medium speed until stiff but not dry in a large bowl with an electric mixer. Set aside. Combine the sugar, corn syrup, and water in a medium heavy saucepan over medium heat and cook, without stirring, swirling the pan gently by the handle from time to time, until the sugar is dissolved and the mixture comes to a boil. Raise the heat to medium-high, cover, and cook for 2 minutes to dissolve any sugar crystals sticking to the sides. Uncover, attach a candy thermometer to the side of the pan, and cook to 244°F.

10 Beating constantly, gradually add the syrup to the egg whites in a thin stream, trying to avoid the beaters. Quickly scrape the bowl well (the syrup will have splattered onto the sides) and continue beating on medium to medium-high speed until the whites are glossy and form stiff peaks. Beat in the extracts and lemon juice. Immediately fold in the raisins and walnuts. You must assemble the cake quickly before the filling sets.

11 To frost the cake, place one of the layers on a cake plate. Spread with about 1 cup of the hard filling. Add the next layer and spread with about 1 more

cup hard filling. Place the third layer on top. Spread the remaining hard filling over the sides and top, making the top thicker than the sides and using the back of a spoon to form swirls and peaks. Let the cake stand for about 1 hour, so that the filling forms a thin crust. To serve, slice with a sharp knife.

HEALTH CLAIM

The fact that Snowdrift is pure vegetable oil and nothing else means that it has the highest possible food value. Snowdrift not only makes things good to eat but is itself a more nourishing food than almost anything else you eat. Snowdrift is much richer than butter, because butter contains salt and water and curds as well as fat, while Snowdrift is all pure fat. You may be interested in the following table of calories which shows the relative fuel value of Snowdrift compared to the other things we eat:

	Calories Per Lb.
Snowdrift	4050
Oleomargarine	3525
Butter	3450
Bacon	3030
Cheese	1950
Sugar	1860
Cereals	1665
Beef	1275
Eggs	720
Milk	325
Vegetables	229

There is more calory value in Snowdrift, pound for pound, than in any of the foods you cook with it.

—Ida C. Bailey Allen, *A New Snowdrift Cookbook* (1920)

8

Sponge Cakes, Angel Food Cakes, and Chiffon Cakes

The kinds of cake most apt to prove injurious are pound cake and rich plum cake; but very little of these should ever be eaten, and if they could be wholly super-seded by the sponge cake *and other light varieties, it would be much better for the health of those who are in the habit of frequenting parties.*

—Sarah Josepha Hale, *The Good Housekeeper* (1841)

Sponge cakes, angel food cakes, and chiffon cakes have one thing in common: they magically puff to magnificent heights in the oven, rising to at least twice their volume. This is thrilling to see, and it happens because of air that is beaten into the eggs.

In the beginning of the eighteenth century, a generous amount of butter was a primary ingredient in many cakes. The sponge cakes that had caught Sarah Hale's fancy were English in origin and contained no "injurious" butter. Instead, they got their lift from whites and yolks beaten separately, then carefully folded together with flour. Originally these cakes were baked on sheets as individual little cakes or biscuits (cookies). When the batter was put into a deep pan—and it is anyone's guess when this happened—it rose up tall and light, earning the name "sponge" for its springy texture.

Even though they didn't require the tedious step of creaming butter with sugar, sponge cakes were no less labor-intensive than pound cakes, because the batter needed long beating. Sarah Hale, who was a leading magazine editor of her day, rec-ommended beating it for a full hour, and *Martha Washington's Booke of Cookery*, written during the seventeenth century, calls for a total of 4 hours. This laborious enterprise was accomplished by simple wooden rods or whisks made of birch or metal. No wonder these cakes were not everyday fare!

The invention of the rotary egg beater around 1870 accelerated the rise in popu-larity of sponge cakes and other representatives of the light brigade. The tube pan, too, was a nineteenth-century invention, though the first ones were square, not round like today's models. The central tube assured the even distribution of heat to the batter, resulting in cakes that cooked more quickly. By the beginning of the twentieth century, these pans had become standard. Making a tube cake was a way for a baker to show off her expertise and demonstrate that she was truly "modern." Angel food cake recipes made their appearance at about the same time as the rotary beater. Unlike sponge cakes, which contained yolks, angel food cakes were made with egg whites only. By then, sugars and flours were ultra-pure, white, and easily obtainable. The angel food cake was the epitome of the most desirable qualities in baking: softness, lightness, and whiteness.

Another type of sponge cake, the génoise, arrived from France during the same period. It was made with whole eggs that were heated before beating so they attained maximum volume, instead of separately beaten yolks and whites. It also contained melted butter, which was folded into the batter immediately before baking.

In the 1920s, an insurance salesman and cooking hobbyist discovered that the addition of vegetable oil to a sponge cake batter made an exceptionally tender cake. Its creator, Harry Baker, achieved fame among Hollywood luminaries for his chiffon cake, and in 1947, he finally sold his secret formula for an undisclosed sum to General Mills. The following year, *Betty Crocker Chiffon Cake Recipes and Secrets* trumpeted an "amazing new cake family!", hailing the cake as "the biggest kitchen news in one hundred years."

Over time the relatively simple tube cakes gave rise to a series of elaborate spin-offs that were almost as rich as their pound cake predecessors. In the mid 1900s, it became fashionable to split sponge cakes into layers and fill and frost them with whipped cream. Angel food cakes were hollowed out, filled with any kind of ice cream, and refrozen. Chiffon cakes, too, were embellished upon. They were chocolatized, nuttified, and covered with toppings and glazes. Génoise cakes were filled and frosted with buttercreams and used in all sorts of desserts, including trifle, charlotte russe, ice cream cakes, and petits fours.

With or without these extravagances, tube cakes have deservedly flourished into the present. Electric mixers have cut beating times from hours to minutes. And today's bakers, unlike those of a century or more ago, can experience the thrill of watching a tube cake rise to enormous heights without a corresponding feeling of exhaustion.

POINTERS FOR SPONGE, ANGEL FOOD, AND CHIFFON CAKES

1. Flour. Always use a soft wheat flour—cake flour or the marvelous unbleached soft wheat flour from Great Valley Mills in Pennsylvania (see Sources, page 526). These low-gluten soft wheat flours are your best insurance that the cakes will be as tender as possible. Always sift the flour before measuring to remove lumps.

2. Eggs. For sponge cakes, the yolks and whites are beaten separately. The yolks should be beaten until they are thick and pale and form a slowly dissolving ribbon when the beaters are lifted. The ribbon should be visible for about 10 seconds before it disappears.

Egg whites must be beaten in a clean, grease-free bowl. Even a tiny bit of fat can prevent whites from whipping into a glorious, billowy texture. Beat until they are shiny and hold a firm shape. When you raise the beaters, they should form firm peaks that curl only slightly at their tips. Do not overbeat. If you do, sometimes you can fix things by adding an unbeaten egg white or two to the overbeaten ones and whipping them briefly.

3. Folding. Use a wide bowl and a large rubber spatula to give you plenty of room to incorporate that all-important air into the batter. Cut down through the batter with the rounded end of the rubber spatula, going to the bottom of the bowl, then, while rotating the bowl about a quarter turn, scrape the broad side of the spatula against the bottom of the bowl and bring it up and above the batter, using a flip of the wrist to move the batter from the edge of the bowl toward the center. Once you get the hang of it, you'll be able to work very quickly. If you're gradually sifting dry ingredients over the eggs and folding them in in installments, don't be too thorough with the first additions, or you may deflate the eggs too much. Only with the final addition should you fold everything together completely.

4. Baking pan. Follow the specific recipe instructions for how to prepare the baking pan. These cakes generally rise far better in ungreased pans. I use a two-piece 10-x-4-inch aluminum tube pan, available in supermarkets and hardware stores. Avoid nonstick tube pans—batters don't cling well to the sides. Wash the pan in soapy water and rinse and dry it thoroughly before use.

5. Baking and cooling. Some recipes call for putting the cake into a cold oven. Tube cakes are cooled upside down with plenty of space underneath for air circulation. Because of their delicate structure, if they were left to cool upright, they might collapse. If your tube pan has "feet," just turn it upside down over a wire rack set on your countertop. For greater air circulation, I invert the pan onto a narrow-necked wine bottle or large funnel. In 2 to 3 hours, it is completely cooled. Don't worry about the cake falling out of the pan; since the pan is not greased, the cake will cling to the sides.

6. Removing the cake from its pan. Use a sharp, narrow, thin-bladed knife, such as a filleting knife. Insert the knife between the cake and the side of the pan, going all the way to the bottom, press the knife firmly against the side, and slowly move it all around the pan to loosen the cake. Do not use a sawing motion. Then run the knife around the central tube. Lift the cake out of the pan by the tube, and run the knife between the bottom of the cake and the base of the pan to release it. Carefully invert the cake onto a wire rack and remove the tube portion of the pan.

7. Cutting the cake. Use a sharp serrated knife and a sawing motion.

ORANGE SPONGE CAKE

*Makes one
10-inch
tube cake,
12 to 16
servings*

This cake, which is made in an untraditional way by beating the flour into the yolks, melts on the tongue. It is high, tender, moist, and loaded with orange flavor. It needs no adornment, though you wouldn't go wrong serving a spoonful of whipped cream and some fresh berries alongside each slice. Note that you do not preheat the oven for this cake.

7 large eggs, separated	$1/4$ cup fresh orange juice
$1^1/2$ cups sugar	$1^1/2$ cups sifted cake flour
1 teaspoon pure orange extract	$1/4$ teaspoon salt
Finely grated zest of 1 orange	$1/2$ teaspoon cream of tartar

1 Have ready a grease-free 10-x-4-inch tube pan with a removable bottom (*not* nonstick).

2 Place the egg yolks, 1 cup of the sugar, the orange extract, zest, orange juice, and flour in a large wide bowl. Beat with an electric mixer on low speed for 1 minute, just to combine. Increase the speed to medium-high and beat for 4 to 5 minutes, until the yolks are very thick and pale and form a ribbon when the beaters are raised. Set aside.

3 In another large bowl, with clean beaters, beat the egg whites and salt with the mixer on medium-low speed until frothy, 1 to 2 minutes. Add the cream of tartar and beat only until the whites form soft peaks when the beaters are raised. Beat in the remaining $1/2$ cup sugar 2 tablespoons at a time, beating for 15 to 20 seconds after each addition. Increase the speed to medium and continue beating until the whites are thick like marshmallow cream and form peaks that curl just a bit at their tips.

4 Use a large wide rubber spatula to scoop the whites onto the yolk mixture. Fold together very gently only until no streaks of white show. Gently scrape the batter into the pan.

5 Adjust an oven rack to the lower third position. Place the pan in the oven and turn the oven on to 350°F. Bake for 45 to 50 minutes, until the cake is golden brown on top and springs back when pressed very gently. Immediately invert the pan onto a narrow-necked bottle. Let cool completely upside down, about 2 hours.

6 Loosen the sides of the cake from the pan with a narrow thin-bladed knife. Run the knife between the cake and the central tube. Lift the cake out of the pan by its tube and release the cake from the bottom of the pan with the knife. Carefully invert the cake onto a cake plate and lift off the pan. This cake is best when very fresh. Cut into portions with a sharp serrated knife.

LET THEM BE LIGHT

In making cakes *it is of the utmost importance that the eggs should be properly and sufficiently beaten; otherwise the cakes will most certainly be deficient in the peculiar lightness characterizing those that are made by good confectioners. Persons who do not know the right way, complain much of the fatigue of beating eggs, and therefore leave off too soon. There will be no fatigue, if they are beaten with the proper stroke, and with wooden rods, and in a shallow, flat-bottomed earthen pan. The coldness of a tin pan retards the lightness of the eggs. For the same reason do not use a metal egg-beater. In beating them do not move your elbow, but keep it close to your side. Move only your hand at the wrist, and let the stroke be quick, short, and horizontal; putting the egg-beater always down to the bottom of the pan, which should therefore be shallow. Do not leave off as soon as you have got the eggs into a foam; they are then only beginning to be light. But persist till after the foaming has ceased, and the bubbles have all disappeared. Continue till the surface is smooth as a mirror, and the beaten egg as thick as a rich boiled custard; for till then it will not be really light.*

—Eliza Leslie, *Miss Leslie's New Receipts for Cooking* (1854)

LEMON SPONGE CAKE

Makes one 10-inch tube cake, 12 to 16 servings

Lemon extract (or essence) was very popular in the nineteenth century, and it was used in all sorts of cakes and cookies. Sponge cake, especially, benefits from lemon's wonderful tartness, and this tall, tender cake is packed with lemon flavor. I make it the traditional way, beating the whites and yolks separately and folding them together with the flour.

7 large eggs, separated	3 tablespoons warm water
1¹/₂ cups sugar	¹/₄ teaspoon salt
Finely grated zest of 1–2 lemons, to taste	¹/₂ teaspoon cream of tartar
1 tablespoon fresh lemon juice	1¹/₂ cups sifted cake flour

1 Have ready a grease-free 10-x-4-inch tube pan with a removable bottom (*not* nonstick).

2 Beat the egg yolks in a large bowl with an electric mixer on medium-high speed for 5 minutes, or until they are thick and lemon colored. On medium-low speed, beat in 1 cup of the sugar 2 tablespoons at a time, beating for 10 to 15 seconds after each addition. Increase the speed to medium-high and beat for 2 minutes. Add the grated lemon zest, lemon juice, and water and beat for 2 minutes, or until pale and the consistency of thick foam. Set aside.

3 In a clean, wide bowl, with clean beaters, beat the egg whites and salt with the mixer on medium-low speed until frothy, about 1 minute. Add the cream of tartar and beat until the whites hold a very soft shape with softly curling peaks. Beat in the remaining ¹/₂ cup sugar 2 tablespoons at a time, beating for about 15 seconds after each addition. Increase the speed to medium and continue beating until the whites form definite peaks that curl just a bit at their tips, less than 1 minute.

4 Sift the flour onto the yolk mixture and fold it in with a few swift broad strokes of a large rubber spatula until it is almost incorporated. Scrape the mixture over the egg whites and fold them together very gently and slowly only until no whites show.

5 Rinse the two pieces of the tube pan with cool tap water and shake off the excess water. Carefully transfer the batter to the pan, and gently smooth the top with the rubber spatula.

6 Adjust an oven rack to the lower third position. Place the pan in the oven and turn the oven on to 350°F. Bake for about 50 minutes, until the cake is golden brown and the top springs back when gently pressed. Immediately invert the pan onto a narrow-necked bottle. Let cool completely upside down, about 2 hours.

7 Loosen the sides of the cake from the pan with a narrow thin-bladed knife. Run the knife between the cake and the central tube. Lift the cake out of the pan by its tube and release the cake from the bottom of the pan with the knife. Carefully invert the cake onto a cake plate and lift off the pan bottom. Cut into portions with a serrated knife.

LEMON SPONGE CLOUD

Makes one 10-inch tube cake, 12 to 16 servings

This cake is spectacular. It rises almost 2 inches above the pan rim and has a fabulous, tender texture. You will need a candy thermometer or a digital probe thermometer. The most scrumptious way to serve the cake is to slather slices generously with softly whipped cream and then spoon lightly sugared sliced fresh peaches or strawberries on top.

1½ cups sifted cake flour	Finely grated zest of 1 lemon
½ teaspoon salt	1 tablespoon fresh lemon juice
8 large eggs, separated	1 teaspoon pure lemon extract
1¾ cups sugar	½ teaspoon cream of tartar
½ cup plus 2 tablespoons water	

1 Have ready a grease-free 10-x-4-inch tube pan with a removable bottom (*not* nonstick).

2 Resift the flour with the salt; set aside.

3 Beat the egg yolks in a large wide bowl with an electric mixer on medium speed for 1 minute. Increase the speed to high and beat until the yolks have increased in volume and are very thick and pale, 5 to 6 minutes. Set aside.

4 Heat 1½ cups of the sugar and ½ cup of the water in a small heavy saucepan over high heat without stirring, swirling the mixture occasionally as it comes to a boil. When the mixture boils and turns clear, cover the pan and boil for 2 to 3 minutes to dissolve any sugar crystals on the sides of the pan. Uncover, attach a candy thermometer or digital probe thermometer, and cook, without stirring, until the temperature reaches 230° to 234°F.

5 Just before the syrup is ready, beat the egg yolks again for a few seconds on high speed. Pour about 2 tablespoons of the syrup onto the yolks, then immediately turn the mixer to high speed and beat for 5 to 10 seconds. Continue adding the syrup in small installments, then beat for a few seconds, until it all has been added. Beat for several minutes longer, until the mixture is cool. Beat in the lemon zest, lemon juice, lemon extract, and the remaining 2 tablespoons water. Add the flour mixture and beat it in on low speed only until incorporated.

6 In another large bowl, with clean beaters, beat the whites with the mixer on medium speed until foamy. Add the cream of tartar and beat until the whites form soft droopy peaks when the beaters are raised. Beat in the remaining $1/4$ cup sugar about 1 tablespoon at a time, beating for about 15 seconds after each addition. Increase the speed to medium-high and beat for a few seconds more, until the whites form peaks that curl a bit at their tips; do not overbeat.

7 Add about one fourth of the whites to the yolks and fold them together with a large rubber spatula, using few broad strokes. Don't be too thorough. Scrape the remaining whites on top and fold together until the mixture is a uniform yellow color. Gently transfer the batter to the tube pan and smooth the top.

8 Adjust an oven rack to the lower third position. Place the pan in the oven and turn on the oven to 350°F. Bake for 50 to 55 minutes, until the cake is well browned, has a few cracks on top, and springs back when gently pressed. Immediately invert the pan onto a narrow-necked bottle. Let cool completely upside down, about 2 hours.

9 Loosen the sides of the cake from the pan with a narrow thin-bladed knife. Run the knife between the cake and the central tube. Lift the cake out of the pan by its tube and release the cake from the bottom of the pan with the knife. Carefully turn the cake out onto a square of waxed paper placed on the countertop. Cover the bottom with a wire rack, and invert again so that the cake is right side up. Transfer the cake to a cake plate. To serve, cut with a serrated knife using a gentle sawing motion.

LADYFINGERS

Makes about 60 ladyfingers

These individual "fingers" of sponge cake are delicious eaten plain with tea or coffee. They're also perfect for molded desserts. Although commercial ladyfingers are a terrific convenience and are fine, homemade ones will have more character. They are best when very fresh, but they keep well in the freezer for 2 to 3 weeks. You will need a large pastry bag, 12 to 14 inches long, and a plain metal tip with a 1/2-inch opening.

3 large eggs, separated	1/2 cup confectioners' sugar
1 large egg white	1 teaspoon pure vanilla extract
1/8 teaspoon salt	1 cup sifted cake flour
1/4 teaspoon cream of tartar	
1/4 cup sugar	Confectioners' sugar for dusting

1 Adjust two oven racks to divide the oven into thirds and preheat the oven to 350°F. Line two 14-x-17-inch baking sheets with cooking parchment or silicone liners and set aside. Insert the tube into the pastry bag and tuck some of the bag into the tube to form a plug. Fold the top of the bag over to form a cuff and stand the bag upright, with the top open, in a tall narrow bowl or 1-quart measure; set aside.

2 In a medium bowl, beat the 4 egg whites and salt with an electric mixer on medium speed until foamy. Add the cream of tartar and beat until soft peaks form. Gradually beat in the sugar 1 tablespoon at a time, then increase the speed to high and beat until the whites form upright, glossy peaks when the beaters are raised. Set aside.

3 In another medium bowl, beat the egg yolks on high speed until pale and slightly thickened, about 2 minutes. Add the confectioners' sugar and vanilla and beat until the mixture is very thick and pale, about 2 minutes more. Fold in the flour. The batter will be very thick. Stir in about one fourth of the beaten whites to lighten it, then fold in another one fourth of the whites. Scrape this mixture onto the remaining whites and fold together gently but thoroughly.

4 Scrape the batter into the pastry bag. Carefully pipe strips of batter about 3 inches long and 3/4 inch wide onto the baking sheets, making 3 rows of 10 strips on each pan and spacing them about 1 inch apart. Using a fine strainer, dust the tops lightly with confectioners' sugar.

5 Bake for 10 to 12 minutes, reversing the sheets from top to bottom and front to back after 6 minutes, until the tops of the ladyfingers are lightly colored and spring back when gently pressed. Slip the parchment or liners off the baking sheets and dislodge the ladyfingers with a firm metal spatula. Place them on wire racks to cool. Store airtight to prevent them from drying out.

HOW TO TEST OVEN TEMPERATURE

The baking of the cake is as important as the mixing. For most kinds the oven should be rather slow. If it be too hot for sponge cake, the cake will sometimes rise very high and fall again. In any case it will be coarse-grained and tough. A good test for sponge cake is to put a piece of white paper into the oven, close the door, and open it in five minutes. If the paper be a rich yellow, the oven is right; but if it be light yellow, the oven is too cool, or if a dark brown, it is too hot.

—Maria Parloa, *Miss Parloa's Kitchen Companion* (1887)

CHARLOTTE RUSSE

*Makes 8
servings*

From the mid-nineteenth century on, American cookbooks almost always had a recipe for charlotte russe, and major hotels often offered the dessert on their menus. In the first decades of the twentieth century, charlotte russe was very popular in large eastern cities of America.

Why all the fuss? It's hard to beat the combination of great cake and great cream. A sponge cake–lined mold is filled with whipped heavy cream or a combination of pastry cream and whipped cream. That's it. The topping of currant jelly is a later addition, but I like it for both color and tartness.

1 large egg	40 Ladyfingers (page 316) or store-bought
1 large egg yolk	
1/2 cup sugar	1/3 cup red currant jelly
1/4 cup cornstarch	
2 cups milk	Whipped cream (flavored with rum, if you wish), for serving
2 tablespoons unsalted butter	
1 cup heavy cream	
1 teaspoon pure vanilla extract	8 candied violets or 2 tablespoons chopped toasted almonds
2 tablespoons confectioners' sugar	

1 Whisk together the egg, egg yolk, sugar, and cornstarch in a medium bowl. Heat the milk in a medium heavy saucepan until it is steaming hot but not quite at a boil. Gradually whisk the hot milk into the egg mixture. Pour the egg-milk mixture into the saucepan and place the pan over medium heat. Stir gently and constantly with a heatproof rubber spatula, scraping the bottom of the pan often, until the mixture is almost boiling. Add the butter and cook, stirring and scraping, until the mixture boils and thickens, about 3 minutes. Reduce the heat to low and continue cooking for 2 to 3 minutes more, stirring constantly. Remove from the heat and scrape the sides of the pan. Place a piece of plastic wrap directly on the surface of the custard, and set it aside to cool completely.

2 In a medium bowl, whip the cream, vanilla, and confectioners' sugar until the cream holds a firm shape. Fold it into the cooled custard.

3 Place about a tablespoon of the custard into each of eight 8-ounce glasses, preferably with sloping sides, such as highball glasses. Tap the bottoms of the glasses gently on the palm of your hand to make a thin layer of custard. Place 5 ladyfingers in each glass, rounded sides against the sides. Spoon about $1/2$ cup custard into each glass and tap on the palm of your hand to level.

4 Heat the currant jelly in a small saucepan over medium heat, stirring, for just a few seconds to liquefy. It should be barely warm. Divide the jelly among the desserts, spooning about 2 teaspoons over the custard in each cup. Cover each glass with plastic wrap and refrigerate 2 to 3 hours, or up to 8 hours to chill and blend the flavors, before serving.

5 To serve, spoon whipped cream onto each portion, and decorate with a candied violet or a sprinkle of chopped toasted almonds.

CHARLOTTE RUSSE

A favorite little dainty of this sort is sold at the city confectionaries that is made in a paper case, size and shape of a common tin cup of the half pint size. A sheet of sponge cake is baked on paper, taken off and cut in pieces that will just fit inside the cases, a bottom piece is put in and then the charlotte is filled with a spoonful of whipped cream, sweetened and flavored but whipped up without gelatine. But they are made for fine parties in paper cases of the shape of small tumblers, wider at top than at bottom so that they can be taken out of the case when served, as the pattern with straight-up sides cannot. These are lined with either cake or lady fingers, but to give them firmness enough to be removed from the cases a little gelatine has to be added to the pure cream.

—Jessup Whitehead, *The American Pastry Cook* (1894)

AMAZING ANGEL FOOD CAKE

Makes one 10-inch tube cake, 12 to 16 servings

There are many ways of making angel food cake, but this method, pardon the pun, takes the cake. I'd never before seen anything like it, and it works like a charm. The cake is covered tightly with foil for the first 10 minutes of baking, uncovered, and then baked for 15 more minutes. I adapted the recipe from one created for Pillsbury's Bake-Off in 1951. The cake rises to the top of the pan and has a meltingly moist and tender texture, as well as a delicious vanilla-almond flavor. Serve it plain, or with berries or peaches and whipped cream.

1 cup sifted cake flour	1 teaspoon cream of tartar
1/2 cup confectioners' sugar	1 cup sugar
13 large egg whites	1 teaspoon pure vanilla extract
1/2 teaspoon salt	1/2 teaspoon pure almond extract

1 Adjust an oven rack to the lower third position and preheat the oven to 475°F. Have ready a grease-free 10-x-4-inch tube pan with a removable bottom (*not* nonstick).

2 Resift the flour with the confectioners' sugar; set aside.

3 In a large wide bowl, beat the whites with an electric mixer on medium speed until frothy, about 1 minute. Add the salt and cream of tartar and continue beating until the whites are thick and fluffy and form soft billowy mounds that droop at their tips. Beat in the sugar 2 tablespoons at a time, beating for a few seconds after each addition. Add both extracts and beat for 30 seconds, or until the whites form slightly stiff peaks that curl at their tips and move slightly when you tilt the bowl.

4 Gradually fold in the flour mixture, sifting about 3 tablespoons at a time evenly over the whites and using a large rubber spatula to fold the two together with a few gentle strokes. Using the spatula, gently transfer the batter to the tube pan. To remove any large air bubbles, run a long narrow metal spatula in 3 or 4 concentric circles through the batter, beginning at the tube and working outward. Smooth the top with the rubber spatula.

5 Cover the pan tightly with heavy-duty foil. Bake for 10 minutes. Quickly

open the oven door and remove the foil. Close the oven door and reduce the temperature to 425°F. Bake for 15 minutes more, or until the cake has risen to the top of the pan, is well browned, and springs back when gently pressed. The cake may have a few cracks. Immediately invert the pan onto a narrow-necked bottle. Let cool completely upside down, 2 to 3 hours.

6 Loosen the sides of the cake from the pan using a narrow thin-bladed knife. Run the knife between the cake and the central tube. Lift the cake out of the pan by its tube, and release the cake from the bottom of the pan with the knife. Carefully turn the cake out onto a wire rack. Cover with a cake plate and invert the two so that the cake is right side up. To serve, cut into portions with a serrated knife.

CHOCOLATE SOUFFLÉ CAKE

Makes one 9-inch cake, 12 servings

When you take a bite of this cake, it feels like a cloud of bittersweet chocolate. The texture results from baking the cake in a water bath. Unlike a soufflé, however, the cake will not fall. This cake doesn't really need anything else, but if you wish, serve it with lightly sweetened whipped cream.

1/2 cup firmly packed dark brown sugar

1/2 cup plus 1/3 cup sugar

3/4 cup water

1 tablespoon instant espresso powder (I use Medaglia d'Oro)

2 ounces (2 squares) unsweetened chocolate, chopped

2 ounces (2 squares) semisweet chocolate, chopped

2/3 cup Dutch-process cocoa

1/4 teaspoon salt

3 large eggs, separated

2 tablespoons coffee liqueur, such as Kahlúa

1/3 cup cake flour (spooned into cup and leveled)

3 large egg whites

1/4 teaspoon cream of tartar

Confectioners' sugar for dusting

1 Adjust an oven rack to the lower third position and preheat the oven to 350°F. Pour 1 inch of boiling water into a large roasting pan about 2 inches deep and place the pan in the oven. Butter a 9-inch springform pan. Coat the inside of the pan with fine dry bread crumbs and knock out the excess. Wrap the outside of the pan tightly in a square of heavy-duty aluminum foil, being careful not to tear the foil.

2 In a medium heavy saucepan, combine the brown sugar, 1/2 cup of the white sugar, the water, and espresso powder. Bring to a boil, stirring until both sugars are dissolved. Remove from the heat and whisk in both chocolates, the cocoa, and the salt until smooth. Whisk in the egg yolks and coffee liqueur. Let cool to room temperature.

3 Whisk the flour into the cooled chocolate mixture. Set aside.

4 In a large bowl, beat the 6 egg whites and cream of tartar with an electric mixer on medium speed until soft peaks form. Gradually beat in the remaining $\frac{1}{3}$ cup sugar, then increase the speed to high and beat until the egg whites form upright, shiny peaks that curl slightly at their tips when the beaters are raised. Add one fourth of the chocolate mixture and fold it in gently with a large rubber spatula. Don't be too thorough. In 3 more additions, gradually fold in the remaining chocolate mixture, just until no whites show. Scrape the mixture into the pan and place the pan in the water bath.

5 Bake for about 35 minutes, until a toothpick inserted into the center of the cake comes out looking moist with a few bits of chocolate sticking to it; do not overbake. Remove the cake from the water bath and set the pan on a wire rack to cool completely.

6 Remove the foil, then the sides of the springform pan. Invert the cake onto a rack and carefully remove the bottom of the pan. Place a dessert plate over the cake and invert again. The cake is delicate, so be careful. Dust the top with the confectioners' sugar. To serve, rinse a knife in hot water and shake off the excess water before making each cut.

ORANGE CHIFFON CAKE

Makes one 10-inch tube cake, 16 servings

Chiffon cakes are similar to sponge cakes, but the addition of oil gives them a tender, fine crumb. Created in the 1920s, they were hailed as the first new cake in a hundred years. I adapted this recipe from a 1948 booklet, *Betty Crocker Chiffon Cake Recipes and Secrets*.

2³/₄ cups sifted cake flour

1¹/₂ cups sugar

1 teaspoon baking powder, preferably nonaluminum

¹/₂ teaspoon salt

Finely grated zest of 1 large orange

Finely grated zest of 1 large lemon

²/₃ cup fresh orange juice

2 teaspoons pure vanilla extract

1 teaspoon pure orange extract

¹/₂ cup vegetable oil

7 large eggs, separated

1 large egg white

¹/₄ teaspoon cream of tartar

1 Adjust an oven rack to the lower third position and preheat the oven to 325°F. Have ready a grease-free 10-x-4-inch tube pan with a removable bottom (*not* nonstick).

2 Place the flour, 1 cup of the sugar, the baking powder, salt, zests, orange juice, extracts, oil, and egg yolks in a large wide bowl and beat with an electric mixer on low speed for 1 minute, until the batter is smooth. Raise the speed to medium-high and beat for 4 minutes, or until thick and fluffy. Set aside.

3 In another large bowl, with clean beaters, beat the 8 egg whites on medium-low speed until foamy. Add the cream of tartar and beat on medium speed until the whites form peaks that droop and curl softly at their tips when the beaters are raised. Beat in the remaining ¹/₂ cup sugar 2 tablespoons at a time, beating for about 15 seconds after each addition. Increase the speed to medium-high and beat until the whites are shiny and form upright peaks when the beaters are raised, about 1 minute; do not overbeat.

4 Spoon about one fourth of the whites onto the yolks and fold them together with a large rubber spatula until partly combined. Scoop the remaining whites onto the mixture and fold them in gently but thoroughly, only until no whites show. Carefully scrape the batter into the pan.

5 Bake for 55 minutes. Raise the heat to 350°F and bake for 15 to 20 minutes more, until the cake is well browned, has a few cracks, and springs back when gently pressed in a few places. Immediately invert the pan onto a narrow-necked bottle. Let cool completely upside down, about 2 hours.

6 Loosen the sides of the cake from the pan with a narrow thin-bladed knife. Run the knife between the cake and the central tube. Lift the cake out of the pan by its tube, and release the cake from the bottom of the pan with the knife. Carefully invert the cake onto a square of waxed paper. Cover with a wire rack and invert again so that the cake is right side up. Transfer the cake to a cake plate. To serve, cut with a serrated knife using a gentle sawing motion.

CHOCOLATE MARBLE CHIFFON CAKE

Makes one 10-inch tube cake, about 16 servings

Marble cakes seem to be an American invention. The first recipe may have been from *Common Sense in the Household* (1874) by Marion Harland, who darkened part of her batter with molasses. In this recipe, half the batter is mixed with cocoa and vanilla and the other half is flavored with almond extract. This is a tall, tender cake.

CHOCOLATE MIXTURE

- 1/3 cup cocoa, preferably Dutch-process
- 1/3 cup sugar
- 1/3 cup boiling water
- 1 teaspoon pure vanilla extract

CAKE

- 2 3/4 cups sifted cake flour
- 1 1/2 cups sugar
- 1 teaspoon baking powder, preferably nonaluminum
- 1/2 teaspoon salt
- 3/4 cup cold water
- 1/2 cup vegetable oil
- 7 large eggs, separated
- 1 large egg white
- 1/4 teaspoon cream of tartar
- 3/4 teaspoon pure almond extract

FROSTING

- 4 tablespoons (1/2 stick) unsalted butter
- 4 ounces (4 squares) unsweetened chocolate
- 2 cups confectioners' sugar
- 1/8 teaspoon salt
- 2 teaspoons pure vanilla extract
- 1/4 cup cream or half-and-half, plus more if needed

1 For the chocolate mixture, whisk together the cocoa, sugar, and boiling water in a small bowl until perfectly smooth; stir in the vanilla and set aside to cool.

2 For the cake, adjust an oven rack to the lower third position and preheat the oven to 325°F. Have ready a grease-free 10-x-4-inch tube pan with a removable bottom (*not* nonstick).

3 Place the flour, 1 cup of the sugar, the baking powder, salt, water, oil, and egg yolks in a large wide bowl and beat with an electric mixer on low speed for 1 minute, just until the batter is smooth. Raise the speed to medium-high and beat for 4 minutes, or until thick and fluffy.

4 In another large bowl, with clean beaters, beat the 8 egg whites on medium-low speed until foamy. Add the cream of tartar, and beat on

medium speed until the whites form peaks that droop and curl softly at their tips when the beater is raised. Beat in the remaining $1/2$ cup sugar 2 tablespoons at a time, beating for about 15 seconds after each addition. Increase the speed to medium-high and beat until the whites are shiny and form upright peaks when the beaters are raised, about 1 minute; do not overbeat.

5 Spoon about one fourth of the whites onto the yolk mixture and fold them together with a large rubber spatula until partly combined. Scoop the remaining whites onto the mixture and fold them in gently but thoroughly, only until no whites show. Carefully transfer half of this batter back to the egg white bowl, and gently fold in the almond extract. Stir the chocolate mixture to be sure it's perfectly smooth and add it to the batter in the other bowl. Fold together gently until the batter is almost an even chocolate color. Carefully pour about one fourth of the chocolate batter into the tube pan. Spoon about one third of the plain batter in 3 or 4 mounds over the chocolate. Continue the layering, making 4 layers of chocolate batter and 3 layers of plain.

6 Bake for 55 minutes. Increase the heat to 350°F and bake for 15 to 20 minutes more, until the cake is well browned, has a few cracks, and springs back when gently pressed in a few places. Immediately invert the pan onto a narrow-necked bottle. Let cool completely upside down, about 2 hours.

7 Loosen the sides of the cake from the pan with a narrow, thin-bladed knife. Run the knife between the cake and the central tube. Lift the cake out of the pan by its tube and release the cake from the bottom of the pan with the knife. Carefully turn the cake out onto a cake plate, bottom side up.

8 For the frosting, melt the butter in a small heavy saucepan over very low heat. Add the chocolate and stir occasionally until the chocolate is melted and the mixture is smooth. Set aside to cool briefly.

9 Put the confectioners' sugar in a medium bowl and add the salt, vanilla, cream or half-and-half, and the chocolate mixture. Whisk together to make a smooth, thick, spreadable frosting; if it is too thick, thin it with additional cream. Quickly, before the frosting sets, spread it all around the sides and top of the cake with a long narrow metal spatula. Let stand until the icing is set. To serve, cut the cake into portions with a serrated knife using a gentle sawing motion.

BLACK WALNUT CHIFFON CAKE

Makes one 10-inch tube cake, 12 to 16 servings

This is a simply gorgeous cake, almost 5 inches tall and frosted with a thin layer of a chocolate icing—serve it with Champagne. Be sure to chop the walnuts very fine. Even if you buy chopped walnuts, you'll need to use a chef's knife to get the pieces smaller, about 1/8 inch. Don't use a food processor, which would make the pieces too fine. You can use regular walnuts if you prefer.

CAKE

- 2 1/2 cups sifted cake flour
- 1 1/2 cups sugar
- 1 teaspoon baking powder, preferably nonaluminum
- 1/2 teaspoon salt
- 2 teaspoons instant espresso powder (I use Medaglia d'Oro)
- 1 teaspoon ground cinnamon
- 3/4 cup cold water
- 1/2 cup vegetable oil
- 2 teaspoons pure vanilla extract
- 7 large eggs, separated
- 1 large egg white
- 1/2 teaspoon cream of tartar
- 1 cup very finely chopped black walnuts

ICING

- 8 tablespoons (1 stick) unsalted butter
- 2 1/2 tablespoons all-purpose flour
- 1/4 teaspoon salt
- 1/2 cup milk, heated, plus more if needed
- 3 cups confectioners' sugar
- 1 teaspoon pure vanilla extract
- 2 ounces (2 squares) unsweetened chocolate, melted

1 For the cake, adjust an oven rack to the lower third position and preheat the oven to 325°F. Have ready a grease-free 10-x-4-inch tube pan with a removable bottom (*not* nonstick).

2 Place the flour, 1 cup of the sugar, the baking powder, salt, espresso powder, cinnamon, water, oil, vanilla, and egg yolks in a large wide bowl and beat with an electric mixer on low speed for 1 minute, just until the batter is smooth. Raise the speed to medium-high and beat for 4 minutes, or until the mixture is thick and fluffy. Set aside.

3 In another large bowl, with clean beaters, beat the 8 whites on medium-low until foamy. Add the cream of tartar and beat on medium speed until the whites form peaks that droop and curl softly at their tips when the beaters are raised. Beat in the remaining $1/2$ cup sugar 2 tablespoons at a time, beating for about 15 seconds after each addition. Increase the speed to medium-high and beat until the whites are shiny and form upright peaks when the beaters are raised, about 1 minute; do not overbeat.

4 Spoon about one fourth of the whites onto the yolks and fold them together with a large rubber spatula, only until partly combined. Scoop the remaining whites onto the mixture and fold them in gently but thoroughly, only until no whites show. Sprinkle the walnuts evenly over the batter and fold them in gently. Carefully scrape the batter into the pan.

5 Bake for 55 minutes. Raise the heat to 350°F and bake for 15 to 20 minutes more, until the cake is well browned, has a few cracks, and springs back when gently pressed in a few places. Immediately invert the pan onto a narrow-necked bottle. Let cool completely upside down, about 2 hours.

6 Loosen the sides of the cake from the pan with a narrow, thin-bladed knife. Run the knife between the cake and the central tube. Lift the cake out of the pan by its tube and release the cake from the bottom of the pan with the knife. Carefully turn the cake out onto a plate, bottom side up.

7 For the icing, melt the butter in a medium heavy saucepan over medium heat. When bubbly, whisk in the flour and salt and cook, whisking constantly, for 2 minutes; do not allow the flour to brown. Remove from the heat and let stand briefly until the bubbles subside, then add the hot milk all at once and whisk until smooth. Return the pan to medium heat and cook, whisking constantly, for 2 minutes. The mixture will separate and curdle. Remove from the heat and set aside to cool until tepid.

8 Gradually whisk the confectioners' sugar into the milk mixture, then whisk in the vanilla. Add the chocolate and whisk until smooth and spreadable but not runny. If necessary, adjust the consistency of the icing with a few droplets of milk. Using a long narrow metal spatula, spread the icing carefully all over the sides and top of the cake and the tube position. Let stand until the icing is set, about 1 hour. To serve, cut the cake into portions with a serrated knife, using a gentle sawing motion.

CLASSIC GÉNOISE

*Makes one
8- or 9-inch
round, or
one 8-inch
square, or
one large
sheet cake*

Génoise is perhaps the most versatile of the sponge cake family. Its firm texture allows it to readily absorb liqueur-spiked sugar syrups, adding moisture to the cake and enabling it to take on any number of flavors. Buttercream icings are particularly good with génoise cakes. Génoise makes excellent layer cakes, tortes, jelly rolls, or ice cream cakes. Plain génoise can be cut up for use in trifle, petits fours, and charlotte russe, and you can also use it to make Boston Cream Pie (page 332).

4 tablespoons (¹/₂ stick) unsalted butter	¹/₂ cup sifted all-purpose flour
4 large eggs	¹/₈ teaspoon salt
¹/₂ cup sifted cake flour	¹/₂ cup sugar
	1 teaspoon pure vanilla extract

1 Melt the butter in a small saucepan over medium heat. Carefully skim the foam off the surface with a small spoon and continue cooking until the butter solids and the clear butter turn light brown. Carefully pour the butter through a very fine mesh strainer into a medium bowl and let cool. (If the butter is hot, it will deflate the batter.)

2 Adjust an oven rack to the center position and preheat the oven to 350°F if using a round or square pan, 375°F if using a jelly-roll pan. Butter the pan. Line the bottom of a round or square cake pan (or a springform pan) with waxed paper or cooking parchment. Or line a jelly-roll pan with a long sheet of waxed paper or parchment, with a 1- or 2-inch overhang at each end. Butter the paper and dust the inside of the pan with all-purpose flour; knock out the excess. Set aside.

3 Warm the whole eggs by covering them with hot tap water (120° to 130°F). Let stand for 10 minutes. Remove and pat dry.

4 Meanwhile, resift the flours with the salt; set aside.

5 Crack the eggs into a large bowl. Add the sugar and vanilla and beat with an electric mixer on medium-high speed for 3 minutes. Increase the speed to high and beat for another 2 minutes, until they are pale and thick and form a ribbon that stays on the surface for a few seconds when the beaters

are lifted. Sift about half of the flour mixture over the eggs and fold in rapidly and gently with a large rubber spatula until almost all of it is incorporated. Sift on the remaining flour and fold rapidly but gently until almost incorporated. Immediately transfer about 1 cup of the mixture to the butter and fold rapidly to combine well, then fold the butter mixture into the egg-flour mixture. Immediately scrape the batter into the pan and carefully spread it level.

6 Bake the round or square cake for 25 to 30 minutes, the jelly-roll cake for 15 to 20 minutes, until it is golden brown, springs back when gently pressed, and shows a faint line of shrinkage at the edges of the pan. Immediately run the tip of a small knife all around the sides to release the cake from the pan. Cover the pan with a wire rack and invert. Carefully remove the pan and paper, cover with another rack, and invert again to cool right side up. Let cool completely before using.

BOSTON CREAM PIE

Makes one 9-inch 2-layer cake, 10 servings

This version of Boston cream pie is extraordinary. The cake, a hot milk sponge, dates to the late 1800s. It is especially tender, light, and delicate. The layers are filled with a beautifully smooth baked cream custard flavored with vanilla and stick cinnamon. (The recipe is from Eliza Leslie's 1851 cookbook, *Directions for Cookery*.) It's rich and sublime, a crème brûlée without the sugar topping. The glaze is a silky-smooth chocolate ganache. Serve small portions of this rich dessert at a fancy tea party or after a fairly light meal. (The photograph is on the cover.)

CUSTARD FILLING

- 2 cups heavy cream
- 1 3-inch cinnamon stick
- 1 vanilla bean, split lengthwise
- $1/4$ cup sugar
- 4 large egg yolks

- $1/2$ cup milk
- 4 tablespoons ($1/2$ stick) unsalted butter, cut into pieces
- 2 large eggs
- $2/3$ cup sugar
- 1 teaspoon pure vanilla extract

HOT MILK SPONGE CAKE

- 1 cup sifted cake flour
- 1 teaspoon baking powder, preferably nonaluminum
- $1/4$ teaspoon salt

GLAZE

- $1/4$ cup heavy cream
- 3 ounces (3 squares) semisweet or bittersweet chocolate, coarsely chopped

1 For the custard filling, place the cream and cinnamon stick in a small heavy saucepan. Scrape the seeds from the vanilla bean into the cream and add the pod. Slowly bring to a boil over medium-low heat; watch closely, or the cream may boil over. Remove from the heat, add the sugar, and stir until dissolved. Set aside to steep for about 1 hour.

2 Adjust an oven rack to the center position and preheat the oven to 325°F. Have ready a 9-inch ovenproof glass pie plate and a shallow baking pan large enough to contain the pie plate. Bring a kettle of water to a boil.

3 If a skin has formed on top of the cream, stir it back in. Strain through a fine-mesh strainer and return to the saucepan. Heat until almost boiling. Meanwhile, in a medium bowl, whisk the egg yolks. Gradually whisk the

hot cream into the egg yolks; don't beat. Strain the mixture through a fine-mesh strainer into the pie plate and set the pie plate in the baking pan. Add boiling water to come halfway up the sides of the pie plate and place in the oven.

4 Bake for 20 to 25 minutes, just until set; the tip of a sharp knife inserted into the center should come out clean. Remove the custard from the water bath and cool to room temperature on a wire rack. (The custard can be made ahead and refrigerated for several hours, or overnight.)

5 For the sponge cake, adjust an oven rack to the center position and preheat the oven to 350°F. Butter a 9-inch layer cake pan, or coat with cooking spray. Line the bottom with a round of waxed paper or cooking parchment. Butter the paper or coat with cooking spray and dust the bottom of the pan lightly with all-purpose flour. Knock out the excess flour and set aside.

6 Resift the cake flour with the baking powder and salt, and set aside.

7 Combine the milk and butter in a small heavy saucepan and set over low heat. In a large bowl, beat the eggs with an electric mixer on high speed for a few minutes, until thickened and light in color. On medium speed, gradually beat in the sugar, then beat on high for 5 minutes. Beat in the vanilla. On low speed, add the sifted dry ingredients, beating only until incorporated. Scrape the bowl, handling the batter as gently as possible.

8 Meanwhile, bring the milk and butter mixture to a boil. Beating on low speed, add the milk mixture in a steady stream to the batter, taking 15 to 20 seconds to do so. As soon as the batter is smooth, scrape it into the cake pan.

9 Bake for 25 to 30 minutes, until the cake is a deep golden brown color, springs back when gently pressed, and pulls away from the sides of the pan; do not overbake. Cool for 10 minutes on a wire rack. Run a small sharp knife around the edges to loosen the cake, cover with a rack, and invert. Remove the pan and paper liner, cover the cake with another rack, and reinvert to cool right side up.

10 To assemble, use a sharp serrated knife to slice the cake horizontally in half. Carefully remove the top half and set it aside. Place the bottom half on a cake plate, cut side up. Spoon the custard onto the cake, spreading it

gently with a small metal spatula to make a smooth layer reaching almost to the edges. Set the top half of the cake right side up on the filling. If you want to serve the cake soon, with an unchilled filling, leave it at room temperature while you make the glaze; otherwise, refrigerate it.

11 For the glaze, bring the cream to a simmer in a small heavy saucepan over medium heat. Add the chocolate and stir briefly with a small whisk until the chocolate is partly melted. Remove from the heat and continue stirring until melted and smooth. Set aside for a few minutes, stirring occasionally, until thickened a bit.

12 To glaze the cake, pour all of the glaze onto the center of the cake and carefully spread it with a long metal spatula right to the edges. Refrigerate for a few minutes to set the glaze, or for 1 to 2 hours, or longer, until chilled. This dessert is best the day it is assembled. Cut into portions with a sharp knife.

THE STORY OF BOSTON CREAM PIE

Just why this classic American dessert is called a pie and not a cake has long been a mystery. Perhaps it was because the cake layers were originally baked in pie tins, as many cakes from the mid-1800s were. "Washington pie plates" were often specified as the pan of choice for many kinds of cakes. They were jelly-cake pans—round, shallow, straight-sided pans of varying diameters, used to make thin layers of cake that were stacked together with jam or jelly in between.

I've found recipes resembling Boston cream pie—two layers of tender cake filled with custard and dusted with confectioners' sugar, but with no chocolate glaze—in manuscripts and in published cookbooks from the late 1800s. These cakes went by various names: cream cake, custard cake, French cake, and, most commonly, Washington pie. But for that time period, I've found the name Boston Cream Pie in print only once, in an 1878 Graniteware booklet. Over time, custard replaced the jam or jelly in Washington pie, but the dessert retained its original name.

The addition of the chocolate glaze was a long time coming. The first Boston cream pie with a chocolate glaze that I've found appears in 1950, in *Betty Crocker's Picture Cook Book*. It took almost 100 years before the transformation of Washington pie into our Boston Cream Pie was complete.

RICE FLOUR, ALMOND, AND RUM BUTTER SPONGE CAKE

Makes one 10-inch tube cake, 12 to 16 servings

This is a luxurious, creamy, luscious extravaganza. The sponge cake is unusual because it's made with rice flour, something that was used a great deal in the nineteenth century in all kinds of baking. The cake is firm and moist and cuts very easily. Rice flour is sold in many supermarkets and health food stores. A particularly fine-quality rice flour can be ordered from Great Valley Mills (see Sources, page 526).

If you want more filling and icing, you can increase the whipped cream ingredients by half.

4 ounces blanched almonds

1 1/2 cups rice flour (spooned into the cup and leveled)

7 large eggs, separated

1 1/2 cups sugar

1/4 cup dark rum (I use Myers's)

1 teaspoon pure almond extract

3 large egg whites

1/2 teaspoon salt

4 tablespoons (1/2 stick) unsalted butter, melted and cooled

WHIPPED CREAM

4 teaspoons instant espresso powder (I use Medaglia d'Oro)

1 tablespoon dark rum

2 cups heavy cream

1/3 cup confectioners' sugar

12–16 chocolate-covered coffee beans

1 Adjust an oven rack to the lower third position and preheat the oven to 350°F. Have ready a grease-free 10-x-4-inch tube pan with a removable bottom (*not* nonstick).

2 Chop the almonds in a food processor, pulsing 10 to 12 times for about 1 second each. Add the rice flour and process for about 30 seconds, until the mixture feels very fine when you rub it between your fingers. Process for a few seconds more if necessary, but be careful not to turn the mixture into a paste. Set aside.

3 In a large wide bowl, beat the egg yolks with an electric mixer on medium speed for 1 minute. Increase the speed to high and beat for 4 to 5 minutes, until the yolks are very pale and thick. Beat in 1 cup of the sugar about 2 tablespoons at a time, beating for a few seconds after each addition, then beat for 4 to 5 minutes more, until the yolks are very thick. On low speed, beat in the rum and almond extracts. Set aside.

4 In another large bowl, with clean beaters, beat the 10 egg whites and salt with the mixer on medium speed until soft peaks form when the beaters are raised. Beat in the remaining $1/2$ cup sugar about 2 tablespoons at a time, beating for 10 to 15 seconds after each addition. Increase the speed to medium-high and beat until the whites form stiff shiny peaks that curl only slightly at their tips.

5 In 3 additions, stir the almond mixture into the yolk mixture. Add about one fourth of the beaten whites and fold them in to lighten the batter. Don't be too thorough. Fold in the remaining whites in 3 more installments, folding in the last addition until no whites show.

6 Drizzle about one third of the butter (which must be no warmer than tepid) over the batter and fold it in with 3 or 4 broad strokes of the spatula. Repeat 2 more times with the remaining butter. Immediately scrape the batter into the tube pan. Smooth the top with the spatula.

7 Bake for 45 to 50 minutes, until the cake is golden brown with a few cracks and springs back when gently pressed. Invert the pan onto a narrow-necked bottle. Let cool completely upside down, about 2 hours.

8 Loosen the sides of the cake from the pan with a narrow thin-bladed knife. Run the knife between the cake and the central tube. Lift the cake out of the pan by its tube, and release the cake from the bottom of the pan with the knife. Carefully turn the cake out onto a wire rack. (The cake can be made 1 day ahead. Wrap in plastic and refrigerate.)

9 For the whipped cream, stir the instant espresso and rum together in a small cup to dissolve the coffee. Place the cream in a chilled bowl and add the coffee mixture and confectioners' sugar. Beat with an electric mixer on medium speed until the cream begins to thicken. Raise the speed to medium-high and continue beating until the cream is very thick and holds a definite shape. Refrigerate if not using immediately.

10 Cut the cake horizontally into thirds with a large, sharp serrated knife.

Remove the top two layers and set aside. Set the bottom layer on a cake plate, cut side up. With a narrow metal spatula, spread with about 1 cup of the whipped cream. Cover with the middle layer and spread with another 1 cup cream. Place the third layer on top, cut side down, and spread the remaining cream over the top and sides. Decorate with the chocolate-covered coffee beans and refrigerate until serving time. (The cake should be assembled several hours ahead.) To serve, cut the cold cake into portions with a sharp serrated knife. Refrigerate leftovers.

THE ORIGINAL PARKER HOUSE
CHOCOLATE CREAM PIE

*Makes one
10-inch 2-
layer cake,
12 to 16
servings*

According to today's Omni Parker House Hotel, this classic dessert was introduced at Boston's Parker House when the original hotel opened in October 1856. The chef at the Parker House was French, and his version is a two-layered French butter sponge cake brushed with a rum-flavored syrup and filled with a generous layer of French pastry cream. More pastry cream is spread on the sides, and toasted sliced almonds are pressed onto the cake. The top of the cake is covered with a thin layer of chocolate fondant icing and decorated with scrolls of white fondant. It is breathtaking to behold and tastes sensational.

Old cookbooks, newspapers, and food journals, however, contain no mention of this dessert, and for good reason: it was too complicated for most cooks, especially since the chocolate icing required the cook to make a fondant first. And for another reason, too: chocolate wasn't a common baking ingredient in the home until many years after the Parker House opened.

For those who want a true culinary adventure, I am including a recipe for fondant and for chocolate fondant icing. The pastry cream and fondant must be made at least 1 day ahead, preferably several. Neither is difficult to make, but you'll need some special equipment: a marble slab measuring about 18 x 24 inches (or a granite countertop), a candy thermometer or digital probe thermometer, and a firm-bladed metal bench scraper or painter's scraper (which you can find in hardware shops). If you don't want to make fondant, you can order an excellent version of it by mail (see Sources, page 524) or simply use the chocolate ganache.

WHITE FONDANT (OPTIONAL)

2½ cups sugar

1 cup milk or water

⅛ teaspoon cream of tartar

RUM SYRUP

⅓ cup water

3 tablespoons sugar

2 tablespoons dark rum (I use
　　Myers's)

TOASTED ALMONDS

1 cup sliced blanched or
　　unblanched almonds

PASTRY CREAM

4 large eggs

¹/₄ teaspoon salt

³/₄ cup sugar

¹/₄ cup cornstarch

3 tablespoons cake flour

3¹/₃ cups milk, heated

3 tablespoons unsalted butter, cut into pieces

2 teaspoons pure vanilla extract

SPONGE CAKE

4 tablespoons (¹/₂ stick) unsalted butter

6 large eggs, separated

1 cup sugar

2 teaspoons pure vanilla extract

1 cup sifted cake flour

¹/₄ teaspoon salt

CHOCOLATE FONDANT ICING

8 ounces white fondant (from above)

Milk, if necessary

4 ounces (4 squares) semisweet or bittersweet chocolate, melted

OR

CHOCOLATE GANACHE

¹/₃ cup heavy cream

6 ounces (6 squares) semisweet or bittersweet chocolate, chopped

1 For the fondant, if using, mist the marble slab with cold water.

2 Combine the sugar and milk or water in a medium heavy saucepan. Cook over medium-high heat, stirring with a wooden spoon to dissolve the sugar, until the mixture begins to seethe. Add the cream of tartar and stir vigorously. The mixture will rise up in the pan. Attach a candy thermometer or digital probe thermometer. Cook, stirring occasionally, until the thermometer registers 236°F, 3 to 4 minutes. Immediately remove from the heat. Rinse a pastry brush in cold water, shake off the excess, and quickly wipe down the sides of the saucepan. Pour the syrup down the center of an 18-x-24-inch marble slab in a narrow strip. *Do not scrape the pan, or the fondant will crystallize.* Let the syrup stand for a few minutes, until its surface wrinkles when you press it gently and an impression of a finger remains. The syrup must still be warm.

3 Using a metal bench or painter's scraper, start scraping the syrup from one edge, working the length from one end to the other in a single long stroke.

Then reverse directions and repeat the process, gradually working your way toward the center of the strip of syrup, up and down and back and forth, smearing the fondant against the marble. As you work, the syrup will turn from clear to cloudy; in about 10 minutes, it will have thickened considerably and be creamy white and stiff. Scrape the blade clean with a knife, then scrape all of the fondant together, pressing it into one lump; it will seem like a giant hard crystal. Let rest on the slab for 10 to 15 minutes.

4 Cut the fondant into 4 pieces. Knead each piece on the marble, like bread dough, until it is smooth, creamy, and supple. When all the pieces have been kneaded, combine them and knead them together briefly. Wrap the fondant securely in plastic wrap and place it in a 1-quart airtight container. Cover and refrigerate for at least 1 day before using; a week or longer is better. (The fondant will keep well for 2 to 3 months.)

5 For the rum syrup, stir the water and sugar in a small heavy saucepan over medium heat until the sugar dissolves and the mixture almost boils. Remove from the heat and let cool to room temperature. Stir in the rum. (The syrup can be made 2 to 3 days ahead; cover and refrigerate. Bring to room temperature before using.)

6 To toast the almonds, adjust an oven rack to the center position and preheat the oven to 350°F.

7 Place the almonds in a shallow rimmed baking pan and toast in the oven until golden brown, about 10 minutes, checking frequently to make sure they don't brown too much. Let cool completely. (If not using that day, transfer them to a zip-top plastic bag and refrigerate. Bring to room temperature before using.)

8 For the pastry cream, beat the eggs and salt in a large bowl with an electric mixer on medium speed until slightly thickened, 3 to 5 minutes. Beat in the sugar about 2 tablespoons at a time, and continue beating until the eggs are very thick and pale and form a slowly dissolving ribbon when the beaters are raised. On low speed, beat in the cornstarch and flour. Slowly beat in the hot milk.

9 Scrape the mixture into a 6-quart saucepan. Cook over medium heat, stirring constantly with a heatproof rubber spatula at first, then, when the mixture becomes lumpy, a wire whisk, until the mixture comes to a boil

and thickens. Boil, whisking constantly, for 2 to 3 minutes. Remove from the heat and whisk in the butter, then the vanilla. Scrape the mixture into a bowl, press a piece of plastic wrap directly on the surface, and let cool to room temperature. Refrigerate overnight. (The pastry cream can be refrigerated for up to 3 days.)

10 For the cake, melt the butter in a small saucepan over medium-low heat; set aside.

11 Adjust an oven rack to the lower third position and preheat the oven to 325°F. Butter the bottom of a 10-inch springform pan and line it with a circle of waxed paper or cooking parchment. Butter the paper and dust it lightly with all-purpose flour. Knock off the excess flour, attach the sides of the pan, and set the pan aside.

12 Beat the yolks in a large wide bowl with an electric mixer on medium-high speed until thickened, about 3 minutes. Beat in $1/2$ cup of the sugar about 2 tablespoons at a time, beating for 20 to 30 seconds after each addition, then beat until the yolks are very thick and pale and form a slowly dissolving ribbon when the beaters are raised, about 3 minutes more. Beat in the vanilla. Beat in the flour and the salt on low speed only until incorporated.

13 In a large bowl, with clean beaters, beat the whites and salt on medium speed until the beaters leave impressions in the whites. Beat in the remaining $1/2$ cup sugar about 2 tablespoons at a time, beating for 20 to 30 seconds after each addition. Continue beating for 1 to 2 minutes longer, until the whites hold a firm shape and form peaks that curl slightly at their tips.

14 Check the butter to be sure it is liquid and no hotter than tepid; if necessary, place the cup briefly in a small pan of warm water. Scoop about one fourth of the whites onto the yolk mixture and fold them together gently with a few broad strokes of a large rubber spatula. Don't be too thorough. Scrape the remaining whites on top, and fold them in gently just until no whites show. Carefully drizzle half the butter on top of the batter, and incorporate it with 2 or 3 broad strokes. Repeat, folding only until no butter shows. Carefully scrape the batter into the pan and smooth the top.

15 Bake for about 40 minutes, until the cake is golden brown and springs back when gently pressed; do not overbake. Cool in the pan on a rack for 10 minutes. Run the blade of a sharp knife around the edges of the cake and

remove the pan sides. Invert the cake onto a cooling rack and remove the bottom of the pan and the paper liner. Replace the liner on the cake bottom, cover with another rack, and invert the two. Let cool completely.

16 For the chocolate fondant icing, if using, place 8 ounces white fondant in the top of a double boiler or in a medium saucepan and set the pan in a larger pan of hot water over medium-low heat. The fondant must melt slowly and not get too hot; if it seems too thick when melted, add a few droplets of milk. Meanwhile, place the chocolate in another small pan, set it in a larger pan of hot water over medium heat, and stir occasionally until the chocolate is melted and smooth. When the fondant is completely melted, place about 2 tablespoons of it into a small zip-top bag, seal the bag, and set it in a pan of hot water to keep the fondant fluid. Add the chocolate to the remaining fondant and whisk together. If the mixture seizes, gradually add a little milk, whisking after each addition until the fondant is smooth and pourable but not runny. Keep it in the hot water (with the heat turned off) until ready to use.

Or, if using the ganache, bring the cream to a simmer in a small heavy saucepan over medium heat. Add the chocolate and stir briefly with a whisk until the chocolate is partly melted. Remove from the heat and continue stirring until melted and smooth. Set aside for a few minutes, until slightly thickened.

17 To assemble, cut out a 10-inch cardboard disk for the cake. Level the top of the cake with a sharp serrated knife, then slice the cake horizontally in half. Remove the pastry cream from the refrigerator, and whisk it until smooth. Place a dab of pastry cream in the center of the cardboard disk and set the bottom layer on it cut side up. Brush half the rum syrup all over the layer and spread with a $^3/_4$-inch layer of pastry cream. Set the second cake layer on the cream and brush with the remaining syrup. With a narrow metal spatula, spread a thin layer of pastry cream all around the sides of the cake. (You may have some pastry cream left over; refrigerate it for another use.) Put the almonds in a shallow pan. Supporting the cake with the palm of one hand, hold it over the pan of almonds and press the nuts gently all around the side of the cake. You'll have more nuts than you need; save the extra for another use.

18 Set the cake on a platter. Whisk the chocolate fondant or ganache until smooth. Remove the pan from the water and dry the bottom of the pan. Immediately scrape the fondant (or ganache, if using) onto the center of the cake and rapidly spread it with a large metal icing spatula right to the edges; don't allow any to run down the sides. Remove the bag of white fondant from the hot water and pat it dry. Press the fondant into one bottom corner of the bag, and snip the corner off to make a small opening. Squeeze the fondant out of the bag in a zigzag pattern all over the top of the cake. Refrigerate the cake for at least 1 hour. (The cake can be assembled up to 1 day ahead.)

19 To serve, rinse a sharp knife in hot water and shake off the excess water before making each cut. Place the portions on dessert plates and let stand at room temperature for about 20 minutes before serving. Refrigerate leftovers.

TO MAKE AND USE A PASTRY BAG

Fold a piece of strong cotton cloth (perhaps a foot square) from two opposite corners, so as to give it a triangular shape. On one side sew together the two edges, thus making a bag shaped like a "dunce's cap." Cut the cloth at the apex just enough to permit a short tin tube, somewhat like a tailor's thimble, to be pushed through.

—Maria Parloa, *Miss Parloa's New Cook Book* (1880)

BANANA-STRAWBERRY TRIFLE

Makes 10 to 12 servings

Génoise is ideal for a trifle. The dense cake soaks up the alcohol and becomes moist and tender without falling apart. The resulting trifle is firm enough to be cut into wedges. Although trifle is traditionally served during the Christmas holidays, I make this one in the spring or early summer, when strawberries are at their best. You must assemble the dessert a day ahead so the flavors and textures have a chance to blend.

CUSTARD

1½ cups milk
1 large egg
2 large egg yolks
½ cup sugar
1½ tablespoons cornstarch
⅛ teaspoon salt
Finely grated zest of 1 lemon
1 teaspoon vanilla extract

Classic Génoise (page 330),
baked in an 8-inch square pan

½ cup dry sherry
6 tablespoons cognac or Grand Marnier
½ cup seedless strawberry jam
1 tablespoon fresh lemon juice
2 firm but ripe bananas (¾ pound)

TOPPING

2 tablespoons sliced or slivered almonds
1 cup heavy cream
2 tablespoons confectioners' sugar

1 For the custard, heat the milk in a medium heavy saucepan over medium heat until it is steaming hot but not quite at a boil. Meanwhile, whisk together the egg, egg yolks, sugar, cornstarch, and salt in a medium bowl until well combined. Gradually whisk in the hot milk. Pour the egg-milk mixture into the saucepan and bring to a boil over medium heat, stirring constantly with a heatproof rubber spatula, scraping the bottom of the pan often. When the mixture has thickened and is bubbling, reduce the heat to low and cook for 2 minutes, stirring constantly. Remove from the heat.

2 Place the saucepan in a pan or bowl of ice and water. Stir occasionally until cooled to room temperature, then stir in the lemon zest and vanilla.

3 Meanwhile, cut the cake into quarters with a sharp serrated knife and cut each quarter into 6 slices. Fit half the cake slices snugly into the bottom of a round glass bowl about 10 inches in diameter and 2 inches deep, trimming the pieces as necessary and pushing them together.

4 Combine the sherry and cognac or Grand Marnier in a cup and drizzle half the mixture evenly over the cake slices in the bowl. Combine the strawberry jam and lemon juice in a small bowl and spread half the mixture over the cake slices. Spoon a thin layer of the cooled custard (about ²/₃ cup) over the jam. Slice the bananas and arrange them over the custard in a single layer. Spoon and spread the remaining custard over the bananas; the cake and bananas should be completely covered. Arrange the remaining cake slices snugly over the custard, trimming them as necessary to fit. Drizzle the remaining sherry mixture evenly over the cake and spread with the remaining strawberry jam mixture. Cover tightly with plastic wrap and refrigerate for at least 8 hours, or overnight, to allow the custard to set and the flavors to blend.

5 Meanwhile, for the topping, adjust an oven rack to the center position and preheat the oven to 350° F.

6 Spread the almonds in a shallow baking pan and toast in the oven, stirring once or twice, until golden brown and fragrant, 5 to 8 minutes. Let cool completely.

7 Shortly before serving, whip the cream with the confectioners' sugar until thick. Spread it evenly over the top of the trifle. Sprinkle with the toasted almonds. (You can add the topping up to 3 hours in advance and refrigerate the trifle.) To serve, cut into wedges, or spoon portions into dessert bowls. Spoon any liquid remaining in the bottom of the dessert dish over the trifle.

MINTED GÉNOISE ICE CREAM CAKE

Makes 12 servings

In this holiday ice cream cake, layers of génoise brushed with crème de menthe–flavored syrup encase mint-flavored vanilla ice cream mixed with chocolate mint candies. The warm bittersweet chocolate sauce complements the mint.

MINT SYRUP

- 1/4 cup sugar
- 1/2 cup hot water (120°–130°F)
- 1 tablespoon crème de menthe liqueur

  Classic Génoise (page 330), baked in an 8-inch springform pan

ICE CREAM

- 1 quart best-quality vanilla ice cream
- 1 tablespoon crème de menthe liqueur
- 12 Andes mint candies, each quartered crosswise

CHOCOLATE SAUCE

- 3/4 cup sugar
- 3/4 cup Dutch-process cocoa
- 1/8 teaspoon salt
- 1 cup milk
- 1/4 cup water
- 1 tablespoon unsalted butter
- 2 teaspoons pure vanilla extract

1 For the syrup, stir the sugar and hot water together in a small bowl to dissolve the sugar. Add the crème de menthe and set aside until cooled to room temperature.

2 Split the cake horizontally into two layers with a sharp serrated knife. Place a round of waxed paper in the bottom of an 8-inch springform pan. Set the bottom génoise layer cut side up in the pan. Brush with half the syrup and set aside.

3 For the ice cream, soften it in a medium bowl only until it is malleable, then stir in the crème de menthe and chocolate mint candies. Immediately spread the ice cream over the cake in the pan. Set the other génoise layer

cut side up on a sheet of plastic wrap and brush with the remaining mint syrup. Quickly and carefully, using the plastic wrap to support the cake, invert the layer onto the ice cream. Press gently into place, wrap securely in plastic wrap, and freeze for at least 2 hours. (The cake can be prepared up to 2 days ahead.)

4 For the chocolate sauce, whisk together the sugar, cocoa, and salt in a medium heavy saucepan. Gradually whisk in the milk and water. Bring to a slow boil over medium heat, stirring occasionally with a heatproof rubber spatula. Add the butter and slowly boil, stirring occasionally, for 3 to 4 minutes, until slightly thickened. Remove from the heat and stir occasionally until the sauce is warm or cool. Stir in the vanilla. (The sauce may be made up to 1 day ahead.) Reheat the sauce before serving.

5 To serve, remove the plastic wrap and the sides of the springform pan. Cut the cake into portions, place on dessert plates, and ladle about 2 tablespoons of sauce over each serving.

ORANGE GÉNOISE WITH CHOCOLATE BUTTERCREAM

*Makes
12 to 16
servings*

I f you're an orange-and-chocolate lover, this is for you: génoise layers flavored with orange zest and brushed with a Grand Marnier syrup, filled
and frosted with a luscious chocolate buttercream.

GRAND MARNIER SYRUP

- ¹/₄ cup sugar
- ¹/₂ cup hot water (120°–130°F)
- 2 tablespoons Grand Marnier

BUTTERCREAM

- 2 tablespoons unsalted butter
- 2 ounces (2 squares)
  unsweetened chocolate,
  chopped
- 1 ounce (1 square) semisweet
  chocolate, chopped

- ¹/₄ cup heavy cream
- 2 teaspoons pure vanilla extract
- 2 cups confectioners' sugar

  Classic Génoise (page 330),
  with the finely grated zest of
  1 orange added in step 5
  during the last moments of
  beating, and baked in a
  9-inch round cake pan

1 For the syrup, stir the sugar and hot water together in a small bowl to dissolve the sugar. Stir in the Grand Marnier and set aside to cool to room
temperature.

2 For the buttercream, combine the butter, chocolates, and cream in a
medium heavy saucepan and heat over low heat, stirring occasionally,
until the chocolate is melted and the mixture is very smooth. Remove from
the heat and stir in the vanilla and confectioners' sugar. Let cool to room
temperature, stirring occasionally (a skin will form as it cools). The buttercream is ready to use when it is firm enough to hold a soft shape. Beat in
the skin before use. Refrigerate if not using within 6 hours, but bring to
room temperature before icing the cake.

3 To assemble, split the cake horizontally into two layers with a sharp serrated knife. Place the bottom génoise layer cut side up on a cake plate and
brush with half the syrup. Spread with about ³/₄ cup of the buttercream. Set

the top génoise layer cut side up on a square of plastic wrap and brush with the remaining syrup. Carefully invert the cake onto the bottom layer, using the plastic wrap to support it. Spread the remaining buttercream on the sides and top. Refrigerate for at least 1 hour (or up to 1 day).

4 To serve, cut into portions with a sharp knife, place on dessert plates, and let stand for about 15 minutes at room temperature before serving.

LEMON GÉNOISE WITH WHITE CHOCOLATE BUTTERCREAM AND RASPBERRIES

Makes 12 to 16 servings

This is a gorgeous cake, brushed with lemon syrup, filled with fresh raspberries, and frosted with a white chocolate buttercream. Make this in the summer, when raspberries are at their peak.

LEMON SYRUP

1/4 cup sugar

1/2 cup hot water (120°–130°F)

2 tablespoons fresh lemon juice or framboise (raspberry liqueur)

BUTTERCREAM

1 3.5-ounce bar white chocolate (I use Lindt), finely chopped

1 8-ounce package cream cheese, at room temperature

2 tablespoons unsalted butter, at room temperature

1 teaspoon pure vanilla extract

1 tablespoon fresh lemon juice

3 cups confectioners' sugar

Classic Génoise (page 330), with the finely grated zest of 1 lemon added in step 5 during the last moments of beating, and baked in a 9-inch layer cake pan

1 cup fresh raspberries

1 For the syrup, stir the sugar and hot water together in a small bowl to dissolve the sugar. Stir in the lemon juice or framboise and set aside to cool to room temperature.

2 For the buttercream, put the white chocolate in a small saucepan, set it in a larger pan of hot water on medium heat, and stir frequently just until the chocolate is melted and smooth. Set aside.

3 In a large bowl, beat the cream cheese, butter, vanilla, and lemon juice with an electric mixer on medium speed until very smooth, about 2 minutes. Add the white chocolate and beat it in on low speed just until incorporated. Gradually beat in the confectioners' sugar, beating only until the buttercream is smooth. Refrigerate briefly, if necessary, to make it firm enough to spread.

4 To assemble, split the cake horizontally in half with a sharp serrated knife. Place the bottom layer cut side up on a plate and brush with half the syrup. Reserve 16 perfect raspberries for the garnish. In a small bowl, gently fold together the remaining raspberries with $3/4$ cup of the white chocolate buttercream. Spread over the génoise. Set the top layer cut side up on a square of plastic wrap and brush with the remaining syrup. Carefully invert the cake onto the filling, using the plastic wrap to support it. Spread the remaining buttercream on the sides and top. Arrange the raspberries in a circle around the border. Refrigerate for at least 1 hour (or up to 1 day) before serving. To serve, cut into portions with a sharp knife.

9 Cheesecakes and Tortes

The cheesecakes made by mid–nineteenth century American cooks bore little resemblance to the sublime, silky creations of today. Many of the recipes began with a distinctly unromantic ingredient: rennet, the lining of a calf's stomach. The rennet, used in cheese making for its coagulating properties, was first soaked in water, releasing an enzyme. When that water was added to warmed milk and allowed to stand for a few minutes, the enzyme caused the milk proteins to set into curds, which were then ladled into a sieve and the watery whey drained off. The curds then were mixed with sugar, flavorings, and sometimes pulverized almonds or dried currants or raisins, and baked in a pan—with or without a pastry crust. Other recipes called for making a custard of eggs and milk and draining it for hours in a sieve until it was firm. Old-fashioned cheesecakes were bland and distinctly curdy.

Our national obsession with smoothness did not begin until after 1920, the year the Breakstone company began marketing cream cheese on a large scale. Cream cheese had originated hundreds of years before in Europe and was imported to America from Holland. Unlike cottage cheese, cream cheese was made without rennet, without heat, and without separating curds from whey. It was simply fresh cream that was allowed to drain in a cloth-lined sieve for about two weeks, until it became spreadable, like ultrathick sour cream. Breakstone's readily available modern version was made in hours, not weeks, and involved treating cream and milk with lactic acid–producing bacteria, which caused the mixture to become firm.

One of the first bakers to use the new cream cheese in cheesecakes was Arnold Reuben, Jr., owner of Reuben's Restaurant in Manhattan. Theater people and other night owls thronged to his place for the smooth creamy dessert, which had a velvety feel on the tongue. Reuben's spawned many imitators, and the New York cheesecake—a particular style, not a specific recipe—was born.

Years later, Leo Linderman, a German immigrant nicknamed Lindy, opened a theater-district restaurant featuring lox and bagels, chicken livers, and other traditional Jewish fare. The star attraction of the menu was his cheesecake, a tall, dense, creamy affair originally baked in a cookie crust. It became the gold standard that established New York as the cheesecake capital of the world. Lindy's restaurant is no more, but his famous cheesecake lives on.

By the 1930s, the traditional pastry crust and its simpler counterpart, the Eastern European zwieback crumb crust, had been replaced by an American timesaver: the graham cracker crust. The crumbs, mixed with butter and sugar, were simply pressed into the pan—no dough to mix, nothing to roll out.

It was left to a Chicago baker and entrepreneur, Charles Lubin, who founded a company that he named after his daughter, to transform the dessert into a national icon. Introduced in 1949, the Sara Lee frozen cheesecake, with a cream cheese filling nestled in a crunchy graham cracker crust and topped with a buttery smooth layer of sour cream, ensured that Americans could have their favorite dessert instantly.

START WITH ONE CALF . . .

Many women of the nineteenth century prepared their own rennet for cheese making. Here's how Elizabeth Ellicott Lea did it.

When the rennet is taken from the calf, wash it, lay it on a plate well covered with salt; put more on in two days, keep it in a cold place; in three or four days it will do to stretch on sticks; hang it up in a dry cool place, with as much salt as will stick to it; when quite dry, put it in a paper bag and hang it up; a piece two inches square soaked in two table-spoonfuls of water will make a cold custard; the same piece salted and dried will do several times.

—Elizabeth Ellicott Lea, *Domestic Cookery* (1853)

CHEESECAKE POINTERS

1. Full-fat, low-fat, and fat-free cream cheese. Cream cheese contains gum stabilizers, which help give cheesecakes their incredible smoothness. Don't use "natural" cream cheese, the type usually sold in health food stores, because it doesn't contain the necessary stabilizers. For most cheesecake recipes, I prefer the reduced-fat cream cheese Neufchâtel, sold under many brand names. (Kraft's "1/3-less-fat cream cheese" is Neufchâtel.) Sometimes, however, I use a mixture of full-fat and reduced-fat cheese. Never use fat-free cream cheese. It is gummy and gluey and has an unpleasant taste.

2. Yogurt cheese. Yogurt cheese can be used as a substitute for cream cheese in many cheesecake recipes. Yogurt cheese is made by draining yogurt in a strainer set over a bowl for a period of hours, or overnight, until it becomes thick and smooth. Be sure to choose a brand that contains no additives, especially gelatin; read the label. Avoid "extra creamy" yogurts, which will not work. Try to find yogurts that contain "active cultures." Many health food stores sell organic yogurts that work well. I generally use low-fat Dannon or Yoplait, brands available in supermarkets everywhere.

3. Baking cheesecakes. A cheesecake is a custard, and custards bake best at low temperatures. Low heat prevents the cheese and egg proteins from curdling, producing a grainy, unpleasant texture. One sure way of achieving a gentle even heat for cheesecakes is to bake them in a water bath. When a cheesecake has baked long enough, the center should be wobbly, not firm. After it cools and has been refrigerated for the specified amount of time, the filling will be firm and not at all runny.

4. Cooling cheesecakes. Cooling some cheesecakes—especially those relatively low in fat—in a turned-off oven instead of at room temperature ensures that the milk and egg proteins, which have set into a creamy custard, don't contract and separate, resulting in a grainy, watery cheesecake. Sour cream toppings also tend to remain intact and not crack when cheesecakes are cooled in the oven.

LINDY'S CHEESECAKE

*Makes one
9-inch
cheesecake,
16 servings*

This is perhaps the most famous and imitated cheesecake of all. Dense and creamy, it is what has become known as New York–style cheesecake. The recipe is linked to the original Lindy's restaurant, which opened in New York City in 1923 and closed in 1967. The late Helen McCully, food editor of *House Beautiful* magazine for many years, claimed to have gotten the recipe from Lindy himself, and I have adapted it from her 1978 version in *Cooking* magazine.

The recipe calls for a pastry crust and an unusual method of baking. Both are essential to the success of the recipe. For baking, the cake is started at a temperature of 525°F, then the oven temperature is reduced to a cool 200°F. The high temperature gives the top of the cheesecake a rich brown color, and the low temperature assures a creamy texture. Be sure to use an oven thermometer to make certain your oven can accommodate these swings in temperature. I've made this with regular and reduced-fat cream cheese and can honestly say I prefer the texture and feel of the latter. A fresh strawberry sauce brings out the flavors of the cheesecake.

PASTRY

- 1/2 cup sugar
- Finely grated zest of 1 lemon
- 4 tablespoons (1/2 stick) cold unsalted butter, cut into 4 pieces
- 1 large egg yolk
- 1 tablespoon water
- 1 teaspoon pure vanilla extract
- 1 cup all-purpose flour

FILLING

- 5 8-ounce packages Neufchâtel cream cheese, at room temperature
- 1 3/4 cups sugar
- 3 tablespoons all-purpose flour
- 1/4 teaspoon salt
- Finely grated zest of 1 orange
- Finely grated zest of 1 lemon
- 1 tablespoon pure vanilla extract
- 5 large eggs
- 2 large egg yolks
- 1/4 cup heavy cream

SAUCE

- 3 cups ripe strawberries, rinsed, patted dry, and stems removed
- 3/4 cup sugar
- 1/3 cup water
- Pinch of salt
- 1 1/2 tablespoons cornstarch
- 2 teaspoons unsalted butter
- 1 teaspoon fresh lemon juice

1 For the pastry, place the sugar and lemon zest in a food processor and process for 5 seconds. Add the butter, egg yolk, water, and vanilla and pulse until the mixture looks granular and lumpy; the butter should be in about $1/4$-inch pieces. Add the flour and pulse rapidly 20 to 30 times, stopping occasionally to scrape the sides and bottom of the bowl, until the mixture almost gathers into a ball. Turn the dough out onto a piece of plastic wrap and press the dough into a 1-inch-thick cake. Wrap and refrigerate for 1 hour.

2 Adjust an oven rack to the lower third position and preheat the oven to 400°F. Butter a 9-inch springform pan. Detach the sides; set aside.

3 Cut off slightly less than one half of the dough. Break it into pieces, and scatter them over the springform bottom. Press firmly and evenly with your fingertips to make a thin layer. Set the bottom crust in the oven and bake until pale golden brown, about 8 minutes. Remove from the oven with a wide metal spatula and set on a cooling rack to cool completely. Increase the oven temperature to 525°F.

4 Shape the remaining pastry into a square. Roll it out on a lightly floured surface to a rectangle slightly larger than 10 x 6 inches. With a large sharp knife, trim away the edges so that the pastry measures 10 x 6 inches. Cut the pastry crosswise into five 2-inch strips. Reassemble the springform pan. Line the sides of the pan with 4 of the pastry strips, pressing the pieces firmly together where their edges meet and pressing the pastry firmly against the pan so that it will stay in place. Cut what you need from the last strip to fill in the last gap. Refrigerate while you prepare the filling.

5 For the filling, beat the cream cheese in a large bowl with an electric mixer on medium speed until smooth. Add the sugar, flour, salt, zests, and vanilla and beat until smooth, 2 to 3 minutes. Beat in the eggs and yolks one at a time, beating only until thoroughly incorporated, about 15 seconds after each. Beat for another 30 seconds. On low speed, beat in the heavy cream. Scrape the mixture into the pan and smooth the top.

6 Bake for 10 minutes, then reduce the heat to 200°F and bake for 1 hour longer; the top will be golden brown. Cool to room temperature on a rack. Cover loosely and refrigerate for at least 6 hours; overnight is best.

7 For the strawberry sauce, if the strawberries are small, reserve 1 cup of the

prettiest ones. If they are large, slice enough to make 1 cup. Set aside. Place the remaining berries in a medium saucepan and crush with a potato masher. Add the sugar, water, salt, and cornstarch. Stir well with a heat-proof rubber spatula, and bring to a boil over medium heat, stirring constantly. Reduce the heat to low and continue cooking, stirring constantly, for 2 minutes, or until the sauce is slightly thickened. Remove from the heat and add the butter, lemon juice, and reserved berries. Cool to room temperature, then refrigerate until chilled. (The sauce can be made a day ahead.)

8 To serve, run a small sharp knife around the edges of the cake to release the pastry and carefully remove the sides of the pan. Rinse a knife in hot water, shake off the excess water, and slice. Serve each portion with a spoonful of the strawberry sauce. Refrigerate leftovers.

RICOTTA CHEESECAKE WITH BLUEBERRY SAUCE

Makes one 9-inch cheesecake, 10 servings

This very special cheesecake, baked in a pastry crust, is smooth and creamy and melts on the tongue. It will be at its creamiest and best if you use homemade ricotta. Making the cheese is not difficult, but if you don't want to bother with it, the cheesecake will be perfectly good with a top-quality commercial whole-milk ricotta. The leftover blueberry sauce is great on pancakes or waffles.

Pastry from Lindy's Cheesecake
  (page 356)

FILLING

1 pound Homemade Ricotta
  Cheese (page 361) or store-
  bought whole-milk ricotta
1 8-ounce package cream cheese
  (do not use low-fat), at room
  temperature
1 cup sugar
¼ teaspoon salt
2 teaspoons pure vanilla extract

4 large eggs
3 large egg yolks
1 cup crème fraîche or sour
  cream

SAUCE

5 cups fresh blueberries, picked
  over, or thawed frozen
  unsweetened blueberries
1½ cups sugar
2 tablespoons fresh lime juice
1 tablespoon cornstarch
2 tablespoons water

1 Prepare the pastry following the directions in steps 1 through 4 on page 357, but reduce the oven temperature to 350°F after baking the bottom crust.

2 For the filling, beat the ricotta in a large bowl with an electric mixer on medium speed until smooth, about 1 minute. Add the cream cheese and beat again until smooth, about 1 minute. Add the sugar, salt, and vanilla and beat for 1 minute more. Beat in the eggs one at a time, beating for 30 seconds after each. Add the egg yolks all at once and beat them in well. On low speed, beat in the crème fraîche or sour cream only until the batter is very smooth. Pour the mixture into the pastry-lined pan.

3 Bake for 1 hour and 15 minutes, or until the cheesecake is golden brown. The filling will rise a great deal, then sink, leaving a higher rim all around. There may be a crack or two on top.

4 Turn off the oven and prop the door open a few inches. Let the cheesecake cool to room temperature in the oven. Run a small sharp knife around the edges of the cake and carefully remove the pan sides. Refrigerate the cheesecake, still on the pan bottom, overnight; cover with plastic wrap once it is thoroughly cold. (The cheesecake can be made up to 2 days ahead.)

5 For the sauce, place 3 cups of the blueberries and the sugar in a food processor and process for 2 minutes. Pour into a medium saucepan. Stir in the lime juice. Combine the cornstarch with the water in a small bowl and add to the berry mixture. Cook over medium heat, stirring gently and constantly with a heatproof rubber spatula, until the mixture thickens and comes to a boil. Reduce the heat to medium-low and cook, stirring, for 2 minutes more. Remove from the heat and stir in the remaining 2 cups berries. Let cool completely, then transfer to a container and refrigerate, covered, until very cold. (The sauce can be made up to 1 day ahead.)

6 To serve, rinse a knife in hot water and shake off the excess water before making each cut. Spoon some of the blueberry sauce over and around each portion. Refrigerate leftovers.

HOMEMADE RICOTTA CHEESE

Makes about 1 1/4 pounds

Homemade ricotta is exquisitely smooth and rich on the tongue. You'll need a large heavy pot: my first choice is enameled cast-iron. A candy thermometer or digital probe thermometer is essential to keep track of the temperature as the milk heats slowly. You'll also need some cheesecloth, a large wire strainer or colander, and a heatproof rubber spatula. Besides using fresh ricotta in a cheese-cake, I like to serve it with ripe melon and fresh strawberries. It's especially good when just made and still warm.

2 1/2 quarts whole milk
  1 cup heavy cream
  1/3 cup fresh lemon juice
  1/4 teaspoon salt

1. Combine the milk, cream, and lemon juice in a 5 1/2- to 6-quart pot. Stir well with a rubber spatula and set the pan over medium-low heat. Attach a candy thermometer or digital probe thermometer to the side of the pot and bring to a simmer. Simmer, without stirring, for about 40 minutes, or until the thermome-ter registers 170°F.

2. Increase the heat to medium and continue to cook, without stirring, until the temperature registers 205°F. The milk will seethe and be on the verge of boiling. Remove the pot from the heat and let stand for 10 to 15 minutes.

3. Rinse a double thickness of cheesecloth, squeeze out the excess water, and line a large strainer or colander with it. Set the strainer in the sink and slowly ladle the ricotta mixture into it. Let the cheese drain for about 1 hour, without stirring, until it is quite thick. Discard the liquid.

4. Transfer the cheese to a bowl and gently stir in the salt. The ricotta is ready to use, or it can be refrigerated, covered, for up to 3 days.

VERY LEMON CHEESECAKE

Makes one 8-inch cheesecake, 8 to 10 servings

Avanilla cream sandwich cookie crust provides a textural contrast to the light and creamy ultra-lemony filling. This is the perfect dessert after a fairly rich meal. Sweetened condensed milk gives the cake its special texture.

CRUST

- 6 vanilla cream sandwich cookies
- 2 tablespoons sugar
- 1 tablespoon unsalted butter, melted

FILLING

- 3 8-ounce packages Neufchâtel cream cheese, at room temperature
- 1 14-ounce can sweetened condensed milk
- 1/4 cup cornstarch
- 1/4 teaspoon salt
- 4 large eggs
  Finely grated zest of 3 lemons
- 1/2 cup fresh lemon juice
- 1 teaspoon pure lemon extract

1 For the crust, adjust an oven rack to the center position and preheat the oven to 350°F. Butter an 8-inch springform pan, detach the sides so the crumbs will brown evenly, and set aside.

2 Put the cookies in a zip-top plastic bag and crush with a rolling pin to make fine crumbs. Place the crumbs in a medium bowl and add the sugar and butter. Toss with a fork to combine well. Press the crumbs into the bottom of the pan. Set the bottom of the pan on the oven rack and bake for 8 minutes. Use a wide metal spatula to remove the crust from the oven and set it on a wire rack to cool. Reduce the heat to 300°F.

3 For the filling, beat the cream cheese in a large bowl with an electric mixer on medium speed until smooth, 1 to 2 minutes. Gradually beat in the condensed milk, and beat for 30 seconds more. Add the cornstarch and salt and beat on low speed until smooth. On medium speed, beat in the eggs one at a time, beating just until each is thoroughly incorporated, 20 to 30 seconds. On low speed, beat in the lemon zest, juice, and extract.

4 Reassemble the springform pan. Scrape the batter into the pan and smooth the top. Place a square of aluminum foil, shiny side up, loosely over the top of the pan. Bake for 50 minutes.

5 Turn the oven off, remove the foil, and let the cake stand in the oven with the door closed for 1 hour longer. Transfer the cake to a wire rack to cool to room temperature, then cover loosely with a paper towel and refrigerate overnight.

6 To serve, run a small sharp knife around the edges of the cake and carefully remove the pan sides. Rinse a knife in hot water and shake off the excess water before making each cut.

CHEESECAKE WITHOUT CHEESE

Half a pound of butter;
Half a pound of sugar;
Eight eggs;
One pint of milk;
A quarter of a pound of currants;
Four ounces of bread;
One table-spoonful of brandy;
One table-spoonful of wine;
One table-spoonful of rose-water;
One small nutmeg;
Half a tea-spoonful of cinnamon.

Put the milk on to boil; beat up four eggs, and stir into it; when it is a thick curd, take it off, and when cool, mash it very fine. Crumb the bread, and mix with the curd. Beat the butter and sugar to a cream; add the curd and bread to it; then whisk the other four eggs thick and light, and pour them into the mixture; then add gradually the brandy, wine, rose-water, and spice, and, lastly, the currants. They may be baked in soup plates, or in small, square tin pans. Cut the paste [pastry] round, line the pan, put in the filling, and turn the paste over, which forms a half circle. Bake in a quick oven.

—Hanna Widdifield, *Widdifield's New Cook Book* (1856)

LEMON CHEESECAKE WITH BLACKBERRY-CASSIS SAUCE

Makes one 9-inch cheesecake, 12 servings

Lemon is one of the most accommodating of flavors. It pairs well with practically anything, in this case, blackberries. The crust and filling are made very quickly with a food processor.

CRUST

18 graham cracker squares

¼ cup sugar, plus more if needed

1 teaspoon ground cinnamon

1 tablespoon cold unsalted butter

1 large egg white

FILLING

1 1-pound container low-fat cottage cheese

1 8-ounce package Neufchâtel cream cheese, at room temperature

1 cup plus 3 tablespoons sugar

¼ cup cornstarch

¼ teaspoon salt

3 large eggs, separated
   Finely grated zest of 1 lemon

¼ cup fresh lemon juice

2 teaspoons pure vanilla extract

SAUCE

1 pound fresh blackberries (about 4 cups), picked over (or use frozen thawed berries, with whatever juices accumulate)

½ cup water

½ cup sugar

1 tablespoon fresh lemon juice

2 tablespoons cornstarch

2 tablespoons crème de cassis liqueur

1 For the crust, adjust an oven rack to the center position and preheat the oven to 325°F. Butter a 9-inch springform pan. Detach the sides and set aside.

2 Crumble the graham crackers into a food processor and process to fine crumbs, about 10 seconds. Add the ¼ cup sugar, cinnamon, and butter and process for 10 to 15 seconds more, until the butter is in tiny pieces. Add the egg white and pulse rapidly about 10 times, only until the crumb mixture is moist looking; do not overprocess. Press the crumbs evenly into the bottom of the pan, sugaring your fingers if the mixture is damp or sticky. Bake for 20 minutes. Remove the bottom of the pan from the oven

with a wide metal spatula and cool completely on a wire rack. Reduce the oven temperature to 300°F.

3 For the filling, process the cottage cheese in the (clean) processor for 2 full minutes, until smooth; stop to scrape the sides of the bowl once or twice. Add the cream cheese and process until smooth, about 30 seconds. Add 1 cup of the sugar, the cornstarch, salt, and egg yolks. Process until smooth. Scrape the bowl and process again. Add the lemon zest, lemon juice, and vanilla and process for 5 to 10 seconds more.

4 Beat the egg whites in a medium bowl with an electric mixer on medium speed until they form soft peaks. On medium speed, gradually add the remaining 3 tablespoons sugar, then continue beating until the whites are shiny and form peaks that curl slightly at their tip when the beaters are raised. Scrape the whites into the food processor and pulse briefly 4 times only, just to incorporate them.

5 Reattach the sides of the pan and scrape the cheesecake batter into the pan. Lay a square of aluminum foil, shiny side up, loosely over the pan and bake for 50 minutes.

6 Turn the oven off, remove the foil, and let the cheesecake stand in the oven with the door closed for 1 hour longer. Transfer to a wire rack, cool completely, then cover loosely with a paper towel and refrigerate overnight.

7 For the sauce, combine the blackberries, water, sugar, and lemon juice in a medium heavy saucepan. Bring to a boil over medium heat, stirring occasionally with a heatproof rubber spatula. Reduce the heat and simmer for 5 minutes. Mix the cornstarch and crème de cassis in a small cup, add to the simmering berries, and immediately stir in gently with the rubber spatula. The sauce will thicken quickly. Simmer for 1 to 2 minutes, and remove from the heat. Cool completely, then cover and refrigerate until very cold. (The sauce can be made 1 day ahead.)

8 To serve, run a small sharp knife around the edges of the cake and carefully remove the pan sides. Rinse a knife in hot water and shake off the excess water before making each cut. Spoon some of the blackberry sauce over each portion.

VANILLA LEMON CHEESECAKE WITH RASPBERRY TOPPING

Makes one 9-inch cheesecake, 12 servings

This is a light-textured, lemony cheesecake, made with homemade yogurt cheese. Be sure the yogurt you use does not contain any gelatin or stabilizers; if it does, the liquid will not drain away from it properly and the cheesecake will be too wet. Start this 2 days before you wish to serve it.

If fresh raspberries are in season, substitute them for the frozen: Combine 3 cups berries with ¼ cup sugar and 1 to 2 tablespoons kirsch or framboise. Let stand for 30 minutes or so before serving.

1 2-pound container low-fat vanilla yogurt (I use Dannon)

CRUST

15 chocolate wafer cookies (I use Famous)
2 tablespoons fine dry bread crumbs
1 large egg white

FILLING

1 8-ounce package Neufchâtel cream cheese, at room temperature
1 cup light sour cream

½ cup sugar
3 tablespoons cornstarch
¼ teaspoon salt
2 large eggs
   Finely grated zest of 1 lemon
2 tablespoons fresh lemon juice

TOPPING

1 cup light sour cream
1 tablespoon sugar
1 large egg white
1 teaspoon pure vanilla extract

2 10-ounce packages frozen raspberries in syrup, thawed

1 Rinse a large square of cheesecloth, squeeze out the excess moisture, and line a strainer with it. Set the strainer over a deep bowl, place the yogurt in the strainer, and refrigerate for 12 to 24 hours, covered loosely with plastic wrap, to drain thoroughly. Discard the liquid, transfer the yogurt cheese to a covered container, and refrigerate until needed; drain off any liquid before using. (The yogurt cheese can be made 1 to 2 days ahead.)

2 For the crust, adjust an oven rack to the center position and preheat the oven to 300°F. Butter a 9-inch springform pan; detach the sides and set aside.

3 Put the chocolate wafers in a zip-top plastic bag and crush into fine crumbs with a rolling pin. Add the bread crumbs and shake to combine well. In a small bowl, beat the egg white with a fork to break it up. Add the crumbs and mix with the fork until thoroughly moistened. Press the crumbs into the bottom of the springform pan. Bake for 20 minutes. Remove from the oven with a wide metal spatula and set on a wire rack to cool.

4 In a large bowl, beat the cream cheese with an electric mixer on medium speed until smooth, about 2 minutes. Add the yogurt cheese and beat for 1 minute. Add the sour cream, sugar, cornstarch, and salt and beat until smooth. Beat in the eggs one at a time, beating only until thoroughly incorporated. Beat in the lemon zest and juice.

5 Reassemble the springform pan, turn the filling into the pan, and spread it level. Bake for 45 minutes; the filling will be very soft and wobbly.

6 Meanwhile, for the topping, whisk together the sour cream, sugar, egg white, and vanilla in a small bowl.

7 Gently spoon and spread the topping evenly over the cheesecake. Bake for another 15 minutes. Turn the oven off and leave the cheesecake in for 1 hour more with the door closed. Cool the cheesecake to room temperature on a wire rack, then refrigerate, uncovered, for at least 8 hours or overnight before serving.

8 To serve, run a small sharp knife around the edges of the cake and carefully remove the pan sides. Rinse a knife in hot water and shake off the excess water before making each cut. Spoon some raspberries and syrup over each portion.

AMARETTO-AMARETTI CHEESECAKE

*Makes one
8-inch
cheesecake,
10 to 12
servings*

Amaretti, crispy Italian almond cookies flavored with apricot kernels, come two to a package wrapped in tissue paper. Amaretto flavors the cheesecake, and a tangy sour cream layer tops the dessert.

CRUST

- 16 amaretti (8 packages)
- 2 tablespoons sugar
- 1 tablespoon unsalted butter, melted

FILLING

- 2 8-ounce packages Neufchâtel cream cheese, at room temperature
- 1/4 teaspoon salt
- 1/2 cup plus 2 tablespoons sugar
- 1 tablespoon cornstarch

- 1/8 teaspoon ground cinnamon
- 1/8 teaspoon freshly grated nutmeg
  Finely grated zest of 1 lemon
- 2 large eggs, separated
- 1 tablespoon fresh lemon juice
- 3 tablespoons Amaretto di Saronno liqueur

TOPPING

- 1 cup light sour cream
- 2 tablespoons sugar
- 1 teaspoon pure vanilla extract
- 1 large egg white

1 For the crust, adjust an oven rack to the center position and preheat the oven to 350°F. Butter an 8-inch springform pan. Detach the sides and set aside.

2 Place the cookies in a zip-top plastic bag and crush into fine crumbs with a rolling pin. Transfer the crumbs to a small bowl and use a fork to mix them with the sugar and butter. Press 3/4 cup of the crumb mixture into the bottom of the pan; reserve the remaining crumbs for later. Bake for 6 minutes, until aromatic and golden. Carefully remove from the oven with a wide metal spatula and cool on a wire rack. Reduce the heat to 300°F.

3 For the filling, beat the cream cheese in a large bowl with an electric mixer on medium speed until smooth, about 2 minutes. Add the salt, 1/2 cup of the sugar, the cornstarch, cinnamon, nutmeg, and lemon zest and beat until smooth, 1 to 2 minutes. Beat in the egg yolks, then the lemon juice and liqueur.

4 In a small bowl, with clean beaters, beat the egg whites on medium speed until foamy. Gradually beat in the remaining 2 tablespoons sugar and beat until the whites form glossy peaks that hold their shape and curl softly at their tips but are not dry. Gently fold the whites into the cheesecake batter.

5 Reassemble the springform pan, pour about half the batter onto the crust, and spread it level. Sprinkle the reserved crumb mixture evenly over the batter and carefully spoon the remaining batter over the crumbs; smooth the top. Bake for 45 minutes; the center will be wobbly.

6 Meanwhile, for the topping, whisk together the sour cream, sugar, vanilla, and egg white in a small bowl.

7 Spread the topping over the hot cheesecake, and bake for another 15 minutes. Turn off the oven and leave the cheesecake in the oven for another 45 minutes with the door closed. Remove from the oven, and cool to room temperature on a rack, then refrigerate, uncovered, for at least 8 hours or overnight before serving.

8 To serve, run a small sharp knife around the edges of the cake and carefully remove the pan sides. Rinse a knife in hot water and shake off the excess water before making each cut.

MAPLE PECAN CHEESECAKE

*Makes one
8-inch
cheesecake,
10 servings*

This is a truly American cheesecake, starring two great American products, pecans and maple syrup. Serve small portions—it is rich.

CRUST

8 graham cracker squares

2 tablespoons sugar

1/2 teaspoon ground cinnamon

1 tablespoon unsalted butter, at room temperature

FILLING

1/2 cup chopped toasted pecans

2 8-ounce packages Neufchâtel cream cheese, at room temperature

2 tablespoons cornstarch

1/4 teaspoon salt

1 large egg

3/4 cup pure maple syrup

TOPPING

1 cup sour cream

1 tablespoon sugar

1 large egg white

1 teaspoon maple extract

1 For the crust, adjust an oven rack to the center position and preheat the oven to 300°F. Butter an 8-inch springform pan; detach the sides and set aside.

2 Place the graham crackers in a zip-top plastic bag and crush them into fine crumbs with a rolling pin. Mix the crumbs with the sugar and cinnamon in a small bowl. Add the butter and mix well with a fork. Press the crumbs into the bottom of the pan. Bake for 20 minutes. Remove the bottom of the pan from the oven with a wide metal spatula and cool on a wire rack.

3 For the filling, toast the pecans by placing them on a heavy baking sheet and bake for about 10 minutes, stirring once or twice, until fragrant. Set aside to cool. Beat the cream cheese in a large bowl with an electric mixer on medium speed until smooth, about 2 minutes. Add the cornstarch, salt, and egg and beat until smooth, 2 to 3 minutes more. On low speed, gradually beat in the maple syrup.

4 Reassemble the springform pan. Pour and spread about half the filling into the pan. Sprinkle evenly with half the toasted pecans. Spoon the remaining filling carefully over the pecans, smooth the top, and sprinkle with the

remaining pecans. Bake for 45 minutes; the filling will be very soft and wobbly.

5 Meanwhile, for the topping, whisk together the sour cream, sugar, egg white, and maple extract in a small bowl until smooth.

6 Gently spoon and spread the topping over the cheesecake and bake for another 15 minutes. Turn the oven off and leave the cheesecake in the oven for 1 more hour with the door closed. Remove from the oven and cool to room temperature on a wire rack, then refrigerate, uncovered, for at least 8 hours before serving.

7 To serve, run a small sharp knife around the edges of the cake and carefully remove the pan sides. Rinse a knife in hot water and shake off the excess water before making each cut.

CHOCOLATE RUM CHEESECAKE

*Makes one
8-inch
cheesecake,
8 to 10
servings*

After much experimentation, I've hit upon a way of making a cheese-cake that uses a lot less fat than traditional methods. Instead of combining the crumbs with ¹/₄ to ¹/₃ cup melted butter, I use an egg white and only 1 tablespoon butter. This chocolate crust is crunchy and delicious, and the chocolaty filling, though relatively low in fat, is sensuous and creamy, almost like mousse.

CRUST

- 18 chocolate graham cracker squares
- ¹/₄ cup sugar
- 1 tablespoon unsalted butter, at room temperature
- 1 large egg white

FILLING

- 3 ounces (3 squares) semisweet chocolate
- 3 tablespoons dark rum (I use Myers's)
- ¹/₄ cup chocolate syrup (I use Hershey's)
- 2 8-ounce packages Neufchâtel cream cheese, at room temperature
- 1 cup sugar
- 2 tablespoons Dutch-process cocoa
- ¹/₄ teaspoon salt
- 1 teaspoon pure vanilla extract
- 2 large eggs

1 For the crust, adjust an oven rack to the center position and preheat the oven to 350°F. Butter an 8-inch springform pan and set aside.

2 Place the graham crackers in a zip-top plastic bag and crush them into fine crumbs with a rolling pin. In a medium bowl, beat together the sugar, butter, and egg white with an electric mixer for about 1 minute, until creamy. Add the graham cracker crumbs and stir with a fork to moisten them thoroughly. Turn the crumbs into the buttered pan and press them into the bottom and about 1¹/₄ inches up the sides. Bake for 10 minutes. If the crust puffs up during baking, carefully tamp it down after removing the pan from the oven. Set aside on a cooling rack. Reduce the heat to 300°F.

3 For the filling, combine the chocolate and the rum in the top of a double boiler or in a small saucepan placed in a larger saucepan of hot water set

over medium heat. Stir occasionally with a small wire whisk until the chocolate is melted and the mixture is smooth. Remove the pan from the water bath and whisk in the chocolate syrup. Set aside.

4 In a large bowl, beat the cream cheese with an electric mixer on medium speed until smooth, about 1 minute. Add the sugar, cocoa, salt, and vanilla and beat until smooth, 1 to 2 minutes. On low speed, beat in the melted chocolate mixture. Scrape the bowl and beat for another 30 seconds. On medium speed, add the eggs one at a time, beating only until each is thoroughly incorporated, 20 to 30 seconds.

5 Scrape the batter into the cooled crust and lay a square of aluminum foil, shiny side up, loosely over the top of the pan. Bake for 45 minutes.

6 Turn the oven off, remove the foil, and leave the cheesecake in the oven with the door closed for another 45 minutes. Remove from the oven and let cool to room temperature on a wire rack, then cover loosely with a paper towel and refrigerate for at least 8 hours, or overnight.

7 To serve, run a small sharp knife around the edges of the cake and carefully remove the pan sides. Rinse a knife in hot water and shake off the excess water before making each cut.

BLACK-AND-WHITE CHEESECAKE

Makes one 9-inch cheesecake, 12 servings

This easy two-toned cheesecake is made with white and dark chocolate. Marbled together, they give the cheesecake a gorgeous look.

CRUST

12 Oreo cookies

2 tablespoons unsalted butter, melted

FILLING

1/2 cup hot fudge topping (I use Mrs. Richardson's)

3 tablespoons heavy cream

1 3.5-ounce bar white chocolate (I use Lindt)

2 8-ounce packages Neufchâtel cream cheese, at room temperature

1 cup sugar

1 tablespoon pure vanilla extract

3 large eggs

1 cup sour cream

1 For the crust, adjust an oven rack to the center position and preheat the oven to 350°F. Butter a 9-inch springform pan. Detach the sides and set aside.

2 Place the cookies in a zip-top plastic bag and crush them into fine crumbs with a rolling pin. Add the melted butter to the bag and squeeze to moisten the crumbs well. Empty the crumbs onto the base of the springform pan, place a square of plastic wrap over them, and press firmly to make a thin, even crust. Remove the plastic wrap. Bake for 10 minutes. With a wide metal spatula, carefully remove from the oven and set on a rack to cool completely. Reduce the heat to 300°F.

3 For the filling, combine the fudge topping with 1 tablespoon of the cream in a small bowl; set aside. Break up the white chocolate into small pieces and place them in a small heavy saucepan or the top of a double boiler. Add the remaining 2 tablespoons cream, set the pan in the double boiler or in a larger pan filled with hot water over medium heat, and stir frequently until the chocolate is melted and the mixture is smooth. Remove the pan from the water and set aside to cool slightly.

4 In a large bowl, beat the cream cheese with an electric mixer on medium speed until smooth, about 2 minutes. Add the sugar and vanilla and beat until smooth, about 1 minute. Beat in the eggs one at a time, beating after each only until thoroughly incorporated. On low speed, beat in the sour cream, then the white chocolate.

5 Stir 1 cup of the batter into the hot fudge mixture. Reassemble the springform pan and add the remaining white batter to the pan. Drop the chocolate mixture by small spoonfuls over the batter. Swirl together with a flourish, using a table knife, but don't overdo it; you want definite streaks of dark chocolate. Place a square of aluminum foil, shiny side up, loosely over the top of the pan. Bake for 1 hour and 10 minutes.

6 Turn off the oven, remove the foil, and leave the cheesecake in the oven with the door closed for 1 hour and 15 minutes. Remove from the oven and let cool on a wire rack to room temperature. The cheesecake will be soft. Loosen it from the sides of the pan with a small sharp knife, but do not detach the sides of the pan. Cover loosely with a paper towel and refrigerate overnight.

7 To serve, run a small sharp knife again along the edges of the cake and carefully remove the pan sides. Rinse a knife with hot water and shake off the excess water before making each cut.

CHOCOLATE BROWNIE CHEESECAKE

Makes one 9-inch cheesecake, 12 servings

Here are two of America's favorite treats in one delicious package—cheesecake with a brownie crust. The cheesecake is smooth, creamy, and low fat. The moist, fudgy brownies are also low in fat. Make this a day ahead.

BROWNIES

- ½ cup all-purpose flour
- ⅔ cup unsweetened cocoa powder
- ½ teaspoon baking powder
- ¼ teaspoon baking soda
- ¼ teaspoon salt
- 1 2½-ounce jar Gerber's baby food prunes
- 2 tablespoons milk
- 2 teaspoons instant espresso powder (I use Medaglia d'Oro)
- 1½ teaspoons pure vanilla extract
- 1 tablespoon vegetable oil

- 3 large egg whites
- 1 cup sugar
- ⅓ cup semisweet or bittersweet chocolate chips

CHEESECAKE

- 4 8-ounce packages Neufchâtel cream cheese, at room temperature
- 1½ cups sugar
- ¼ teaspoon salt
- 1 tablespoon pure vanilla extract
- 4 large eggs

1 For the brownies, adjust an oven rack to the center position and preheat the oven to 325°F. Butter a 9-inch square baking pan and set aside.

2 Sift together the flour, cocoa, baking powder, baking soda, and salt. In a small bowl, briskly whisk together the prunes, milk, espresso powder, vanilla, and oil.

3 In a large bowl, beat the egg whites and sugar with an electric mixer on medium speed for 30 seconds, then beat on high for 2½ minutes, or until the mixture is the consistency of marshmallow cream. Beat in the prune mixture. Sprinkle the cocoa mixture on top and fold it in gently but thoroughly. Fold in the chocolate chips. Spread the batter in the pan.

4 Bake for 25 to 28 minutes, until a toothpick comes out moist or with a few chocolate crumbs sticking to it; do not overbake. Transfer the pan to a wire rack to cool. Reduce the heat to 300°F.

5 For the cheesecake, butter a 9-inch springform pan and set aside. In a large bowl, beat the cream cheese with an electric mixer on medium speed until smooth, about 2 minutes. Beat in the sugar, salt, and vanilla until smooth. Beat in the eggs one at a time, beating only until each is thoroughly incorporated. Scrape the bowl and beat for another 30 seconds.

6 To assemble the cheesecake, cut the brownie, still in the pan, in half. Break one portion into small (about 1-inch) pieces. Place the brownie pieces in the bottom of the springform pan, covering it almost completely. Pour in half the cheesecake batter and spread it level. Break up the remaining brownies into small pieces and press them onto the batter. Spoon the remaining batter on top and spread it level.

7 Lay a square of aluminum foil, shiny side up, loosely over the top of the pan. Bake for 1 hour.

8 Turn off the oven, remove the foil, and let the cheesecake stand in the oven with the door closed for 1 hour longer. Remove from the oven and cool to room temperature on a wire rack, then cover the pan loosely with a paper towel and refrigerate overnight before serving.

9 To serve, run a small sharp knife around the edges of the cake and carefully remove the pan sides. Rinse a knife in hot water and shake off the excess water before making each cut.

WHITE CHOCOLATE–CRANBERRY CHEESECAKE

Makes one 9-inch cheesecake, 12 to 16 servings

Dried cranberries, cooked and turned into a "jam," combine with a white chocolate and yogurt cheese mixture in a delicious sweet-tart cheesecake. Start a day ahead so that the yogurt has ample time to drain. Be sure to use yogurt that contains no gelatins, gums, starch, or artificial ingredients. At all costs, avoid yogurts that are labeled "extra creamy": they will not work in this recipe.

1 2-pound container plain nonfat yogurt

CRANBERRY MIXTURE
1 cup (5 ounces) dried cranberries
1/2 cup sugar
1/2 cup water

CRUST
24 vanilla wafer cookies (I use Nabisco)
1 tablespoon vegetable oil

FILLING
1 3.5-ounce bar white chocolate (I use Lindt)
2 tablespoons milk
1 tablespoon pure vanilla extract
1 8-ounce package Neufchâtel cream cheese, at room temperature
1 cup light sour cream
1 cup sugar
1/4 cup cornstarch
1/4 teaspoon salt
3 large eggs

1 Rinse a large square of cheesecloth, squeeze out the excess moisture, and line a large strainer with it. Set the strainer over a bowl and spoon the yogurt into it. Cover loosely with plastic wrap and refrigerate for at least 24 hours to drain thoroughly. Discard the liquid. Place the yogurt cheese in a covered plastic container and refrigerate until needed; pour off any liquid before using. (The yogurt cheese can be made up to 2 days ahead.)

2 For the cranberry mixture, combine the cranberries, sugar, and water in a small heavy saucepan. Bring to a boil over high heat. Cover, reduce the heat to medium-low, and simmer until the fruit is plump and soft, about 10 minutes. Let cool, covered, until just warm, then place in a food processor and process to a puree, about 2 minutes. Set aside.

3 For the crust, adjust an oven rack to the center position and preheat the oven to 350°F. Butter a 9-inch springform pan; detach the sides and set aside.

4 Place the cookies in a zip-top plastic bag and crush them into fine crumbs with a rolling pin. Place in a medium bowl, add the oil, and combine thoroughly with a fork. Press the crumbs into the bottom of the pan. Bake for 10 minutes, or until golden brown. Remove from the oven with a wide metal spatula and cool on a wire rack. Reduce the heat to 300°F.

5 For the filling, break the white chocolate up into small pieces and place it into a small saucepan or the top of a double boiler. Add the milk, set the pan in the double boiler or in a larger pan filled with hot water over medium heat, and stir gently with a small wire whisk until the chocolate is melted and the mixture is smooth. Remove from the heat and whisk in the vanilla; set aside.

6 In a large bowl, beat the yogurt cheese, cream cheese, sour cream, sugar, cornstarch, and salt with an electric mixer on low speed for 1 minute. Beat on medium-high until smooth, about 2 minutes. Beat in the chocolate mixture. On medium speed, beat in the eggs one at a time, beating after each only until thoroughly incorporated, then beat for another 30 seconds. Scrape the cranberry mixture onto the batter. With a large rubber spatula, quickly fold in the cranberries, using only 3 or 4 strokes, so that the batter is streaked with the fruit; don't be too thorough.

7 Reassemble the springform pan. Turn the batter into the pan, smooth the top, and set a square of aluminum foil, shiny side up, loosely over the top of the pan. Bake for 1 hour and 10 minutes.

8 Turn off the oven, remove the foil, and let the cheesecake cool in the oven with the door closed for another 1 hour and 15 minutes. Remove from the oven and let cool to room temperature, then loosely cover with a paper towel, and refrigerate overnight.

9 To serve, run a small sharp knife around the edges of the cake and carefully remove the pan sides. Rinse a knife in hot water and shake off the excess water before making each cut.

TROPICAL CHEESECAKE

Makes one 9-inch cheesecake, 8 to 10 servings

Coconut, pineapple, and guava make a refreshing and pretty glaze for this cheesecake. The filling is a combination of cottage cheese, low-fat cream cheese, and low-fat sour cream, easily made in a food processor. Bake and glaze the cheesecake a day ahead. Leftovers are great for breakfast.

CRUST
- 36 vanilla wafer cookies (I use Nabisco)
- 1/4 cup sugar
- 1 large egg white
- 1 tablespoon unsalted butter, at room temperature

FILLING
- 1 1-pound container low-fat cottage cheese
- 1 8-ounce package Neufchâtel cream cheese

- 1 cup light sour cream
- 1/2 cup canned unsweetened coconut milk
- 1/2 cup sugar
- 2 teaspoons pure coconut extract
- 3 tablespoons all-purpose flour
- 3 large eggs

GLAZE
- 3/4 cup frozen pine-orange-guava concentrate, thawed
- 1/2 cup plus 2 tablespoons water
- 1 teaspoon unflavored gelatin

1 For the crust, adjust the oven rack to the center position and preheat the oven to 350°F. Butter a 9-inch springform pan and set aside.

2 Place the cookies in a zip-top plastic bag and crush into fine crumbs with a rolling pin. In a medium bowl, beat together the sugar, egg white, and butter with an electric mixer until creamy, about 1 minute. Add the cookie crumbs and combine thoroughly with a fork. Press the crumbs into the bottom and about 1½ inches up the sides of the pan. Bake for 12 to 13 minutes, until golden brown. Remove from the oven and cool on a wire rack. Reduce the heat to 300°F.

3 For the filling, rinse a large square of cheesecloth and squeeze out the excess moisture. Open up the cheesecloth and place the cottage cheese in the center. Bring the corners of the cheesecloth over the cheese and twist firmly to squeeze as much liquid from the cottage cheese as you can. Place the cottage cheese in a food processor and process for 2 minutes, or until smooth. Add the cream cheese and process for 1 to 2 minutes more. Add the sour cream, coconut milk, sugar, and coconut extract and process for 20 to 30 seconds. Add the flour and eggs and process for about 15 seconds. Scrape the work bowl and process for 5 seconds more. The batter will be thin.

4 Pour the batter into the crust. Cover the top of the pan loosely with a square of aluminum foil, shiny side up, and bake for 1^1/$_2$ hours.

5 Turn off the oven, remove the foil, and let the cheesecake stand in the oven with the door closed for 1 more hour. Remove from the oven and cool to room temperature, then refrigerate for an hour or so.

6 For the glaze, put about 2 dozen ice cubes in a 13-x-9-inch metal pan and add about 1 inch of cold water. Set aside. Combine the fruit concentrate with ^{1}/$_2$ cup of the water in a medium saucepan. Sprinkle the gelatin over the remaining 2 tablespoons cold water in a small cup. Bring the fruit mixture to a boil over high heat and boil for 2 minutes, stirring occasionally. Remove from the heat and let cool for about 1 minute. Scrape the gelatin mixture into the fruit mixture and stir briefly to dissolve. Place the pan in the ice water bath and stir gently with a rubber spatula until cold and syrupy, about 15 to 20 minutes.

7 Remove the cheesecake from the refrigerator and carefully pour the glaze over the top. Chill overnight before serving.

8 To serve, run a small sharp knife around the edges of the cake and carefully remove the pan sides. Rinse a knife in hot water and shake off the excess water before making each cut.

DOUBLE CHOCOLATE RASPBERRY SOUFFLÉ TORTE

Makes one 8-inch torte, 8 servings

This delicate, melt-in-your-mouth torte is flavored with chocolate and raspberry liqueur. Be sure to use a top-quality chocolate. I like Lindt, but there are many other excellent imported brands to choose from, such as Valrhona. The torte is best at room temperature, so make it in the afternoon to serve that night. When it's refrigerated, the torte's texture becomes dense. This is a late-twentieth-century dessert.

TORTE

- 3 ounces (3 squares) semisweet or bittersweet chocolate, finely chopped
- 2 tablespoons framboise (raspberry liqueur) or Grand Marnier
- 3 tablespoons unsalted butter, at room temperature
- 3/4 cup sugar
- 1 large egg
- 1/4 cup evaporated milk
- 1/4 cup Dutch-process cocoa
- 2 tablespoons cornstarch
- 4 large egg whites
- 1/8 teaspoon salt
- 1/4 teaspoon cream of tartar

SAUCE

- 1 pint fresh raspberries
- 1/3 cup sugar

Confectioners' sugar for dusting

Mint sprigs

1 For the torte, adjust an oven rack to the lower third position and preheat the oven to 300°F. Butter the bottom and sides of an 8-inch springform pan and set aside.

2 Combine the chocolate and raspberry liqueur in a small heavy saucepan. Set the pan over low heat and stir occasionally with a small whisk until the chocolate is melted and the mixture is smooth. Set aside.

3 In a medium bowl, beat together the butter and 1/2 cup of the sugar with an electric mixer on medium-high speed until smooth and fluffy, 2 to 3 minutes. Add the egg and beat for 1 minute. On low speed, gradually beat in the evaporated milk. (The mixture will look curdled). Whisk the melted

chocolate until it is smooth, and beat it in only until thoroughly combined. Add the cocoa and cornstarch and beat only until incorporated.

4 In a large bowl, with clean beaters, beat the egg whites with the salt on medium speed until foamy. Add the cream of tartar and beat until the whites form soft peaks that curl at their tips when the beaters are raised. Beat in the remaining ¹/₄ cup sugar 1 tablespoon at a time, and beat until the whites are shiny and form almost stiff peaks when the beaters are raised; they should curl just a bit at their tips.

5 Gently fold one fourth of the egg white mixture into the chocolate mixture; do not be too thorough. Repeat the procedure with the remaining egg white mixture, one third at a time, thoroughly folding in the last addition. Spoon the batter into the pan and smooth the top.

6 Bake for 45 to 50 minutes, until a toothpick inserted into the center comes out looking slightly wet with a few crumbs sticking to it. Check after 40 minutes to prevent overbaking. The torte will seem soft and jiggly.

7 Meanwhile, for the sauce, puree the raspberries with the sugar in a food processor, about 2 minutes. Pass the puree through a fine strainer to remove the seeds. Refrigerate.

8 When you remove the torte from the oven, immediately run the tip of a small sharp knife around the edges. Cool the torte on a wire rack, then carefully remove the sides of the springform pan.

9 To serve, rinse a sharp knife in hot water and shake off the excess before making each cut. Pool ¹/₄ cup of raspberry sauce on each dessert plate. Use a narrow metal spatula to lift and remove the slices of the torte from the pan bottom (careful: it is delicate), placing the slices on the sauce. Dust the torte with confectioners' sugar and decorate with mint sprigs.

CHOCOLATE CHESTNUT TORTE

Makes one 9-inch torte, 10 to 12 servings

Fresh chestnuts and chocolate give this cake a gossamerlike texture. Make it in the fall, when chestnuts come on the scene. You will spend a bit of time working with the chestnuts, but the results are well worth your effort. This is a festive dessert to serve at Thanksgiving or any special autumn occasion. It's best when freshly baked.

1 pound fresh chestnuts

TORTE

8 ounces (8 squares) bittersweet chocolate, finely chopped

¼ cup dark rum (I use Myers's)

8 tablespoons (1 stick) unsalted butter, at room temperature

1 cup sugar

7 large eggs, separated

¼ teaspoon salt

WHIPPED CREAM

1 cup heavy cream

1 teaspoon pure vanilla extract

2 tablespoons confectioners' sugar

1 To prepare the chestnuts, make an X in the flat side of each with a small sharp knife. Place the chestnuts in a medium heavy saucepan and add water to cover by 1 to 2 inches. Bring to a boil over medium heat. Cover, reduce the heat to low, and simmer slowly until the chestnuts are tender when tested with the tip of a sharp knife, about 45 minutes. Remove from the heat and let cool in the cooking water until you can handle them without burning your fingers.

2 One at a time, remove the chestnuts from the water and peel away their shells and skin. Pat dry on paper towels. Pass them through a food mill with medium to fine holes. Reserve 2 cups of puree for the recipe and freeze the rest for another time. (The chestnuts can be prepared 2 to 3 days ahead and refrigerated.)

3 For the torte, adjust an oven rack to the lower third position and preheat the oven to 350°F. Butter a 9-inch springform pan. Wrap the outside of the pan with a double thickness of heavy-duty foil; set aside. Bring a kettle of water to a boil.

4 Combine the chocolate with the rum in a small saucepan. Set the pan in a larger pan of hot water over medium heat and whisk occasionally until the chocolate is melted and the mixture is smooth. Remove from the water and set aside.

5 In a large bowl, beat the butter with an electric mixer on medium speed until soft and creamy, about 1 minute. Gradually beat in $^3/_4$ cup of the sugar, and continue beating for 2 to 3 minutes, until the mixture is fluffy and light. Beat in the egg yolks one at a time, beating well after each. Add the chestnut puree and beat for 1 minute. Scrape the chocolate mixture into the batter (it's all right if the chocolate is still warm) and beat on low speed just until incorporated.

6 In a large clean bowl, with clean beaters, beat the whites with the salt on medium speed until soft peaks form. Beat in the remaining $^1/_4$ cup sugar 1 tablespoon at a time, beating for about 20 seconds after each addition. Beat on medium-high speed until the whites form stiff, glossy peaks when the beaters are raised. Stir about one fourth of the whites into the chocolate mixture to lighten it. Gradually fold in the remaining whites in 3 additions, folding in the last of the whites only until no whites show. Scrape into the pan and smooth the top.

7 Set the pan in a larger baking pan and add boiling water to come halfway up the sides of the springform pan. Bake for 45 to 60 minutes, until the cake springs back when gently pressed in the center and a toothpick inserted into the center comes out with some chocolate sticking to it. Remove the cake from the water bath and cool on a wire rack. When the torte is completely cool, remove the foil from the cake pan. Run a small sharp knife around the edges of the cake and carefully remove the pan sides.

8 For the cream, whip the cream with the vanilla and confectioners' sugar in a medium bowl with an electric mixer until thickened but not stiff. Refrigerate the cream until serving time.

9 To serve, rinse a knife in hot water and shake off the excess water before making each cut. Place the portions on dessert plates, with a spoonful of the whipped cream alongside each.

Cookies

10

The cookie recipes in the earliest American cookbooks were straightforward mixtures of butter, sugar, flour, and flavoring. Amelia Simmons's brisk directions for Cookies in *American Cookery* are typical:

One pound sugar boiled slowly in half pint of water, scum well and cool, add 1 teaspoon pearlash, dissolved in milk, then two and a half pounds of flour, rub in 4 ounces of butter, and two large spoons of finely powdered coriander seed, wet with above; make rolls half an inch thick and cut to the shape you please; bake fifteen or twenty minutes in a slack oven—good three weeks.

Though recipes like these are not the stuff of today's food fantasies, they were convenient. Unlike cake batters, which had to be beaten for an hour or more and often took hours to bake, cookies could be mixed in moments and baked in a mere six or seven minutes. Even the name "cookie," from the Dutch *koekje,* suggested something approachable and cozy. These handy sweet nibbles stored well—"good three weeks"—in Miss Simmons's terse words. Nineteenth-century cookbook authors were in step with Miss Simmons's cookie sensibilities. The same cookies—beloved for their keeping qualities—appear over and over again: ginger cookies (or cakes, as cookies were often called), macaroons, and jumbles, a tender butter cookie that was good fresh or stale.

It was not until the early twentieth century that recipes began to take a more adventurous turn. The Civil War and its accompanying shortages had transformed foods previously deemed fit only for animal consumption into mainstays of the American diet. As a result, cookies displayed flashes of ingenuity in the years after the war, with novel additions like oatmeal and peanut butter. *Mrs. Rorer's New Cook Book* of 1902 featured other new ingredients, including chocolate and pistachios.

In the 1940s, the products that had been flooding into the American marketplace created an explosion in cookie diversity. *Watkins Cook Book* (1943) offered dozens of recipes that joyfully incorporated the latest choices: sweetened condensed milk, packaged shredded coconut, bran, and even Wheaties. By the end of the Second World War, ready-made foods had become more important than ever: 37 percent of all women were working outside the home, yet they still had to rush home to do all the meal preparation. Packaged cookies appeared on grocery store shelves in increasing number and variety, but many homemakers still preferred to bake their own from scratch.

Fortunately for them, baking was even easier than ever, thanks to better kitchen equipment, which had reached a pinnacle of modernism. Gas and electric ranges, with reliable thermostats, were now the norm. No more wood or coal to burn or flues or dampers to adjust. The turn of a dial was all it took to turn the oven on and to select a precise temperature. The position of shelves could also be adjusted in the oven to accommodate several baking sheets at one time. These innovations were light years ahead of the kitchen equipment available only a few decades earlier. Electric mixers, which debuted in the 1920s, had become beloved kitchen helpers of harried housewives.

By the time the first Pillsbury Bake-Off was held in 1949, cookies were all the rage, and the repertoire had dramatically expanded beyond the handful of prosaic choices in Miss Simmons's day. Fourteen of the one hundred finalist recipes were for cookies. They contained exotic ingredients like Brazil nuts, sesame seeds, peanut brittle, figs, dates, and malted milk. They sported tempting names like Chocolate-Filled Tea Cookies, Marshmallow Fudge Bars, Praline Butter Nuggets, and Sea-Foam Nut Squares, and came in a range of styles: drop, rolled, shaped, filled, icebox, and bars. By 1953, the number of cookie finalists had doubled.

While the cookie revolution shows the American penchant for change and experimentation, cookie making is still the friendly, no-fuss activity that it was in Amelia Simmons's day.

CHRISTMAS ROCKS

Makes 24 large cookies

"Rocks" got their name not from their texture but because of their bumpy appearance. These large, semisoft oatmeal cookies are chockful of golden raisins, rolled oats, and chocolate chips. Popular in the nineteenth century, particularly in New England, rocks often included nuts and dried fruit.

1³/₄ cups all-purpose flour

¹/₂ teaspoon baking soda

¹/₂ teaspoon salt

¹/₂ teaspoon pumpkin pie spice

4 tablespoons unsalted butter (¹/₂ stick), at room temperature

1 cup sugar

1 teaspoon pure vanilla extract

2 large eggs

³/₄ cup unsweetened applesauce

1 cup old-fashioned or quick-cooking (not instant) rolled oats

1 cup golden raisins

²/₃ cup semisweet chocolate chips

1 Adjust two oven racks to divide the oven into thirds and preheat the oven to 375°F. Line two baking sheets with cooking parchment or silicone liners; set aside.

2 Sift together the flour, baking soda, salt, and pumpkin pie spice; set aside.

3 In a medium bowl, beat the butter with an electric mixer on medium speed until smooth. Add the sugar and vanilla and beat for 3 to 4 minutes. Beat in the eggs until incorporated, then beat in the applesauce. With a wooden spoon, stir in the flour mixture until thoroughly moistened, then stir in the oats, raisins, and chocolate chips. The batter will be stiff.

4 Spoon rounded teaspoons of the cookie dough onto the baking sheets in mounds, spacing them 2 inches apart, 12 mounds to a sheet.

5 Bake for 14 to 16 minutes, reversing the sheets from top to bottom and front to back once to ensure even browning, until the cookies are golden brown and the tops spring back when gently pressed. Do not overbake: the cookies should remain soft. Transfer them to wire cooling racks with a wide metal spatula and let cool completely. Store airtight.

JUMBLES

Makes 48 cookies

This is an especially tender, crispy, buttery cookie, and only mildly spicy, despite the presence of a whole nutmeg. I adapted the recipe from *Seventy Five Receipts, for Pastry, Cakes, and Sweetmeats*, by Eliza Leslie (1828). Jumbles, sometimes spelled "jumbals," are one of the best and oldest American cookies. The butter-and-egg-enriched dough was traditionally flavored with rose water or lemon essence (extract), and cooks commonly added caraway or anise seeds. Though American jumbles have evolved into a simple ring shape, the traditional form for this cookie was a figure eight, or double ring, after their name, which derives from the Latin *gemel*, meaning "twin."

Neither Miss Leslie's recipe nor mine contains caraway or anise seeds, though you could certainly add 1 tablespoon of either to the dough if you wish. I brush the hot baked cookies with sugar and rose water, which contributes a delightful perfume and flavor, but you may omit this step. Despite the fact that the cookies contain no chemical leaveners, they spread and flatten out quite a bit during baking. You must make the dough a day ahead, as it needs to be thoroughly chilled before using.

DOUGH

- 3 large eggs
- 1 cup (2 sticks) unsalted butter, at room temperature
- 1 cup sugar
- 1/4 teaspoon salt
- 1 whole nutmeg, grated (2–2 1/2 teaspoons)
- 1/2 teaspoon ground mace
- 1/2 teaspoon ground cinnamon
- 1 teaspoon pure lemon extract
- 1 3/4 cups all-purpose flour

GLAZE (OPTIONAL)

- 2/3 cup sugar
- 1/4 cup rose water

1 For the dough, beat the eggs in a medium bowl with an electric mixer on medium-high speed until they are very thick and pale, about 5 minutes. Set aside.

2 In a large bowl, beat the butter with the mixer on medium speed until smooth and creamy, about 1 minute. Beat in the sugar about 2 tablespoons at a time, beating for a few seconds after each addition. Beat in the salt, nutmeg, mace, cinnamon, and lemon extract and beat for 3 to 4 minutes, until light and fluffy. Slowly beat in the eggs about one fourth at a time, then beat on medium-high speed for 1 minute. On low speed, gradually add the flour, beating only until incorporated. Cover the bowl tightly with plastic wrap and refrigerate overnight.

3 Lightly flour your work surface and scrape the dough onto the flour. Turn to coat all surfaces with flour, and pat the dough into a 1-inch-thick rectangle. Cut the dough into 24 cubes. Work with half the dough at a time; cover and refrigerate the rest. (You can refrigerate the dough you're not using for up to 3 days, or freeze it for up to 2 months.)

4 Adjust two oven racks to divide the oven into thirds and preheat the oven to 350°F. Line two baking sheets with cooking parchment or silicone liners.

5 Roll each piece of dough under your palms into a 10- to 11-inch rope about $1/4$ inch in diameter. Cut each piece crosswise in half. Slightly overlap the ends of each piece to form a ring, press to seal the ends, and smooth the joint. Place the rings about 2 inches apart on the baking sheets, 12 to a sheet.

6 Bake for about 15 minutes, until the edges of the cookies are darker than the rest of the cookie and the bottoms are golden brown; do not overbake. Rotate the baking sheets from top to bottom and front to back once during baking to ensure even browning.

7 For the glaze, if using, combine the ingredients in a small bowl or cup as soon as the cookies come out of the oven, stirring just to mix (the sugar will not dissolve). Immediately brush the tops of the cookies with the glaze, using half of it for the first batch; you may have to brush the cookies twice. Let them cool completely on their baking sheets. Repeat with the remainder of the dough. Store the cookies airtight at room temperature.

ONE-TWO-THREE-FOUR COOKIES

*Makes
12 large
cookies*

The original version of this recipe appeared in the 1884 edition of Mrs. D. A. Lincoln's *Boston Cooking School Cook Book*. By then volume measurements of ingredients, rather than weights, were becoming the norm, and the recipe called for 1 cup butter, 2 cups sugar, 3 cups flour, and 4 eggs: hence its name. I've divided the recipe by four.

This cookie is reminiscent of snickerdoodles, a New England favorite, possibly with German roots. The 1997 *Joy of Cooking* suggests the name may be derived from the German word *schneckennudeln,* which roughly means "crinkly noodles." But *The American Heritage Cookbook* (1964) offers an alternative explanation: "New England cooks had a penchant for giving odd names to their dishes—apparently for no other reason than the fun of saying them. Snickerdoodles come from a tradition of this sort that includes Graham Jakes, Jolly Boys, Brambles, Tangle Breeches, and Kinkawoodles."

These are large, fairly thin cookies with an irresistible texture: crunchy outside and tender-chewy inside.

$^2/_3$ cup all-purpose flour	4 tablespoons ($^1/_2$ stick) unsalted butter, at room temperature
$^1/_8$ teaspoon baking soda	$^1/_2$ cup sugar
$^1/_4$ teaspoon cream of tartar	1 large egg, separated
$^1/_8$ teaspoon salt	
$^1/_4$ teaspoon ground cinnamon	

1 Adjust an oven rack to the center position and preheat the oven to 350°F. Line a baking sheet with cooking parchment or a silicone liner.

2 Sift the flour with the baking soda, cream of tartar, salt, and cinnamon; set aside.

3 In a large bowl, beat the butter and $^1/_4$ cup of the sugar with an electric mixer for 3 to 4 minutes on medium speed until smooth and fluffy. In a small bowl, beat the egg yolk until it is slightly thickened. Gradually add the remaining $^1/_4$ cup sugar to the egg yolk, and continue to beat for 2 to 3 minutes. Beat the egg yolk into the butter mixture.

4 In a small bowl, with clean beaters, beat the egg white until stiff but not dry. Beat into the butter mixture on low speed to combine well. Stir in the flour mixture to make a stiff dough.

5 Lightly dust a piece of waxed paper with flour. Scrape the dough onto the flour and dust it with a bit more flour. Pat the dough into a 3-x-4-inch rectangle and cut it into twelve 1-inch squares. Roll each piece of dough into a ball and place them about 3 inches apart on the prepared baking sheet. Flatten the cookies with the bottom of a glass to a thickness of about $1/4$ inch.

6 Bake for about 12 minutes, only until the cookies are golden with porous-looking tops. Don't overbake them, or they'll be too crisp and dry. Set the pan on a wire rack to cool for about 2 minutes. Then carefully lift the cookies off with a wide metal spatula and set them on a cooling rack. They are great warm and best the day they're made.

GINGERBREAD LITTLE CAKES

Makes about 24 cookies

In the old days, many types of cookies were called cakes, and gingerbread was made from a dough, cut into various shapes, and baked. What we call gingerbread—the moist and spicy cake—didn't become popular until the late 1800s, after the development of baking powder and baking soda. These cookies are soft and spicy, with an extra kick from crystallized ginger. They are easily made in a saucepan.

2¼ cups all-purpose flour

½ cup finely chopped crystallized ginger

½ cup firmly packed light or dark brown sugar

½ cup molasses (I use Grandma's)

2 teaspoons ground ginger

1 tablespoon ground cinnamon

1 teaspoon ground cardamom

1½ teaspoons baking soda

8 tablespoons (1 stick) unsalted butter, at room temperature, cut into 8 tablespoon-sized pieces

1 large egg, lightly beaten

1 Combine 1 tablespoon of the flour with the crystallized ginger in a small bowl and toss to coat; set aside.

2 Combine the brown sugar, molasses, ground ginger, cinnamon, and cardamom in a medium heavy saucepan. Bring to a boil over medium heat, stirring occasionally with a wooden spoon. Immediately add the baking soda and stir as the mixture becomes thick and foamy and rises to the top of the pan. Remove from the heat and stir in the butter until melted. Stir in the egg. Gradually stir in the remaining flour in 3 or 4 additions, adding the chopped ginger after the second addition. The dough will be stiff.

3 Scrape the dough onto a sheet of waxed paper and knead it briefly to mix well. Cool to room temperature.

4 Adjust two oven racks to divide the oven into thirds and preheat the oven to 325°F. Line two baking sheets with cooking parchment or silicone liners.

5 Transfer the dough to an unfloured work surface and pat or roll it to a ³⁄₈-inch thickness. Cut into shapes with cookie cutters and transfer to the bak-

ing sheets, spacing them about 2 inches apart. Gather the scraps, pat or roll them out again, and cut more cookies.

6 Bake for about 15 minutes, reversing the sheets from top to bottom and front to back once during baking, until the cookies look puffy and feel soft; do not overbake. Let cool on the pans for 5 minutes, then, with a wide metal spatula, carefully transfer them to racks to cool completely. Store airtight. These keep fresh for days.

PEPPERED GINGERSNAPS

*Makes 24
cookies*

For centuries, ginger was one of the most popular spices in cookies and in cookery. Amelia Simmon's *American Cookery* (1796) contains several recipes for ginger cookies. These large, crisp, old-fashioned cookies are spiced with a generous amount of ginger and a small amount of pepper. The dough is chilled, then each cookie is shaped by hand. These stay crisp for several days at room temperature.

1³/₄ cups all-purpose flour

2 teaspoons baking soda

¹/₄ teaspoon salt

¹/₄ teaspoon freshly ground black pepper

1 tablespoon ground ginger

1 teaspoon ground cinnamon

8 tablespoons (1 stick) unsalted butter, at room temperature

¹/₂ cup sugar

¹/₂ cup firmly packed dark brown sugar

¹/₄ cup molasses (I use Grandma's)

1 large egg

1 large egg white

¹/₄ cup sugar for coating

1 Sift together the flour, baking soda, salt, pepper, ginger, and cinnamon; set aside.

2 In a large bowl, beat the butter with an electric mixer on medium speed until smooth, about 1 minute. Add both sugars and the molasses and beat for 2 to 3 minutes. Add the egg and egg white and beat until the mixture is fluffy, 1 to 2 minutes. With a wooden spoon, stir in the flour mixture to make a stiff dough. Cover and refrigerate for at least 1 hour. (The dough can be frozen for up to 1 month.)

3 Adjust two oven racks to divide the oven into thirds and preheat the oven to 375°F. Line two baking sheets with cooking parchment or silicone liners.

4 Turn the chilled dough out onto a sheet of plastic wrap and pat it into a 6-x-4-inch rectangle, using the plastic wrap to help shape the rectangle. Flour your hands if the dough is sticky. Cut the dough into twenty-four 1-inch squares. Place the sugar in a small bowl. Roll one piece of dough into a ball, drop it into the sugar, and toss to coat with the sugar. Repeat with

the remaining dough, placing the cookies 2 to 3 inches apart on the baking sheets, 12 to a sheet.

5 Bake for 12 to 14 minutes, rotating the sheets from top to bottom and front to back halfway during baking, until the tops of the cookies develop cracks and are a rich brown. With a wide metal spatula, transfer them to wire cooling racks and cool completely. They will become crisp as they cool. Store airtight. The cookies can also be frozen for up to 2 weeks.

LEMON-HONEY DROP COOKIES

Makes 30 cookies

Drop cookies were just about the most popular kind of cookie in the nineteenth century because they required no special shaping. These golden, tender, old-fashioned drop cookies get their zing from lemon zest and lemon extract. An extra jolt of lemon comes from the glaze and the garnish of strips of lemon zest.

DOUGH

1³/₄ cups cake flour

1 teaspoon baking powder, preferably nonaluminum

¹/₂ teaspoon salt

8 tablespoons (1 stick) unsalted butter, at room temperature

¹/₂ cup plus 2 tablespoons sugar

Finely grated zest of 1 lemon

1 teaspoon pure lemon extract

1 large egg

¹/₃ cup honey

¹/₄ cup plain yogurt

GLAZE

1 cup confectioners' sugar

2 tablespoons fresh lemon juice

Zest of 1 lemon removed in strips with a vegetable peeler and cut into thin strips about 1 inch long or removed with a zester

1 Adjust two oven racks to divide the oven into thirds and preheat the oven to 350°F. Line two baking sheets with cooking parchment or silicone liners; set aside.

2 Sift the flour with the baking powder and salt; set aside.

3 In a large bowl, beat the butter with an electric mixer on medium speed until smooth, about 1 minute. Add the sugar, lemon zest, and extract, and beat for 2 to 3 minutes. Add the egg and beat for 1 minute more. Beat in the honey. Gently stir in half the flour mixture, using a rubber spatula. Stir in the yogurt, then the remaining flour.

4 Using two regular teaspoons, pick up a slightly rounded mound of dough with one spoon and use the other spoon to push the batter off onto the baking sheet, spacing them 2 to 3 inches apart, 15 cookies per sheet.

5 Bake for 12 to 15 minutes, rotating the sheets from top to bottom and front to back once during baking until the cookies are barely sand colored; do not overbake.

6 Meanwhile, for the glaze, whisk together the confectioners' sugar and lemon juice in a small bowl until smooth. Cover tightly.

7 As soon as the cookies are done, brush them with the glaze and arrange a few strips of zest on each cookie. Carefully transfer the cookies with a wide metal spatula to cooling racks and cool completely. Store airtight. The cookies will keep for 2 to 3 days or can be frozen for up to 2 weeks.

DO IT AGAIN

Amelia Simmons's *American Cookery* (1796) has two recipes for drop cookies. One is called simply Butter Drop. The second name is more puzzling: Butter Drop Do.

Students of the period know that "do." is an abbreviation of "ditto," and signified that in this case, the recipe was made with the same ingredients as the preceding one. The abbreviation would often appear in a recipe in which the quantity of an ingredient was identical, as in "1 teaspoon cinnamon, do. nutmeg, do. mace."

BIZCOCHITOS

Makes about 48 cookies

These New Mexican cookies were traditionally made at Christmastime, but nowadays they appear at any time of the year—and with good reason. They're crisp, tender, somewhat flaky and crumbly, like shortbread, and mildly flavored with anise seeds.

Lard is definitely the preferable fat for these cookies. Unlike butter, which is about 16 percent water, lard contains no water, a difference that makes the butter version of the cookies less flaky and tender than those made with lard.

The two most common supermarket brands of lard are John Morrell's and Armour. They're fine, and you'll be happy with the results, but if you have access to some home-rendered lard, the cookies will be even better.

$2^2/_3$ cups all-purpose flour	1 large egg
$1^1/_2$ teaspoons baking powder, preferably nonaluminum	4 teaspoons brandy
	$1^1/_2$ teaspoons anise seeds
$1/_2$ teaspoon salt	
1 cup lard or unsalted butter (2 sticks), at room temperature	$1/_4$ cup sugar
	$1/_2$ teaspoon ground cinnamon
$1/_2$ cup sugar	

1 Sift the flour with the baking powder and salt; set aside.

2 In a large bowl, beat the lard or butter with an electric mixer on medium speed until soft and smooth, about 1 minute. Gradually beat in the sugar, then beat on medium-high speed for 3 to 4 minutes. Add the egg and beat for 1 minute. Beat in the brandy on low speed, then the anise seed. On low speed, gradually beat in the flour mixture, beating only until thoroughly incorporated and the dough gathers into a mass. Scrape the dough onto a sheet of plastic wrap and shape into a 1-inch-thick disk. Wrap securely and refrigerate for 1 to 2 hours, or up to 2 days.

3 Adjust two racks to divide the oven into thirds and preheat the oven to 350°F.

4 Turn the dough out onto a lightly floured surface, divide it in half, and coat

both sides lightly with flour. (Wrap and refrigerate one piece of dough.) If the dough is very firm, tap it gently with a rolling pin to flatten it and soften it slightly. For thin, crisp cookies, roll the dough to a scant $1/4$ inch; for thicker cookies, like shortbread, roll the dough about $3/16$ inch thick. Cut out cookies with any shape cutters you like (diamonds, circles, stars, animals) and place about 1 inch apart on ungreased baking sheets. Gather the scraps from both batches of dough and press them together. Roll out and cut as before. If the dough is too soft, wrap in plastic, and refrigerate about 30 minutes before rolling. (Don't roll out scraps more than once, or the cookies will be tough.)

5 Combine the sugar and cinnamon, and sprinkle lightly over the cookies.

6 Bake for 10 to 14 minutes, until the cookies are golden brown. Reverse the sheets from top to bottom and front to back once during baking to ensure even browning. Cool the cookies on the baking sheets for 1 minute, then transfer them to wire racks with a wide metal spatula to cool completely. Store airtight.

FUDGY CHOCOLATE STRIPPERS

Makes 36 cookies

The dough for these cookies is shaped into logs, baked, and then filled with a creamy chocolate mixture. The soft and fudgy cookies are cut into diagonal strips for serving.

1⅓ cups all-purpose flour

⅓ cup unsweetened cocoa powder

¾ teaspoon baking soda

¼ teaspoon salt

⅛ teaspoon ground cloves

3 tablespoons unsalted butter, at room temperature

1 cup sugar

1 teaspoon espresso powder (I use Medaglia d'Oro)

1 teaspoon pure vanilla extract

1 2½ ounce jar Gerber's baby food prunes

1 large egg

½ cup sweetened condensed milk

2 ounces (2 squares) unsweetened chocolate, chopped

1 Adjust an oven rack to the center position and preheat the oven to 350°F.

2 Sift the flour, cocoa, baking soda, salt, and cloves together; set aside.

3 In a medium bowl, combine the butter, sugar, espresso, vanilla, prunes, and egg. Beat with an electric mixer on high speed until smooth and creamy, about 2 minutes. Add the flour mixture and stir in well with a rubber spatula. The batter will be thick and sticky.

4 Coat two sheets of waxed paper with vegetable cooking spray. Divide the dough into 3 even mounds on one of the waxed paper sheets. Coat the tops lightly with cooking spray. Transfer one of the mounds to the second sheet of waxed paper and roll it, using your palms, into a cylinder 12 inches long and 1 inch thick. (If the waxed paper slides on the countertop as you work, hold the paper down with one hand and use the second hand to roll the dough.) Using the waxed paper to help you, carefully transfer the log to a nonstick or lightly buttered baking sheet, placing the log parallel to one short side, about 2 inches from the end. Repeat with the remaining dough, placing the cylinders about 4 inches apart.

5 Bake for 13 to 14 minutes, until the strips of dough are soft with long cracks; do not overbake.

6 Meanwhile, combine the condensed milk and chocolate in the top of a double boiler or in a small heavy saucepan set in a larger pan of hot water over medium heat. Stir occasionally until the chocolate is melted and the mixture is smooth and thick. Remove from the heat, but leave the pan in the water bath to keep the chocolate warm. Immediately use the back of a teaspoon to make a shallow trench about 1 inch wide down the length of each strip. Place the warm chocolate mixture in small spoonfuls in each trench and use the back of the teaspoon to spread the filling evenly. With a wide metal spatula, carefully transfer the strips to a cutting surface. Let stand until completely cool and the chocolate filling is set, 30 to 60 minutes.

7 With a large knife, cut each strip into 12 cookies on a sharp angle. These are best the day they're baked.

AS EASY AS FALLING OFF A LOG

When making Ginger Snaps, Cookies, etc., if the dough is shaped in long narrow rolls and chilled on ice or left in a cold place over night it may be sliced off instead of rolling. This saves a good deal of time and is very satisfactory.

—Larkin Housewives' Cook Book (1915)

SPICY ICEBOX OATMEAL CRISPS

Makes about 36 cookies

This is a straightforward icebox cookie, and the dough comes together very quickly. It must be refrigerated overnight before baking. The cookies are thin, dark, crisp, and crunchy.

²/₃ cup all-purpose flour

¹/₂ teaspoon baking soda

¹/₄ teaspoon salt

1 teaspoon ground cinnamon

¹/₂ teaspoon ground allspice

¹/₂ teaspoon freshly grated nutmeg

¹/₄ teaspoon ground cloves

¹/₄ teaspoon freshly ground black pepper

8 tablespoons (1 stick) unsalted butter, at room temperature

1 teaspoon pure vanilla extract

1 cup firmly packed light brown sugar

1 large egg

1¹/₂ cups old-fashioned or quick-cooking (not instant) rolled oats

1 Sift the flour with the baking soda, salt, cinnamon, allspice, nutmeg, cloves, and black pepper; set aside.

2 In a large bowl, beat the butter with an electric mixer on medium speed until smooth, about 1 minute. Add the vanilla and brown sugar and beat for 2 to 3 minutes. Add the egg and beat it in well. Stir in the flour mixture with a wooden spoon, then stir in the oats.

3 Place the dough on a large piece of plastic wrap and form it into a log about 9 inches long and 2 inches wide, using the plastic wrap to help you shape the dough. Wrap tightly in the plastic wrap and refrigerate overnight. (The dough can be frozen for up to 1 month; thaw overnight in the refrigerator.)

4 Adjust two oven racks to divide the oven into thirds and preheat the oven to 350°F. Line two baking sheets with cooking parchment or silicone liners.

5 Using a sharp knife, cut the dough into ¹/₄-inch-thick slices. Place the slices on the baking sheets, spacing them 2 inches apart.

6 Bake for 12 to 14 minutes, until the cookies are dark brown. Rotate the sheets from top to bottom and front to back once to ensure even baking. Cool the cookies completely on the baking sheets on racks. Store airtight. These stay fresh for several days.

THE ICEBOX COMETH

Before the age of commercial ice, many families built icehouses on the banks of a farm pond. In the winter, when the water had frozen solid, the ice was cut into blocks, packed in sawdust to insulate it, and stored in the icehouse, where it would keep for many months. To use the ice in the home, however, special containers had to be designed to house both the ice and the food.

These iceboxes, or nonelectric refrigerators, date back to 1803. Thomas Moore, a Maryland farmer, devised a storage chest with an upper compartment for holding ice and a lower one for keeping food. A drip pan on the bottom of the chest captured the water as the ice melted. The pan was emptied periodically, and new ice was added as needed.

For the next few decades, icemen driving horse-drawn carts delivered the ice. To let the iceman know how much he should leave, owners placed a card in the window indicating the desired amount. Since the iceboxes were often kept on a porch outside the house, deliveries could be made even if no one was at home.

When the compression process for manufacturing ice was developed in the mid-1840s, ice became widely available. Eliza Leslie wrote that an icebox was a convenience "no family should be without," and it soon became a fixture in American homes. Iceboxes made it possible to keep perishable foods fresh for several days, and they also led to a new class of desserts. By the mid-1800s, recipes for charlotte russe and other gelatin-based desserts began appearing regularly in cookbooks. The icebox gave rise to other baking classics. In 1924, a recipe for an icebox cake was published in *Everybody's Cookbook,* and the February 1929 issue of the *Ladies' Home Journal* trumpeted another creation of the new cooling appliance: "The ice-box cookie is the new and improved 1929 model home-made cookie."

BIG LEMON-FROSTED SUGAR COOKIE SQUARES

Makes 20 cookies

These huge, crisp old-fashioned sugar cookies are enriched with a little wheat germ. They're easy to make and a great favorite with both kids and adults.

DOUGH

1³/₄ cups all-purpose flour

1 teaspoon baking powder, preferably nonaluminum

¹/₄ teaspoon baking soda

¹/₄ teaspoon salt

¹/₄ cup untoasted wheat germ

8 tablespoons (1 stick) unsalted butter, at room temperature

1 cup sugar

1 teaspoon pure vanilla extract

1 large egg

1 large egg white

1 tablespoon milk

Finely grated zest of 1 lemon

GLAZE

1 large egg white

2 cups confectioners' sugar

2–3 teaspoons fresh lemon juice

Colored sugar sprinkles for decoration (optional)

1 For the dough, sift together the flour, baking powder, baking soda, and salt into a bowl. Stir in the wheat germ; set aside.

2 In a large bowl, beat the butter with an electric mixer on medium speed until smooth, about 1 minute. Add the sugar and vanilla and beat for 2 to 3 minutes. Add the egg, egg white, milk, and lemon zest and beat in well. With a wooden spoon, gradually stir in the flour mixture to form a moist dough.

3 Scrape the dough onto a sheet of plastic wrap and pat it into a rectangle about 1 inch thick, using the plastic wrap to help you. Wrap tightly and refrigerate for at least several hours, or overnight.

4 Adjust two oven racks to divide the oven into thirds and preheat the oven to 400°F.

5 Roll the dough on a lightly floured surface into a 12-x-15-inch rectangle, checking occasionally to make sure the dough isn't sticking. With a large

sharp knife, cut the dough into twenty 3-inch squares. Carefully transfer the squares to two ungreased baking sheets, spacing them about 2 inches apart, 10 on each sheet.

6 Bake for 10 to 12 minutes, until the cookies are deep golden brown and have cracks on top. Rotate the sheets from top to bottom and front to back about halfway during baking to ensure even browning. With a wide metal spatula, transfer the cookies to cooling racks to cool completely.

7 For the glaze, beat the egg white in a small bowl until foamy. Add the confectioners' sugar and 2 teaspoons of the lemon juice and beat until smooth. The icing should be just thick enough to spread over the cookies with a pastry brush. If it is too thick, gradually beat in droplets of lemon juice until the consistency is right. Brush a thin layer of icing over the cookies and sprinkle with the sugar sprinkles, if using. Let the icing set.

ORANGY "FIG NEWTON" DIAMONDS

Makes 20 cookies

This is my version of Fig Newtons, one of the most popular cookies of the twentieth century. Two layers of tender, buttery pastry enclose a honey-orange-fig filling. The delicate dough must be prepared ahead, but it rolls out easily as long as it's cold. The filling is quickly made in a food processor.

DOUGH

1²/₃ cups all-purpose flour

1 teaspoon baking powder, preferably nonaluminum

¹/₂ teaspoon salt

6 tablespoons unsalted butter (³/₄ stick), at room temperature

¹/₃ cup sugar

1 teaspoon pure vanilla extract

¹/₃ cup honey

1 large egg

FILLING

1 pound dried Black Mission figs
    Finely grated zest of 1 large orange

3 tablespoons sugar

¹/₄ cup boiling water

2 tablespoons honey

2 tablespoons fresh orange juice

1 large egg yolk, beaten with 1 teaspoon milk for glaze

1 For the dough, sift together the flour, baking powder, and salt; set aside.

2 In a large bowl, beat the butter with an electric mixer on medium speed until smooth, about 1 minute. Add the sugar and vanilla and beat for 2 to 3 minutes. Beat in the honey, then the egg. With a wooden spoon, gradually stir in the flour mixture to make a fairly stiff dough.

3 Transfer the dough to a sheet of plastic wrap and pat it into a 5-x-8-inch rectangle, using the plastic wrap to help you. Wrap securely and refrigerate for at least 8 hours, or overnight.

4 Adjust an oven rack to the center position and preheat the oven to 375°F. Butter a 9-inch square baking pan and set aside.

5 For the filling, cut off any tough stems from the figs and discard. Place the figs in a food processor and pulse 6 times, or until chopped medium-fine. Add the orange zest and process for 20 seconds. In a measuring cup, dis-

solve the sugar in the boiling water. Stir in the honey and orange juice until thoroughly combined. With the motor running, pour the mixture through the feed tube and process until smooth, 1 to 2 minutes, stopping to scrape the sides of the bowl twice. Spoon the fig mixture into a bowl.

6 Divide the dough in half. Roll one half out on a lightly floured surface to a 9-inch square. Press the dough into the bottom of the prepared pan. Place small mounds of the filling all over the dough and spread it evenly with the back of a spoon. Roll out the second piece of dough to a 9-inch square and carefully place it over the fig filling. Pat it gently in place. Brush the egg yolk glaze evenly over the top (you may not need it all), and prick the dough with a fork in about 6 places.

7 Bake for about 30 minutes, until deep golden brown on top. Cool in the pan on a wire rack for 30 minutes.

8 Run a small knife around the edges of the pan to release the pastry. Cover the pan with a wire rack and invert the two. Remove the pan, cover the pastry with another wire rack, and invert again to cool completely right side up.

9 Transfer the pastry to a cutting board and use a large sharp knife to cut into 5 strips. To make diamond shapes, cut each strip on an angle into 4 cookies. (The trimmings are a treat for the cook.) Store airtight.

CHOCOLATE-SECRET WALNUT COOKIES

Makes 24 cookies

The original inspiration for these cookies was a 1949 Pillsbury Bake-Off recipe that won $10,000. It featured a brown sugar–butter dough wrapped around mint chocolate wafers, and it was a trend-setter.

The Droste chocolate pastilles used in this recipe are thin chocolate disks with a deep, rich chocolate taste. They are available in candy and gourmet shops as well as some supermarkets.

Make the dough a few hours ahead of time, or even the day before, since it needs to chill thoroughly.

1 1/3 cups all-purpose flour
1/2 teaspoon baking soda
1/4 teaspoon salt
8 tablespoons (1 stick) unsalted butter, at room temperature
1/2 cup sugar
1/4 cup firmly packed light brown sugar

1 teaspoon vanilla extract
1 large egg
1 tablespoon water
24 Droste bittersweet chocolate pastilles (from 2 packages)

24 walnut halves

1 Sift the flour, baking soda, and salt together; set aside.

2 In a large bowl, beat the butter with an electric mixer on medium speed until smooth, about 1 minute. Beat in both sugars about 2 tablespoons at a time, beating for a few seconds after each addition. Beat in the vanilla, and beat for 3 to 4 minutes. Add the egg and beat on medium-high speed for 1 minute, then beat in the water. On low speed, gradually add in the flour mixture, beating only until completely incorporated. Cover the bowl tightly with plastic wrap and refrigerate for at least several hours, or overnight.

3 Adjust two oven racks to divide the oven into thirds and preheat the oven to 375°F. Line two baking sheets with cooking parchment or silicone liners; set aside.

4 Scrape the dough onto a lightly floured work surface and pat it into a 1-inch-thick rectangle. Cut into 24 cubes. Working quickly so that the dough doesn't soften too much, roll each piece into a ball and flatten to a round about $1/4$ inch thick. Wrap a pastille in each piece of dough and place seam side down on the baking sheets, spacing the cookies about 2 inches apart, 12 cookies to a sheet. Press a walnut half onto the top of each cookie.

5 Bake until the cookies are golden brown, 10 to 12 minutes. Rotate the sheets from top to bottom and front to back once during baking to ensure even browning. Let cool on the baking sheets for a minute or two, then use a wide metal spatula to transfer the cookies to wire cooling racks to cool completely. Store airtight at room temperature. The cookies can be frozen for up to 1 week.

PEANUT BUTTERSCOTCH CHEWS

*Makes 16
cookies*

Peanuts, not a nut but a legume, are highly nutritious. It wasn't until George Washington Carver extolled the virtues of peanuts that they became accepted by the American public. The candylike batter for this cookie is made quickly in a saucepan.

1 cup all-purpose flour	$1/3$ cup evaporated milk
$1/2$ teaspoon baking soda	1 large egg
$1/4$ teaspoon salt	1 teaspoon pure vanilla extract
1 teaspoon ground cinnamon	$1/3$ cup dry-roasted peanuts, finely
4 tablespoons ($1/2$ stick) unsalted butter	chopped
1 cup firmly packed light brown sugar	

1 Adjust an oven rack to the center position, and preheat the oven to 325°F. Butter an 8-inch square baking pan and set aside.

2 Sift the flour with the baking soda, salt, and cinnamon; set aside.

3 Melt the butter in a medium heavy saucepan over medium-low heat. Add the brown sugar and stir constantly with a wooden spoon for 1 minute, or until the mixture smells toasty. Add the evaporated milk, raise the heat to medium, and stir occasionally as the mixture comes to a boil. Boil for exactly 1 minute, stirring once or twice. Let cool until warm.

4 Beat in the egg with the wooden spoon until smooth, then beat in the vanilla. Stir in the flour mixture only until incorporated, then the peanuts. Spread the batter evenly in the prepared pan.

5 Bake for about 30 minutes, until a toothpick comes out moist with a few crumbs sticking to it. Do not overbake—these should be very moist. Cool on a wire rack for about 5 minutes, then tamp down the sides of the "cake" with your fingertips to level it. Cool completely, and cut into squares.

CHEWY COCONUT MACAROONS

Makes 20 cookies

Macaroons have been popular for centuries. Sometimes called "Maca-ronies" or "Macaroonies," they were traditionally made with almonds, pounded in a mortar with a pestle, and flavored with rose water. Sugar beaten with egg whites bound the mixture together. These macaroons are held together with sweetened condensed milk and flour. They're crunchy on the outside, chewy on the inside, and loaded with coconut.

1/2 cup cake flour	1 14-ounce can sweetened
2 1/2 cups loosely packed sweetened	condensed milk
flaked coconut	1 1/2 teaspoons pure vanilla extract

1 Adjust an oven rack to the center position and preheat the oven to 250°F. Line a baking sheet with cooking parchment or a silicone liner; set aside.

2 In a large bowl, combine the flour and coconut, tossing well with your fingertips to coat the coconut with the flour. Add the condensed milk and vanilla and stir with a wooden spoon or spatula until well combined. The mixture will be stiff.

3 Spoon rounded regular teaspoonsful of the mixture onto the baking sheet, spacing them 2 inches apart and making 20 mounds.

4 Bake for 30 minutes, rotating the baking sheet from front to back once during baking. Increase the heat to 350°F and bake for 6 to 10 minutes more, only until the macaroons are golden brown all over; do not overbake. Carefully transfer to cooling racks with a wide metal spatula and cool completely. Serve very fresh.

ESPRESSO MERINGUE COOKIES

Makes about 36 cookies

Plain meringue cookies were quite popular in the nineteenth century. Don't make these on humid days, because they tend not to dry out sufficiently. Superfine sugar is sold in most supermarkets. If you can't find it, you can process granulated sugar in a food processor for a minute.

4 large egg whites

¹/₄ teaspoon salt

¹/₄ teaspoon cream of tartar

1 cup superfine sugar

1¹/₂ tablespoons instant espresso powder (I use Medaglia d'Oro)

1 teaspoon pure vanilla extract

About 36 coffee beans

Cocoa for dusting

1 Adjust two oven racks to divide the oven into thirds and preheat the oven to 225°F. Line two baking sheets with cooking parchment or silicone liners; set aside.

2 In a large bowl, beat the egg whites and salt with an electric mixer on medium speed until foamy. Add the cream of tartar and continue beating until the whites form softly curling peaks when the beaters are raised. Beat in the sugar 2 tablespoons at a time, beating for about 30 seconds after each addition. Beat in the espresso and vanilla, then increase the speed to high and beat until the meringue forms stiff, shiny, unwavering peaks when the beaters are raised.

3 Using a regular teaspoon, heap spoonfuls of the meringue onto the baking sheets, spacing them about 2 inches apart; work quickly, before the sugar dissolves. Top each mound with a coffee bean and dust lightly with cocoa.

4 Bake for about 1¹/₂ hours, rotating the sheets from top to bottom and front to back once about halfway through the baking. To test for doneness, carefully try to lift one or two meringues off the baking sheet. They may feel soft, but if they come off easily, they are done.

5 Turn the oven off and prop the door open slightly with the handle of a wooden spoon. Let the meringues cool completely in the turned-off oven, at least 2 hours. Store airtight. The meringues keep fresh for about a week.

GIANT PASSOVER CHOCOLATE–PINE NUT MERINGUE SMOOCHES

Makes 16 cookies

These meringue kisses are like no other. Huge, filled with chocolate and nuts, they're crusty on the outside and chewy on the inside. A treat at Passover, they're a big hit any time of the year.

You'll need to line your baking sheets with cooking parchment or silicone liners. Don't make meringues on a damp or rainy day; they don't like humidity.

$^1/_3$ cup pine nuts	1 teaspoon pure vanilla extract
4 large egg whites	2 ounces (2 squares) bittersweet
$^1/_8$ teaspoon salt	chocolate, cut into small
1 cup sugar	pieces

1 Toast the pine nuts in a small heavy skillet over medium-high heat for 3 to 4 minutes, stirring occasionally, until golden brown. Remove from the pan and set aside to cool.

2 Adjust an oven rack to the center position and preheat the oven to 250°F. Line a baking sheet with cooking parchment or a silicone liner; set aside.

3 Beat the egg whites and salt in a large bowl with an electric mixer on medium speed until the whites form soft peaks when the beaters are lifted. Beat in the sugar about 2 tablespoons at a time, beating for 15 to 30 seconds after each addition. Beat in the vanilla, then increase the speed to high and beat for 3 to 4 minutes, until the meringue forms very stiff, shiny peaks when the beaters are raised. Gently fold in the pine nuts and chocolate.

4 Working quickly, drop the mixture by large spoonfuls onto the prepared baking sheet, spacing them 1 to 2 inches apart and making 16 mounds.

5 Bake for 1 hour, or until the surfaces of the meringues feel dry and you can pick one off the liner without it sticking.

6 Turn off the oven, prop the door open slightly with the handle of a wooden spoon, and let the meringues sit in the oven for another 30 minutes. Transfer them to a large serving platter. These are best when very fresh.

HAMANTASCHEN

Makes 20 cookies

These triangular cookies are a traditional treat for the joyous Jewish holiday of Purim, also known as the Feast of Esther. But I've found the cookies at any time of the year in bakeshops all across the country. Normally, the filling for the cookies is made from a puree of prunes (*lekvar*) or from ground poppy seeds sweetened with honey. I like to use golden Calimyrna figs. The dough and filling must chill overnight.

PASTRY

- 6 tablespoons (³/₄ stick) unsalted butter, at room temperature
- 2 ounces cream cheese
- ²/₃ cup sugar
- 1 teaspoon pure vanilla extract
- 1 large egg
- 1³/₄ cups all-purpose flour
- 1¹/₂ teaspoons baking powder, preferably nonaluminum
- ¹/₄ teaspoon salt

FILLING

- 12 ounces dried Calimyrna figs
- 3 tablespoons sugar
- 3 tablespoons boiling water
- 1 tablespoon light corn syrup
- 1 tablespoon fresh lemon juice

1 For the pastry, beat the butter, cream cheese, sugar, and vanilla in a large bowl with an electric mixer on medium speed until creamy, smooth, and fluffy, 2 to 3 minutes. Add the egg and beat on high speed until smooth. Add the flour, baking powder, and salt and mix on low speed just until incorporated. Scrape the mixture onto a sheet of plastic wrap, wrap securely, and refrigerate overnight.

2 Meanwhile, prepare the fig filling: Put the figs in a food processor and pulse 6 times to chop, then process continuously for 30 seconds. Place the sugar in a measuring cup and stir in the boiling water until the sugar dissolves. Add the corn syrup and lemon juice and combine thoroughly. With the processor running, gradually add the sugar mixture and process until smooth, about 2 minutes, stopping once or twice to scrape the sides of the work bowl. Transfer to a small bowl, cover, and refrigerate overnight.

3 Divide the dough in half. Shape each half into a 10-inch-long cylinder. Cut each roll into 10 pieces, and quickly roll each piece into a ball. Place the balls on a tray lined with plastic wrap and refrigerate.

4 Measure level tablespoons of the fig mixture and place them on another tray lined with plastic wrap. Moisten your hands and shape each mound into a domed disk measuring 1 1/2 inches in diameter.

5 Adjust two oven racks to divide the oven into thirds and preheat the oven to 400°F. Coat two nonstick baking sheets lightly with cooking spray. Set aside.

6 To shape the hamantaschen, remove a ball of dough from the refrigerator and place it on a 6-inch square of waxed paper. With your fingertips, flatten the dough into a 3- to 3 1/2-inch circle and smooth the edges. Place a round of fig mixture on the center of the circle of dough. Form the point of a triangle by folding in two sides of the circle, pressing them against the edges of the filling and leaving the rest of the filling exposed. Pinch the edges firmly to seal; be careful not to enclose any filling in the "pinches." Remove the cookie from the waxed paper and place it on one of the baking sheets. Repeat with the remaining dough and filling, placing 10 cookies on each sheet, leaving 1 to 2 inches of space between them.

7 Bake for 12 to 15 minutes, until the cookies are a light golden brown. Rotate the baking sheets from top to bottom and front to back about halfway during baking to ensure even browning. Use a wide metal spatula to transfer the cookies to wire cooling racks. Let cool completely. Store in airtight containers. These stay fresh for 2 to 3 days.

CASHEW AND GOLDEN RAISIN BISCOTTI WITH WHITE CHOCOLATE GLAZE

Makes about 30 biscotti

Biscotti have taken the country by storm in recent years. Simple in concept, they were traditionally made with only a few ingredients. We have Americanized them by adding all sorts of wonderful ingredients. No matter, they're still biscotti (this Italian word means "twice-baked"). These are crisp, crunchy, nutty, and mildly spiced. Glazing biscotti may seem like gilding the lily, but the white chocolate does marvelous things for the cookies. If you're a dunker, go ahead and take the plunge.

DOUGH

1¼ cups all-purpose flour

¾ teaspoon baking powder, preferably nonaluminum

¼ teaspoon baking soda

½ teaspoon freshly grated nutmeg

¼ teaspoon ground mace

2 large eggs

2 teaspoons pure vanilla extract

¾ cup sugar

¾ cup dry-roasted salted cashews

¾ cup golden raisins

GLAZE

1 3.5-ounce bar white chocolate (I use Lindt), finely chopped

1 tablespoon milk

1 Adjust an oven rack to the center position and preheat the oven to 300°F. Line a baking sheet with cooking parchment or a silicone liner; set aside.

2 For the dough, sift the flour with the baking powder, baking soda, nutmeg, and mace; set aside.

3 In a large bowl, beat the eggs, vanilla, and sugar with an electric mixer on medium speed for about 2 minutes, until thickened and light in color. Stir in the flour mixture, then the cashews and raisins. Place large spoonfuls of batter diagonally, touching one another, across the baking sheet, and spread them into one big log about 15 inches long and 3½ to 4 inches wide. Square off the ends.

4 Bake for about 45 minutes, rotating the sheet from front to back once during baking, until the log is golden brown and the top feels dry. Do not underbake. Carefully slide the log onto a cutting board. While it is still hot,

use a sharp serrated knife and a sawing motion to cut it crosswise into $^1/_2$-
to $^3/_4$-inch-thick slices.

5 Stand the slices upright and space them about $^1/_2$ inch apart on the baking
sheet, and return the pan to the oven. Bake for 20 minutes more, or until
golden brown. Let cool completely on the baking pan on a rack.

6 For the glaze, place the white chocolate in a small microwave-safe bowl
with the milk. Microwave on low power for 1 minute. Stir the chocolate
mixture and continue microwaving until the chocolate is melted and
smooth, about 1 minute longer. Or, to melt the chocolate on top of the
stove, put the chocolate and milk in a small saucepan, place it in a larger
saucepan of hot water set over medium-low heat, and stir occasionally
until melted and smooth.

7 Turn the cooled biscotti cut side up and drizzle with the white glaze. Let
stand until the glaze is set. Store airtight. These stay fresh for days.

WHITE CHOCOLATE CHUNK BROWNIES

Makes 16 brownies

These fudgy, moist dark chocolate brownies, studded with chunks of white chocolate, have an almost candylike texture.

1 3.5-ounce bar white chocolate (I use Lindt)
1 cup all-purpose flour
$^2/_3$ cup Dutch-process cocoa
$^1/_2$ teaspoon baking powder, preferably nonaluminum
$^1/_4$ teaspoon salt
5 tablespoons unsalted butter
$^2/_3$ cup sugar

$^2/_3$ cup firmly packed dark brown sugar
1 teaspoon instant espresso powder (I use Medaglia d'Oro)
1 2$^1/_2$-ounce jar Gerber's baby food prunes
1 large egg
2 large egg whites
2 teaspoons pure vanilla extract

1 Adjust an oven rack to the center position and preheat the oven to 325°F. Butter a 9-inch square baking pan.

2 With a large sharp knife, cut the white chocolate bar into pieces along its marked lines, then cut each piece crosswise in half; set aside. Sift the flour, cocoa, baking powder, and salt together; set aside.

3 Melt the butter in a medium heavy saucepan over low heat. Remove from the heat and stir in both sugars, the espresso, and the prunes with a wooden spoon. Stir in the egg and egg whites one at a time, until thoroughly incorporated. Stir in the vanilla. Add the flour mixture and stir until thoroughly moistened. Stir in the white chocolate. Spread the batter evenly in the prepared pan.

4 Bake for 30 minutes, or until a toothpick comes out with a few moist crumbs attached; do not overbake. Cool completely on a wire rack, and cut into 16 squares with a small sharp knife.

CARAMEL PECAN CANDY BAR COOKIES

Makes 20 bars

These cookies have a buttery, crunchy brown sugar base and a chewy topping made from chopped pecans and purchased caramel candies. The cookies are amazingly easy to make.

4 tablespoon (¹/₂ stick) unsalted butter, at room temperature

¹/₃ cup firmly packed light brown sugar

¹/₄ teaspoon salt

2 teaspoons pure vanilla extract

²/₃ cup all-purpose flour

40 caramels (I use Kraft)

2 tablespoons evaporated milk

¹/₂ cup finely chopped pecans

1 Adjust an oven rack to the center position and preheat the oven to 375°F. Butter an 8-inch square baking pan; set aside.

2 In a large bowl, beat the butter, brown sugar, salt, and 1 teaspoon of the vanilla with an electric mixer on medium speed for 2 to 3 minutes. Stir in the flour thoroughly with a wooden spoon. The dough will be crumbly. Press the dough firmly and evenly into the bottom of the prepared pan.

3 Bake for 15 minutes. Remove the pan from the oven and gently pat the crust back in place with a pot holder to level it. (Leave the oven on.)

4 Meanwhile, melt the caramels with the evaporated milk in a small heavy saucepan over low heat, stirring occasionally until smooth, about 15 minutes. Stir in the remaining 1 teaspoon vanilla.

5 Scrape the caramel mixture over the hot crust and, holding the pan with pot holders, tilt it gently from side to side to level the caramel. Sprinkle evenly with the pecans. Bake for 15 minutes more, or until the caramel topping is bubbly and puffy. Cool completely on a wire rack. Cut into bars with a small sharp knife.

CHOCOLATE MINT BROWNIE BARS

Makes 25 to 30 bars

Bar cookies, brownies included, are a twentieth-century invention. Brownies made their first appearance in cookbooks around 1906. By the 1920s, recipes for them were everywhere.

These brownies will remind you of Mystic Mint cookies. A fudgy brownie layer is topped with a thin layer of mint-flavored icing and drizzled with a bitter chocolate glaze.

BROWNIES

- 1 cup all-purpose flour
- ½ teaspoon baking powder, preferably nonaluminum
- ¼ teaspoon salt
- 6 tablespoons (¾ stick) unsalted butter
- ¼ cup evaporated milk
- 1 cup Dutch-process cocoa
- 1 cup firmly packed light brown sugar
- ½ cup sugar
- 2 teaspoons pure vanilla extract
- 4 large egg whites

ICING

- 1 cup confectioners' sugar
- 1 tablespoon evaporated milk
- 1 tablespoon unsalted butter, at room temperature
- ½ teaspoon mint extract

GLAZE

- 1 ounce (1 square) unsweetened chocolate
- 1 tablespoon unsalted butter

1 For the brownies, adjust an oven rack to the center position and preheat the oven to 325°F. Butter a 9-inch square baking pan; set aside.

2 Sift the flour with the baking powder and salt; set aside.

3 Melt the butter in a medium heavy saucepan over medium heat. Stir in the evaporated milk and cocoa and cook, stirring, for 1 minute. Add both sugars and cook, stirring, for 1 minute more. Remove from the heat and stir in the vanilla extract. Let cool slightly.

4 With a wooden spoon, add the egg whites one at a time to the butter mixture, stirring until the batter is smooth and shiny. Add the flour mixture and stir just to incorporate thoroughly. Scrape the batter into the prepared pan.

5 Bake for 25 minutes, or until the brownie "cake" barely springs back when gently pressed and a toothpick inserted into the center comes out slightly moist with a few crumbs sticking to it; do not overbake. Cool completely on a wire rack.

6 For the icing, beat the confectioners' sugar, evaporated milk, butter, and mint extract in a small bowl until smooth. Spread evenly over the brownies. Refrigerate for about 1 hour to set the icing.

7 For the glaze, heat the chocolate in a small microwave-safe dish in the microwave oven on high for 45 seconds. Add the butter and microwave on high for 20 seconds. Stir well and microwave for a few seconds more if necessary, until completely smooth. Or, to make the glaze on top of the stove, place the chocolate and butter in a custard cup, set the cup in a saucepan filled with 1 inch hot water, and heat over medium heat, stirring occasionally, until melted and completely smooth. Drizzle the hot glaze over the icing, letting some white spots show through. Refrigerate to set the glaze, 30 minutes or longer.

8 Run the tip of a small sharp knife around the brownies to release them from the sides of the pan, then cut into 5 even strips. Using a narrow metal spatula, carefully remove the strips from the pan and cut each crosswise into 5 or 6 pieces. Place on a tray, cover with plastic wrap, and refrigerate. Serve straight from the refrigerator.

MARSHMALLOW FUDGE BARS

*Makes
24 bars*

These bars are like layered rocky road cookies. A thin brownie layer with pecans is topped with marshmallows and spread with chocolate fudge frosting.

CAKE LAYER

²/₃ cup all-purpose flour

2 tablespoons Dutch-process cocoa

¹/₄ teaspoon baking powder, preferably nonaluminum

¹/₄ teaspoon salt

8 tablespoons (1 stick) unsalted butter, at room temperature

³/₄ cup sugar

1 teaspoon pure vanilla extract

2 large eggs

¹/₂ cup chopped pecans

24 soft marshmallows, snipped in half with scissors

FROSTING

¹/₂ cup firmly packed light or dark brown sugar

¹/₄ cup water

3 ounces (3 squares) unsweetened chocolate

4 tablespoons (¹/₂ stick) unsalted butter

1¹/₂ teaspoons pure vanilla extract

1¹/₂ cups confectioners' sugar

2–3 tablespoons heavy cream

1 For the cake layer, adjust an oven rack to the center position and preheat the oven to 350°F. Lightly butter a 13-x-9-inch baking pan. Line the pan with a sheet of aluminum foil, carefully pressing the foil into the corners without tearing it and leaving any overhanging edges. Butter the foil (don't use cooking spray) and set the pan aside.

2 Sift the flour with the cocoa, baking powder, and salt; set aside.

3 In a large bowl, beat the butter with an electric mixer on medium speed until smooth, about 1 minute. Add ¹/₄ cup of the sugar and the vanilla and beat for 30 seconds. Beat in the remaining ¹/₂ cup sugar about 2 tablespoons at a time, beating for 10 to 15 seconds after each addition, then beat for 3 to 4 minutes. Add the eggs one at a time, beating well after each. On low speed, add the flour mixture, mixing only until incorporated. Stir in the pecans. Place large spoonfuls of batter all over the bottom of the pre-pared pan and spread them together with the back of the spoon to make a thin, even layer.

4 Bake for 15 to 20 minutes, until the layer is just set and a toothpick comes out with a few bits of chocolate batter sticking to it. Quickly place the marshmallows, cut side down, on top of the hot cake. Return to the oven for 3 minutes, then cool completely on a wire rack.

5 For the frosting, bring the brown sugar, water, and chocolate to a boil in a medium saucepan over medium heat, stirring occasionally. Boil, stirring constantly, for 3 minutes. Remove from the heat and stir in the butter until it melts, then the vanilla. Let cool to room temperature.

6 Stir the confectioners' sugar into the chocolate mixture. Gradually add enough heavy cream to make a smooth, thick, spreadable frosting. Spread the frosting evenly over the marshmallow layer. Let stand until the frost-ing is set, about 1 hour.

7 To serve, remove the cake from the pan by lifting the edges of foil. Cut into bars with a large sharp knife; run the knife under warm tap water occasion-ally and shake off the excess water if the marshmallows stick to it. Store airtight.

MAPLE DATE BARS

*Makes
20 bars*

This is my homage to two transcontinental gifts to the American sweet tooth: dates from California and maple syrup from the Midwest and the Northeast. Use whole pitted dates; packaged chopped dates are of inferior quality.

12 ounces moist pitted dried dates, preferably Medjool, cut into small pieces

$^1/_3$ cup pure maple syrup

$^3/_4$ cup water

Finely grated zest of 1 lemon

1 cup all-purpose flour

$^1/_4$ teaspoon baking soda

$^1/_4$ teaspoon salt

8 tablespoons (1 stick) unsalted butter, at room temperature

$^2/_3$ cup sugar

1 cup old-fashioned or quick-cooking (not instant) rolled oats

1 Combine the dates, maple syrup, and water in a medium heavy saucepan and bring to a boil over medium heat, stirring occasionally. Cook, stirring frequently, until the mixture is thick, like jam, 10 to 12 minutes. Watch carefully, and stir constantly toward the end of cooking to prevent scorching. Stir in the lemon zest, and set aside to cool completely.

2 Adjust an oven rack to the center position and preheat the oven to 400°F. Butter an 8-inch square baking pan and set it aside.

3 Sift the flour with the baking soda and salt; set aside.

4 In a large bowl, beat the butter with an electric mixer on medium speed until smooth, about 1 minute. Add the sugar and beat for 2 to 3 minutes. Stir in the flour mixture, then the oats; the mixture will be crumbly. Press 2 cups of the oatmeal mixture firmly and evenly over the bottom of the prepared pan. Spread with the cooled date mixture and sprinkle the remaining oatmeal mixture over the top. Press it in place gently but firmly (don't pack it down), to make a smooth even layer.

5 Bake for about 25 minutes, or until golden brown. The topping may puff and crack a bit. Cool completely in the pan on a wire rack. Using a small sharp knife, loosen the "cake" from the sides of the pan, then cut into bars. Store airtight.

CHOCOLATE HONEY DATE AND WALNUT BARS

Makes 24 to 36 bars

In these moist, chewy bars, chocolate and dates turn into an almost candylike confection. You will be hard-pressed to identify the dates as such, but they're absolutely essential to the cookies' charm. The walnuts add a crunchy contrast. Be sure to use whole pitted dates; packaged chopped dates are inferior and too sugary. These are welcome in lunch boxes.

²/₃ cup unsweetened cocoa

³/₄ cup plus 2 tablespoons
    all-purpose flour

¹/₂ teaspoon salt

8 tablespoons (1 stick) unsalted
    butter

¹/₃ cup honey

1 cup sugar

3 large eggs

2 teaspoons pure vanilla extract

1 pound moist pitted dried dates,
    preferably Medjool, each cut
    with scissors into 3 or 4 pieces

1 cup coarsely broken walnuts

1 Adjust an oven rack to the center position and preheat the oven to 350°F. Butter a 13-x-9-inch baking pan, or coat with cooking spray; set aside.

2 Sift the cocoa, flour, and salt together; set aside.

3 Place the butter in a medium saucepan over medium heat. When it is partially melted, stir in the honey with a wooden spoon. Remove from the heat and stir in the sugar. Add the eggs one at a time, stirring only until thoroughly mixed in. Stir in the vanilla. Gradually stir in the flour mixture until the batter is smooth. Add the dates and walnuts and mix them in.

4 Scrape the batter into the prepared pan. Spread and pat with a rubber spatula to make an even layer.

5 Bake for 25 to 30 minutes, until the cake barely springs back when gently pressed and a toothpick comes out with a few crumbs sticking to it; do not overbake. Cool to room temperature in the pan on a wire rack. Cut into bars with a sharp knife. Store in an airtight container, or simply cover the pan tightly with foil and leave at room temperature; the bars can also be frozen for up to 2 weeks.

APRICOT COCONUT WALNUT BARS

Makes 16 dessert bars or 48 cookies

This recipe won me second prize in the junior division at the tenth Pillsbury Bake-Off when I was nineteen years old. These bars consist of a thick tart filling of apricots sandwiched between two butter-crumb layers loaded with coconut and walnuts. Serve large portions as a dessert or smaller pieces as a bar cookie. If you decide on the former, accompany them with lightly sweetened whipped cream.

1 pound dried apricots	$3/4$ cup ($1^1/2$ sticks) unsalted butter, at room temperature
2 cups water	
2 cups plus 2 tablespoons sugar	1 cup sweetened shredded coconut
$1^2/3$ cups all-purpose flour	
$1/2$ teaspoon baking soda	1 cup walnuts

1 Combine the apricots with the water in a medium heavy saucepan. Bring to a boil over medium-high heat. Reduce the heat to low, cover, and simmer, stirring occasionally, until the fruit is tender, about 40 minutes. Strain over a bowl and cool for 5 minutes. Reserve $1/4$ cup of the apricot juice. Set the saucepan aside.

2 Combine the apricots, the reserved juice, and 1 cup plus 2 tablespoons of the sugar in a food processor and process until smooth, about 30 seconds. Scrape the puree into the saucepan you used to cook the apricots. (There's no need to wash the food processor.) Bring the apricot puree to a boil over medium-high heat, stirring occasionally. Cook, stirring almost constantly, for 5 minutes. Remove from the heat and let cool to room temperature.

3 Adjust an oven rack to the center position and preheat the oven to 400°F. Butter a 13-x-9-inch baking pan, or coat with cooking spray; set aside.

4 Sift the flour with the baking soda; set aside.

5 Process the remaining 1 cup sugar and the butter in the food processor for 45 seconds. Scrape the work bowl, add the coconut and walnuts, and pulse 4 times. Add the flour mixture and pulse 6 times. Scrape the work bowl and pulse *very quickly* 6 to 8 more times, until the mixture is crumbly and just barely holds together. Transfer the mixture to a large sheet of waxed paper

and break up any lumps with your fingertips. (If your kitchen is very warm, refrigerate the mixture briefly for easier handling.)

6 Press 2¹/₂ cups of the crumb mixture over the bottom and halfway up the sides of the prepared pan. Bake for 10 minutes, or until the crust is lightly colored. Remove from the oven; leave the oven on.

7 Spread the apricot mixture evenly over the hot crust. Sprinkle the remaining crumb mixture on top and pat the crumbs gently into place. Bake until the top is golden brown, 20 to 25 minutes. Cool in the pan on a wire rack. Cut into dessert bars or into bar cookies.

BUTTERCRUNCH LEMON CHEESE BARS

Makes 16 bars

A buttery and crunchy pastry crust lies underneath a tangy lemon filling made with cottage cheese. The secret of these bars is to process the cheese until it has lost its graininess and is completely smooth. These need to be refrigerated for 8 hours, or overnight, before serving. Serve them straight from the refrigerator.

CRUST

6 tablespoons (¾ stick) unsalted butter, at room temperature

¼ teaspoon ground mace

¼ teaspoon salt

¼ cup firmly packed dark brown sugar

¾ cup plus 2 tablespoons all-purpose flour

FILLING

1 cup cottage cheese

Finely grated zest of 1 large lemon

3½ tablespoons fresh lemon juice

1 cup sugar

2 tablespoons all-purpose flour

¼ teaspoon baking powder, preferably nonaluminum

1 large egg

2 large egg whites

1 For the crust, adjust an oven rack to the lower third position and preheat the oven to 350°F. Butter an 8-inch square baking pan and set aside.

2 In a large bowl, beat the butter, mace, and salt with an electric mixer on medium speed until smooth and creamy, about 1 minute. Add the brown sugar and beat for 2 to 3 minutes. Add the flour and beat it in on low speed until thoroughly combined. Press the crust firmly and evenly into the prepared pan.

3 Bake for 20 minutes.

4 Meanwhile, for the filling, process the cottage cheese in a food processor for 2 minutes, or until very smooth. Add the lemon zest, lemon juice, sugar, flour, baking powder, egg, and egg whites and process for 10 seconds. Scrape the work bowl and process for another 10 seconds.

5 Pour the filling over the hot crust. Bake for 25 to 30 minutes, until the filling has puffed slightly and is set; do not overbake. Let cool to room temperature, then refrigerate for at least 8 hours, or overnight. To serve, cut into 16 bars and serve cold.

Variation

Substitute 1 tablespoon finely grated blood orange zest and $1/4$ cup blood orange juice for the lemon zest and juice.

Fruit Desserts

Desserts are like unto the ruffles or trimmings on a garment; they must be used with judgment or they will spoil the entire meal. Avoid heavy desserts where meats have formed a large portion of the dinner.

—Mrs. Rorer, *Mrs. Rorer's New Cook Book* (1902)

A century ago, the average American housewife had a number of options at her disposal if she wanted to follow Mrs. Rorer's sensible advice. Homey fruit cobblers, crumbles, crisps, and Bettys were so commonplace and simple to prepare that few nineteenth-century cookbooks bothered giving recipes for them. All the cook had to do was put some fruit in a baking pan, sweeten it with sugar or molasses, add a bit of spice, and top it with some sort of biscuitlike dough or pastry. If she wanted shortcake, she baked the biscuit dough first, then split and filled it with fresh fruit. Happily, this popular custom has persisted into the twenty-first century, and the informal baked-fruit-with-topping genre is among the most satisfying of all desserts.

Cobblers are fruit baked under a layer of tender pastry. The pastry is thicker than a piecrust and may be a leavened biscuit dough or a regular pastry dough. Crisps are so-called because the fruit is covered with a layer of crunchy, crumbly topping, made by cutting butter into flour, as for a pie dough, but omitting the liquid. Nuts are often added for extra crunch. Crumbles are an English relative of our crisps, with oatmeal added to the topping, and Bettys are made by layering fruit and dried bread crumbs in a pan. The bread acts as a thickener, absorbing the fruit's juices as the dessert bakes.

A tremendous variety of fresh fruit was available to cooks in the eastern and southern states throughout the eighteenth and nineteenth centuries. The second edition of Amelia Simmons's *American Cookery,* published in 1796 in Albany, New York, contains recipes using apples, currants, cranberries, apricots, grapes, gooseberries, pears, damson plums, quinces, raspberries, strawberries, cherries, mulberries, peaches, and a few others. Mary Randolph's classic work, *The Virginia House-Wife* (1824), published hundreds of miles south, features recipes using these same fruits. For eating out of season, fruits were preserved in syrups, jams, or jellies, or they were dried.

America's beloved strawberries grew wild throughout the original colonies. Roger Williams, founder of Providence, Rhode Island, wrote that the strawberry "is the wonder of all the Fruits growing naturally in those parts." Because wild berries were so plentiful then, few people bothered to cultivate them. But as the popula-

SARAH TYSON RORER

Though few cooks today know Mrs. Rorer's name, we've all been influenced by her work in the field of cookery. From the mid-1880s through the mid-1930s, Sarah Tyson Rorer was a cookbook author, cooking teacher, magazine editor, food chemist, nutritionist, dietician, product spokesperson, renowned public speaker and lecturer, and wife and mother. Her most famous works are *Mrs. Rorer's Philadelphia Cook Book* (1886), and *Mrs. Rorer's New Cook Book* (1902). Her advice on diet from a century ago is thoroughly up to date. She advocated healthful eating, favoring vegetables, fruits, and small portions of meat, and she stressed the importance of a moderate intake of fat.

Mrs. Rorer believed that a woman's place was in the home. She said, "I believe that work outside is so disagreeable and unpleasant that the Lord gave it to the men to do. Let them have it." In other regards, she was the epitome of modernity. She appeared at her standing-room-only demonstrations gowned in silk and an apron, and at the conclusion of preparing a four- or five-course meal from scratch in under an hour, her clothing was always spotless. All her efforts were intended to prove that with a basic knowledge of cookery and organization, kitchen work need not be messy or drudgery, but something a woman could feel proud of.

Mrs. Rorer's life encompassed most of the major changes of the twentieth century. She was born in 1847, at a time when cast-iron ranges were replacing brick ovens, the Oregon Trail was at its peak, and the fastest way to get around was by horse. She died in 1937, when airplanes were transporting passengers around the world and homes were equipped with electric stoves, mixers, and refrigerators.

tion spread, cultivation began in the early part of the nineteenth century. By the 1880s more than 100,000 acres of strawberries were under cultivation, compared to only 1,400 at the turn of the century. In a single night in June 1847, the Erie Railroad transported 80,000 baskets of strawberries to New York City on its milk train. Today, strawberries are grown in all fifty states, with about 75 percent of the crop coming from California.

Over time, apples would become the nation's most popular fruit, both for eating and cooking. Unlike strawberries, many varieties could be stored fresh for months in a root cellar, packed in sand or between layers of hay or straw. We have Johnny Appleseed (John Chapman) to thank for spreading apples from the east to the Midwest early in our country's history. Born in 1774 in Massachusetts, Johnny Appleseed was a lover of nature, and early in his life he developed a passion for apples. Soon after the Lewis and Clark expedition ended in 1806, people began the westward migration across the country. Knowing how important apples were to Americans, Johnny Appleseed planted orchards stretching from Pennsylvania to Iowa. He tended his seedlings and gave them to newly arrived settlers.

Along with the familiar fruits, exotic fruits began appearing during colonial times. The pineapple, in particular, attained celebrity status because a fresh one was expensive and rare, and, as a centerpiece, it made a beautiful topic of conversation. Less affluent hostesses sometimes rented pineapples by the day from a confectioner for just that purpose. Over time, because of the extravagance such a display represented, the pineapple came to be a symbol of hospitality. Faster ships in the late 1800s made pineapples more accessible to the population as a whole, but it wasn't until 1899, when pineapple canning began in Hawaii, that the fruit became available for the first time to a worldwide mass market.

Canned pineapple became a sensation. It was served in salads, fruit cocktails, pies, sherbets, and in all sorts of other desserts. And in the 1920s, someone thought to turn the whole baked-fruit-dessert-with-topping idea literally upside down, and the pineapple upside-down cake was born. This idea is still so appealing that we continue to make variations on the theme using all sorts of other fruits. Mrs. Rorer would approve.

OLD-FASHIONED STRAWBERRY SHORTCAKE

Makes 6 servings

Strawberry shortcake must be made with the ripest, most succulent, in-season berries, or not at all. Whoever was inspired to make the first strawberry shortcake is anybody's guess, but recipes for biscuits began appearing in American cookbooks in the early 1800s. The earliest printed recipe I know of for strawberry shortcake dates to 1841, but it probably appeared well before that, once chemical leaveners were used to make biscuits. Given the abundance of both wild and cultivated strawberries in America, strawberry shortcake may well have been a culinary inevitability. In *Food and Drink in America,* Richard J. Hooker suggests that it is probably of New England origin. Lydia Maria Child, a Massachusetts native, had a recipe for Short Cake in her 1829 book *The American Frugal Housewife.* Although there is no instruction for serving the shortcake with strawberries or any other fruit, this may have been something taken for granted.

The following recipe for strawberry shortcake uses a rich, tender biscuit dough, made especially moist by the addition of cooked egg yolk, a technique employed by James Beard. The shortcakes should be baked just before serving, but you can cut them out ahead of time and refrigerate for up to 2 hours.

STRAWBERRIES

- 2 pints ripe strawberries
- 2–4 tablespoons sugar

SHORTCAKES

- 2 cups all-purpose flour
- 1/4 cup sugar
- 1 tablespoon baking powder, preferably nonaluminum
- 1/4 teaspoon salt
- 5 tablespoons cold unsalted butter, cut into tablespoon-sized pieces
- 3 hard-cooked large egg yolks
- 3/4–1 cup heavy cream

- 1 tablespoon unsalted butter, melted
- 1 tablespoon sugar

WHIPPED CREAM

- 1 cup heavy cream
- 1/2 teaspoon pure vanilla extract

- 2–4 tablespoons unsalted butter, melted

1 Prepare the strawberries about 1 hour before serving. Rinse, pat dry on paper towels, hull, and halve, quarter, or slice, depending on their size. Place them in a medium bowl, taste them, and add sugar according to their sweetness. Set aside.

2 For the shortcakes, adjust an oven rack to the center position and preheat the oven to 375°F.

3 Combine the flour, sugar, baking powder, and salt in a medium bowl. Add the chilled butter and cut it in with a pastry blender or work it in using your fingertips until the particles are very fine. Force the egg yolks through a fine sieve and stir them into the flour mixture. (If you wish, use a food processor to cut the butter into the flour until the mixture is very fine; add the whole egg yolks and pulse them in until very fine, then transfer the mixture to a medium bowl.)

4 Add ³/₄ cup of the heavy cream and stir gently with a fork until the dough is moistened and just holds together. It should be fairly stiff, but if necessary, add more cream a little at a time, stirring until the dough just gathers together. Scrape the dough onto a lightly floured work surface and dust all surfaces lightly with flour. Pat the dough gently to a scant ³/₄-inch thickness. With a floured 3-inch round cutter, cut out 4 biscuits and place them 2 inches apart on an ungreased heavy baking sheet. Gather the scraps and form them as gently as possible into a smooth mass. Pat the dough out again and cut 2 more biscuits. Place them on the baking sheet. (If you are not ready to bake, refrigerate them, lightly covered with plastic wrap, for up to 2 hours. Bring to room temperature before baking.)

5 Brush the tops of the biscuits lightly with the melted butter and sprinkle them with the sugar. Bake for about 15 minutes, or until golden brown and a toothpick inserted into the center comes out clean. Let stand for 2 to 3 minutes on the baking sheet, just until cool enough to handle.

6 Meanwhile, for the whipped cream, whip the cream with the vanilla until it holds a soft shape. Refrigerate until ready to serve.

7 Using a sharp serrated knife, carefully split the hot biscuits horizontally in half. Brush the cut surfaces with melted butter and spoon some of the strawberry juices over them. Place the bottom halves of the shortcakes on

dessert plates and heap them with the strawberries and any remaining juices. Spoon large dollops of cream over the berries, cover with the tops of the shortcakes, and serve immediately.

PERFECT SHORTCAKE

My mother made strawberry shortcake in a small dripping pan and of a very rich biscuit dough. When this was baked to flaky perfection it was turned on to a platter and split in two. The top half was laid aside and the bottom part lavishly spread with butter. Over this the berries (already crushed in a blue and white porcelain bowl) were thickly poured. Then the top half was laid over this (still piping hot), fulsomely buttered, while the remainder of the berries completely canopied the whole. The juice ran off and made a crimson lake on which the shortcake rested. It was then set in the oven to "ripen" for a few minutes. A pitcher of cream on the table acted as accompaniment for those who wanted it. When we had shortcake we had but little else, nor needed more. Here was a dish complete in itself, perfect in quality, adequate in quantity, and presenting a feast sufficient for gods or epicurean man.

—Della T. Lutes, *The Country Kitchen* (1935)

APPLE BROWN BETTY

*Makes 8
servings*

This is an old classic American recipe that probably came about as a way of using up stale bread and whatever fruit happened to be around, which probably meant apples. Use day-old firm-textured bread, such as French or Italian. A small amount of rye crumbs (about $1/3$ cup) adds a nice tang. For the apples, any tart semifirm kind will work. Macoun, Winesap, Jonathan, and Newtown Pippin are all good choices.

3 tablespoons unsalted butter

2 cups loosely packed coarsely
   torn bread ($1/2$-inch pieces)
   from day-old bread (see
   above)

$1/3$ cup sugar

$1/3$ cup firmly packed light brown
   sugar

1 teaspoon ground cinnamon

$1/4$ teaspoon ground allspice

$1/4$ teaspoon ground mace

$1/8$ teaspoon salt

2 pounds tart semifirm apples
   (about 5 medium or 4 large),
   quartered, cored, peeled, and
   sliced crosswise $1/4$ inch thick

$1/2$ cup apple cider
   Finely grated zest of 1 lemon

2 tablespoons fresh lemon juice

1 teaspoon pure vanilla extract

1 Adjust an oven rack to the center position and preheat the oven to 375°F.

2 Melt the butter in a 10-inch skillet over medium-low heat and cook until the butter solids and liquid are golden brown, about 8 minutes. Remove from the heat and stir in the bread crumbs; set aside.

3 In a large bowl, combine both sugars, the cinnamon, allspice, mace, and salt. Add the apples, apple cider, lemon zest, lemon juice, and vanilla and combine well. Turn half of the apple mixture (including half the liquid) into an 8-inch square baking pan. Sprinkle with half the crumbs. Place the remaining apple mixture on top, spreading it evenly, and sprinkle with the remaining crumbs.

4 Bake for 1 hour, until the fruit is tender, the juices bubbly, and the crumb topping golden brown. Halfway during cooking, use a wide metal spatula to press down on the apple mixture. When the Betty is done, remove from the oven and press down again with the metal spatula. Cool on a wire rack until warm, and serve.

APPLE-PLUM CRISP

Makes 8 servings

Apples and plums make a splendid crisp. The plums add both sweetness and tartness and turn the filling a beautiful burgundy color. I like to use first-of-the-season McIntosh apples, since they have a fabulous buttery texture. Lacking these, use any tart late-season mature apple, such as Sweet Sixteen, Cameo, Braeburn, Northern Spy, or York Imperial.

TOPPING

- 1 cup all-purpose flour
- ½ cup firmly packed dark brown sugar
- 8 tablespoons (1 stick) cold unsalted butter, cut into tablespoon-sized pieces
- 1½ teaspoons ground cinnamon

FILLING

- 6 cups (about 2 pounds), cored, peeled, and sliced McIntosh apples
- ½ cup sugar
  Finely grated zest of 1 lemon
- 1 tablespoon fresh lemon juice
- 1 pound Italian prune plums, halved and pitted

1 Adjust an oven rack to the center position and preheat the oven to 400°F. Butter a 9-inch square baking pan and set aside.

2 For the topping, place all the ingredients in a food processor and pulse until the butter is chopped into small pieces. Or, place all the ingredients in a large bowl and cut in the butter with a pastry blender or two knives until the particles resemble coarse crumbs; set aside.

3 For the filling, toss the apples with the sugar, lemon zest, and lemon juice in a large bowl to combine well. Add the plums and mix them in gently.

4 Place the filling in the prepared pan and spread the fruit out evenly with your fingers. Sprinkle the topping evenly over to cover the fruit completely. Bang the pan on the countertop a few times to settle the topping among the pieces of fruit, and pat it gently in place without packing it down. Wipe the rim of the pan clean.

5 Bake for 35 to 45 minutes, until the topping is well browned, the juices are thickened, and the fruit is tender when pierced with the tip of a small sharp knife. Cool on a wire rack (the crisp will sink as it cools), and serve warm or at room temperature.

GINGERED McINTOSH CRISP

Makes 8 to 10 servings

First-of-the-season McIntosh apples make a sensational crisp. Here the fruit is flavored with crystallized ginger, lemon, and vanilla and covered with a buttery cinnamon topping. You can add a cup of blueberries or raspberries if you like. This is best served warm, and it is especially good with a scoop of vanilla ice cream, vanilla frozen yogurt, or lightly sweetened whipped cream. When McIntosh apples aren't available, substitute Macoun, Braeburn, or Rome Beauty, or use a combination of two or three types.

TOPPING

- 1 cup all-purpose flour
- 1/2 cup firmly packed light or dark brown sugar
- 1 teaspoon ground cinnamon
- 1/4 teaspoon ground mace
- 8 tablespoons (1 stick) cold unsalted butter, cut into tablespoon-sized pieces

FILLING

- 1/2 cup sugar
- 1/4 cup finely chopped crystallized ginger
- Finely grated zest of 1 lemon
- 2 tablespoons fresh lemon juice
- 1 teaspoon pure vanilla extract
- 3 pounds McIntosh apples (about 8 medium), quartered, cored, peeled, and thinly sliced

1 Adjust an oven rack to the center position and preheat the oven to 400°F. Butter a 2¹/₂-quart ovenproof dish, such as a 9-inch square or 10 inch round dish; set aside.

2 For the topping, process the flour, brown sugar, cinnamon, and mace in a food processor for 10 seconds. Add the butter and pulse 8 to 10 times, until the butter is chopped into medium-small pieces; set aside.

3 For the filling, combine the sugar, ginger, lemon zest, lemon juice, and vanilla in a large bowl. Add the apples and fold together gently until the fruit is well moistened. Spread in the prepared baking dish and distribute the crumb mixture evenly on top.

4 Bake for 45 to 50 minutes, until the filling is bubbly and the top is browned. Cool on a wire rack, and serve warm or at room temperature.

NECTARINE-RASPBERRY CRISP

*Makes
8 to 10
servings*

Yellow nectarines reach their peak in the market just as our raspberries ripen. The two are wonderful together, either raw or cooked. Do not use white nectarines in this dessert. They are too sweet and watery. The topping for this crisp is extra crunchy and buttery.

TOPPING

- 1 cup all-purpose flour
- 1/2 cup firmly packed light brown sugar
- 1 teaspoon freshly grated nutmeg
- 1/4 teaspoon salt
- 8 tablespoons (1 stick) cold unsalted butter, cut in tablespoon-sized pieces
- 1/2 cup old-fashioned or quick-cooking (not instant) rolled oats

FILLING

- 2 tablespoons sugar
- 1/2 teaspoon freshly grated nutmeg
  Pinch of salt
  Finely grated zest of 1 lemon
- 2 1/2 pounds firm but ripe yellow nectarines (8–9), halved, pitted, and sliced into 1/2-inch wedges
- 2 cups fresh red or golden raspberries
- 2 tablespoons fresh lemon juice

1 Adjust an oven rack to the lower third position and preheat the oven to 400°F. Lightly butter a 2 1/2-quart baking dish, such as a 12-x-8-inch or round 10-x-2-inch pan.

2 For the topping, place the flour, brown sugar, nutmeg, and salt in a food processor. Pulse a few times to combine. Add the butter and pulse until it is in small pieces. Add the oats and process for 1 to 2 seconds, just to combine. Set aside.

3 For the filling, combine the sugar, nutmeg, salt, and lemon zest in a large bowl. Add the nectarines, raspberries, and lemon juice and fold everything together gently with a large rubber spatula. Spread the filling evenly in the baking dish.

4 Sprinkle the crumb mixture on top of the fruit, and spread it evenly with your hands to completely cover the fruit. Pat the filling gently in place, without packing it down.

5 Bake for 1 hour, or until the topping is lightly browned and the juices are thickened and bubbly. Cool on a wire rack, and serve warm or at room temperature. Refrigerate leftovers.

SPOON SCIENCE

A spoon means that the material should lie as much above the edge of the spoon as the bowl sinks below it. A heaping teaspoon means that the material should be twice as high above the edge of the spoon as the bowl sinks below it. A level teaspoon should hold sixty drops of water. . . . A speck is what can be placed within a quarter inch square surface.

— *The Pillsbury Cook-Book* (1914)

Got that?

RASPBERRY COBBLER

Makes 8 to 10 servings

Cobblers are an old American dessert, and they may be made with just about any fruit. In this recipe, raspberries are topped with a biscuit batter, a sugar-cornstarch mixture is sprinkled over it, and boiling water is poured over that. The raspberry juices become slightly thickened, the biscuit layer emerges tender and buttery, and the top of the cobbler has a shiny, crisp crust of sugar. The unusual method comes from my friend Pat Gray, who found it in a magazine twenty years ago.

6 cups (3 pints) fresh raspberries	1/2 teaspoon salt
2 tablespoons fresh lemon juice	4 tablespoons (1/2 stick) cold unsalted butter, cut into tablespoon-sized pieces
1 1/4 cups all-purpose flour	
1 1/2 cups sugar	
1 teaspoon baking powder, preferably nonaluminum	2/3 cup milk
	1 1/2 tablespoons cornstarch
	1 cup boiling water

1 Adjust an oven rack to the center position and preheat the oven to 350°F.

2 Carefully spread the raspberries in a 2 1/2-quart shallow baking dish, such as a 12-x-8-inch or 10-inch round dish. Drizzle with the lemon juice; set aside.

3 Sift the flour, 1/4 cup of the sugar, the baking powder, and salt into a medium bowl. Cut the butter in with a pastry blender or two knives until the particles resemble coarse crumbs. Add the milk and stir only until the dry ingredients are moistened. Using two small teaspoons, one to scoop up the batter and the other to scrape it onto the fruit, place about half of the batter in small mounds all around the edges of the dish. Spread the batter evenly with the back of a spoon. Place the remaining batter by spoonfuls over the fruit in the center and spread carefully into an even layer, covering the fruit completely.

4 Mix the remaining 1 1/4 cups sugar with the cornstarch in a small bowl. Sprinkle evenly over the batter. Carefully pour the boiling water all over the top.

5 Bake for 50 minutes. Increase the temperature to 400°F and bake for about 10 minutes longer, until the cobbler is well browned and the juices are bubbly. Cool on a wire rack, and serve warm or at room temperature.

Variations

You can use just about any fruit or fruit combination that strikes your fancy. Figure on 6 cups of fruit total.

1. Rhubarb. Cut the stalks into $^1/_2$-inch pieces. Mix the fruit with $^1/_4$ cup sugar and 1 to 2 teaspoons grated fresh ginger; replace the lemon juice with 1 tablespoon vanilla extract.

2. Rhubarb-Strawberry. Use 4 cups cut-up rhubarb and 2 cups sliced strawberries, mixed with $^1/_4$ cup sugar. Add $^1/_2$ teaspoon ground cinnamon to the fruit.

3. Blueberry, Raspberry, and Blackberry. Use 2 cups of each fruit.

4. Peach. Peel, pit, and cut 2 pounds of the fruit into $^1/_2$-inch slices; you should have 6 cups. Combine with the lemon juice, $^1/_2$ teaspoon pumpkin pie spice, and $^1/_2$ teaspoon almond extract.

5. Peach, Raspberry, and Blueberry. Use 2 cups of each fruit. Peel and dice the peaches. Season with the lemon juice, $^1/_2$ teaspoon ground cinnamon, and 2 teaspoons pure vanilla extract.

SHERRY COBBLER

The old-fashioned meaning of *cobbler* was a drink. Here's how Miss Leslie prepared one:

Lay in the bottom of a large tumbler, two table-spoonfuls of powdered loaf sugar, and squeeze over it (through a strainer) the juice of a large lemon that has been softened by rolling under your hand. Then half fill the tumbler with ice, broken very small. Add a large glass of very good sherry wine. Take another tumbler, and pour the liquid back and forward from glass to glass, till completely mixed without stirring. Sip it through a clean straw, or one of the tubes made on purpose.

—Eliza Leslie, *Miss Leslie's New Cookery Book* (1857)

Sounds mighty refreshing!

PEACHES AND CREAM COBBLER

Makes 6 to 8 servings

My, oh my, this is about as good as it gets: peaches and cream and cream cheese and egg yolks, baked under a tender, buttery biscuit crust. In the oven, the dessert creates its own custardy sauce. Make it only when peaches are really fine.

PASTRY

- 1¼ cups all-purpose flour
- ¼ cup sugar
- ½ teaspoon baking soda
- ¼ teaspoon salt
- 5 tablespoons cold unsalted butter, cut into tablespoon-sized pieces
- ⅔ cup buttermilk

FILLING

- 3 pounds ripe peaches (about 9 medium)
- 4 ounces cream cheese
- ½ cup sugar
- 1 teaspoon pure vanilla extract
- ⅛ teaspoon pure almond extract
- 1 teaspoon pumpkin pie spice
- 2 large egg yolks
- ½ cup heavy cream

Milk for brushing

1 tablespoon sugar

1 For the pastry, sift the flour, sugar, baking soda, and salt into a large mixing bowl. Add the butter and cut it in with a pastry blender or two knives until the butter pieces are pea-sized. Stir in the buttermilk with a fork just until the dough gathers into a ball. Sprinkle your work surface lightly with flour and scrape the dough onto it. Toss the dough about to coat it lightly with flour.

2 You will need a 2½-quart baking dish, either a 9-inch square or a 10-inch round for the cobbler. Pat or roll the dough out into a 9-inch square or 10-inch round, depending on your baking dish. The dough is soft and tender, so handle it gently. Carefully transfer the dough to a cookie sheet, using two large spatulas or pastry scrapers, and refrigerate.

3 Adjust one oven rack in the center and the other at the lowest position. Set a large baking sheet on the lower rack to catch any juices that may bubble over, and preheat the oven to 400°F.

4 For the filling, prepare to peel the peaches by bringing a large pot of water to a boil. Drop in 3 peaches at a time and blanch for 30 to 40 seconds. Immediately remove the peaches with a slotted spoon and place them in a large bowl of cold water. As soon as the peaches are cool, remove from the water and strip off their skins with a sharp paring knife. If you're working with freestone peaches, cut them in half along their natural dividing line, twist the halves gently in opposite directions, and separate the halves. Remove the pits and slice each peach half into 4 or 5 wedges. If you have cling peaches, slice the peeled peaches into wedges and cut the pieces off the pits.

5 Beat the cream cheese in a large bowl with an electric mixer until smooth. Add the sugar, vanilla and almond extracts, and pumpkin pie spice and beat for 2 to 3 minutes. Add the egg yolks and beat for 1 minute. Beat in the cream on low speed just until combined. Fold in the peaches. Turn into the baking dish.

6 Carefully place the pastry on top (it should just come to the edges of the dish) and brush lightly with milk. Sprinkle with the sugar and pierce the pastry in 6 to 8 places with the tip of a sharp paring knife.

7 Place the dish on the center oven shelf and bake for 45 to 50 minutes, until the top is a deep golden brown and the filling bubbles up around the edges. Cool on a wire rack, and serve warm or at room temperature. Refrigerate leftovers.

Variations

1. If you like nuts in your cobbler toppings, add 1/3 cup chopped walnuts or pecans to the flour mixture before stirring in the buttermilk.

2. To make a softer batter that you drop in spoonfuls over the filling, increase the buttermilk to 3/4 cup. Drop 8 to 10 mounds of batter evenly over the filling, brush each lightly with milk, and sprinkle with sugar.

3. Add 1 cup raspberries or 1 cup blueberries, picked over, to the peaches when folding them into the cream cheese mixture.

APPLE-CRANBERRY COBBLER

Makes 8 servings

Cranberries tint the apples a seductive pink color in this homey, tart, old-fashioned cobbler. McIntosh is my first-choice apple, and the fruit on our own tree ripens at just about the time cranberries first begin appearing in the markets in the fall. But you can make the cobbler with any apple that becomes soft and tender during a brief baking. Macouns are another good choice. No thickener is used in the fruit mixture: cranberries have lots of natural pectin, as do apples.

FILLING

- ½ cup sugar
- ¾ teaspoon pumpkin pie spice
- ¾ cup fresh orange juice (grate the zest for the batter first)
- ¼ cup water
- 1½ cups fresh or frozen (not thawed) cranberries
- 2 tablespoons dark rum (I use Myers's)
- 6 cups peeled and cubed (½-inch) McIntosh or other tart apples (about 1½ pounds)

BATTER

- 1 cup all-purpose flour
- ¼ cup sugar
- 1 teaspoon baking powder, preferably nonaluminum
- ¼ teaspoon baking soda
- ¼ teaspoon salt
- 4 tablespoons (½ stick) cold unsalted butter, cut into 4 pieces
- Grated zest of 1 orange
- ⅔ cup buttermilk
- 1 pint vanilla frozen yogurt

1 Adjust an oven rack to the center position and preheat the oven to 400°F.

2 For the filling, combine the sugar, pumpkin pie spice, orange juice, water, and cranberries in a medium heavy saucepan. Cook over medium-high heat, stirring gently and constantly with a heatproof rubber spatula, until the mixture comes to a boil. Cover, reduce the heat to low, and simmer for about 5 minutes, mashing the fruit with the spatula, until the cranberries are tender and the sauce is slightly thickened. Stir in the rum and apples. Let cool.

3 For the batter, sift the flour, sugar, baking powder, baking soda, and salt to-

gether into a medium bowl. Add the butter and cut it in with a pastry blender or two knives until the particles resemble coarse meal. Add the orange zest and buttermilk and stir with a fork just until the batter is thoroughly moistened.

4 Transfer the fruit mixture to a 9-inch square pan or round 10-x-2-inch baking dish. Spoon the batter on top in 8 even mounds, 7 around the side and one in the middle, leaving space between them.

5 Bake for about 35 minutes, until the filling is bubbly and the top is well browned. Cool on a rack, and serve warm or at room temperature accompanied by the frozen yogurt.

TO KEEP APPLES FOR WINTER USE

Put them in casks or bins, in layers well covered with dry sand, each layer being covered. This preserves them from air, from moisture, and from frost; it prevents their perishing by their own perspiration, their moisture being absorbed by the sand; at the same time it preserves the flavor of the apples, and prevents their wilting. Pippins have been kept in this manner sound and fresh till mid-summer; and how much longer they would have kept is not known. Any kind of sand will answer, but it must be perfectly dry. If apples are immersed in grain of any kind, they will keep good all the year round, and the grain will not in any way be the worse for it.

—Mrs. E. A. Howland, *The New England Economical Housekeeper* (1845)

APRICOT-BERRY CRUMBLE

Makes 8 to 10 servings

Crumbles are baked fruit desserts with a topping containing oats. According to Richard Sax's *Classic Home Desserts,* they are an English version of American crisps. This crumble, while still maintaining the simplicity of its ancestors, is a bit more sophisticated. Fresh apricots, raspberries, and blueberries, flavored with a few kernels of apricot pits, lemon zest, lemon juice, and sugar, bake under a generous topping.

FILLING

- 2 pounds ripe but firm apricots (14–16), halved and pitted; 8 apricot pits reserved, cracked with a hammer and kernels removed
- 1 cup firmly packed light brown sugar
  Finely grated zest of 1 lemon
- 1¹/₂ cups fresh raspberries
- 1¹/₂ cups fresh blueberries, picked over
- 2 tablespoons fresh lemon juice

TOPPING

- 1 cup all-purpose flour
- ¹/₄ teaspoon salt
- 1 teaspoon ground cinnamon
- ³/₄ cup old-fashioned or quick-cooking (not instant) rolled oats
- 10 tablespoons (1¹/₄ sticks) cold unsalted butter, cut into 10 tablespoon-sized pieces

1 Adjust an oven rack to the lower third position and preheat the oven to 375°F.

2 Place the apricots in a 2¹/₂-quart baking dish, such as a 10-inch round, 9-inch square, or 12-x-8-inch rectangular dish.

3 For the filling, place the apricot kernels and ¹/₄ cup of the brown sugar in a food processor and process for about 30 seconds, until the kernels are finely ground. Add the lemon zest and process for 5 to 10 seconds. Scrape the mixture over the apricots (set the processor bowl aside) and combine well with your fingers. Scatter the raspberries and blueberries over the apricots, and drizzle with the lemon juice. Set aside.

4 For the topping, add the flour, salt, cinnamon, oats, and the remaining brown sugar to the food processor and process for 10 seconds. Add the butter and pulse only until the mixture resembles coarse crumbs: stop to check the mixture after every 3 or 4 pulses. Spread the mixture evenly over the fruit, but don't pack it down.

5 Bake for 50 to 60 minutes, until the topping is crisp and browned and the fruit is bubbly and tender. Test with the tip of a small sharp knife. Cool the crumble on a wire rack, and serve warm or at room temperature.

Variations

Figure on 8 cups total fruit, and balance the sweet with the tart. Don't be afraid to use some dried fruits, such as sour cherries or blueberries, with fresh in-season fruits.

1. In the fall, make this with apples (Braeburn or Cameo are good varieties) and cranberries. Use about 6 cups peeled, thinly sliced apples and 2 cups chopped cranberries. Substitute grated orange zest and orange juice for the lemon.

2. Pears and pineapple, about 4 cups of each, with about 1 teaspoon grated fresh ginger, are another good combination. Or use $1/2$ teaspoon crushed anise seeds instead of the ginger, and 1 tablespoon Pernod. Almond flavoring also goes well with these fruits, and since they're so juicy, a few crushed amaretti cookies can be mixed with them.

3. In the spring, use 6 cups cut-up rhubarb and 2 cups sliced strawberries. Substitute orange zest and juice for the lemon, and sprinkle the fruit with a tablespoon of pure vanilla extract, too.

RHUBARB RASPBERRY CRUNCH BARS

Makes 9 servings

This dessert is a showcase for rhubarb and raspberries. The filling is baked between layers of a crunchy, buttery brown-sugar crumb mixture that will remind you of butterscotch. And the filling's bright red color is sensational! A rosy pink topping of whipped heavy cream and raspberries adds the finishing touch to a basically simple dessert.

FRUIT

- 1 pound trimmed rhubarb, cut into 1/2-inch pieces (4 cups)
- 1 cup plus 2 tablespoons sugar
- 2 1/2 tablespoons cornstarch
  Pinch of salt
- 1 1/2 cups fresh raspberries
- 1 tablespoon framboise (raspberry liqueur) or 1/2 teaspoon pure almond extract

TOPPING

- 8 tablespoons (1 stick) unsalted butter, melted
- 1 teaspoon ground cinnamon
- 1 cup old-fashioned or quick-cooking (not instant) rolled oats
- 1 cup firmly packed dark brown sugar
- 1 1/3 cups all-purpose flour

RASPBERRY CREAM

- 1 cup heavy cream
- 2 tablespoons sugar
- 1/2 teaspoon pure vanilla extract
- 1/2 cup fresh raspberries

  Raspberries for topping (optional)

1 For the fruit, combine the rhubarb in a bowl with the sugar; cover and let stand for several hours, until the sugar is dissolved and the rhubarb has released its liquid. (The rhubarb can be prepared the night before and refrigerated.)

2 Adjust an oven rack to the center position and preheat the oven to 325°F.

3 Drain the rhubarb well in a strainer set over a large bowl. Measure the juices; add water, if necessary, to make 1 cup. Place the liquid in a medium heavy saucepan and stir in the cornstarch and salt until dissolved. Cook over medium heat, stirring constantly with a heatproof rubber spatula, until the mixture thickens and boils. When it is translucent, reduce the heat to medium-low and continue cooking and stirring for 1 minute

longer. The sauce will be thick. Remove from the heat and stir in the rhubarb, raspberries, and the framboise or almond extract. Set aside.

4 For the topping, stir the melted butter with the cinnamon in a large bowl. Add the oats, brown sugar, and flour and stir well to moisten the dry ingredients: use your fingers to be sure everything is thoroughly combined and the mixture is damp but crumbly. Press 2 cups of the crumbs into the bottom of an ungreased 9-inch square baking pan. Spoon the rhubarb mixture over the crust, and sprinkle evenly with the remaining crumb mixture. Pat the crumbs gently to compact them slightly.

5 Bake for 55 to 65 minutes, until the topping is well browned. Cool on a wire rack until warm or at room temperature.

6 Meanwhile, for the raspberry cream, whip the cream with the sugar and the vanilla in a small bowl until softly thickened. Mash the $1/2$ cup raspberries with a fork just to break them up a bit, and add them to the cream. Continue whipping until the cream is thick and holds its shape. Cover and refrigerate.

7 To serve, cut the dessert into 9 squares and set on dessert plates. Top each square with a dollop of the whipped cream. Decorate with additional raspberries, if desired. Serve at once.

PLUM KUCHEN

Makes 8 to 10 servings

Kuchen is German for "cake," and many such cakes—thick batters spread in a thin layer and baked—are made with fruit. You can use almost any kind of fruit, such as apples, peaches, or apricots, but this kuchen made with Italian prune plums is especially fine. The batter is very easy to make, and it bakes into an exquisitely delicate and light cake. When prune plums are in season, I bake and freeze several of these cakes for a taste of summer in the wintertime.

BATTER

1½ cups sifted all-purpose flour
1½ teaspoons baking powder, preferably nonaluminum
½ teaspoon salt
½ teaspoon freshly grated nutmeg
⅓ cup sugar
5 tablespoons cold unsalted butter, cut into tablespoon-sized pieces

1 large egg
⅓ cup milk
1½ teaspoons pure vanilla extract

25–30 Italian prune plums (1½–2 pounds), halved and pitted

TOPPING

¼ cup sugar
1 teaspoon ground cinnamon
3 tablespoons unsalted butter, melted

1 Adjust an oven rack to the lower third position and preheat the oven to 400°F. Butter or grease a 13-x-9-inch baking pan (do not use cooking spray) and set aside. (If you plan to freeze the kuchen, butter the pan and line it with aluminum foil, leaving any overhanging edges of foil alone.)

2 For the batter, resift the flour with the baking powder, salt, nutmeg, and sugar into a large bowl. Cut in the butter with a pastry blender or two knives until the mixture resembles coarse crumbs.

3 In a small bowl, lightly beat the egg with a fork. Stir in the milk and vanilla, and pour into the flour mixture. Stir with the fork until the mixture is thoroughly moistened. Place small spoonfuls of the batter in the prepared pan, spacing them 1 to 2 inches apart. Spread them with the back

of the spoon into a very thin even layer, swirling the spoon back and forth in a figure-eight pattern. Arrange the plums cut side down in tightly packed rows on top of the batter.

4 For the topping, combine the sugar with the cinnamon in a small bowl. Brush the plums with the melted butter, and sprinkle the cinnamon sugar evenly over them.

5 Bake for 35 to 45 minutes, until the fruit juices have almost stopped bubbling and a toothpick inserted into the cake portion comes out clean. Cool in the pan on a wire rack until warm or at room temperature.

Note: To freeze the kuchen, grasp the edges of the foil and carefully lift the cooled cake out of the pan. Set the cake on a baking sheet and place in the freezer. When it is solidly frozen, peel off the foil and wrap the cake securely in plastic wrap, then in heavy-duty foil. Store in the freezer for up to 6 months. To reheat, unwrap the frozen cake, set it on a baking sheet, and tent it loosely with the foil. Bake in a preheated 300°F oven for 20 to 30 minutes, until it is completely thawed and slightly warm.

OLD-FASHIONED PINEAPPLE UPSIDE-DOWN CAKE

Makes one 10-inch cake, 8 to 10 servings

Pineapple upside-down cake dates to the 1920s. Traditionally it is made with canned pineapple, with maraschino cherries filling the holes in the pineapple rings. I much prefer fresh pineapple, and that is what I use when I can get the ones from Maui—picked ripe and bursting with flavor. Pineapples do not get any sweeter once picked, so it is important to buy a completely ripe one. I use macadamia nuts instead of the cherries. A cast-iron skillet will give you the best results.

1 fresh pineapple (3–4 pounds)

TOPPING

4 tablespoons ($^1/_2$ stick) unsalted butter

$^3/_4$ cup firmly packed light brown sugar

About $^1/_2$ cup whole macadamia nuts (salted or unsalted)

CAKE

1$^1/_2$ cups sifted all-purpose flour

$^1/_2$ teaspoon baking soda

$^1/_4$ teaspoon salt

6 tablespoons ($^3/_4$ stick) unsalted butter, at room temperature

$^3/_4$ cup sugar

2 teaspoons pure vanilla extract

2 large eggs

$^3/_4$ cup buttermilk

1 To prepare the pineapple, cut 1 to 2 inches off the top and stem end with a chef's knife. Stand the pineapple upright on a work surface, and cut away the skin in strips, cutting deeply enough to remove any "eyes." Turn the pineapple sideways and cut into 8 to 10 $^1/_2$-inch-thick circles. Use a small cookie cutter to remove the pineapple core and to make pineapple rings.

2 Adjust an oven rack to the center position and preheat the oven to 350°F.

3 For the topping, melt the butter in a 10-inch cast-iron skillet over medium heat. Add the brown sugar, and cook, stirring with a wooden spoon, until the mixture is thick and bubbly and the sugar has almost dissolved. Remove from the heat and carefully arrange the pineapple in the syrup, pressing the rings down. Fill in the spaces with macadamia nuts. Set aside.

4 For the cake, resift the flour with the baking soda and salt; set aside.

5 In a large bowl, beat the butter with an electric mixer on medium speed until smooth and creamy, about 1 minute. Add $1/4$ cup of the sugar and the vanilla and beat for 2 minutes. Beat in the remaining $1/2$ cup sugar about 2 tablespoons at a time, beating each addition in thoroughly, then beat for 2 minutes. Beat in the eggs one at a time, beating for 1 minute after each. Using a rubber spatula, stir in the flour mixture in 3 additions, alternating with the buttermilk, beginning and ending with the flour and stirring only until the batter is smooth. Pour the batter over the fruit and spread it level.

6 Bake for about 40 minutes, until the cake is well browned and springs back when gently pressed in the center and a toothpick comes out clean. Run the tip of a small sharp knife all around the edges to release the cake. Cover with a dessert platter, hold it firmly in place, and invert the two. Wait for 1 minute, then carefully lift off the skillet. If any fruit or nuts have stuck to the pan, place them back on the cake. Serve warm or at room temperature.

MAPLE-PEAR UPSIDE-DOWN CAKE

Makes one 10-inch cake, 8 servings

Maple syrup, cooked down to a glaze and topped with fresh pears, becomes the "topping" for this twist on an old American classic. The cake is tender and delicate and low in fat. You'll need a 10-inch cast-iron or nonstick skillet.

1/2 cup pure maple syrup

3 medium pears (Bosc or Anjou), quartered, cored, peeled, and each quarter cut lengthwise in half

1 1/4 cups sifted all-purpose flour

3/4 teaspoon baking powder, preferably nonaluminum

1/4 teaspoon baking soda

1/4 teaspoon salt

1/4 teaspoon ground ginger

6 tablespoons (3/4 stick) unsalted butter, at room temperature

2/3 cup sugar

1 teaspoon pure vanilla extract

2 large eggs

1/2 cup buttermilk

1 Adjust an oven rack to the lower third position and preheat the oven to 350°F.

2 Place the maple syrup in a heavy 10-inch cast-iron or nonstick skillet and boil over high heat until thick and full of large bubbles, 2 to 3 minutes. Remove from the heat, and arrange the pears in the syrup in an attractive pattern. Return to high heat and boil until the syrup is thick and bubbly again, shaking the pan from time to time to prevent the pears from sticking. Remove from the heat.

3 Resift the flour with the baking powder, baking soda, salt, and ginger; set aside.

4 In a medium bowl, beat the butter with an electric mixer on medium speed until smooth, about 1 minute. Add the sugar and vanilla and beat on medium-high speed for about 3 minutes, until smooth and creamy. Beat in the eggs one at a time, beating for 1 minute after each addition. Stir in half the flour mixture gently with a rubber spatula until well combined. Add all the buttermilk and stir it in. Add the remaining flour mixture and stir in only until the batter is smooth. Spoon the batter evenly over the pears and spread it level.

5 Bake for about 30 minutes, until the cake is a deep golden brown and springs back when gently pressed and a toothpick inserted into the center comes out clean. Immediately run the tip of a small sharp knife around the edges to release the cake. Place a heatproof cake plate over the skillet. Invert the two, wait a few seconds, and carefully lift off the skillet. If any fruit has stuck to the pan, place it back on the cake. Serve warm (best) or at room temperature.

FRESH SOUR CHERRY UPSIDE-DOWN CAKE

Makes one 12-x-8-inch cake, 8 to 10 servings

Sour cherry season is fleeting. The cherries come in for about two weeks in August, and they will not wait. We use as many as we can fresh, and freeze the rest whole in bags. This cake is wonderful warm from the oven.

TOPPING

- 4 tablespoons (1/2 stick) unsalted butter
- 1/2 cup firmly packed light or dark brown sugar
- 1/2 teaspoon ground cinnamon
- 1 pound fresh sour pie cherries, pitted (about 2 1/2 cups pitted), or canned sour pie cherries packed in water, drained

CAKE

- 2 cups sifted cake flour
- 1/4 teaspoon baking soda
- 1/2 teaspoon salt
- 1/2 teaspoon freshly grated nutmeg
- 8 tablespoons (1 stick) unsalted butter, at room temperature
- 1/2 teaspoon pure almond extract
- 1 cup sugar
- 2 large eggs
- 1/2 cup sour cream

TOPPING

- 1 cup heavy cream
- 2 tablespoons sugar
- 1/2 teaspoon pure vanilla extract

1 Adjust an oven rack to the center position and preheat the oven to 350°F.

2 For the topping, melt the butter in a small saucepan over medium heat. Add the brown sugar and stir constantly until smooth. Spread the mixture in a buttered 2 1/2-quart baking dish, such as a 12-x-8-inch or a 10-inch round dish. Arrange the cherries in a single layer over the brown sugar mixture; set aside.

3 For the cake, resift the flour with the baking soda, salt, and nutmeg; set aside.

4 In a large bowl, beat the butter with an electric mixer on medium speed until smooth, about 1 minute. Add the almond extract and 1/4 cup of the

sugar and beat for 1 minute. Beat in the remaining ³/₄ cup sugar about 3 tablespoons at a time, beating for 15 to 20 seconds after each addition, then beat on medium-high speed for 3 minutes. Scrape the bowl and beaters. Beat in the eggs one at a time, beating for 1 minute after each addition. On low speed, beat in the flour mixture in 3 additions, alternating with the sour cream, beginning and ending with the flour and beating only until smooth. Scrape the batter over the cherries and spread it level.

5 Bake for about 40 minutes, until the cake is golden brown and springs back when gently pressed and a toothpick inserted into the center comes out clean. Immediately cover the baking dish with a rimmed platter, grasp the platter and dish with pot holders, and invert the two. Slowly lift off the baking dish. If any fruit has stuck to the pan, place it back on the cake. Let cool until warm or room temperature.

6 Meanwhile, for the topping, whip the cream with the sugar and vanilla in a medium bowl until it holds a firm shape.

7 To serve, cut the cake into squares and place a spoonful of the cream alongside each portion.

KENTUCKY STACK CAKE

Makes one 6-layer cake, about 20 servings

Six thin layers of molasses cake interspersed with chunky, mildly spiced applesauce make up this classic cake from the mountains of Appalachia. I became intrigued with the dessert after visiting Carlos Manning and his wife at their home and apple ranch in the mountains of West Virginia a few years ago. Mrs. Manning called it "Molassy Cake," and said she'd learned to make it from her mother. Carlos used to make his own molasses, but he now devotes his time to nurturing heirloom apple varieties.

Since stack cake keeps well, Mrs. Manning said, it is a handy thing to have around in case company drops by. Recipes for the cake part of this multilayered masterpiece vary: some are biscuitlike, others tender cake, like this one. But the filling is always made from dried apples and flavored with spices of one's choosing. Some recipes say to spread the filling on every layer, including the top, while others say to leave the top plain. I opt for the latter. Assemble the cake 2 days before serving; it becomes almost puddinglike on standing. I love it with lightly sweetened whipped cream or with a scoop of vanilla ice cream.

I adapted the cake recipe from a small paperback, *Antique Cookbook,* written by Bertha Barnes.

FILLING

- 1 pound dried apples
- 6 cups water
- 1 cup sugar
- 2 teaspoons apple pie spice (or use 1 teaspoon ground cinnamon, 1/2 teaspoon ground allspice, 1/2 teaspoon ground mace, and 1/4 teaspoon ground cloves)

CAKE

- 4 cups sifted all-purpose flour
- 1 1/2 teaspoons baking powder, preferably nonaluminum
- 1/4 teaspoon baking soda
- 1/2 teaspoon salt
- 1/2 teaspoon ground cloves
- 1 cup (2 sticks) unsalted butter, at room temperature
- 1 cup sugar
- 3 large eggs
- 1 1/2 cup molasses (I use Grandma's)
- 1/4 cup milk

Confectioners' sugar for dusting

1 For the filling, put the apples and 4 cups of the water in a large heavy pot, cover, and cook over medium heat until the apples swell and the water is absorbed, about 30 minutes. Check the apples frequently, pushing them down into the water periodically with a wooden spoon. As they become soft, break them up into chunky pieces with a potato masher—they will not be completely tender.

2 Add the remaining 2 cups water and cook for another 20 minutes, or until the apples are soft but not quite tender, stirring often to make sure they aren't sticking to the bottom of the pot. When the water is almost completely absorbed, add the sugar and spice and stir well. Continue cooking, stirring frequently, for a few minutes more to blend the flavors and evaporate the last of the water. Mash the apples with the potato masher to make a chunky, thick applesauce. Remove from the heat, uncover, and let cool to room temperature. (The applesauce can be covered and refrigerated for up to 3 days. Bring to room temperature before using.)

3 For the cake, adjust an oven rack to the center position and preheat the oven to 350°F (if you are using more than two pans, adjust two racks to divide the oven into thirds). Butter two, four, or six 9-inch round layer cake pans. Line the bottoms with rounds of waxed paper or cooking parchment, butter the paper, and dust the sides and bottoms with flour. Knock out the excess flour, and set aside. (You'll be making 6 layers of cake in all; if you need to reuse pans, repeat the buttering, lining, and flouring after the first layers are baked and cooled.)

4 Resift the flour with the baking powder, baking soda, salt, and cloves; set aside.

5 In a large bowl, beat the butter with an electric mixer on medium speed until smooth, about 1 minute. Beat in the sugar about $1/4$ cup at a time, beating for a few seconds after each addition. Scrape the bowl and beaters and beat on medium-high speed for 5 minutes. Beat in the eggs one at a time, beating well after each addition.

6 Combine the molasses and milk in a small bowl. On low speed, add the flour mixture to the batter in 4 additions, alternating with the liquid, beginning and ending with the flour and beating only until smooth.

7 Use 1 cup of batter (measured with a dry measuring cup) for each layer. Spread it evenly in the prepared pans with the back of a spoon or an offset metal spatula to make a thin layer, about $1/4$ inch thick. Bake for 12 to 15 minutes, until the layers just spring back when gently pressed and there is a faint line of shrinkage away from the sides of the pans. Cool the layers in the pans for 5 minutes. Loosen the cake from the sides of the pans with the tip of a small sharp knife, cover the pans with wire racks, and invert. Carefully lift off the pans and papers, leaving the layers to cool upside down.

8 To assemble the cake, place one of the layers with its original top side down on a cake plate and spread with about $1^1/3$ cups of filling: since the filling is thick and the cake is very tender, the best way of doing this is to place small spoonfuls of filling all around the outer edge of the layer, a few more in the middle, and then spread them carefully together with the back of the spoon. Repeat with the remaining layers and filling, leaving the top layer plain. Cover and refrigerate for 2 days before serving.

9 Bring the cake to room temperature before serving. Dust the top with confectioners' sugar and cut the cake with a heavy sharp knife.

FRESH APRICOT CAKE

*Makes one
9-inch cake,
8 servings*

Fresh apricots from California begin arriving in produce markets in June. But even supermarket apricots taste great in this cake.

1 1/2 cups sifted all-purpose flour

1 1/2 teaspoons baking powder, preferably nonaluminum

1/4 teaspoon salt

8 tablespoons (1 stick) cold unsalted butter, cut into tablespoon-sized pieces

3/4 cup sugar

1/2 cup chopped toasted, skinned hazelnuts (see page 28)

2 large eggs

1/3 cup milk

1 teaspoon pure vanilla extract

8 medium apricots (1–1 1/4 pounds), halved and pitted

2 tablespoons unsalted butter, melted

1 teaspoon ground cinnamon

1 Adjust an oven rack to the center position and preheat the oven to 350°F. Butter a 9-inch springform pan; set aside.

2 Resift the flour with the baking powder and salt into a large bowl. Cut in the butter with a pastry blender or two knives until the mixture resembles coarse crumbs. Stir in 1/2 cup of the sugar and the hazelnuts.

3 Beat the eggs lightly with a fork in a small bowl, and add the milk and vanilla. Add to the flour mixture and stir with a fork just until the mixture is moistened. Spread the batter in the prepared pan. Arrange the apricot halves cut side down on top of the batter and brush with the melted butter. Combine the remaining 1/4 cup sugar with the cinnamon and sprinkle evenly over the apricots and batter.

4 Bake for 1 hour, or until a toothpick inserted in the center comes out clean. Cool in the pan on a wire rack until warm or at room temperature.

5 To serve, remove the sides of the pan and set the cake, still on the pan bottom, on a dessert platter.

HONEYED APPLE TORTE

Makes one 9-inch torte, 8 to 10 servings

This buttery cake is topped with slices of apples that have been cooked in honey and lemon juice. As the torte bakes, the apples sink into it. Be sure to use a firm, tart apple variety that will hold its shape when cooked. Newtown Pippin, Granny Smith, Northern Spy, Rome, and Winesap are all good candidates. Select medium apples instead of large ones for a more attractive appearance.

1/3 cup apple blossom honey (or other honey)

2 tablespoons fresh lemon juice (grate the zest first)

3 medium-firm tart cooking apples (about 1 1/4 pounds), quartered, cored, peeled, and each quarter cut lengthwise into 2 wedges

1 1/4 cups sifted unbleached all-purpose flour

1 teaspoon baking powder, preferably nonaluminum

1/4 teaspoon salt

6 tablespoons (3/4 stick) unsalted butter, at room temperature

3/4 cup sugar

1 teaspoon pure vanilla extract
Finely grated zest of 1 lemon

1/4 cup firmly packed light brown sugar

2 large eggs

TOPPING

1 tablespoon sugar

1/2 teaspoon ground cinnamon

1 Bring the honey and lemon juice to a simmer in a 12-inch nonstick skillet over medium heat, stirring occasionally. Add the apple wedges, cut side down, and cook, stirring gently and frequently with a heatproof rubber spatula, for 10 to 15 minutes, until the apples are translucent and almost tender when tested with the tip of a sharp paring knife. Set aside to cool.

2 Adjust an oven rack to the center position and preheat the oven to 350°F. Butter a 9-inch springform pan, or coat with cooking spray; set aside.

3 Resift the flour with the baking powder and salt; set aside.

4 In a large bowl, beat the butter with an electric mixer on medium speed until smooth, about 1 minute. Add 1/4 cup of the sugar, the vanilla, and lemon zest and beat on medium-high speed for 1 minute. Beat in the remaining $1/2$ cup sugar, then the brown sugar about $1/4$ cup at a time, beating for 20 to 30 seconds after each addition, then beat for 4 minutes. Beat in the eggs one at a time, beating for 1 minute after each addition. On low speed, beat in the flour mixture only until the batter is smooth.

5 Spread the batter evenly in the prepared pan. Arrange the cooled apple slices on top in an attractive pattern of concentric circles, leaving a bit of space between the wedges. Press the apple slices slightly into the batter.

6 For the topping, combine the sugar with the cinnamon and sprinkle evenly over the apples and batter.

7 Bake for 1 hour, or until the cake is nicely browned and springs back when gently pressed. Cool completely in the pan on a wire rack. Remove the sides of the pan and cut into portions with a sharp serrated knife.

PRACTICAL APPLES

Take a deep, brown baking-pan; butter it; fill it with apples, peeled, cut in quarters, and cored; add a large spoonful of cinnamon, two teacups of brown sugar, one teacupful of good cider, if you have it; if not, a little water; cover with a common pie-crust; bake about four hours; then break the crust into the pan with the apples and juice. To be eaten with sugar and cream.

—Mrs. Putnam, *Mrs. Putnam's Receipt Book* (1860)

12

Pies and Tarts

It is far more difficult to give directions for making good pastry, than to give directions for making good puddings; for, though all the materials are of the best quality, and all the proportions accurately given, the result depends almost entirely on dexterity and skill in compounding them.

—Mrs. Bliss, *The Practical Cook Book* (1853)

Pies and tarts—both sweet and savory—were made in Europe long before the *Mayflower* landed at Plymouth Rock in 1620. But during the almost four hundred years since then, American cooks have elaborated on fillings and come up with innumerable variations using the plentiful and diverse fruits that grow here.

By 1796, Amelia Simmons was able to present three apple pie recipes and one for currant pie in her *American Cookery*; six tart recipes, including apple, cranberry, apricot, gooseberry, orange, and grapes; and numerous puddings—many of which are actually pies—with apple turning up again along with pumpkin (or pompkin, as she called it), orange, lemon, and quince. This is an astonishing number for a slim volume—sixty-four pages—that covers all branches of cookery. There are many more recipes for savory pies as well.

What accounts for this variety? The diversity and newness of some of the ingredients certainly kindled the spirit of culinary experimentation, which was important since baking was more likely a weekly than an everyday activity in the seventeenth and eighteenth centuries. Fruit pies had the advantage of keeping well. Rather than being reserved for dessert, pies were a mainstay of the hearty meals that were served for breakfast on farms.

Another reason pies became so popular was that they were convenient to bake in a brick oven. Typically, breads went into the oven first, when the temperature was at its highest, and then fruit pies followed. The heat of the "falling oven"—brick retains heat remarkably well for many hours, the temperature falling gradually after the wood coals have been raked out—was ideal because it cooked the crust without burning the fruit and sugar inside. Custard pies went in after the fruit pies. Enough heat still radiated from the bricks to brown the crusts, but it was gentle and did not curdle the custards.

The pies of Miss Simmons's time were fairly simple to make. Until the nineteenth century, most pies were made without thickeners. Sometimes the fruits—apples, peaches, or apricots—were cooked to evaporate their moisture before they were put into the crust, which would eliminate the need for any thickener. But for many pies, the fruit was sliced and put directly into a pastry-lined pan, seasoned with sugar and spice, covered with a top crust, and baked. Berries and cherries were usually tossed with a bit of flour and sugar before baking, but these seem to be exceptions to the rule.

Though methods for making pie filling have been refined in modern times, piecrust techniques haven't changed in a hundred and fifty years. The basic ingredients were—and still are—flour, butter (or lard), salt, and liquid. Although butter and lard, or a combination, were the fats of choice, solidified drippings from meat roasts were also popular. Mrs. Bliss, the author of *The Practical Cook Book,* made her crusts the way we do today, by cutting the fat into the flour and salt and mixing in enough water, sometimes with an egg, to hold the pastry together. The "dexterity and skill" she refers to are just a matter of handling the dough gently, and I give you plenty of tips to ensure success.

PIECRUST AND TART SHELL POINTERS

1. Flour. Most of these recipes use a mixture of all-purpose flour (unbleached or bleached) and bleached cake flour, a soft wheat, or low-gluten, flour. This combination approximates pastry flour and produces a more tender crust. If you can get unbleached white pastry flour, you may substitute it for both these flours. Unbleached soft wheat flour can be used instead of cake flour with excellent results. Great Valley Mills in Pennsylvania makes it (see Sources, page 526).

2. Fats. Many of today's piecrust recipes use a combination of butter and vegetable shortening—the butter for the flavor and the shortening for tenderness. I prefer all butter. Because butter's water content (shortening contains no water) can contribute to the development of gluten, making for a tougher pastry, I add some egg yolk and cider vinegar to the dough, both of which inhibit gluten formation.

3. Mixing pastry doughs. I prefer to use the food processor. By cutting the fat into the flour with the processor blade, you create many more butter pieces than you could with a pastry blender or two knives, making for a more even distribution of the fat and producing tender and flaky pastry. Use quick pulses while adding the liquid, pulsing just until the dough *begins* to come together. Then stop and press the dough pieces together by hand. Handling the dough minimally will ensure tenderness.

4. Chilling the dough. All doughs benefit from resting in the refrigerator for an hour or so. The gluten has a chance to relax, which makes rolling the dough easy. You can leave the dough refrigerated, securely wrapped in plastic, for 2 or 3 days. Or, enclose the wrapped dough in a zip-top freezer bag and freeze for up to 1 month.

5. Rolling the dough. The less flour you use, the better. I use a pastry cloth, an 18-x-24-inch piece of canvas, which makes it possible to use less flour. You can purchase canvas at a fabric shop, or buy a pastry cloth from a gourmet shop or bakery supply catalog (see Sources, page 524).

If the dough feels too firm when you take it from the refrigerator, tap it a few times with the rolling pin. Roll from the center of the dough outward and don't let the rolling pin roll over the edge of the dough, or you'll compress it too much. Rotate the disk of dough occasionally as you roll. Once it is rolled to the proper size—don't worry about rough edges at this point—you can put it into the pan.

6. Making a pie or tart shell. I like to use Pyrex pie plates for pies. Pyrex is a good conductor of heat and shows the color of the pastry so you can see when it's done. Tart pans are always metal. Fold the circle of dough in half, then in half again. Place the point of the dough in the center of the pie plate or tart pan, and carefully unfold the dough so that it lines the pan. Do not stretch the dough. To make sure it hugs the sides of the pan, lift an edge and gently nudge the dough down into the pan, then continue as you move around the circle. I cut away excess pastry with kitchen shears, leaving a $^1/_2$ inch overhang. If the directions say to flute the dough, fold the edge under itself, toward the side of the pan, and pinch the dough to form a high-standing rim. Press an index finger against the inside of the folded rim of dough and pinch the dough on either side of the finger to make a V. Repeat, making a pattern of Vs all round the top of the crust. Refrigerate for at least 30 minutes before baking. If at any time the pastry is too soft to work with, refrigerate briefly to firm it up.

If making a double-crust pie, use the larger piece of dough for the bottom crust. Roll it out, line the pan, but don't trim off the excess pastry. Refrigerate while you prepare the filling.

7. Baking a single-crust pie or a tart shell. To help the pastry keep its shape during baking, line the chilled crust with a square of aluminum foil. Leave the edges of the foil pointing upward. Pour in enough dried beans to fill the shell; a 2-pound bag should do it. Put the shell in the preheated oven and bake according to the recipe. Cool completely before using. The beans can be used again and again.

FLAKY PIECRUST

This is my favorite basic pastry for all-butter single and double-crust pies. It is quick to make, easy to roll out, and deliciously tender and flaky. Although the dough is easily mixed by hand, I always use the food processor. The speed with which the metal blade chops the butter into the flour and incorporates the liquid minimizes gluten development. The amount of liquid may be a little bit more than you need, so add it very slowly toward the end of mixing. The dough should be moist enough to just hold together, but not at all wet or sticky.

SINGLE PIECRUST
Makes enough for one 9-inch pie shell

- 1 cup all-purpose flour
- 1/3 cup cake flour
- 1/4 teaspoon salt
- 8 tablespoons (1 stick) cold unsalted butter, cut into tablespoon-sized pieces
- 1/4 cup ice water
- 1 large egg yolk
- 1/2 teaspoon cider vinegar

DOUBLE PIECRUST
Makes enough for a double-crusted 9-inch pie or two 9-inch pie shells

- 2 cups all-purpose flour
- 2/3 cup cake flour
- 1/2 teaspoon salt
- 1 cup (2 sticks) cold unsalted butter, cut into tablespoon-sized pieces
- 1/2 cup ice water
- 1 large egg yolk
- 1 teaspoon cider vinegar

1 *If using a food processor,* pulse the flours and salt together for 5 seconds. Add the butter and pulse 4 times for about 1 second each, just to cut it into smaller pieces. Combine the water, egg yolk, and cider vinegar in a measuring cup. Pulsing rapidly, gradually pour the liquid through the feed tube in a thin stream until the dough forms several large clumps and *almost* gathers into a ball, 20 to 30 pulses. Watch closely. You may not need to add all the liquid.

   If making the dough by hand, combine the flours and salt in a large bowl. Add the butter and cut it into the flour with a pastry blender or two knives until the mixture resembles coarse meal. Combine the water, egg yolk, and cider vinegar in a measuring cup. Sprinkle in the liquid gradually, about 1 tablespoon at a time, tossing the mixture with a fork and stirring just until the dough gathers into a ball. You may not need to add all the liquid.

2 Transfer the dough to a sheet of plastic wrap. For a single crust, gently press the dough together to form a 1-inch-thick disk. For a double crust, press the dough together and divide it into two pieces, one slightly larger than the other. Form each piece into a 1-inch-thick disk. Wrap the dough securely in plastic and refrigerate for at least 1 hour. (The dough can be made up to 2 days ahead.) *For a fully baked single crust, continue as directed below. If making a double-crust pie, follow the instructions in the particular recipe.*

3 Put the dough on a lightly floured surface and flatten it slightly by tapping it all over with a rolling pin. Roll the dough into a 12-inch circle, placing the pin on the center of the dough and rolling out, without pressing down, and using as little flour as possible. Turn the dough about a quarter turn with each roll. Avoid running the pin over the edge of the dough, which would compress it. Don't be concerned about rough edges.

4 Fold the circle of dough in half, then in half again, and place the point in the center of a 9-inch pie plate, preferably Pyrex. Carefully unfold the dough and fit it into the pan by nudging it gently into the pan without stretching it. Trim the excess pastry to a ¹/₂-inch overhang. Fold the edge back under itself, toward the side of the pan, and pinch the double thickness to make a high-standing rim. Flute it by pinching it at ¹/₂-inch intervals into an attractive zigzag pattern. Refrigerate for 1 hour.

5 Adjust an oven rack to the center position and preheat the oven to 400°F.

6 Line the chilled pastry shell with a square of aluminum foil, pressing the foil gently over the bottom and sides. Fill the shell with dried beans. Bake for about 20 minutes, until the edges of the pastry just begin to brown. Remove from the oven and carefully lift out the foil and beans. Prick the bottom of the pastry evenly with a fork, return to the oven, and continue baking until golden brown and cooked through, 10 to 15 minutes more. Check frequently to make sure the pastry isn't puffing up—if it is, prick it gently with a toothpick. Cool completely on a wire rack before filling.

$25,000 APPLE PIE

*Makes one
9-inch pie,
8 to 10
servings*

A recent pie-baking contest that I judged at the Culinary Institute of America in Hyde Park, New York, was a study in contemporary flavors. The students, vying for scholarship money, had put just about anything they could think of into their creations: cream, blood oranges, bourbon, cranberries, ginger, and even mesquite bean jelly. But in the end, the simplest and most old-fashioned pie won the day. Its sweet-tart apple flavor snapped my taste buds to attention with the first bite. A small amount of cinnamon and brown sugar enhanced the apple taste without overwhelming it. The apple textures were varied and combined perfectly with the tender yet flaky pastry. And the apples were perfectly cooked.

The day before, we had visited an apple orchard in the picturesque Hudson River Valley, where contestants literally had their pick of the crop, but only one student did so. Meri Jo Leach chose five different varieties—Cortland, McIntosh, Crispin (also known as Mutsu), Empire, and Ginger Gold —to capture the $25,000 grand prize.

For the best results, use a mixture of apple varieties for taste and texture. Two or three types are better than just one alone.

1 Double Piecrust (page 472)

FILLING

1/2 cup sugar

1/4 cup firmly packed light brown sugar

3/4 teaspoon ground cinnamon

3 tablespoons all-purpose flour

1/4 teaspoon salt

2 1/2 pounds apples, quartered, cored, peeled, and each quarter cut lengthwise in half, then crosswise into thin slices (6–7 cups)

1 tablespoon fresh lemon juice

2 tablespoons cold unsalted butter, cut into small pieces

2 tablespoons heavy cream

1 tablespoon sugar

1 Adjust one oven rack to the lowest position and the second in the center of the oven. Set a baking sheet on the lower rack and preheat the oven to 450°F.

2 Roll the larger piece of dough out on a lightly floured surface to a 12-inch circle. Fit it into a 9-inch pie plate, without stretching it. Leave the excess dough hanging over the edges. Refrigerate.

3 For the filling, combine both sugars, the cinnamon, flour, and salt in a large bowl. Break up any lumps of brown sugar with your fingertips. Add the apples and lemon juice and combine well.

4 Roll the second piece of dough out on the lightly floured surface to an 11-inch circle. Spoon the apple mixture into the bottom crust, mounding it slightly in the center. Distribute the pieces of butter over the apples, and brush the edges of the overhanging pastry lightly with water. Carefully place the second circle of pastry on top of the apples. Press the edges of dough together firmly, and trim away the excess, leaving a ¹/₂-inch overhang. Fold the overhang under itself to form a standing rim, and flute it. Cut 6 slits in the top of the pastry in a spoke pattern with the tip of a small sharp knife. Brush the pastry with the cream and sprinkle with the sugar.

5 Place the pie on the baking sheet and bake for 20 minutes. Transfer the pie and the baking sheet to the center shelf and reduce the temperature to 375°F. Continue baking for another 45 minutes, or until the crust is golden brown, the juices are bubbling up through the slits, and the apples are tender when tested with the tip of a sharp knife. Cool for several hours on a wire rack before serving.

MOCK APPLE PIE

The modern Ritz cracker pie has an ancestry reaching back more than 130 years. Here's one example:

Six soda crackers pounded and mashed in two cups of cold water for twenty-minutes, the rind and juice of two lemons, two and a half cups of white sugar; mix well together; bake in puff-paste; this quantity will make three pies, and taste like green apples.

—S. Annie Frost, *The Godey's Lady's Book Receipts and Household Hints* (1870)

RHUBARB-STRAWBERRY PIE

*Makes one
9-inch pie,
8 servings*

Strawberries and rhubarb have worked their magic together in sauces, compotes, puddings, crisps, and pies ever since cooks first thought to combine the two. Be sure to make this pie only in the early summer, when rhubarb is tender and strawberries are bursting with flavor. Start the filling 6 to 8 hours ahead or the night before; macerating the rhubarb in the sugar overnight coaxes out the excess juices, which would otherwise make the pie unpredictably runny.

FILLING

1 1/2 pounds trimmed rhubarb, cut
    into 1/2-inch pieces (6 cups)

1 3/4 cups sugar

1/4 teaspoon ground cloves

1/4 teaspoon ground ginger

1/4 teaspoon ground allspice
    Finely grated zest of 1 orange

3 tablespoons fresh orange juice

1/4 cup cornstarch

1 pint ripe strawberries, rinsed,
    patted dry, hulled, and sliced

2 tablespoons cold unsalted
    butter, cut into small pieces

1 Double Piecrust (page 472)

1 tablespoon sugar

1 For the filling, combine the rhubarb, sugar, and spices in a large bowl. Cover and let stand at room temperature for at least 6 to 8 hours, or overnight. Refrigerate if your kitchen is warm.

2 Stir the rhubarb mixture to dissolve any remaining sugar. Set a strainer over a bowl, transfer the rhubarb mixture to it, and let drain for about 1 hour.

3 Measure the juice, and add water if necessary to make 1 1/4 cups. Put the juice in a medium saucepan and whisk in the orange zest, orange juice, and cornstarch. Cook over medium heat, stirring gently and constantly with a heatproof rubber spatula, until the mixture boils and thickens, then cook, stirring gently, for 2 minutes more. Remove from the heat and let cool to room temperature.

4 Meanwhile, adjust one oven rack to the lowest position and the second in the center of the oven. Set a baking sheet on the lower rack and preheat the oven to 450°F.

5 Roll the larger piece of dough out on a lightly floured surface to a 12-inch circle. Fit it into a 9-inch pie plate, without stretching it. Leave the excess dough hanging over the edges. Refrigerate.

6 Roll out the second piece of pastry on the lightly floured surface to an 11-inch circle.

7 In a large bowl, fold together the rhubarb, cooled cornstarch mixture, and strawberries. Spoon the mixture into the bottom crust, mounding it slightly in the center. Distribute the pieces of butter over the filling. Brush the edges of the overhanging pastry lightly with water and cover the pie with the top crust, pressing the edges to seal. Trim away the excess pastry, leaving 1/2-inch overhang. Fold the overhang under itself to make a standing rim and flute it. Cut 6 slits in the top crust in a spoke pattern with the tip of a small sharp knife. Brush the pastry lightly with cold water and sprinkle it with the sugar.

8 Place the pie on the baking sheet and bake for 20 minutes. Transfer the pie and the baking sheet to the center shelf and reduce the temperature to 375°F. Continue baking for another 45 to 50 minutes, or until the crust is well browned and you can see thickened juices bubbling through the slits. Cool the pie on a wire rack for several hours before serving (if you cut the pie too soon, the filling may run). This pie is delicious slightly cold; I like to cool it for 2 to 3 hours, then refrigerate it for 2 to 3 hours.

"THE PERSIAN APPLE"

Rhubarb stalks, or the Persian apple, is the earliest ingredient for pies, which the spring offers. The skin should be carefully stripped, and the stalks cut into small bits, and stewed very tender. These are dear pies, for they take an enormous quantity of sugar. Seasoned like apple pies.

—Mrs. Child, *The American Frugal Housewife* (1829)

GOOSEBERRY PIE

Makes one
8-inch pie,
8 servings

Gooseberries are tart, almost transparent, marble-sized green berries, only edible when cooked. They thrive in cool climates, growing on low bushes in most of the northern and Midwest states. In colonial times, gooseberries were a much used and much loved staple, appearing in pies, tarts, preserves, sauces, puddings, fools, and vinegars. Gooseberry recipes were still common in early- to mid-nineteenth-century American cookbooks, but they petered out toward the end of the century. Today, happily, the berries are becoming increasingly available at farmers' markets in June and July. Be sure to use green berries for this pie. As gooseberries ripen, they turn a beautiful burgundy color, but they lose a lot of their tantalizing zing.

Preparing gooseberries takes a lot of patience, which might account for their declining popularity as the twentieth century approached. The blossom ends and stems (tops and tails) must be removed from each berry. You can either pinch them off with your fingers or use scissors to snip them off. This tart, delicious pie is well worth the effort. Serve it with vanilla frozen yogurt or vanilla ice cream.

FILLING
4¹/₂ tablespoons all-purpose flour
³/₄ cup sugar
    Pinch of salt
4 cups topped and tailed
    gooseberries (about 1¹/₄
    pounds)

2 tablespoons cold unsalted
    butter, cut into small pieces

1 Double Piecrust (page 472)

1 tablespoon sugar

1 Adjust one oven rack to the lowest position and the second in the center of the oven. Set a baking sheet on the lower rack and preheat the oven to 450°F.

2 For the filling, combine the flour, sugar, and salt in a small bowl; set aside.

3 Roll the larger piece of dough out on a lightly floured surface to a 12-inch circle. Fit it into an 8-inch pie plate, without stretching it. Leave the excess dough hanging over the edges.

4 Roll the second piece of dough out on the lightly floured surface to an 11-inch circle. Place one third of the gooseberries in the pie shell and sprinkle one third of the sugar mixture evenly over them. Repeat twice with the remaining gooseberries and sugar mixture. Distribute the pieces of butter over the filling, and brush the edges of the overhanging pastry lightly with water. Carefully place the second circle of pastry on top of the gooseberries. Press the edges of dough together firmly, and trim away the excess dough, leaving a 1/2-inch overhang. Fold the overhang under itself to form a standing rim, and flute it. Cut 6 small slits in the top of the pastry in a spoke pattern with the tip of a small sharp knife. Brush the pastry with water and sprinkle with the sugar.

5 Place the pie on the baking sheet in the oven and bake for 20 minutes. Transfer the pie and its baking sheet to the center shelf and reduce the temperature to 375°F. Continue baking for another 45 to 50 minutes, or until the crust is well browned and the juices are bubbling up through the slits. Cool for several hours on a wire rack before serving. You can refrigerate the pie overnight after it has cooled; bring to room temperature before serving.

AMARETTI CHERRY PIE

Makes one 9-inch pie, 8 servings

Cherry pies go way back in our baking history, certainly to colonial times. Sour pie cherries, picked fresh off the tree and pitted as soon as possible, make the best pies. Use thawed frozen cherries if fresh are unavailable. Make the pie early in the day so that the filling has hours to cool and compose itself and will not ooze when cut. Vanilla ice cream or frozen yogurt is mandatory with this pie.

1 Double Piecrust (page 472)

FILLING

3/4 cup sugar

3 tablespoons quick-cooking tapioca

Pinch of salt

2 pounds fresh sour pie cherries, pitted (5 cups)

6 amaretti cookies (3 packages), finely crushed (scant 1/3 cup)

1/2 teaspoon pure almond extract

2 tablespoons cold unsalted butter, cut into small pieces

1 tablespoon sugar

1 Adjust one oven rack to the lowest position and the second in the center of the oven. Set a baking sheet on the lower rack and preheat the oven to 450°F.

2 Roll the larger piece of dough out on a lightly floured surface to a 12-inch circle. Fit it into a 9-inch pie plate, without stretching it. Leave the excess dough hanging over the edges. Refrigerate.

3 For the filling, combine the sugar, tapioca, and salt in a large bowl. Add the cherries (with any accumulated juices), amaretti, and almond extract and fold together gently; set aside for 15 minutes.

4 Meanwhile, roll the second piece of dough out on the lightly floured surface to an 11-inch circle. Spoon the cherry mixture into the bottom crust, and distribute the pieces of butter evenly over it. Brush the edges of the overhanging pastry lightly with water. Carefully place the second circle of pastry on top of the cherries. Press the edges of dough together firmly, and trim the excess dough, leaving a 1/2-inch overhang. Fold the overhang under itself to form a standing rim, and flute it. Cut 6 slits in the top of the

pastry in a spoke pattern with the tip of a small sharp knife. Brush the pastry with water and sprinkle with the sugar.

5 Place the pie on the baking sheet and bake for 20 minutes. Transfer the pie and the baking sheet to the center shelf and reduce the temperature to 375°F. Continue baking for another 50 minutes, or until the crust is golden brown, and the juices are bubbling up through the slits. Cool for several hours on a wire rack before serving. You can refrigerate the pie for an hour or two to make sure the filling sets.

WHEN IS IT DONE?

There can be no positive rules as to the exact time of baking each article. Skill in baking is the result of practice, attention, and experience. Much, of course, depends on the state of the fire, and on the size of the things to be baked, and something on the thickness of the pans or dishes.

—Eliza Leslie, *Seventy-Five Receipts* (1828)

BLUEBERRY PIE WITH AMARETTI STREUSEL

Makes one 9-inch pie, 10 servings

Amaretti, the Italian almond cookies, make a marvelously crunchy and flavorful streusel topping. Some of the streusel is sprinkled over the bottom of the pie shell to absorb the blueberry juices and to keep it crisp. There is no starchy thickener in the filling. Instead, beaten egg whites keep the filling together. It will not run when cut. This is a very easy pie to make. Be sure to make it only during the summer months, when blueberries are really fine.

TOPPING

12 amaretti cookies (6 packages)

1/3 cup all-purpose flour

1/2 cup sugar

1 teaspoon ground cinnamon

3 tablespoons cold unsalted
   butter

FILLING

2 large egg whites

1/8 teaspoon salt

4 cups fresh blueberries, picked
   over

2 tablespoons sugar

1 tablespoon fresh lime juice

1 Single Piecrust (page 472),
   baked

1 Adjust an oven rack to the center position and preheat the oven to 400°F.

2 For the topping, place the amaretti in a zip-top plastic bag and crush them coarsely with a rolling pin. Set aside.

3 Combine the flour, sugar, and cinnamon in a small bowl. With a pastry blender or two knives, cut in the butter until the particles resemble fine crumbs. Stir in the crushed amaretti.

4 For the filling, beat the egg whites and salt in a medium bowl with an electric mixer until the whites hold a firm shape but are not dry. Add the blueberries, sugar, and lime juice and fold in gently but thoroughly, trying not to break the berries.

5 Sprinkle 1/4 cup of the crumb mixture over the bottom of the pie shell.

Spread the filling over the crumbs, and sprinkle the remaining crumb mixture over the filling, using your fingertips to spread the crumb mixture evenly over the berries, without packing it down.

6 Bake until the filling is bubbling at the edges, about 45 minutes. If the edges are browning too much toward the end of baking, tent the pie loosely with foil. Cool for several hours on a wire rack before serving.

FRESH PINEAPPLE PIE

*Makes one
9-inch pie,
8 servings*

When you have a fresh pineapple that's really good, you owe it to yourself to make this pie. Pineapples from Maui are picked ripe and have the best taste of any that I've found in the markets. I've tried several thickeners, and quick-cooking tapioca works best. The fruit juices thicken without becoming pasty, and they glimmer around the pieces of pineapple. Be sure to let the fruit mixture stand at least 15 minutes before filling the pie shell, or the tapioca will not be able to do its job.

1   Double Piecrust (page 472)

FILLING
¼   cup quick-cooking tapioca
¾   cup sugar
6   cups cut-up fresh pineapple
     (½-inch chunks)

1½   teaspoons finely grated lime
     zest
1   tablespoon fresh lime juice
2   tablespoons cold unsalted
     butter, cut into small pieces

1   tablespoon sugar

1   Adjust one oven rack to the lowest level and the second in the center of the oven. Set a baking sheet on the lower rack and preheat the oven to 450°F.

2   Roll the larger piece of dough out on a lightly floured surface to a 12-inch circle. Fit it into a 9-inch pie plate, without stretching it. Leave the excess dough hanging over the edges. Refrigerate.

3   For the filling, combine the tapioca and sugar in a large bowl. Add the pineapple, lime zest, and juice and mix together thoroughly. Let stand for at least 15 minutes.

4   Meanwhile, roll the second piece of dough out on the lightly floured surface to an 11-inch circle. Spoon the pineapple mixture into the bottom crust, mounding it slightly in the center. Distribute the pieces of butter over the pineapple, and brush the edges of the overhanging pastry lightly with water. Carefully place the second circle of pastry on top of the pineapple. Press the edges of dough together firmly, and trim away the excess, leaving a ½-inch overhang. Fold the overhang under itself to form a stand-

ing rim, and flute it. Cut 6 slits in the top of the pastry in a spoke pattern with the tip of a small sharp knife. Brush the pastry with water and sprinkle with the sugar.

5 Place the pie on the baking sheet in the oven and bake for 20 minutes. Transfer the pie and the baking sheet to the center shelf and reduce the temperature to 375°F. Continue baking for another 45 to 50 minutes, or until the crust is well browned and the juices are bubbling up thickly through the slits. Cool for several hours on a wire rack before serving.

THE PERIPATETIC PINEAPPLE

Pineapples are native to tropical America. Early explorers took them to other parts of the world, and by the late 1400s, the fruit was being cultivated in the West Indies. Columbus saw pineapples on the island of Guadaloupe on an expedition in 1493. There, the pineapple was known to the natives as *na-na,* meaning "fragrance-fragrance." The French word for pineapple, *anana,* and the Spanish, *ananas,* are probably derived from this word. The Spanish also called the pineapple *piña,* because it resembled a pinecone. In the 1800s, pineapples were imported fresh to North America from the West Indies, where they became a favorite.

Over time, pineapple cultivation spread to many of the world's tropical regions. Just when the fruit arrived on the Hawaiian Islands is uncertain, though it's been suggested that Captain Cook may have introduced it there in the late 1700s. The plants grew well in the islands' climate and rich volcanic soil. Because the islands were so far from a major land mass, much of the fruit shipped from there didn't survive the long ocean voyages. Preserving was the answer. In 1892, Captain Kidwell, an English horticulturist, started the first pineapple cannery on the island of Oahu. The industry thrived and continues to this day. Canning made it possible for pineapples to be transported anywhere in the world.

LEMON MERINGUE PIE

Makes one 9-inch pie, 8 servings

Lemon meringue pie, with its flaky crust, custardy lemon filling, and billowy meringue, is justifiably one of America's most loved desserts. According to food historian William Woys Weaver, the pie is about two hundred years old, having been introduced in the early 1800s by noted Philadelphia baker and cooking teacher Mrs. Elizabeth Goodfellow. This recipe makes a sensationally high pie with generous amounts of filling and meringue. To give the meringue a silken texture, the egg whites and sugar are heated before beating.

FILLING

- 1/2 cup cornstarch
- 1 1/2 cups sugar
- 1/4 teaspoon salt
- 2 1/4 cups water
- 2 large eggs
- 6 large egg yolks
- 4 tablespoons (1/2 stick) unsalted butter, cut into tablespoon-sized pieces
- Finely grated zest of 2 large lemons
- 1/3 cup fresh lemon juice
- 1/2 teaspoon pure vanilla extract

MERINGUE

- 6 large egg whites
- 2 tablespoons water
- 3/4 teaspoon cream of tartar
- 3/4 cup sugar
- Pinch of salt
- 1 teaspoon pure vanilla extract

- 1 Single Piecrust (page 472), baked

1 Adjust an oven rack to the lower third position and preheat the oven to 325°F.

2 For the filling, combine the cornstarch, sugar, and salt in a large saucepan. Gradually whisk in the water until smooth. Place the pan over medium heat and stir constantly with a heatproof rubber spatula until the mixture thickens, boils, and becomes translucent. Remove from the heat.

3 In a medium bowl, whisk the eggs and yolks together just until combined. Whisk in about 1/2 cup of the hot cornstarch mixture, then whisk in another $\frac{1}{2}$ cup. Add the egg mixture to the remaining cornstarch mixture in the saucepan and whisk together thoroughly. Bring to a boil over medium heat, stirring constantly with the rubber spatula, and cook, stirring, for 3 to 4 minutes. Remove from the heat and stir in the butter, then the lemon zest. Gradually stir in the lemon juice, then the vanilla. Place a piece of plastic wrap directly on the surface of the filling and set aside.

4 For the meringue, stir the whites, water, cream of tartar, sugar, and salt together in a medium stainless steel bowl with a rubber spatula. Half fill a large skillet with hot tap water, and set it over medium heat. When the water reaches a simmer, place the bowl with the egg white mixture in the pan and stir gently but constantly with the spatula until the mixture turns milky white and feels hot to a fingertip, 2 to 3 minutes. Scrape the mixture into a large bowl, add the vanilla, and beat with an electric mixer on medium speed until the whites form fluffy, firm peaks that curl slightly at their tips when the beaters are raised.

5 Scrape the hot filling into the pie shell. Place about half of the meringue in dollops all around the edges of the filling. Using the back of a spoon, spread the meringue to the edges of the pastry, partially covering it. Scrape the rest of the meringue onto the center of the filling and spread it to cover the filling completely. Swirl the meringue attractively with the back of the spoon.

6 Bake for about 30 minutes, until the meringue is just lightly browned. Cool on a wire rack for about 1 hour, then refrigerate for at least several hours (4 to 6 hours is best) before serving.

7 This pie is best on the day it is made. To serve, rinse a sharp knife in hot water and shake off the excess water before making each cut. Refrigerate leftovers.

HAZELNUT-STREUSEL SWEET POTATO PIE

Makes one 9-inch pie, 8 to 10 servings

Sweet potato pies were very popular with nineteenth-century cooks. Here's a contemporary rendition with a terrific hazelnut streusel topping that is a great contrast to the smooth, creamy filling. I make it for Thanksgiving.

FILLING

1 1/2 pounds sweet potatoes

2/3 cup sugar

1/2 teaspoon ground mace

1/2 teaspoon freshly grated nutmeg

1/4 teaspoon salt

2 teaspoons pure vanilla extract

3 large eggs

3/4 cup heavy cream

1 Graham Cracker Crust (page 493), baked

TOPPING

1/4 cup all-purpose flour

1/4 cup firmly packed dark brown sugar

3/4 teaspoon ground cinnamon

2 tablespoons cold unsalted butter

1/2 cup chopped toasted, skinned hazelnuts (see page 28)

1 For the filling, cook the sweet potatoes in the microwave oven or a steamer. If microwaving, prick each one with a fork and microwave on high power for 15 minutes, or until completely tender. If using a steamer, be sure there's enough water in the pan, and steam them, covered, until tender, 30 to 40 minutes. Cool, cut in half, scoop out the flesh, and mash with a fork or potato masher. You need 1 2/3 cups for the filling. (The sweet potatoes can be prepared a day or two ahead and refrigerated, covered.)

2 Adjust an oven rack to the center position and preheat the oven to 350°F.

3 In a food processor, process the sweet potatoes, sugar, mace, nutmeg, salt, vanilla, eggs, and cream for 20 seconds. Scrape the work bowl and process for 15 to 20 seconds longer, until smooth. Pour the mixture into the graham cracker crust.

4 For the topping, combine the flour, brown sugar, and cinnamon in a small

bowl. With a pastry blender or two knives, cut in the butter until the mixture resembles coarse crumbs. Stir in the hazelnuts.

5 Sprinkle the topping over the filling. Bake for 45 minutes, or until the sides are puffed and set but the center of the pie jiggles when you move the pan.

6 Cool on a wire rack until the filling firms up, at least 2 to 3 hours. Cut into wedges and serve. (You can refrigerate this pie for about 1 hour before serving to ensure that the filling is set.)

ABOUT HAZELNUTS

Hazelnuts (also called filberts or cobnuts) have been cultivated in the United States since 1857. About 97 percent of all the filberts grown in America come from Oregon.

To bring out their rich flavor, the nuts must be roasted to a golden brown color, and the skins should be rubbed off with a towel (see page 28).

BLACK BOTTOM PIE

*Makes one
9-inch pie,
8 servings*

This special-occasion pie has a gooey chocolate bottom. It's set in a graham cracker crust, topped with a delicate, pure white, rum-flavored chiffon made with an Italian meringue. The whole thing is simply voluptuous. I've developed the recipe over a number of years. Marjorie Kinnan Rawlings, author of *The Yearling,* also wrote a marvelous cookbook, *Cross Creek Cookery* (1942), in which she includes a similar recipe. Here is how she felt about Black Bottom Pie:

> I think this is the most delicious pie I have ever eaten . . . so delicate, so luscious, that I hope to be propped up on my dying bed and fed a generous portion. Then I think that I should refuse outright to die, for life would be too good to relinquish. The pie seems fussy to make, but once a cook gets the hang of it, it goes easily.

CHOCOLATE BOTTOM

- ½ cup sugar
- ⅓ cup Dutch-process cocoa
- 2 tablespoons cornstarch
- ⅛ teaspoon salt
- 1¼ cups milk
- 3 ounces (3 squares) semisweet chocolate, coarsely chopped
- 2 tablespoons unsalted butter

- 1 Graham Cracker Crust (page 493), baked

FILLING

- 1½ teaspoons unflavored gelatin
- 2 tablespoons cold water
- ¼ cup sugar
- 1 tablespoon cornstarch
- ⅛ teaspoon salt
- 1 cup milk
- 1 teaspoon pure vanilla extract
- 2 tablespoons light rum
- 4 large egg whites
- ¼ teaspoon cream of tartar
- ½ cup sugar
- 3 tablespoons water

Pecan halves

1 For the chocolate bottom, whisk together the sugar, cocoa, cornstarch, and salt in a medium heavy saucepan. Gradually whisk in the milk. Place the pan over medium-high heat and cook, stirring gently and constantly with a heatproof rubber spatula, until the mixture is steaming hot and almost

boiling. Add the chocolate and continue cooking and stirring, scraping the bottom and sides of the pan well with the spatula, until the mixture boils and thickens. Reduce the heat to low and cook, stirring, for another 2 minutes. Add the butter. If the mixture is lumpy, whisk to make it smooth. Remove from the heat and place the saucepan in a larger pan of ice and water. Stir occasionally with the spatula until the mixture cools to room temperature and thickens.

2 Spread the chocolate mixture over the bottom of the graham cracker crust and refrigerate for 2 hours. (Save the ice water bath.)

3 For the filling, sprinkle the gelatin over the cold water in a small cup, and let stand for 5 minutes to soften. Combine the sugar, cornstarch, and salt in a medium heavy saucepan. Gradually whisk in the milk until smooth. Cook over medium-high heat, stirring constantly with a heatproof rubber spatula, until the mixture boils and thickens slightly. Reduce the heat to low and continue cooking and stirring gently for 1 minute longer. Off the heat, scrape in the gelatin and stir for about 1 minute to dissolve. Place the saucepan in a larger pan of ice and water and stir just until the mixture reaches room temperature; do not let it get cold. Remove the pan from the ice water bath and stir in the vanilla and rum. Set aside. (Save the ice water bath.)

4 Place the egg whites in a medium stainless steel bowl and set the bowl over a basin of warm water. Stir the whites with a fork until they are warm, then beat them with an electric mixer on medium speed until foamy. Add the cream of tartar and continue beating until soft peaks form. Set aside while you make the sugar syrup.

5 Place the sugar and water in a small heavy saucepan—do not stir. Set the pan over high heat and swirl the pan occasionally as the mixture comes to a boil. When the sugar is dissolved and the mixture is boiling, cover and boil over high heat for 1 minute to dissolve any sugar crystals on the sides of the pan. Uncover and continue cooking until the syrup reaches 240°F on a candy thermometer or digital probe thermometer, 1 to 2 minutes.

6 Meanwhile, when the sugar syrup is almost ready, resume beating the egg whites on medium speed until they form stiff peaks. When the syrup

reaches the correct temperature, slowly pour the hot syrup onto the whites, beating constantly, avoiding the beaters. Continue beating at high speed for several minutes more, until the meringue forms stiff, shiny peaks and is cool. Set aside.

7 Return the pan with the gelatin mixture to the ice bath and stir with the rubber spatula until the mixture begins to set. Remove from the ice bath and gently whisk in about 1 cup of the meringue until smooth. In 3 additions, gently fold the gelatin mixture into the remaining meringue.

8 Remove the crust from the refrigerator and carefully spoon the meringue mixture over the chocolate layer, mounding it slightly in the center; it may not all fit. Refrigerate the pie, reserving any excess filling at room temperature. After 20 minutes, when the top of the pie has set, carefully spoon any remaining chiffon mixture over the center. Refrigerate for at least 6 hours before serving.

9 Decorate the pie by arranging pecan halves in a ring on top. To serve, rinse a sharp knife in hot water and shake off the excess water before making each cut. Refrigerate leftovers.

GRAHAM CRACKER CRUST

Makes one 9-inch crust

The substitution of a graham cracker crumb crust for the usual flour and butter (or lard) crust was nothing short of revolutionary, and utterly American in its timesaving reliance on a convenience food. According to Jean Anderson, writing in *The American Century Cookbook,* the first recorded instance of a printed graham cracker crust recipe was in 1923. Since then, the recipe, which originally called for melted butter and an egg, has been further streamlined by eliminating the egg (and increasing the butter). My crust contains far less butter than most versions.

Baking the crust in a foil-lined pan, then removing the foil and returning the crust to the pan, ensures that the crust won't remain glued to the pan when you cut your pie. I learned this technique from Maida Heatter's *Book of Great Desserts.*

18 graham cracker squares	1 tablespoon cold unsalted butter
¼ cup sugar, plus more if needed	1 large egg white
1 teaspoon ground cinnamon	

1 Adjust an oven rack to the center position and preheat the oven to 325°F.

2 Line a 9-inch pie plate with a square of aluminum foil. Fold the excess foil out and away from the rim.

3 In a food processor, process the graham crackers until they are fine crumbs, about 10 seconds. Add the sugar, cinnamon, and butter and process for 10 to 15 seconds, until the butter is in small bits. Add the egg white and pulse rapidly about 10 times, only until the crumb mixture is moist looking; do not process until it forms a ball.

4 Coat the lined pie plate with cooking spray and press the mixture firmly into the bottom and up the sides. Make sure the crust is not too thick where the bottom meets the sides (sugar your fingers as necessary if the mixture is sticky).

5 Bake for 15 minutes, or until the crust is lightly browned and smells aromatic. Let cool completely on a wire rack. Lift up the edges of the foil and lift the crust from the pan. Carefully peel away the foil, supporting the crust with one hand as you go. Replace the crust in the pie plate.

BLACK BOTTOM BANANA CREAM PIE

Makes one 9-inch pie, 8 servings

This is a combination of two of my favorite pies, banana cream and chocolate cream. Be sure the bananas you use are ripe—the skins should have some brownish spots.

CHOCOLATE BOTTOM

1/2 cup sugar

1/3 cup Dutch-process cocoa

2 tablespoons cornstarch

1/8 teaspoon salt

3/4 cup milk

1 ounce (1 square) semisweet chocolate, coarsely chopped

1 tablespoon unsalted butter

1 Single Piecrust (page 472), baked

CUSTARD

1 large egg

1/2 cup sugar

2 tablespoons cornstarch

1/4 teaspoon salt

1 cup milk

1 tablespoon unsalted butter

1 teaspoon pure vanilla extract

2 ounces cream cheese

2 medium-large bananas (12 ounces)

TOPPING

1 cup heavy cream

2 tablespoons confectioners' sugar

1/2 ounce (1/2 square) semisweet chocolate, coarsely chopped

1 For the chocolate bottom, whisk the sugar, cocoa, cornstarch, and salt in a small heavy saucepan. Gradually whisk in the milk. Place over medium heat and cook, stirring gently and constantly with a heatproof rubber spatula, until steaming hot and almost boiling. Add the chocolate and continue cooking, stirring constantly and scraping the bottom of the pan, until the mixture comes to a boil and thickens. Reduce the heat to low and continue cooking, stirring, for another 2 minutes. Remove from the heat and stir in the butter. Cool to room temperature.

2 Stir the chocolate mixture well, and spread it evenly in the bottom of the

pie shell. Refrigerate for at least 1 hour, until the chocolate layer is completely chilled and set.

3 For the custard, whisk together the egg, sugar, cornstarch, and salt in a small bowl. Heat the milk in a medium heavy saucepan over medium heat until it is steaming hot but not quite boiling. Gradually whisk the hot milk into the egg mixture. Return the mixture to the saucepan and stir gently and constantly over medium heat with a heatproof rubber spatula, scraping the bottom of the pan often, until slightly thickened. Add the butter and cook until the mixture boils and thickens further, 3 to 4 minutes; if the custard seems lumpy, switch to a whisk. Reduce the heat to low and continue cooking, stirring constantly, for 2 to 3 minutes more. Cool to room temperature, stirring occasionally.

4 Stir the vanilla into the custard. Add the cream cheese. Beat with an electric mixer until smooth. Set aside.

5 Slice the bananas and arrange them, slightly overlapping, on the chocolate layer. Spoon the custard over the bananas and carefully spread it to cover the bananas completely.

6 For the topping, whip the cream with the confectioners' sugar until thick. Spread it over the custard layer. Sprinkle the chopped chocolate over the cream. Refrigerate for 3 to 4 hours before serving. To serve, rinse a sharp knife in hot water and shake off the excess water before making each cut. Refrigerate leftovers.

BUTTERSCOTCH CREAM PIE

*Makes one
9-inch pie,
8 servings*

True butterscotch is sugar cooked with butter, and that is the first step in making the filling for this pie. Evaporated milk adds a silky smoothness. You must make this a day ahead so the filling has time to set.

FILLING

- 2 tablespoons unsalted butter
- ³/₄ cup plus 2 tablespoons firmly packed dark brown sugar
- 1 cup evaporated milk
- ¹/₃ cup cornstarch
- ¹/₈ teaspoon salt
- 3 large egg yolks
- 2 cups milk
- 2 teaspoons pure vanilla extract

1 Single Piecrust (page 472), baked

TOPPING

- 1 cup heavy cream
- 2 tablespoons confectioners' sugar
- Ground cinnamon

1 For the filling, melt the butter in a medium heavy saucepan over medium heat. Add the brown sugar and cook, stirring constantly with a wooden spoon, for 2 minutes. Add ¹/₄ cup of the evaporated milk 1 tablespoon at a time, stirring after each addition. Continue cooking and stirring until the mixture comes to a boil, and boil for 30 seconds. Remove from the heat.

2 In a medium bowl, whisk together the cornstarch, salt, egg yolks, and the remaining ³/₄ cup evaporated milk until smooth. Heat the milk in a saucepan until it is almost boiling. Very gradually at first, slowly whisk the milk into the egg yolk mixture. Then whisk this into the brown sugar mixture and set the pan over medium heat. Cook, stirring constantly with a heatproof rubber spatula, until the mixture thickens and boils. Cook, stirring and scraping with the spatula, for 2 minutes more. Strain the mixture into a clean bowl and stir in the vanilla.

3 Place the bowl in a pan of ice and water and stir constantly but gently until the filling feels cool to the touch. Pour the filling into the pastry shell and refrigerate overnight.

4 For the topping, when you are ready to serve (or an hour or two before), whip the cream with the confectioners' sugar until thick. Spread it over the filling, and dust lightly with cinnamon. Serve cold. Refrigerate leftovers.

FUDGY BROWNIE ICE CREAM PIE

Makes one 9-inch pie, 8 to 10 servings

This is a dream dessert for a party: a hot fudge sundae in a walnut brownie crust. You can make the crust early in the day and assemble the pie just before serving. Bottled hot fudge sauce saves you the effort of making your own, but be sure to buy a top-quality one. (Or substitute caramel sauce if you wish.) And if you want to go all out, why not serve portions of the pie with gobs of whipped cream, a sprinkling of nuts, and a maraschino cherry?

BROWNIE CRUST

- 4 tablespoons (1/2 stick) unsalted butter
- 1 ounce (1 square) unsweetened chocolate
- 1/2 cup Dutch-process cocoa
- 1 1/3 cups plus 2 tablespoons sugar
- 1/4 teaspoon salt
- 1/4 cup warm water
- 2 teaspoons pure vanilla extract

- 2 large eggs, separated
- 1/4 cup all-purpose flour
- 1/2 cup finely chopped walnuts
- 1 large egg white

- 1 quart vanilla ice cream or frozen yogurt

- 1 16.5-ounce jar hot fudge topping (I use Mrs. Richardson's)

1 For the crust, adjust an oven rack to the center position and preheat the oven to 350°F. Butter a 9-inch pie plate and dust with fine dry bread crumbs. Tap out the excess and set aside.

2 Melt the butter and chocolate in a medium heavy saucepan over low heat. Stir with a whisk until smooth. Whisk in the cocoa and raise the heat to medium. Cook, whisking constantly, for 1 minute. Stir in 1 1/3 cups of the sugar and cook for 1 minute. Remove from the heat and whisk in the salt, water, vanilla, and egg yolks. Stir in the flour, then the walnuts.

3 Whip the 3 egg whites in a small bowl with an electric mixer on medium speed until they form soft peaks. Gradually beat in the remaining 2 tablespoons sugar, and continue beating until the whites form stiff, shiny peaks that curl slightly at their tips when the beaters are raised. Using a large rubber spatula, fold one third of the whites into the chocolate mixture, then fold in the remaining whites only until no whites show. Scrape the mixture into the pie plate.

4 Bake for 30 minutes, or until puffed. Turn the oven off and leave the pan in the oven for another 5 minutes. Remove from the oven and cool completely on a wire rack, 3 to 4 hours. The crust sinks a bit in the middle as it cools.

5 When ready to serve, place scoops of the ice cream in the brownie crust, piling them in. Spoon the chocolate sauce over the ice cream, without covering it completely. Serve immediately.

FLAKY TART PASTRY

Makes enough for one 9- or 10-inch tart shell or one 13-inch free-form tart

A crunchy, flaky all-butter pastry is best for most tarts. The small amount of sugar helps with the browning and retards gluten development. The amount of water may be a bit more or a bit less than you need, so add it slowly toward the end of mixing. The dough should be moist enough to just hold together, but not at all wet or sticky.

1¼ cups all-purpose flour	10 tablespoons (1¼ sticks) cold unsalted butter, cut into tablespoon-sized pieces
¼ cup cake flour	
1 tablespoon sugar	
½ teaspoon salt	¼ cup ice water, plus more if needed

1 *If using a food processor,* pulse the flours, sugar, and salt together for 5 seconds. Add the butter and pulse 4 times for about 1 second each, just to cut it into smaller pieces. Pulsing rapidly, gradually pour the ice water through the feed tube in a thin stream until the dough almost gathers into a ball and forms several large clumps, 20 to 30 pulses. Watch closely. You may not need to add all the water. Or, if the dough seems dry, add 1 teaspoon additional water at a time, pulsing a few times after each addition.

If making the dough by hand, combine the flours, sugar, and salt in a large bowl. Add the butter pieces and cut it into the flour with a pastry blender or two knives until the mixture resembles coarse meal. Sprinkle in the water about 1 tablespoon at a time, tossing the mixture with a fork and stirring just until the dough gathers into a ball. You may not need to add all the water. Or, if the dough seems dry, add 1 teaspoon more water at a time, tossing well with the fork, until the dough just holds together when pressed.

2 Transfer the dough to a sheet of plastic wrap and press it together to form a 1-inch-thick disk. The dough can be used right away, or wrapped securely in plastic and refrigerated for up to 2 days. For a baked tart shell, continue as directed below. If making a free-form tart shell, follow the directions in the individual recipe.

3 Put the dough on a lightly floured surface and flatten it slightly by tapping it all over with a rolling pin. Roll the dough into a 13-inch circle, placing the pin on the center of the dough and rolling out, without pressing down, and using as little flour as possible. Turn the dough about a quarter turn with each roll. Avoid running the pin over the edges of the dough, which would compress it. Don't be concerned about rough edges.

4 Fold the circle of dough in half, then in half again, and place the point in the center of a 9- or 10-inch tart pan with a removable bottom. Carefully unfold the dough and fit it into the pan by nudging it gently into the pan without stretching it. Trim the excess to a $^1/_2$-inch overhang. Fold the overhang over into the pan, pressing it firmly against the sides to form a double layer. Then press the sides of pastry so that it extends $^1/_4$ inch above the rim. Refrigerate until ready to fill. If baking the shell without a filling, refrigerate for at least 1 hour.

5 To bake the tart shell, adjust an oven rack to the center position and place a baking sheet on the rack. Preheat the oven to 375°F.

6 Line the chilled tart shell with a square of aluminum foil, pressing the foil gently over the bottom and sides. Fill the shell with dried beans. Place the shell on the baking sheet and bake for about 20 minutes, until the edges of the pastry just begin to brown. Remove from the oven and carefully lift out the foil and beans. Prick the bottom of the pastry evenly with a fork, return to the oven, and continue baking until golden brown and cooked through, 15 to 20 minutes more. Check frequently to make sure the pastry isn't puffing up; if it is, prick it gently with a toothpick. Cool completely on a wire rack before filling.

WARM PEAR AND ALMOND CUSTARD TART

Makes one
9-inch tart,
8 servings

I don't know why pears and almonds go together so well, but they do. For this tart, the pears are poached in a lemon-flavored sugar syrup and then baked in a custard flavored with a splash of almond extract. Chopped sliced almonds are sprinkled on top and toasted during the final 20 to 30 minutes of baking. This tart is best served warm, but refrigerated leftovers make a marvelous breakfast.

FILLING

1 1/2 cups water

1 1/2 cups sugar

2 tablespoons fresh lemon juice

5 firm but ripe Bartlett or Anjou pears (about 2 pounds)

3 large eggs

1/8 teaspoon salt

3/4 cup milk

1/2 teaspoon pure almond extract

1/2 teaspoon pure vanilla extract

1 tart shell made with Flaky Tart Pastry (page 500), baked

2 tablespoons sliced almonds, chopped

1 For the filling, bring the water and 1 cup of the sugar to a boil in a medium heavy saucepan. Reduce the heat and simmer for 5 minutes. Remove from the heat and stir in the lemon juice.

2 Cut each pear lengthwise in half and use a small sharp knife to remove the core and fibrous tissue. Peel the pear halves, dropping them into the sugar syrup as you go. Bring to a simmer over medium heat, cover, and simmer, adjusting the heat as necessary, until the pears look translucent and are tender when tested with a toothpick, about 15 minutes. Remove the pears with a slotted spoon and set them on several thicknesses of paper towels to drain well.

3 Adjust an oven rack to the center position and preheat the oven to 325°F.

4 Whisk together the eggs and salt in a medium bowl. Add the remaining 1/2 cup sugar and whisk in briefly. Stir in the milk and both extracts. Pour a thin layer of the mixture into the tart shell. Arrange 8 pear halves, cut sides down, in a circle around the edge of the pastry shell. Place the remaining 2 pear halves in the center. Carefully pour in the remaining custard.

5 Bake for 1 hour. Sprinkle the almonds over the exposed pear halves and bake until the custard is set, another 20 to 30 minutes. Test by inserting the tip of a small sharp knife into the center of custard—it should just come out clean; do not overbake. Cool completely in the pan on a wire rack, about 3 hours.

6 Remove the rim of the pan and set the tart, still on the pan bottom, on a serving platter. Serve at room temperature. Refrigerate leftovers, and serve cold.

HOW DO YOU KNOW IF THEY'RE RIPE?

The best way to tell if a pear is ripe and ready to eat is to press it gently at the stem end. And I mean gently. It should give just a little. The pear should also smell fruity, but sometimes it doesn't. When you go shopping for pears, you may find every one you test is hard and implacable. Not to worry. Bring them home and leave them in a paper bag. Test them every day or so. Some may ripen before others because they were picked at different times. If the pear is fully ripe, use it immediately, or refrigerate it for no more than a day or two.

LEMON CREAM TART

*Makes one
9-inch tart,
8 servings*

This takeoff on key lime pie, made with lemons and a vanilla cookie crust, is deliciously tangy and refreshing. In the nineteenth century, fresh milk would not keep long without refrigeration, so Florida cooks used sweetened condensed milk in their key lime pies.

CRUST

36 vanilla wafer cookies

3 tablespoons sugar

4 tablespoons (1/2 stick) unsalted butter, melted

FILLING

3 large eggs

1 14-ounce can sweetened condensed milk

Finely grated zest of 2 lemons

1/2 cup fresh lemon juice

Confectioners' sugar for dusting

8 candied violets (optional)

1 For the crust, adjust an oven rack to the center position and preheat the oven to 325°F.

2 Put the cookies in a zip-top plastic bag and crush with a rolling pin to make fine crumbs. Transfer the crumbs to a bowl and add the sugar and melted butter. Combine well with a fork. Press the mixture into the bottom and up the sides of a 9-inch tart pan with a removable bottom. Bake for 15 minutes, or until golden brown.

3 Meanwhile, for the filling, whisk the eggs in a medium bowl. Whisk in the condensed milk and the lemon zest. Very gradually whisk in the lemon juice.

4 When the crust is ready, remove it from the oven and pour in the filling. Return the pan to the oven and bake for another 30 minutes, or until the filling has puffed slightly and is set. Let cool completely on a wire rack.

5 Remove the rim of the pan and set the tart, still on the pan bottom, on a serving platter. Refrigerate for several hours, or overnight, before serving.

6 To serve, dust the tart with confectioners' sugar and decorate with the candied violets, if desired. Serve cold.

RUSTIC APRICOT-ALMOND TART

*Makes one
10-inch tart,
8 servings*

This is one of the easiest and most satisfying of tarts. The pastry is made in an old-fashioned way that results in an especially crunchy crust: no fancy shaping and no fancy pans. You'll need a 13-inch pizza pan.

FILLING

1/3 cup sliced almonds, blanched or unblanched

2 tablespoons unbleached all-purpose flour

Flaky Tart Pastry (page 500)

2 pounds apricots (about 14 large), halved and pitted

3/4 cup sugar

1/2 teaspoon pumpkin pie spice

2 tablespoons cold unsalted butter, cut into small pieces

1 Adjust an oven rack to the center position and preheat the oven to 400°F.

2 For the filling, set aside 2 tablespoons of the almonds. Place the remaining almonds and the flour in a food processor and process until fine, about 30 seconds.

3 Roll the pastry dough out on a lightly floured surface to a 13-inch circle. Carefully transfer the pastry circle to an ungreased 13-inch pizza pan and spread with the flour-almond mixture, leaving a 1¹/₂-inch border all around. Arrange the apricot halves cut side down over the flour mixture, overlapping a few in the center if necessary. Combine the sugar with the pumpkin pie spice in a small bowl. Reserve 1 tablespoon, and sprinkle the remaining sugar mixture evenly over the apricots. Scatter the butter pieces over them, then sprinkle the reserved almonds on top. Bring the exposed edges of the pastry up over the outer layer of apricots, pressing firmly to adhere to the fruit. Brush the edges of the pastry lightly with water and sprinkle with the reserved sugar mixture.

4 Bake for 50 to 60 minutes, until the filling is bubbly and the pastry is well browned. Cool the tart on the pan on a wire rack, then carefully transfer the tart to a large serving platter with a wide metal spatula.

RUSTIC APRICOT-PISTACHIO TART

Makes one 10-inch tart, 8 to 10 servings

This informal tart is quick and easy to make since the pastry is shaped free-form and baked on a pizza pan. Serve plain or with whipped cream or vanilla ice cream.

Flaky Tart Pastry (page 500)

FILLING

$^2/_3$ cup shelled pistachios (salted or unsalted)

$^2/_3$ cup sugar

$^1/_4$ teaspoon ground cardamom

2 tablespoons all-purpose flour

2 pounds apricots (about 14 large), halved and pitted

2 tablespoons cold unsalted butter, cut into small pieces

1 Adjust an oven rack to the center position and preheat the oven to 400°F.

2 Roll the dough out on a lightly floured surface to a 13-inch circle. Don't be concerned about rough or uneven edges. Place the dough on an ungreased 13-inch pizza pan.

3 For the filling, coarsely chop $^1/_3$ cup of the pistachios; set aside. Place $^1/_3$ cup of the sugar, the cardamom, the remaining $^1/_3$ cup pistachios, and the flour in a food processor and process for about 30 seconds, until the nuts are finely chopped.

4 Spread the pistachio mixture evenly over the crust, leaving a $1^1/_2$-inch border all around. Arrange the apricot halves cut sides down in concentric circles on the sugar-pistachio mixture. Bring the exposed edges of the pastry up over the apricots and press the pastry firmly in place. Brush the edges of the pastry lightly with water, and sprinkle with 1 tablespoon of the remaining $^1/_3$ cup sugar. Sprinkle the rest of the sugar over the apricots. Sprinkle the chopped pistachios over the fruit. Scatter the pieces of butter on top.

5 Bake for about 1 hour, until the pastry is well browned and the fruit juices are bubbly. Cool the tart on the pan on a wire rack. Serve warm or at room temperature.

NUT CASE

Pistachio nuts, which originated in the Middle East, were first imported into the United States in the 1880s. They didn't become really popular until the 1930s, when the nuts—dyed a gaudy red to set them apart from other nuts— were sold in vending machines. Around that time, an enterprising American plant scientist, William E. Whitehouse, traveled to Persia (modern-day Iran) to collect pistachio seeds for planting in California. The dry desertlike climate of California's interior proved ideal for the nut. But pistachio trees require seven to ten years to mature, and it wasn't until 1950 that a single stand-out tree emerged.

Plantings continued throughout the 1960s, and in 1976, the first commercial crop of 1.5 million pounds was harvested. Today more than 96,000 acres in California are planted with pistachio trees, yielding more than one hundred times the first harvest.

RUSTIC RED PLUM TART

Makes one 11-inch tart, 10 servings

Red plums (there are several varieties to choose from in the summer) have a firmer texture than prune plums, and they give this tart a gorgeous color. Ground walnuts keep the crust from becoming soggy. This tart should be served plain—it needs nothing else.

Flaky Tart Pastry (page 500)

WALNUT MIXTURE

- 1/4 cup walnuts
- 1/4 cup all-purpose flour
- 1/2 teaspoon ground cinnamon

TOPPING

- 1 1/2 pounds ripe red plums (about 9)
- 1/3 cup sugar
- 1/2 teaspoon ground cinnamon
- 1/4 teaspoon freshly grated nutmeg

GLAZE

- 1/4 cup apricot preserves
- 1 tablespoon water

1 Roll the dough out on a lightly floured surface to a 14-inch circle. Carefully transfer the dough to an ungreased 13-inch pizza pan; leave the excess hanging over the rim. Refrigerate if your kitchen is warm.

2 Adjust an oven rack to the center position and preheat the oven to 400°F.

3 For the walnut mixture, process the walnuts, flour, and cinnamon in a food processor for 20 seconds, or until the nuts are very finely ground; do not overprocess. Set aside.

4 For the topping, cut through the "seam" of each plum to divide the plum into two halves, then slice each half into 6 wedges, cutting the wedges off the pit as you go.

5 Sprinkle the walnut mixture evenly over the tart dough, leaving a 1 1/2-inch border all around. Arrange a circle of plum wedges, touching one another, around the edge of the walnut mixture. Form a second circle of plum slices inside the first, with the tips of the slices slightly overlapping the outer circle. Form a third, and possibly a fourth, circle with the remaining plum wedges; the walnut mixture should be completely covered.

6 Combine the sugar, cinnamon, and nutmeg. Set aside 1 tablespoon and sprinkle the remainder evenly over the plums. Bring the exposed edges of the pastry up over the plums, pressing it firmly in place. Brush the pastry edges lightly with cold water and sprinkle with the reserved sugar mixture.

7 Bake for about 50 minutes, until the pastry is well browned. Set the pan on a cooling rack while you prepare the apricot glaze.

8 For the glaze, combine the apricot preserves and water in a small heavy saucepan and bring to a boil over medium heat. Boil, stirring constantly, for 1 minute. Brush the glaze carefully over the plums and inner part of the pastry edge. Let cool completely.

BRIOCHE APPLE TART

Makes one 10-inch tart, 10 to 12 servings

This deliciously indulgent apple extravaganza will melt in your mouth. Apples cooked in a caramel syrup are combined with a bit of Calvados-flavored cream, spread in a buttery brioche crust, and baked. You must prepare the brioche dough at least 1 day ahead, and you can do the same for the filling. Make this early in the day you plan to serve it, since it needs to cool for a few hours. Use tart, crisp apples that will hold their shape during cooking, such as Jonamac, Roxbury Russett, Ashmead's Kernel, Rubinette, Winesap, or a combination. You can serve this plain, or with lightly sweetened whipped cream or small scoops of vanilla ice cream.

FILLING

Finely grated zest of 1 lemon

1/3 cup fresh lemon juice

3 pounds crisp, tart apples, quartered, cored, peeled, and sliced crosswise 1/2 inch thick

4 tablespoons (1/2 stick) unsalted butter

1/2 cup sugar

1/4 teaspoon salt

1/4 teaspoon ground cinnamon

3/4 pound chilled Brioche Dough (page 128)

EGG GLAZE AND TOPPING

1 large egg

2 teaspoons milk

1 tablespoon Calvados or 2 teaspoons pure vanilla extract

1/2 cup heavy cream or mascarpone cheese

Confectioners' sugar for dusting

1 For the filling, combine the lemon zest and juice in a large bowl. Toss the apples in the lemon mixture.

2 Melt the butter in a large skillet over medium-high heat. Stir in the sugar, salt, and cinnamon. Cook, stirring constantly, until the sugar melts and the syrup is caramel colored. Add the apple and lemon mixture and stir well. Cover the pan and cook over medium heat, stirring once or twice, until the caramel melts, about 5 minutes. The apples should be tender but not falling apart. Pour the mixture into a large strainer set over a bowl and allow to drain for several minutes.

3 Return the sugar mixture to the pan and cook over high heat, stirring constantly, for 2 to 3 minutes, until the liquid reduces to a thick syrup. Return the apples to the pan and stir them gently to coat well. Remove from the heat and let cool to room temperature. (If making a day ahead, transfer the cooled apple mixture to a bowl, cover, and refrigerate. Bring to room temperature before continuing.)

4 Meanwhile, butter a 10-inch quiche dish or glass pie plate; set aside. Roll the brioche dough out on a lightly floured surface to a 13-inch circle. Fit the dough into the pan, without stretching it. Fold any overhanging dough back into the pan to make a slightly thicker rim, and press firmly. Cover the dough loosely with a kitchen towel and let rise at room temperature until it is a bit puffy, about 1 1/2 hours.

5 Adjust an oven rack to the lower third position and preheat the oven to 400°F.

6 For the egg glaze, beat together the egg and milk in a small bowl. Prick the bottom of the brioche dough at 1-inch intervals with a fork, and brush some of the glaze lightly all over the bottom and sides. Add the Calvados or vanilla and cream or mascarpone to the leftover egg glaze and whisk until smooth. Add to the cooled apple mixture and fold together gently. Turn the mixture into the quiche dish and smooth the top.

AS THEY LIVE AND BREATHE

New-crop apples make the best pies. Once an apple is picked, it never gets any better. It's crucial to store apples in the refrigerator; do not leave them out on the counter. Even after they are harvested, apples live and breathe just like us, and cold helps to retard spoilage. If you live near an apple orchard, hand-pick your own apples.

7 Bake for 15 minutes. Reduce the heat to 325°F and bake until the pastry is deep brown and the filling is set, 40 to 45 minutes more. If the edges of the pastry are browning too much, cover the tart loosely with aluminum foil toward the end of baking. Let cool to room temperature on a wire rack.

8 Just before serving, dust the top with confectioners' sugar. Refrigerate leftovers, but bring to room temperature before serving.

FRESH ORANGE TART

Makes one 9-inch tart, 8 servings

This is a wonderfully refreshing dessert after a filling meal. Make it in the winter, when oranges are at their best. Choose the juiciest oranges, which will feel the heaviest. This tart should be eaten within a few hours of being prepared.

FILLING

- 12 large seedless oranges (about 5 pounds), plus more if needed
- 1/2 cup sugar
- 2 tablespoons cornstarch
- 1/8 teaspoon salt
- 1 teaspoon pure vanilla extract
- 1/3 cup orange marmalade
- 1 tart shell made with Flaky Tart Pastry (page 500), baked

1 For the filling, place an orange on its side on a work surface and slice off about 1/2 inch from the top and bottom with a small sharp knife. Stand the orange upright and remove the peel and white pith in strips with a downward curving motion of the knife, rotating the orange as you work. Hold the orange over a bowl and remove the sections by cutting between the membranes and letting the sections fall into the bowl. Squeeze the membranes to release more juice. Repeat with the remaining oranges. Transfer the oranges and juice to a large strainer set over a bowl and set aside to drain.

2 Measure the orange juice. You should have 1 cup. If not, squeeze more oranges until you do.

3 In a small heavy saucepan, stir together the sugar, cornstarch, and salt. Gradually stir in the orange juice. Cook over medium heat, stirring constantly and gently with a heatproof rubber spatula, until the mixture boils and thickens. Reduce the heat to low and cook, stirring, for 1 minute more. Remove from the heat and stir in the vanilla. Let the sauce cool to room temperature, stirring occasionally.

4 Place the marmalade in a small saucepan set over medium heat, and bring to a boil, stirring occasionally. Immediately remove from the heat and pour the marmalade into the prepared tart shell. Use the back of a teaspoon to spread it evenly over the bottom. Arrange about half the orange sections in an attractive pattern over the marmalade, overlapping them slightly. Spoon and spread about $^1/_3$ cup of the cooled sauce evenly over the oranges. Arrange the remaining oranges in a pretty pattern over the first layer. Spoon and spread the rest of the sauce evenly over the orange slices. Refrigerate for at least 4 hours, but no longer than 8 hours (or the crust will become too soft), before serving.

ORANGE OR LEMON TART

Take 6 large lemons, rub them well in salt, put them into salt and water and let rest 2 days, change them daily in fresh water, 14 days, then cut slices and mince as fine as you can and boil them 2 or 3 hours till tender, then take 6 pippins [apples], pare, quarter, and core them, boil in 1 pint fair water till the pippins break, then put the half of the pippins, with all the liquor to the orange or lemon, and add one pound of sugar, boil all together one quarter of an hour, put into a gallipot [earthen pot] and squeeze thereto a fresh orange, one spoon of which, with a spoon of the pulp of the pippin, laid into a thin royal paste, laid into small shallow pans or saucers, brushed with melted butter, and some superfine sugar sifted thereon, with a gentle baking, will be very good.

N.B. Pastry pans, or saucers, must be buttered lightly before the paste is laid on. If glass or china be used, have only a top crust.

—Amelia Simmons, *American Cookery* (1796)

FRESH APRICOT TART

*Makes one
11-inch tart,
10 servings*

A thin layer of pastry cream in a buttery almond crust makes a sensational base for poached fresh apricots. Be sure the apricots are firm, or they will quickly turn to mush in the poaching liquid. Since this recipe has several components, you could make the pastry and pastry cream a day ahead. Then all you will have left to do is poach the apricots and bake the tart. The whole thing is brushed with an apricot glaze, which gives the tart a beautiful shine.

Spanish settlers brought apricots to this country in the eighteenth century. The fruit flourished in California's interior valleys, where days are warm and nights cool. Today California grows a number of apricot varieties and produces more than 95 percent of this country's apricots. Much of the fruit is dried, but the hardiest varieties are shipped fresh all over the country from mid-May through early July.

PASTRY

- 1/3 cup slivered almonds
- 1 1/3 cups all-purpose flour, plus more if needed
- 2 tablespoons confectioners' sugar
- 1/4 teaspoon salt
- 10 tablespoons (1 1/4 sticks) cold unsalted butter, cut into tablespoon-sized pieces
- 2 tablespoons ice water

PASTRY CREAM

- 1 cup milk
- 3 large egg yolks
  Pinch of salt
- 1/3 cup sugar
- 2 tablespoons cornstarch
- 1 tablespoon cold unsalted butter
- 1/2 teaspoon pure lemon extract

POACHED APRICOTS

- 3 cups water
- 1 cup sugar
- 1 vanilla bean, split lengthwise, seeds scraped from the pod (pod and seeds reserved)
- 2 pounds firm but ripe apricots (about 14 large), halved, pitted, and each half cut into 2 wedges

APRICOT GLAZE

- 1/3 cup apricot jam

1 For the pastry, place the almonds in a food processor and process until finely chopped, about 10 seconds. Add the 1^1/$_3$ cups flour, confectioners' sugar, and salt and process for 15 to 30 seconds, until the nuts and flour are about the same consistency. Add the butter and pulse 10 times for about 1 second each; the butter should be in small pieces. Pulsing rapidly, pour the water through the feed tube and pulse just until the dough gathers into large clumps.

2 Turn the dough out onto an unfloured work surface, and form it into a 10-inch log; it should not be sticky. If it is, dust it lightly with a little flour. With a short end facing you, use the heel of your hand to rapidly smear walnut-sized portions of the dough away from you, beginning at the far end, until all the pastry has been used. Reshape the dough into a log, and repeat the procedure twice more. Flatten the dough into a disk and place it in an 11-inch tart pan with a removable bottom. Carefully press the dough evenly over the bottom and up the sides of the pan, so it extends about ^{1}/$_8$ inch above the rim. Refrigerate for at least 1 hour. (The tart shell can be covered with plastic wrap and refrigerated for up to 1 day.)

3 For the pastry cream, heat the milk in a medium heavy saucepan just until it reaches a boil. Remove from the heat. In a small bowl, whisk the egg yolks with the salt. Gradually whisk in the sugar and whisk vigorously until the mixture becomes thick and pale, 2 to 3 minutes. Whisk in the cornstarch. Whisk in a few tablespoons of the hot milk. Gradually add the remaining milk, whisking until smooth. Scrape the mixture into the saucepan, add the butter, and cook over medium heat, stirring with a heat-proof rubber spatula, until the mixture is very hot. Keep stirring and scraping the bottom and sides of the pan with the rubber spatula until the mixture gets lumpier, like large-curd cottage cheese. Switch to the whisk, reduce the heat to medium-low, and continue cooking and stirring for 1 to 2 minutes, until the mixture is smooth and thick. Remove from the heat and whisk in the lemon extract. Scrape the pastry cream into a small bowl and press a piece of plastic wrap directly on the surface. Cool to room temperature, then refrigerate. (The pastry cream can be made up to 1 day ahead.)

4 Adjust an oven rack to the center position and place a baking sheet on the rack. Preheat the oven to 375°F.

5 Line the pastry shell with a square of aluminum foil and fill the shell with dried beans. Place the tart pan on the baking sheet in the oven and bake for 20 minutes. Remove the baking sheet with the tart pan, carefully lift out the foil and beans, and gently prick the bottom of the pastry all over with a fork. Return the tart pan and baking sheet to the oven, reduce the temperature to 350°F, and continue baking until the tart shell is evenly browned, 20 to 25 minutes more. Check after the first few minutes to be sure it isn't puffing up in places; if it is, carefully prick the puffs with a toothpick. Let cool completely on a rack.

6 For the poached apricots, combine the water, sugar, and vanilla seeds and pod in a medium heavy saucepan. Bring to a boil over medium-high heat, stirring occasionally, and boil for 2 to 3 minutes. Add the apricots (there should be enough liquid to just cover them), cover the pan, and remove from the heat. Set aside for 2 to 5 minutes, until the apricots are cooked through and tender but not mushy. Remove the apricots with a slotted spoon and set them on several thicknesses of paper towels to drain thoroughly. Reserve the poaching liquid.

7 To assemble the tart, remove the sides from the tart pan and carefully transfer the shell to a dessert platter. Gently whisk the chilled pastry cream until smooth, and spread it evenly in the pastry shell. Arrange the apricots in concentric circles over the pastry cream, placing them close together.

8 For the glaze, boil the apricot jam with 1 tablespoon of the reserved poaching liquid in a small heavy saucepan, stirring constantly, until very thick, bubbly, and translucent, 2 to 3 minutes. Immediately brush the hot glaze over the apricots. Drizzle any remaining glaze in the gaps between the apricots. Refrigerate. The tart can be served as soon as the glaze is set. If it has chilled longer and is very cold, bring it to room temperature before serving.

MAPLE-PECAN TART

Makes one 9-inch tart, 8 servings

This tart comes close to a pecan pie, but the maple syrup gives it an entirely different character. Be sure to use pure maple syrup. Allow the tart to cool completely before serving so the filling will not be runny when you cut it. A dollop of lightly sweetened whipped cream on the side is really wonderful.

Flaky Tart Pastry (page 500)

FILLING

1 1/2 cups pecan halves or large pieces
1 cup pure maple syrup
2 teaspoons pure vanilla extract
3 large eggs
1/4 teaspoon salt

1 Adjust an oven rack to the center position, set a baking sheet on the rack, and preheat the oven to 450°F.

2 Roll the pastry out on a lightly floured surface to an 11-inch circle. Fit the dough loosely into a 9-inch tart pan with a removable bottom, without stretching the dough. Fold the overhanging pastry into the pan, pressing it firmly against the sides to form a double layer. Press the sides of the pastry so that it extends 1/4 inch above the rim.

3 For the filling, toast the pecans by placing them in a single layer on a heavy baking sheet. Bake for 4 to 5 minutes, stirring once or twice, until fragrant. Remove from the baking sheet and set side to cool. Return the baking sheet to the oven. Whisk together the maple syrup, vanilla, eggs, and salt in a medium bowl until smooth. Pour into the tart shell and sprinkle the pecans on top.

4 Place the tart pan on the baking sheet and bake for 10 minutes. Reduce the heat to 325°F and continue baking for another 20 minutes, or until the filling is set and the pastry is lightly browned. Let cool completely in the pan on a wire rack.

5 Remove the rim of the pan and set the tart, still on the pan bottom, on a serving platter. Serve at room temperature.

PUMPKIN SWIRL CHEESECAKE TART

Makes one 9-inch tart, 8 servings

A spicy pumpkin mixture swirled with a smooth cream cheese batter and baked in a flaky tart shell makes a festive dessert for Thanksgiving. I serve this instead of pumpkin pie. Rum-flavored whipped cream topping adds an extra bit of holiday spirit.

FILLING

- 2 8-ounce packages Neufchâtel cream cheese
- $3/4$ cup sweetened condensed milk
- $1/4$ teaspoon salt
- 2 teaspoons pure vanilla extract
- 3 large eggs
- $2/3$ cup canned solid-pack pumpkin (not pumpkin pie filling)
- $1/2$ teaspoon ground cinnamon
- $1/4$ teaspoon ground ginger
- $1/4$ teaspoon ground allspice

- 1 tart shell made with Flaky Tart Pastry (page 500), baked

TOPPING

- 1 cup heavy cream
- 1 tablespoon dark or light rum
- 2 tablespoons confectioners' sugar

Ground cinnamon for dusting

1 Adjust an oven rack to the center position and preheat the oven to 300°F.

2 In a medium bowl, beat the cream cheese with an electric mixer on medium speed until very smooth. Add $1/2$ cup of the condensed milk and beat until smooth. Add the salt, vanilla, and 2 of the eggs and beat only until incorporated.

3 In a small bowl, whisk together the pumpkin, cinnamon, ginger, allspice, the remaining $1/4$ cup condensed milk, the remaining egg, and $1/2$ cup of the cream cheese mixture until smooth. Pour the pumpkin mixture over the remaining cream cheese mixture, and fold together with only 2 or 3 strokes of a rubber spatula to make a two-tone batter. Turn the mixture into the tart shell and smooth the top.

4 Bake for 50 minutes. Turn the oven off and leave the tart in the oven for another 45 minutes with the door closed. The top may have a few cracks.

5 Remove the tart from the oven and cool to room temperature on a wire rack; then refrigerate for 6 hours or longer.

6 For the topping, whip the cream, rum, and confectioners' sugar with an electric mixer until thick. Remove the rim of the tart pan and spread the cream over the pumpkin layer. Dust the top with cinnamon. Transfer the tart, still on the pan bottom, to a dessert platter. To serve, rinse a sharp knife in hot water and shake off the excess water before making each cut. Refrigerate leftovers.

CHOCOLATE TART IN A CHOCOLATE CRUST

Makes one 10-inch tart, 8 to 10 servings

This tart is not at all difficult to make, and you can get the whole thing ready a day ahead except for the whipped cream topping, which takes only a few minutes to put together. Dutch-process cocoa gives the pastry a deeper chocolate taste than regular cocoa, but either one will work.

PASTRY

- 1 cup all-purpose flour
- 1/4 cup unsweetened cocoa, preferably Dutch-process
- 1/4 teaspoon salt
- 4 tablespoons (1/2 stick) cold unsalted butter
- 1/2 cup confectioners' sugar
- 1 large egg yolk
- 1 teaspoon pure vanilla extract
- 3 tablespoons ice water, plus more if needed

FILLING

- 1 14-ounce can sweetened condensed milk
- 1/2 cup unsweetened cocoa, preferably Dutch-process
- 6 ounces cream cheese
- 1 large egg
- 1 large egg yolk
- 2 teaspoons pure vanilla extract

TOPPING

- 1 cup heavy cream
- 2 tablespoons confectioners' sugar
- 1 ounce (1 square) semisweet chocolate, finely chopped

1 For the pastry, stir together the flour, cocoa, and salt in a medium bowl. With a pastry blender or two knives, cut in the butter until the mixture resembles fine meal. In a small bowl, combine the confectioners' sugar, egg yolk, vanilla, and water with a fork. Add gradually to the flour mixture, tossing and stirring with the fork until the dough just gathers into a ball. If the dough seems dry, add a bit more water. Shape the pastry into a 1-inch-thick disk, wrap securely in plastic wrap, and refrigerate for 30 minutes.

2 Roll the dough out on a lightly floured surface to a 13-inch circle. Fit it into a 10-inch tart pan with a removable bottom, without stretching it. Trim

away the excess pastry, leaving a $^1/_2$-inch overhang. Fold the overhang into the pan, pressing it firmly against the sides to form a double thickness. Refrigerate.

3 Adjust an oven rack to the lower third position and place a baking sheet on the rack. Preheat the oven to 350°F.

4 For the filling, stir together the condensed milk and cocoa in a medium bowl. Beat in the cream cheese with an electric mixer until the mixture is very smooth. Beat in the egg, egg yolk, and vanilla extract just until smooth. Turn the mixture into the pastry-lined pan.

5 Set the pan on the baking sheet in the oven and bake for about 30 minutes, until the top is set and springs back when lightly pressed; do not overbake. Let cool completely in the pan on a wire rack.

6 For the topping, whip the cream with the confectioners' sugar until thick. Remove the rim of the tart pan and set the tart, still on the pan bottom, on a dessert platter. Spread the cream on top of the tart (make fancy swirls with the back of a teaspoon if you wish), and sprinkle with the chopped chocolate. Refrigerate until ready to serve. Serve very cold.

SOURCES FOR BOOKS, EQUIPMENT, AND INGREDIENTS

Books

ONLINE SOURCES

Several internet sites offer all kinds of used old cookbooks and other titles for sale.

www.addall.com This is an umbrella site that provides listings from several other sites. When you visit it, click on "used books" on the home page. Sometimes you'll have the option of choosing from several copies of the same book, offered by different independent booksellers.

www.alibris.com or **www.abebooks.com** Alibris does a much better job of keeping its listings current than abebooks; the listings on abebooks are often outdated.

www.amazon.com You can access rare books by clicking your way from amazon's home page to "books" and then to "rare."

INDEPENDENT BOOKSELLERS

There are hundreds of independent booksellers who have old cookbooks and/or facsimiles in their inventory. Here are some I've used.

Food Heritage Press
P. O. Box 163
Ipswich, MA 01938–0163
800–398–4474
Fax: 978–356–8306
Website: www.foodbooks.com

Founded by Joseph M. Carlin in 1995, this company offers out-of-print cookbooks and many facsimiles through its catalog. The website has a valuable link called "Resource Guide for Food Writers." While you can't order titles online at the time of this writing, you can see what's available and either call to place an order or download a form to fill out and fax to the company. Call for a catalog.

Food Words

P. O. Box 42568

Portland, OR 97242-0568

503-232-3470

e-mail: foodword@spiritone.com

This bookshop is owned by Johan and Kay Mathiesen. Their catalogs are full of humor and wonderful old and not-so-old cookbooks.

The Reynolds

185 Main Avenue

South Hampton, NH 03827

603-394-0200

e-mail: oldeport@ttlc.net

Philip K. Reynolds offers rare and hard-to-find cookbooks in his catalog. You can also query him for a particular book by calling or emailing.

The Wine and Food Library

1207 West Madison Street

Ann Arbor, MI 48103

734-663-4894

e-mail: jblong@umich.edu

For nearly thirty years, this business, owned by Jan and Dan Longone, has been an invaluable source for old, rare, and out-of-print books on cookery and wine. Request a catalog.

HISTORICAL NEWSLETTER

Food History News

S. L. Oliver

1061 Main Road

Islesboroo, ME 04848

e-mail: sandyo@prexar.com

Food historian Sandy Oliver has been publishing her informative, chatty newsletter quarterly for thirteen years. It's essential reading for anybody interested in food history. To subscribe, write or e-mail her.

Equipment

Many department stores and specialty cookware shops will have what you need, but here are a few retail and mail-order sources that sell all kinds of baking equipment.

The Baker's Catalogue

P.O. Box 876
Norwich, VT 05055-0876
800-827-6836
Website: www.bakerscatalogue.com

A publication of King Arthur Flour, *The Baker's Catalogue* is issued several times a year. It offers all kinds of baking pans, baking stones, measuring cups, spoons, bench scrapers, marble slabs, cherry pitters, cookie and doughnut cutters, pastry brushes, pastry canvases, silicone liners, bannetons, and many more baker's needs, including many food items (see page 525). The company also has an excellent retail store.

Bridge Kitchenware

214 East 52nd Street
New York, NY 10022
800-274-3435
Website: www.bridgekitchenware.com

This venerable New York City institution is a cook's heaven. Bakers will find just about anything they might need there. Visit the retail store or shop online.

New York Cake and Baking Distributors

56 West 22nd Street
New York, NY 10010
800-94-CAKE-9; 212-675-CAKE

This is the mother of all baking stores. Just about anything you could want, including candy-making tools and specialty products, is here. They also sell ready-made fondant. The company offers a large catalog.

Sweet Celebrations

7009 Washington Avenue South

Edina, MN 55439

800-328-6722

Website: www.sweetc.com

Formerly known as Maid of Scandinavia, this company sells all kinds of baking equipment, cardboard cake disks, silicone liners, and candy-making equipment and ingredients.

Williams-Sonoma

Mail Order Department

P.O. Box 7456

San Francisco, CA 94120-7456

800-541-2233

Website: www.williams-sonoma.com

Although Williams-Sonoma made its reputation selling well-made cookware, cooking utensils, and baking equipment, the company's focus has shifted in recent years to high-end cookware and food products. However, the company still sells food processors, heavy-duty mixers, and some baking equipment.

OLD COOKING EQUIPMENT AND UTENSILS

I've bought some marvelous items through eBay, including a Dover egg beater from 1893; an antique cast-iron gem pan made in Erie, Pennsylvania; a Washington pie plate; several doughnut cutters from the end of the nineteenth century, and some old books and baking pamphlets.

Ingredients

The Baker's Catalogue

P.O. Box 876

Norwich, VT 05055-0876

800-827-6836

Website: www.bakerscalogue.com

If you can't find King Arthur flours locally, you can order them by mail. The catalog also offers pure maple syrup, nuts (including black walnuts), dried fruits (including diced citron), flavoring extracts, chocolate, cocoa, various seeds, dry yeast, and much more.

Chukar Cherry Company

320 Wine Country Road
P. O. Box 510
Prosser, WA 99350
800-624-8544
Website: www.chukar.com
e-mail: chukar@chukar.com

This company offers many dried fruits and berries, including blueberries and cran-berries, as well as cherries.

Dairy Fresh Candies

57 Salem Street
Boston, MA 02113
800-336-5536
Website: shop.store.yahoo.com/dairyfreshcandy

This store carries excellent citron, available in halves or diced. I prefer the halves because I can cut them into any size I want, and they keep better than cut citron. The company also sells many kinds of nuts, extracts, dried and candied fruits, and baking chocolate and cocoa.

Giusto's Vita-Grain

241 East Harris Avenue
South San Francisco, CA 94080
415-873-6566

This company is a great source of organic baking flours.

Great Valley Mills

1774 County Line Road
Barto, PA 19504
800-688-6455

The star attraction here is the unbleached soft wheat flour, a cake or pastry flour that is untreated with chemicals. They also sell unbleached hard wheat flour (bread flour), hard whole wheat flour, soft whole wheat flour, rye flour, rice flour, cracked wheat, fine yellow cornmeal, coarse yellow cornmeal, and many kinds of mixers and food items. Call for a catalog.

Hoppinjohns

800-828-4412

Website: www.hoppinjohns.com

John Martin Taylor, author of wonderful cookbooks about the foods of the South, sells many food items online, including terrific whole-grain grits, stone-ground white cornmeal, and fine white corn flour (finely ground cornmeal). I use the cornmeal for cornmeal breads and muffins, and the corn flour for some cakes.

Penzeys Spices

P. O. Box 933

W19362 Apollo Drive

Muskego, Wisconsin 53150

800-741-7787

Website: www.penzeys.com

The company is famous for pure extracts of vanilla (including double-strength), almond, lemon, and orange; whole vanilla beans and nutmegs; cinnamon sticks and ground cinnamon (real Vietnamese cassia cinnamon, and others); and many other spices. Call for a catalog.

Spices, Etc.

P.O. Box 2088

Savannah, GA 31402

800-827-6373

e-mail: spices@spicesetc.com

Website: www.spicesetc.com

This company carries spices, many natural extracts, and other food items. As far as I know, it is the only company that sells natural coconut flavoring. Thick and creamy, it's essential for coconut cakes, pastries, and desserts. Call for a catalogue.

The Vanilla.COMpany

800-757-7511

Website:www.vanilla.com

This online company, founded and owned by Patricia Rain, is dedicated to promoting and selling pure, natural vanilla worldwide as extracts and whole beans. The site is also a source of vanilla lore, history, and recipes.

BIBLIOGRAPHY

Acton, Eliza. *Modern Cookery in All Its Branches*. Philadelphia: John E. Potter, 1863.

All about Home Baking. New York: General Foods, 1933.

Allen, Ida C. Bailey. *A New Snowdrift Cook Book*. New York: Southern Cotton Oil Trading, 1920.

———. *Ida Bailey's Modern Cook Book*. New York: Garden City Publishing, 1924.

Anderson, Jean. *The American Century Cookbook*. New York: Clarkson Potter, 1997.

Andrews, Mary E. McKean. *Recipe Book*. Manuscript. Cambridge, Mass.: Schlesinger Library.

Appleton, Mary. *Recipe Book*. Manuscript. Cambridge, Mass.: Schlesinger Library.

Barnes, Bertha. *Antique Cookbook*. Jefferson City, Mo.: Modern Litho-Print, 1980.

Beecher, Catharine. *Miss Beecher's Domestic Receipt-Book*. New York: Harper & Brothers, 1846.

Bennion, E. B., and G.S.T. Bamford. *The Technology of Cake Making*. 6th ed. New York: Chapman & Hall, 1997.

Bliss, Mrs. *The Practical Cook Book; Containing Upwards of One Thousand Receipts*. Philadelphia: Lippincott, Grambo, 1853.

Blot, Pierre. *Handbook of Practical Cookery*. New York: D. Appleton, 1867.

Brenner, Joël Glenn. *The Emperors of Chocolate*. New York: Random House, 1999.

Bryan, Mrs. Lettice. *The Kentucky Housewife*. Facsimile of the 1839 edition. Paducah, Ky.: Image Graphics (no date).

Buckeye Cookery and Practical Housekeeping. Facsimile of the 1877 edition. Austin, Tex.: Steck-Warlick, 1970.

Butruille, Susan G. *Women's Voices from the Western Frontier*. Boise, Idaho: Tamarack Books, 1995.

Chadwick, Mrs. J. *Home Cookery: A Collection of Tried Receipts*. Facsimile of the 1853 edition. Birmingham, Ala.: Oxmoor House, 1984.

Child, Mrs. *The American Frugal Housewife*. Facsimile of the 1829 edition. New York: Harper & Row, 1972.

The Complete Bread, Cake, and Cracker Baker in Two Parts. 5th ed. Chicago: Confectioner and Baker Publishing, 1881.

Cornelius, Mrs. *The Young Housekeeper's Friend*. Boston: Brown, Taggard and Chase, 1859.

Corriher, Shirley O. *CookWise*. New York: William Morrow, 1997.

Crowen, Mrs. T. J. *The American Lady's System of Cookery*. Auburn, N.Y.: Derby and Miller, 1850.

———. *Every Lady's Cook Book*. Toledo, Ohio: Sawyer, Brother, 1856.

David, Elizabeth. *English Bread and Yeast Cookery*. Notes by Karen Hess. New York: Viking Press, 1980.

Davidson, Alan. *The Oxford Companion to Food*. Oxford: Oxford University Press, 1999.

De Baca, Margarita C. *New Mexico Dishes*. Albuquerque: Albuquerque Printing, 1983.

De Gouy, Louis P. *The Gold Cook Book*. New York: Greenberg, 1947.

———. *The Pie Book*. New York: Greenberg, 1949.

De Voe, Thomas F. *The Market Book*. Facsimile of the 1862 edition. New York: Burt Franklin, 1969.

———. *The Market Assistant*. Facsimile of the 1867 edition. Detroit: Gale Research, 1975.

Eckhardt, Linda West. *Pears*. San Francisco: Chronicle Books, 1996.

Editors of *American Heritage*. *The American Heritage Cookbook*. American Heritage Publishing, 1964.

Egerton, John. *Southern Food: At Home, on the Road, in History*. New York: Alfred A. Knopf, 1987.

Farmer, Fannie Merritt. *The Boston Cooking School Cook Book*. Boston: Little, Brown, 1907.

———. *The Original Boston Cooking-School Cook Book*. Facsimile of the 1896 edition. New York: Hugh Lauter Levin Associates, 1996.

Farr, Sidney Saylor. *More than Moonshine: Appalachian Recipes and Recollections*. Pittsburgh: University of Pittsburgh Press, 1983.

The First Texas Cook Book. Facsimile of the original 1883 edition. Austin, Tex.: Eakin Publications, 1986.

Franklin, Linda Campbell. *300 Years of Kitchen Collectibles*. 4th ed. Iola, Wis.: Krause Publications, 1997.

Frost, S. Annie. *The Godey's Lady's Book Receipts and Household Hints*. Philadelphia: Evans, Stoddart, 1870.

Fussell, Betty. *Masters of American Cookery*. New York: Times Books, 1983.

Giger, Mrs. Frederick Sidney, ed. *Colonial Receipt Book: Celebrated Old Recipes Used a Century Ago by Mrs. Goodfellow's Cooking School.* Philadelphia: John C. Winston, 1907.

Gilbert, Fabiola C. *Historic Cookery.* State College: New Mexico College of Agriculture and Mechanic Arts, 1956.

Given, Meta. *Meta Given's Modern Encyclopedia of Cooking.* 2 vols. Chicago: J. G. Ferguson, 1959.

Glasse, Hannah. *The Art of Cookery Made Plain and Easy.* Facsimile of the 1805 edition, with notes by Karen Hess. Bedford, Mass.: Applewood Books, 1997.

Gregory, Annie R. *Woman's Favorite Cookbook.* Chicago: International Publishing, 1902.

Hale, Sarah Josepha. *The Good Housekeeper.* Facsimile of the 1841 edition, with an introduction by Janice Bluestein Longone. Mineola, N.Y.: Dover Publications, 1996.

Hall, Elizabeth M. *Practical American Cookery and Domestic Economy.* New York: C. M. Saxton, Barker, 1860.

Hanley, Rosemary, and Peter Hanley. *America's Best Recipes: State Fair Blue Ribbon Winners.* New York: Galahad Books, 1983.

Harland, Marion. *Marion Harland's Complete Cookbook.* Indianapolis: Bobbs-Merrill, 1906.

———. *Common Sense in the Household.* Facsimile of the 1871 edition. Birmingham, Ala.: Oxmoor House, 1985.

Hart, Richard N. *Leavening Agents.* Easton, Pa.: Chemical Publishing, 1914.

Hearn, Lafcadio. *Creole Cook Book.* Fascimile of *La Cuisine Creole* (1885). Gretna, La.: Pelican Publishing, 1967.

Heatter, Maida. *Maida Heatter's Book of Great Desserts.* New York: Alfred A. Knopf, 1974.

Henderson, Mary F. *Practical Cooking and Dinner Giving.* New York: Harper & Brothers, 1877.

Hess, John L. and Karen Hess. *The Taste of America.* Columbia: University of South Carolina Press, 1977.

Hess, Karen. *The Carolina Rice Kitchen: The African Connection.* Columbia: University of South Carolina Press, 1992.

Hill, Annabella P. *Mrs. Hill's Southern Practical Cookery.* Facsimile of *Mrs. Hill's New Cook Book,* 1872 edition. Columbia: University of South Carolina Press, 1995.

Hines, Mary Ann, Gordon Marshall, and William Woys Weaver. *The Larder Invaded. Reflections on Three Centuries of Philadelphia Food and Drink.* Philadelphia: Library Company of Philadelphia and Historical Society of Pennsylvania, 1987.

Home Helps: A Pure Food Cook Book. Chicago: N. K. Fairbank, 1910.

Hooker, Richard J. *Food and Drink in America.* New York: Bobbs-Merrill, 1981.

Horry, Harriott Pinckney. *A Colonial Plantation Cookbook: The Receipt Book of Harriott Pinckney Horry, 1770.* Ed. by Richard J. Hooker. Columbia: University of South Carolina Press, 1984.

Howard, Maria Willett. *Lowney's Cook Book.* Boston: Walter M. Lowney, 1908.

Howland, Mrs. E. A. *The New England Economical Housekeeper.* Worcester, Mass.: self-published, 1846.

Irving, Washington. *Diedrich Knickerbocker's A History of New-York.* Facsimile of the 1854 edition. Tarrytown, N.Y.: Sleepy Hollow Press, 1981.

Larkin Housewives' Cook Book. Buffalo, N.Y.: Larkin, 1915.

Lawrence, James M., and Rux Martin. *Sweet Maple.* Shelburne, Vt.: Chapters Publishing, 1993.

Lea, Elizabeth Ellicott. *A Quaker Woman's Cookbook: The Domestic Cookery of Elizabeth Ellicott Lea.* Ed. by William Woys Weaver. Philadelphia: University of Pennsylvania Press, 1982.

Lee, Mrs. N.K.M. *The Cook's Own Book and Housekeeper's Register.* Boston: Munroe and Francis, 1845.

Leslie, Eliza. *The Lady's Receipt Book; a Useful Companion for Large or Small Families.* Philadelphia: Carey and Hart, 1847.

———. *Miss Leslie's Directions for Cookery.* 1851. Reprint, with an introduction by Janice Bluestein Longone, Mineola, N.Y.: Dover Publications, 1999.

———. *Miss Leslie's New Cookery Book.* Philadelphia: T. B. Peterson, 1857.

———. *Miss Leslie's New Receipts for Cooking.* Philadelphia: T. B. Peterson, 1854.

———. *Seventy-five Receipts, for Pastry, Cakes, and Sweetmeats.* Facsimile of the first edition, 1828. Chester, Conn.: Applewood Books (no date).

Levenstein, Harvey. *Paradox of Plenty: A Social History of Eating in America.* New York: Oxford University Press, 1993.

Lincoln, Mrs. D. A. *Boston Cooking School Cook Book.* 1884. Reprint, with an introduction by Janie Bluestein Longone. Mineola, N.Y.: Dover Publications, 1996.

Longone, Jan. "Professor Blot and the First French Cooking School in New York, Part 1." *Gastronomica* 1, no. 2 (2001): 65–71.

———. "Professor Blot and the First French Cooking School in New York, Part 2." *Gastronomica* 1, no. 3 (2001): 53–59.

Luce, William. *The Belle of Amherst*. New York: Samuel French, 1976.

Lundy, Ronni. *Shuck Beans, Stack Cakes, and Honest Fried Chicken*. New York: Atlantic Monthly Press, 1991.

Lutes, Della T. *The Country Kitchen*. Boston: Little, Brown, 1935.

Martha Washington's Booke of Cookery. Transcribed by Karen Hess. New York: Columbia University Press, 1995.

McCay, Clive M., and Jeanette B. McCay. *The Cornell Bread Book: 54 Recipes for Nutritious Loaves, Rolls, and Coffee Cakes*. New York: Dover Publications, 1980.

Moss, Kay, and Kathryn Hoffman. *The Backcountry Housewife: A Study of Eighteenth-Century Foods*. Gastonia, N.C.: Schiele Museum, 1994.

Oddo, Sandra. *Home Made: Recipes from the Nineteenth Century, Rescued, Reinterpreted, and Commented Upon*. New York: Atheneum, 1972.

Oliver, Sandra. *Saltwater Foodways*. Mystic, Conn.: Mystic Seaport Museum, 1995.

Parkinson, George and Eleanor. *The Complete Confectioner, Pastry-Cook, and Baker*. Philadelphia: Leary & Getz, 1844.

Parloa, M. *The Appledore Cook Book*. Boston: Andrew F. Graves, 1872.

Parloa, Maria. *Miss Parloa's New Cook Book*. Boston: Estes and Lauriat, 1880.

———. *Miss Parloa's Kitchen Companion*. 20th ed. Boston: Estes and Lauriat, 1887.

Parloa, Maria, et al. *Chocolate and Cocoa Recipes*. Dorchester, Mass.: Walter Baker, 1923.

———. *Choice Recipes*. Dorchester, Mass.: Walter Baker, 1902.

Patent, Greg. "Boston Cream Pie." *Gastronomica* 1, no. 4 (2001): 82–87.

The Pillsbury Cook-Book. Minneapolis: Pillsbury Flour Mills, 1914.

Pillsbury's Best 1000 Recipes: Best of the Bake-Off Collection. Chicago: Consolidated Book Publishers, 1959.

Plante, Ellen M. *The American Kitchen, 1700 to the Present*. New York: Facts on File, 1995.

Porter, Mrs. M. E. *Mrs. Porter's New Southern Cookery Book*. Facsimile of the 1871 edition. New York: Promontory Press, 1974.

Prudhomme, Paul. *Chef Paul Prudhomme's Louisiana Kitchen*. New York: William Morrow, 1984.

Putnam, Mrs. *Mrs. Putnam's Receipt Book, and Young Housekeeper's Assistant*. Boston: Ticknor, Reed, and Fields, 1849.

———. *Mrs. Putnam's Receipt Book, and Young Housekeeper's Assistant.* Enlarged ed. New York: Phinney, Blakeman & Mason, 1860.

Pyler, E. J. *Baking Science & Technology.* 3rd ed., 2 vols. Marrian, Kan.: Sosland Publishing, 1988.

Randolph, Mary. *The Virginia House-Wife.* Facsimile of the first edition, 1824, with notes by Karen Hess. Columbia: University of South Carolina Press, 1984.

Ranhofer, Charles. *The Epicurean.* Facsimile of the 1893 edition. New York: Dover Publications, 1971.

Rawlings, Marjorie Kinnan. *Cross Creek Cookery.* New York: Scribner's, 1942.

Rhett, Blanche S. *Two Hundred Years of Charleston Cooking.* Ed. by Lettie Gay. Columbia: University of South Carolina Press, 1976.

Root, Waverly, and Richard de Rochemont. *Eating in America: A History.* New York: William Morrow, 1976.

Rorer, Mrs. S. T. *Good Cooking.* Philadelphia: Curtis Publishing, 1898.

———. *Mrs. Rorer's Philadelphia Cook Book.* Philadelphia: Arnold, 1886.

Rorer, Sarah Tyson. *Mrs. Rorer's Cakes, Icings, and Fillings.* Philadelphia: Arnold, 1905.

———. *Mrs. Rorer's New Cook Book.* Philadelphia: Arnold, 1902.

Rose, Peter G. *Foods of the Hudson.* Woodstock, N.Y.: Overlook Press, 1993.

———, ed. and trans. *The Sensible Cook: Dutch Foodways in the Old and the New World.* Syracuse, N.Y.: Syracuse University Press, 1989.

The Royal Baker. New York: Royal Baking Powder, 1877.

Rudmani, Giuseppi. *The Baker's Manual.* New York: J. Hancy, 1879.

Rundell, Maria Eliza. *A New System of Domestic Cookery by A Lady.* Facsimile of the 1806 edition. Youngstown, N.Y.: Old Fort Niagara Association, 1998.

Rutledge, Sarah. *The Carolina Housewife.* Facsimile of the 1847 edition. Columbia: University of South Carolina Press, 1979.

Sax, Richard. *Classic Home Desserts.* Boston: Houghton Mifflin, 1994.

Simmons, Amelia. *American Cookery.* Facsimile of the 2nd ed., 1796. Bedford, Mass.: Applewood Books, 1996.

Sloat, Caroline, ed. *Old Sturbridge Village Cookbook.* Chester, Conn.: Globe Pequot Press, 1984.

Smallzried, Kathleen Ann. *The Everlasting Pleasure.* New York: Appleton-Century-Crofts, 1956.

Spaulding, Lily May, and John Spaulding, eds. *Civil War Recipes: Receipts from the Pages of Godey's Lady's Book.* Lexington: University Press of Kentucky, 1999.

Spicer, Dorothy Gladys. *From an English Oven.* New York: Women's Press, 1948.

Spring, James W. *Boston and the Parker House.* Boston: J. R. Whipple Corporation (privately printed), 1927.

Spurling, Hilary. *Elinor Fettiplace's Receipt Book.* Middlesex, England: Penguin Books, 1987.

Stieff, Frederick Philip. *Eat, Drink, and Be Merry in Maryland.* 1932. Reprint, Baltimore: Johns Hopkins University Press, 1998.

Stork, John, and Walter Dorwin Teague. *Flour for Man's Bread.* Minneapolis: University of Minnesota Press, 1952.

Strong, L.A.G. *The Story of Sugar.* London: George Weidenfeld & Nicholson, 1954.

Taylor, Hoppin' John Martin. *The Fearless Frying Cookbook.* New York: Workman, 1997.

———. *Hoppin' John's Lowcountry Cooking.* Boston: Houghton Mifflin, 2000.

Trager, James. *The Food Chronology.* New York: Henry Holt, 1995.

Tyree, Marion Cabell. *Housekeeping in Old Virginia.* Facsimile of the 1879 edition. Louisville, Ky.: Favorite Recipes Press, 1965.

Ward, Artemis. *The Grocer's Encyclopedia.* New York: James Kempster Printing, 1911.

Watkins Cook Book. Racine, Wis.: Whitman Publishing, 1943.

Weaver, William Woys. *Pennsylvania Dutch Country Cooking.* New York: Abbeville Press, 1994.

———. *Sauerkraut Yankees. Pennsylvania German Foods & Folkways.* Philadelphia: University of Pennsylvania Press, 1983.

———. *35 Receipts from "The Larder Invaded."* Philadelphia: Library Company of Philadelphia and Historical Society of Pennsylvania, 1986.

Weigley, Emma Seifrit. *Sarah Tyson Rorer.* Philadelphia: The American Philosophical Society, 1977.

Weild, John. *Bakers' Guild; or the Art of Baking.* Boston: self-published, 1870.

Whitehead, Jessup. *The American Pastry Cook.* 7th ed. Chicago: Jessup Whitehead, 1894.

Widdifield, Hannah. *Widdifield's New Cook Book.* Philadelphia: T. B. Peterson, 1856.

Wihlfahrt, Julius Emil. *A Treatise on Flour, Yeast, Fermentation, and Baking.* Fleischmann, 1915.

Wolcott, Imogene. *The New England Yankee Cookbook*. Reprint of *The Yankee Cookbook*, 1939. Louisville, Ky.: Favorite Recipes Press, 1939.

Wood, Ed. *World Sourdoughs from Antiquity*. Berkeley, Calif.: Ten Speed Press, 1996.

Yanner, Fred. M. *The Modern Cake Baker, Pastry Cook, and Confectioner*. Kansas City, Mo.: Hudson-Kimberly, 1894.

Ziemann, Hugo, and Mrs. F. L. Gillette. *The Original White House Cookbook*. Facsimile of the 1887 first edition. Old Greenwich, Conn.: Devin Adair, 1983.

INDEX

Y